Richard Coer de Lyon

 MIDDLE ENGLISH TEXTS SERIES 

The Middle English Texts Series is designed for classroom use. Its goal is to make available to teachers, scholars, and students texts that occupy an important place in the literary and cultural canon but have not been readily available in student editions. The series does not include those authors, such as Chaucer, Langland, or Malory, whose English works are normally in print in good student editions. The focus is, instead, upon Middle English literature adjacent to those authors that teachers need in compiling the syllabuses they wish to teach. The editions maintain the linguistic integrity of the original work but within the parameters of modern reading conventions. The texts are printed in the modern alphabet and follow the practices of modern capitalization, word formation, and punctuation. Manuscript abbreviations are silently expanded, and *u/v* and *j/i* spellings are regularized according to modern orthography. Yogh (ȝ) is transcribed as *g*, *gh*, *y*, or *s*, according to the sound in Modern English spelling to which it corresponds; thorn (þ) and eth (ð) are transcribed as *th*. Distinction between the second person pronoun and the definite article is made by spelling the one *thee* and the other *the*, and final *-e* that receives full syllabic value is accented (e.g., *charité*). Hard words, difficult phrases, and unusual idioms are glossed either in the right margin or at the foot of the page. Explanatory and textual notes appear at the end of the text, often along with a glossary. The editions include short introductions on the history of the work, its merits and points of topical interest, and brief working bibliographies.

This series is published in association with the University of Rochester.

Medieval Institute Publications is a program of
The Medieval Institute, College of Arts and Sciences

WESTERN MICHIGAN UNIVERSITY

RICHARD COER DE LYON

Edited by

Peter Larkin

TEAMS • Middle English Texts Series • University of Rochester

MEDIEVAL INSTITUTE PUBLICATIONS

Western Michigan University

Kalamazoo

This book is printed on acid-free paper.

Library of Congress Cataloging-in-Publication Data

Richard Coeur de Lion (Romance)
Richard Coer de Lyon / edited by Peter Larkin.
pages cm. -- (Middle English texts series)
Text in Middle English; introduction and notes in English.
Includes bibliographical references.
Summary: "Richard Coer de Lyon is a fourteenth-century Middle English verse account of the exploits of Richard the Lion-Hearted, king of England, during the Third Crusade" -- Provided by publisher.
ISBN 978-1-58044-201-5 (paperbound : alk. paper)
1. Richard I, King of England, 1157-1199--Romances. 2. Richard Coeur de Lion (Romance) 3. Crusades--Poetry. 4. Romances, English. I. Larkin, Peter, 1955- editor. II. Title.
PR2065.R4 2015
821'.1--dc23

2014043013

ISBN 978-1-58044-201-5

P 5 4 3 2 1

Contents

ACKNOWLEDGMENTS

In completing this edition of *Richard Coer de Lyon*, I have incurred numerous and substantial debts. I am deeply grateful to Russell A. Peck, General Editor of the series. His careful and learned editorial assistance has been invaluable, and his graciousness and patience extraordinary. I wish also to thank Assistant Editors, Martha M. Johnson-Olin and Pamela M. Yee, and Kara L. McShane, Sharon E. Rhodes, Alison Harper, Jenny Boyar, and Kyle Huskin, Staff Editors. To say that their keen scrutiny of text and manuscripts have greatly improved the edition would be an understatement of a very high order. I wish also to thank Alan Lupack, who made numerous and valuable suggestions in his careful review of the manuscript in its final stages. Without such enormous assistance, this edition would be far less accurate and much less useful. I also gratefully acknowledge the efforts of Pat Hollahan and the staff of Medieval Institute Publications, who brought the volume to completion. It is my privilege to thank the National Endowment of the Humanities for its continued and generous support of this Series. To all who helped with this edition, I am deeply grateful.

For permission to use MS Cambridge, Gonville and Caius College 175/96, my base manuscript, I thank Mark Statham, the Librarian of Gonville and Caius College. In addition, I thank The John Rylands Library, The University of Manchester, for allowing use of Deansgate 15843, Wynkyn de Worde's 1509 printing of *Kynge Rycharde cuer du lyon*. I have used this printing to complete gaps in the base manuscript. In recording textual variants, I also thank The British Library for permission to use the following manuscripts: MS London, BL Additional 31402; MS London, BL Egerton 2862; and MS London, BL Harley 4690. For the use of MS London, College of Arms HDN 58, I thank The College of Arms whose Archivist, Robert Yorke, was especially helpful. For use of MS Edinburgh, National Library of Scotland Advocates' 19.2.1, I wish to thank the National Library of Scotland. I am also grateful to the Bodleian Library for permission to use MS Oxford, Bodleian 21802.

As is evident in my Introduction and Explanatory Notes, I have made substantial use of the scholarship of John Finlayson, Alan Ambrisco, Geraldine Heng, John Gillingham, Nicola McDonald, Jay Rubenstein, and D. A. Trotter, among others. Either directly or indirectly, they demonstrate the continued relevance and vitality of *Richard Coer de Lyon*, and I gratefully acknowledge my debt to them. For his expert help with the German Introduction to Brunner's 1913 edition of Richard, I wish to thank Paul Listen. In addition, I am grateful to Gerald Malsbury for his able and good-natured assistance with Latin sources of the romance. I also owe a debt of gratitude to a group of graduate students for their comments on earlier stages of this edition. Finally, for their patience and support during the long process of completing this edition, I wish to thank my wife, Ashley, and my daughters, Lindsay and Mia. It is my wish to dedicate this edition to them.

Introduction

Richard Coer de Lyon recounts in verse the exploits, both historical and fanciful, of Richard I, King of England. One of a handful of "crusading poems" in Middle English, its main subject is Richard's participation in the Third Crusade.[1] Like other crusading poems, *The Sultan of Babylon* and *The Siege of Milan*, for example, *Richard Coer de Lyon* exhibits the stock conventions of *chansons de geste*: fierce battles between vast, religiously-opposed forces, duels between leaders that test each other's faith, Christian contempt for Saracens who are portrayed as polytheistic pagan idolaters, and divine interventions — both angelic visitations and the appearance of warrior-saints on the battlefield — that set the record right. The plot is punctuated by numerous atrocities, and, of course, reckless heroism, single combat, and violent siege warfare.[2] Scholars such as D. A. Trotter note that poems of the Charlemagne cycle anachronistically project onto the Carolingian past concerns of the crusade era.[3] In another typical manipulation, these works present Charlemagne as a pious Old Testament Warrior.[4] *Richard* offers distortions of a different sort. For example, the romance often remains close to the historical record in its presentation of the recent past, but it frequently depicts its Christian king not as pious but as a demonic warrior.

To elaborate, the work relates the exploits of an historical figure of the recent past whose crusade was well documented. Found in the Auchinleck manuscript and dated to the early fourteenth century, the oldest text — MS Edinburgh, National Library of Scotland Advocates' 19.2.1 — was composed barely one hundred years after Richard's death in 1199. Many of the episodes resemble accounts from such crusade chronicles as Ambroise's *Estoire de la guerre sainte* and the *Itinerarium perigrinorum et gesta regis Ricardi*.[5] Indeed, all manuscripts and printings of *Richard*, even those characterized by fabulous interpolations,

---

[1] Hamel provides an expansive view of what constitutes a Middle English crusading poem: "*Siege of Jerusalem*," pp. 177–79. For a more narrow set of criteria applied to French texts, see Trotter, *Medieval French Literature*, pp. 13–20.

[2] In addition to Hamel and Trotter, noted above, see White's discussion of the conventions of crusading literature: "Saracens and Crusaders." Indicative of the lack of a clear distinction between "history" and "literature" in a medieval context, White demonstrates that chronicles and *chansons* made use of the same rhetorical conventions. In *Saracens* and in *Sons of Ishmael*, Tolan presents a broad discussion of the medieval West's misrepresentation of Islam.

[3] Trotter, *Medieval French Literature*, p. 21.

[4] Trotter, *Medieval French Literature*, pp. 13–20.

[5] Early discussions of *RCL*'s chronicle sources include Jentsch, "Quellen," and Paris, "Le Roman." For correspondences between *RCL* and specific chronicles, see, e.g., the Explanatory Notes to the following lines: 11–19; 1291; 1669; 1810; 1856; 1919; 2479; 2635–36; and 2713–20.

present historically traceable, albeit embellished details of Richard's crusade. With notable geographic specificity, each describes Richard's preparations, his adventures in Sicily, including the pillage of Messina, his conquest of Cyprus, the capture of Acre and massacre of Muslim prisoners, the march to Jaffa, Saladin's (Salâh al-Dîn) destruction of castles and poisoning of wells, Richard's victory at Arsuf and rebuilding of Ascalon, his celebrated defense of Jaffa, his truce with Saladin, his return to England to deal with his brother John's intrigues, and finally, his death on the continent while laying siege to a vassal's castle.[6]

The work represents its hero and the knights who follow him as authentic crusaders motivated by papal appeals and spiritual rewards. In contrast to such figures as Charlemagne and Turpin, Richard and his company are not only holy warriors — soldiers of Christ (*miles Christi*) — they are also pilgrims. Bound by twin vows, they have obligated themselves to go on crusade and to worship at the Holy Sepulcher in Jerusalem. For fulfilling these vows, for discharging their debt to the papacy, and for completing their pilgrimage, crusaders were granted indulgences, namely, the remission of spiritual and temporal penalties. Having "taken the cross," they wear an emblem intended to offer protection against both creditors and assailants as they seek vengeance against God's enemies in the Holy Land.[7]

But the poem's representation of Richard is not always "historical," diverging not only from chronicle sources but also from the conventions of *chansons de geste*, an epic genre often considered historical in nature.[8] And while the violent, fearless, and aggressive warrior found in the poem frequently resembles the historical figure, on a number of occasions, *Richard* presents the king as uncourtly and unchivalric, and it frequently identifies him as a devil.[9] Some texts even depict Richard as a demonic cannibal. Of course, the historical Richard was no cannibal, nor was he uncourtly or unchivalric. Despite these distortions and despite the poem's extreme, even savage, Christian militancy — most notably displayed in Richard's divinely sanctioned massacre of Muslim prisoners at Acre (lines 3745–54) —

---

[6] Historically, the Duke of Austria captured and imprisoned Richard after his crusade. *RCL* places these events before Richard's crusade.

[7] See lines 1323–28, 1387, 1348–82, 1429–30,1699–1701, and 6954. Merrilees, "Crusade," p. 16. Trotter, *Medieval French Literature*, p. 17. On the traditions of pilgrimage and holy war, and for discussions of crusading vows and crusading privileges and obligations, see Brundage, *Medieval Canon Law*. For a discussion of the ritual of taking the cross in England, see Brundage, "'Cruce Signari.'" Concise introductions to the backgrounds of the crusades include Cowdrey, "Pope Urban II's Preaching," Painter, "Western Europe," Peters, Introduction to *First Crusade*, pp. 1–24, and Trotter, *Medieval French Literature*, pp. 13–20.

[8] See, for example, Finlayson, "'*Richard, Coer de Lyon*,'" and Trotter, *Medieval French Literature*, pp. 20–23.

[9] Richard's unchivalric acts include wrapping his hand in wax during the exchange of blows episode, an unfair and brutal ploy (lines 777–98), and his cannibalizing of Saracen princes before Saladin's emissaries (lines 3409–3562). His uncourtly acts include not sharing food with a minstrel, an uncharacteristic rudeness (lines 664–76), and his barbaric consumption of the lion's heart (lines 1105–09). At least six out of a possible eight texts refer to Richard as either a "devylle" or "fende" "of helle," "fiend" being synonymous with "devil" (*MED*, s.v. *fend* (n.), sense 2a). Two of the eight MSS are defective: because of a lacuna, L does not contain the line; and though the line in E ends with the phrase "com fro helle," the first half of the line is illegible. See the Textual Note to line 2580.

Richard became one of the most popular romances in medieval England.[10] To understand both these distortions and this popularity, it will be useful to examine the work's complex and lengthy textual history.

DEMONIZING THE PAST: THE TEXTUAL HISTORY OF *RICHARD COER DE LYON*

Richard survives in seven manuscripts dated from the early fourteenth to the late fifteenth century, and in two printings from 1509 and 1528. Internal evidence — the narrator's repeated reference to a French source, for example (see lines 21, 5098 and 7008) — suggests an Anglo-Norman original, but this presumed text is now lost, and the witnesses that remain vary considerably, no text having served as the source for another. Following Brunner, who produced a critical edition, scholars classify these texts into two versions, *a* and *b*.[11] Five manuscripts have been identified within the *b* group: MS Edinburgh, National Library of Scotland Advocates' 19.2.1 (L); MS London, BL Egerton 2862 (E); MS London, College of Arms HDN 58 (A); MS Oxford, Bodleian 21802 (D); and MS London, BL Harley 4690 (H). The *a* version survives in two manuscripts: MS Cambridge, Gonville and Caius College 175/96 (C), and MS London, BL Additional 31042 (B); and in two printings: Wynkyn de Worde's 1509 London printing (*Kynge Rycharde cuer du lyon*, Oxford, Bodleian Crynes 734; and Manchester, John Ryland's Library Deansgate 15843) (W), and de Worde's 1528 printing (*Kynge Rycharde cuer du lyon*, Oxford, Bodleian S. Seld. D. 45 (1); and London, BL C.40.c.51) $(W)^2$.[12]

The shorter version, *b*, is considered more historically accurate than *a*, which contains a number of "romantic" interpolations, two of which are particularly notorious.[13] While witnesses of *b* refer to Richard's historical mother, Eleanor of Aquitaine, *a* provides the hero with a demonic mother who cannot witness the consecration of the host. Most infamously, this version depicts Richard, an anointed king and crusader, repeatedly cannibalizing Saracen flesh.[14] For a number of reasons, not least of which is the defective condition of manuscripts, determining the precise relation between *a* and *b* has been difficult. For example, E, which represents Richard's second act of cannibalism, is the only member of

---

[10] Lines 3745–54 are quoted at p. 19 below. For a discussion of *RCL*'s Christian militancy, see Hamel, "*Siege of Jerusalem*," pp. 184–85. Discussions of the work's popularity include Heng, *Empire*, p. 110; and Pearsall, "English Romance," p. 58n2.

[11] In addition to following Brunner's classification of texts, scholars generally adopt his letter designations of manuscripts and printings. For a thorough description of the manuscripts, see Guddat-Figge's *Catalogue*; for manuscripts and printings, see Brunner, *Der Mittelenglische Versroman* (hereafter *Löwenherz*), pp. 1–18.

[12] An additional fragment is extant — MS Badminton House 704.1.16 — but too little survives to identify the version it represents: see Davis, "Another Fragment."

[13] As Laura Hibbard states, "The shorter, more sober *b* version . . . like its various antecedents, undoubtedly omits much, is inexact in chronological detail, and somewhat subject to patriotic exaggeration concerning its hero, and to depreciation of his rivals and enemies, but on the whole the narrative is fairly authentic" (*Mediæval Romance*, p. 149).

[14] For references to Eleanor of Aquitaine in *b*, see the Explanatory Note to line 2040. For Richard's demonic origins, see lines 35–250 and related Explanatory Notes. Richard's first act of cannibalism occurs in lines 3027–3124, and his second, in lines 3409–3655.

the *b* group to depict the king consuming Saracen flesh, but defects and lacunae — E begins at line 1857 — prevent determining whether this manuscript included other "romantic accretions" that characterize the *a* group, Richard's first act of cannibalism, to name one. Efforts to identify the portions of the poem that represent direct translations from the lost Anglo-Norman original remain speculative.[15] As to extant texts, it is generally presumed that *a* represents a later version that was produced by adding a series of romance elements, legends, and folk motifs to *b*. To recite a speculative route of development, an intermediate revision, *b*, added the following elements to an "historical" poem about Richard's crusade: the Three Days' Tournament (lines 252–426), Richard's pilgrimage to the Holy Land (lines 615–50), and his captivity in Germany, which features the exchange of blows episode, his love affair, and the lion fight (lines 657–1242).[16] These interpolations occur at the beginning of the narrative and do not alter the episodes of Richard's crusade.[17] The texts in *a* incorporate a later set of revisions, some quite fantastic. These include, most notably, the demon-mother episode (lines 35–250), Richard's journey of revenge to Germany (lines 1465–1647), Richard's acts of cannibalism (lines 3027–3124; and lines 3409–3655), and a series of non-historical crusade adventures that disparage the French king and amplify the role of Fouke Doyly and Thomas of Multon.[18]

That a Middle English romance about Richard I should be subjected to frequent revision has surprised few scholars. For his achievements and personal bravery during the Third Crusade, Richard became, even to contemporaries, a heroic figure. As John Gillingham notes, "No earlier or later king took on a challenge remotely comparable with the task of taking a fleet and an army to the eastern end of the Mediterranean and there facing, even facing down, an adversary as formidable as the great Saladin."[19] With this king, the difficulty of distinguishing fact from fantasy is frequently observed: "many of the apparently 'fabulous' aspects of Richard's career are, in fact, to be found in contemporary or slightly later chronicles, and many of the extraordinary 'heroic' achievements are little more than heightenings of his real life."[20] Richard's celebrated — and attested — defense of Jaffa, for example, defies credulity.[21]

---

[15] See, e.g., Paris, "Le Roman," pp. 356–58; Brunner, *Löwenherz*, pp. 51–70; and Loomis, Review, pp. 457–63, and "Pas Saladin," p. 510.

[16] For variations on this speculated route of development, see Paris, "Le Roman," pp. 354–58; Loomis, Review, p. 462; Hibbard, *Mediæval Romance*, pp. 149–55; and Finlayson, "'*Richard, Coer de Lyon*,'" p. 160. While Richard's German imprisonment refers to an historical event, his actual captivity occurred after, not before, the Crusade.

[17] E, which depicts Richard's second cannibalism, stands as an exception in the "historical" *b* group: see the Explanatory Note to lines 3027–3124.

[18] Scholars note that Sir Thomas Multon and Sir Fouke D'Oyly were actual Lincolnshire knights, but they played no part in Richard's crusade: see, in particular, Finlayson, "Legendary Ancestors." Not present in W or W^2, these non-historical adventures include the sieges of Sudan Turry, Orglyous, and Ebedy (lines 3971–4620); the conquest of Nineveh (lines 5187–5380), and the siege of Babylon (lines 5381–5892). Brunner (*Löwenherz*, pp. 15–17) discusses the differences between *a* and *b* and provides a useful chart on the transmission of passages in each text.

[19] Gillingham, *Richard I*, p. 1.

[20] Finlayson, "Legendary Ancestors," p. 300 (references omitted).

[21] See, e.g., Runciman, *History of the Crusades*, 3:69–73.

In establishing a context for the poem's various "accretions," Richard I's transformation from a military hero of the crusades into a legendary hero of the English nation is worth noting. As the historian Ranulph Higden (c. 1280–1364) observes about excessive praise for national heroes, this process was well under way by the mid-fourteenth century: "Perhaps it is the custom of each nation [*nationi*] to exalt one of its own with excessive praise: just as the Greeks boast of their Alexander, the Romans of their Augustus, the English of their Richard, and the French of their Charlemagne, thus the Britons elevate their Arthur."[22] As a result of Richard's achievements and growing fame, legends and folktale motifs became attached to the historical figure, and the relatively undistorted relation between "history" and narrative in version *b* was altered — "romanticized" — during the text's centuries-long period of production. Summarizing an early view of this process, Laura Hibbard observes, "The elaborated *a* version shows how strong a magnet the story of Richard was, not only for floating scraps of tradition about the king, but also for anecdotes and *motifs* that originally had no connection with him."[23] In contrast to Hibbard's view of haphazard additions, another point must be made, one to be developed later. As D. A. Trotter observes, "Legends concerning historical figures were perhaps an inevitable development from the role of literary, and especially epic, texts. The two readily available models, the heroic and the Biblical, the latter assisted by the typological approach adopted in medieval exegesis, provided a ready source of inspiration."[24]

The interpolations found in *b* — the Three Days' Tournament, Richard's captivity in Germany and his related adventures — have been viewed as lending romantic elements to the poem.[25] While Richard's savage, uncouth consumption of the lion's heart has raised a few eyebrows, the result, the hero's assumption of a nickname, is a familiar romance convention. Also conventional are the Three Days' Tournament and its disguises, the love affair, the exchange of blows, and the lion fight. Routinely encountered in medieval romance, these adventures broaden Richard's appeal by linking him to heroes of both epic and romance.[26] Recognizing these additions in *b* as "romantic" commonplaces, early critics considered their incorporation with the king's historical material to be poorly handled.[27]

Understandably, the fabulous interpolations encountered in *a* have been even more troubling. One example is the demon-mother episode. In the *a* version's initial episode, Henry, Richard's father, is urged to take a wife by his barons. Agreeing, Henry dispatches envoys who are to find the fairest woman alive. After encountering the king of Antioch and his lovely daughter on an exquisite ship, the envoys return to England where Henry quickly marries the daughter, Cassodorien. During the ceremony, though, she swoons before the elevation of the host. In the course of their marriage, she and Henry have two sons, Richard

[22] Higden, *Polychronicon*, 5.336 (my translation); compare Gillingham, *Richard I*, p.1.

[23] Hibbard, *Mediæval Romance*, p. 151.

[24] Trotter, *Medieval French Literature*, p. 25.

[25] L, the oldest text, contains none of these interpolations and is considered closest to the original.

[26] In discussing analogues to Richard's lion fight, Broughton cites both biblical and romance figures: Samson, David, Gawain in *La Mule Sans Frein*, and Guy of Warwick. As to the exchange of blows, an early form of dueling, he cites the following romances: *La Mule Sans Frein*, *The Turk and Gawain*, *Lanzelet*, and *Wolfdietrich* (*Legends of Richard I*, pp. 116–22). Of course, *Sir Gawain and the Green Knight* must be added to this list. See also Finlayson, "Legendary Ancestors," p. 303.

[27] See Finlayson's summary of negative critiques: "'*Richard, Coer de Lyon*,'" pp. 158–59.

and John, and a daughter, Topyas. After her initial swoon, the queen manages to avoid witnessing the sacrament until an earl, with the king's permission, attempts unsuccessfully to prevent her from leaving mass early. Carrying her daughter but dropping John, Cassodorien escapes by flying through the roof of the church never to be seen again (lines 43–234).

The similarities between this episode and a legend concerning Richard's ancestor, Black Fulk of Anjou, have not gone unnoticed.[28] As related by Gerald de Barri, Fulk married a lady of unearthly beauty who, like Cassodorien, could not witness the host's elevation. Compelled to remain in church by Fulk's men, she escaped with two children by flying through the window of the church. The inability of each of these women to witness the elevation, not to mention their ability to fly, indicates their demonic status. As de Barri notes, Richard I often referred to this legend in jest, stating, "Since we have all come from the devil, we are all going to return to the devil."[29] Noted previously, Richard's demonic pedigree hardly accords with those of the heroes of *chansons de geste*, epic works that usually idealize monarchs, Charlemagne, for example.[30]

Of course, the same might be said of his cannibalism. In *Richard*, Richard commits two acts of cannibalism. Only the first bears a relation to the historical record of his crusade. During the actual siege of Acre, and in our poem as well, Richard became ill with a fever. While chronicles report that during a later illness, Richard longed for pears and peaches, in *Richard* the fevered king longs for pork: "But aftyr pork he was alongyd" (line 3071).[31] Since swine is an unclean food to Muslims and Jews, it is hardly surprising that no pork could be found in the Holy Land. Worried about his king, an old knight suggests that a "yonge and fat" (line 3088) Saracen be slain, flayed, and roasted with the proper spices and served to the king as pork. The aroma will enhance the king's appetite; and when he has eaten well of this meal, he will sleep, sweat out his fever, and be healed (lines 3077–3102). The knight's remedy proves effective, and Richard is soon back in battle, slaughtering Saracens.[32] At day's end, though, Richard fears the fever will return and requests that the cook bring him "The hed of that ylke swyn / That I of eet," (lines 3198–99). Faced with losing his own head or producing that of the swine, the cook presents the Saracen's head:

"Loo, here the hed, my lord, mercy!"
Hys swarte vys whenne the kyng seeth, — *When the king sees his swarthy (black) face*
Hys blake berd and hys whyte teeth,

[28] See, e.g., Brunner, *Löwenherz*, pp. 59–60; Loomis, Review, p. 465; and Broughton, *Legends of Richard I*, pp. 78–86.

[29] Giraldus Cambrensis, *Liber de principis instructione*, 3.28, p. 301 (my translation); cited by Broughton, *Legends of Richard I*, pp. 78–79. Chapman, who classifies Cassodorien as a fairy mistress of the "Swan Maiden type," cites a number of other related legends, "Demon Queen," pp. 393–95.

[30] See, e.g., Trotter's discussion of "Charlemagne's portrayal in the style of an old testament warrior-king . . ." in *Medieval French Literature*, p. 25.

[31] Identified by chroniclers as *Arnaldia* or *Léonardia*, the disease Richard suffered from was likely scurvy or trench mouth, as Gillingham notes (*Richard I*, pp. 160, 217); see Explanatory Notes to lines 3027 and 3071.

[32] The historical Richard reportedly recovered from his illness quickly after sweating off his fever (Richard of Devizes, *Chronicon*, p. 81; cited by Heng, *Empire*, p. 77).

Hou hys lyppys grennyd wyde:
"What devyl is this?" the kyng cryde,
And gan to lawghe as he were wood (lines 3210–15).

While the king unknowingly consumes Saracen flesh in this first instance, his second act of cannibalism is quite deliberate. After Richard wins Acre, Saladin sends emissaries with treasure to win the release of high–born Muslim hostages. At a dinner for these emissaries, Richard serves them the heads of "The Sarezynys of most renoun" (line 3414). Then, in their presence, he consumes with relish the head of another Saracen prince. Before sending these emissaries away, he delivers a chilling message for Saladin:

Say hym it schal hym nought avayle
Though he forbarre oure vytayle, *block our food supplies*
Brede, wyne, flesshe, fysshe and kunger, *conger eel*
Of us non schal dye for hungyr,
Whyle that we may wenden to fyght, *go*
And slee the Sarezynes dounryght, *outright*
Wassche the flesche and roste the hede.
With oo Sarwzyn I may wel fede, *one; fully feed*
Wel a nyne or a ten, *No less than*
Of my goode, Crystene men."
Kyng Richard sayd: "I you waraunt,
Ther is no flesch so noryysshaunt, *nourishing*
Unto an Ynglyssche Crysten man,
Partryk, plover, heroun, ne swan, *Partridge*
Cow, ne oxe, scheep, ne swyn,
As is the flessh of a Saryzyne! (lines 3537–52)

As with the episode of the demon mother, scholars note a number of parallels. In an encomiastic section of his chronicle, Richard of Devizes, a contemporary of the king, presents Saladin's brother, Safadin, praising the English monarch as a great warrior. Among other comments, Safadin states of Richard, "Indeed, it was said of him that he ate his enemies alive."[33] In addition to this comment, a compliment not intended to be taken literally, scholars connect his cannibalism to accounts of crusader cannibalism in *La Chanson d'Antioche* and in chronicles of the First Crusade.[34] An oft cited passage from the anonymous *Gesta Francorum et aliorum Hierosolimitanorum* records crusader cannibalism at Ma'arra: "While we were there some of our men could not satisfy their needs, either because of the long stay or because they were so hungry, for there was no plunder to be had outside the walls. So they ripped up the bodies of the dead, because they used to find bezants hidden in their entrails, and others cut the dead flesh into slices and cooked it to eat."[35] Other narratives report cannibalism at the siege of Antioch. *La Chanson d'Antioche*, for example,

[33] Richard of Devizes, *Chronicon*, trans. Appleby, p. 77.

[34] Brunner, *Löwenherz*, p. 65; Hibbard, *Mediæval Romance*, pp. 151–52; Broughton, *Legends of Richard I*, pp. 108–09; Tattersall, "Anthropophagi," p. 249; Heng, *Empire*, p. 334n3; and Akbari, "Hunger," pp. 211–12. See Ambrisco's discussion of these references in "Cannibalism," pp. 508–11.

[35] *Gesta Francorum*, trans. Hill, p. 80. Fulcher of Chartres provides a similar account in *A History of the Expedition to Jerusalem*, pp. 112–13.

describes the Tarfurs' cannibalism of Turkish corpses during the rigors of the siege. Identified as poor, barefoot, and degenerate soldiers, this group, acting on the suggestion of Peter the Hermit, cannibalized Turkish corpses and pillaged cemeteries for more bodies.[36] Despite their gruesome actions, the Tarfurs at times celebrate their cannibalism, even taunting the Turks on the walls of Antioch: "The pilgrims ate with pleasure, without bread and without salt, saying as they did, 'This is most tasty, better than any pork or even cured ham. Cursed be anyone who would die now where there is such abundance!'"[37]

Another noted parallel is found in Adémar of Chabannes's *Chronicon*. In an account of Roger I of Tosny's campaign in the Reconquista of Iberia, Adémar relates a story from which Roger gained the nickname, "Moor-Eater." Each day, Roger would slaughter one of his Saracen prisoners, and, after dismembering the body like a pig, he would boil the remains in a cauldron. Then he would serve one portion as a sumptuous meal to the Saracens while pretending to eat the other portion with his men in another house. Roger allowed one prisoner to escape so that news of his cannibalism would spread. Having instilled fear in this way, he caused the Saracen king Musetus to sue for peace.[38]

The connections between these accounts and Richard's cannibalism are not difficult to discern: the conflation of Saracen flesh with pork; the skinning and preparing of corpses in a manner typical of other meat;[39] the performance of cannibalism to frighten the enemy; and the notion of an abundance of food derived from enemy corpses. Nor is it difficult to see how a redactor might have derived these interpolations by combining Safadin's statement that Richard ate his enemies with the Tarfurs' or Roger's enthusiastic consumption of dead Saracens. Though a process of redaction may be plausible, it need not be successful. As noted, the early assessment of the interpolations in both *b* and in *a* is quite negative. Critics assert that the work is a "blend of fact and fiction . . . impenetrable to the discrimination of historians;" a composite romance that, "drawing on all the Matters," clothes Richard's "romantic career"[40] with the commonplaces of the romance genre; it is "most remarkable for the streak of crude brutality which it displays, as in the lion-heart episode and Richard's cannibalistic orgies at Acre," and even "the technical skills of the author, the vigour and authenticity of the battle-scenes" cannot "disguise the shapelessness

[36] Ambrisco, "Cannibalism," p. 508, citing *Chanson d'Antioche*, ed. Duparc-Quioc, 1:4039–4118; see also Cordery, "Cannibal Diplomacy."

[37] *Chanson d'Antioche*, 1:4073–75, translated by Rubenstein in "Cannibals and Crusaders," p. 549. In William of Tyre's account, Bohemond, not the Tarfurs, slays and roasts a Saracen at the siege of Antioch, but he only pretends to cannibalize his victim (*Chronicon*, 4.23.266); discussed by Rubenstein, "Cannibals and Crusaders," p. 541. See also Ambrisco's discussion of the Tarfurs, "Cannibalism," pp. 508–10.

[38] Adémar de Chabannes, *Ademari Cabannensis*, 3.55.174; see Broughton, *Legends of Richard I*, p. 110.

[39] McDonald discusses the recipe in *RCL* that transforms "a young Muslim into a plate of pork (the meat that is the ubiquitous mark of a Christian diet) . . . by subjecting the unfamiliar flesh to the normal rules of English cooking" ("Eating People," pp. 134–35, 147n28).

[40] Barron, *English Medieval Romance*, pp. 180–81.

of the narrative and laborious circumstancing of each incident, the real drama of history being rejected in favor of the sham of interminable Saracen-baiting."[41]

According to John Finlayson, such judgments, too dependent upon Brunner's edition of the *a* version, misrepresent *Richard*'s literary nature and relations to history. Finlayson asserts that "the two 'families' of manuscripts represent not the usual degrees of scribal corruption and derivation from a lost original which stemmatic editing assumes, but are instead two different works or versions of the deeds and life of Richard I . . . ."[42] In his view, the original *Richard* was "a work of a vigorously heroic type," that was modified to produce *b*, which is not a romance of adventure but a heroic epic, in essence, a *chanson de geste* of Richard: "The dominant matter of *Richard* is not love, the marvellous or the divinely inspired supernatural, but battle: not individual jousts, but combat against the Saracens in order to regain the Holy Places."[43] The *a* version expands *b*, moving a heroic poem in the direction of such "ancestral" romances as *Guy of Warwick*, narratives whose first half depicts a chivalric hero engaged in individual adventures before the hero, in the second half, becomes pious or socially engaged. Finlayson argues that the *b* version of *Richard Coer de Lyon* constitutes "exemplary history presented in the epic mode . . . it is quite successful in its own unmodish pursuits—the blending of heroic action with militant, Christian nationalism."[44]

As Finlayson and others note, the distinction between history and fiction was often a blurred one for a medieval audience.[45] Manuscript contexts, though, can serve as evidence of contemporary opinion of a work's generic status, and several contexts support Finlayson's argument that *b* was perceived as historical and *a* as a romance. In H, the text of *Richard* occurs as a supplement "to a carefully written historical MS," a *Brut*; and in A, *Richard* is inserted into an exemplar of Robert of Gloucester's *Metrical Chronicle*.[46] C, a witness of the "romanticized" *a* version, occurs in a collection of romances.[47] For a number of reasons, some having to do with editorial assumptions, others with the relation between history and

---

[41] Pearsall, "Development," p. 100. This quotation as well as the quotation from Barron above display a debt to Finlayson's summary in "'*Richard, Coer de Lyon*,'" pp. 158–59.

[42] Finlayson, "Legendary Ancestors," pp. 299–300. For Brunner's stemma of *RCL*, see *Löwenherz*, p. 14.

[43] Finlayson, "'*Richard, Coer de Lyon*,'" p. 168.

[44] Finlayson, "'*Richard, Coer de Lyon*,'" p. 180.

[45] In addition to Finlayson's discussion in "'*Richard, Coer de Lyon*,'" pp. 167–70, see Field's treatment of the relation between "history" and "romance" in medieval England, "Romance as History," and, more generally, Fleischman, "On the Representation."

[46] Guddat-Figge, *Catalogue*, pp. 205–06, 216. Finlayson offers a more detailed discussion of manuscript contexts in "'*Richard, Coer de Lyon*,'" pp. 161–65.

[47] The contexts of the remaining manuscripts are less conclusive. While two exemplars of *b* — A and H — appear in historical contexts, E appears within a collection of popular romances. The context of the oldest manuscript, L, is debatable: situated in the famous Auchinleck Manuscript, it is surrounded by romances, as well as religious and historical material. *RCL* is the only text in D, a holster book. From the *a* group, C is found within a collection of romances, but B, the only other manuscript in *a*, appears in a mixed context that includes religious and historical works, lyrics, and romances. Finlayson makes a number of different arguments in "'*Richard, Coer de Lyon*,'" pp. 161–65. See also Akbari, "Hunger," p. 200.

romance, Finlayson's arguments that the two versions of *Richard* should be viewed as distinct works is gaining acceptance among scholars.

Finlayson argues against applying the stemmatic method to the poem's disparate texts. This approach attempts "to establish a text which approximates as closely as possible the author's lost original work in cases where the original has been lost, but where multiple copies have survived."[48] Just as Finlayson argues against applying this method to *Richard*, scholars now consider Middle English romances to constitute a category for which the recovery of a lost, ideal text may not be a suitable goal. Commenting upon the range of textual variation in surviving manuscripts of *King Horn* and *Bevis of Hamtoun*, Derek Pearsall describes a process of textual production that may also apply to *Richard Coer de Lyon*:

> Whoever composed these poems, whether booksellers' hacks, clerics, or genuine *disours* [reciters], they were evidently written for performance, and became to that extent the property of the *disours*. It is their memories of a written text, modified in performance-from-memory . . . that would provide, directly or indirectly, the basis for the extant written copies. These processes of 'recomposition' do not produce garbled texts, or texts necessarily inferior to the original, since the capacities and ambitions of the re-composer are little if at all different from those of the original composer. There is no ideal text, from which succeeding copies degenerate by a process of scribal corruption and decomposition: rather the text exists in an open and fluid state, the successive acts of writing down being no more than arbitrary stages in the continuously evolving life of the poem.[49]

While Finlayson's argument that the two versions represent distinct works has prevailed, critics have paid less attention to the exemplary, epic history of *b* than to *a*, now conceived as a popular romance. No longer considered a degenerate epic corrupted by poorly integrated romantic accretions, scholars view the *a* version as a coherent if provocative whole that gives voice to historical and cultural forces that prevailed during its period of production. Such forces find representation in a number of ways, through generic and historic distortions, for example.

HEROIC TRANSFORMATIONS

Texts of *Richard Coer de Lyon* were continuously produced from at least the early fourteenth century — the date of L, the Auchinleck manuscript (National Library of Scotland Advocates' 19.2.1) — until 1528, the date of the last printed edition.[50] Over this span, historical and cultural forces transformed England and its monarchy. At the beginning of this period, Richard I is not only king of England but also the ruler of an Angevin empire. Stretching from the English channel to the Pyrenees, his continental holdings dwarf those in England, a situation that may justify his having spent two-thirds of his political life in France.[51] After Richard's death in 1199, the monarchy progressively lost its continental

[48] Baker, "Editing Medieval Texts," p. 429.

[49] Pearsall, "Middle English Romance," pp. 41–42.

[50] If the speculative date of the Anglo-Norman original — 1250 — is considered, as well as the license that John Purfoot secured to publish *RCL* in 1568–69 (see Heng, *Empire*, p. 110), then the period of textual production extends to three hundred years.

[51] Gillingham, *Richard I*, p. x.

possessions so that by the end of the Hundred Years' War, England retained only a single town in France, Calais. As the realm developed a geographic boundedness through these losses, other developments fostered the emergence of a collective identity. In the contest of Anglo-Norman, British, and English identities that characterized Angevin England, an English identity prevailed. By the late twelfth century, the Anglo-Norman elites were already identifying themselves as English, a self-identification that coincided with the rise of the English vernacular as the speech of the realm.[52] In 1258, for example, Henry III confirmed the provisions of Oxford in both French and in English;[53] and by 1362, English had replaced French in Parliament and as the language of law. The translation of the original French version of *Richard* into English, a displacement repeatedly emphasized by the narrator, exemplifies as well the rise of the vernacular.

War, a noted mechanism for the production of identity, characterizes the period of the poem's English textual production. In addition to wars against Scotland and Wales, England was constantly fighting France, most notably in the Hundred Years' War (1337–1453). In addition the crusades with their collective traumas, notably the memory of cannibalism, continued, but the West did not fare well after the Third Crusade, losing Antioch in 1268 and Acre in 1291.[54] Constantinople fell in 1453, marking an end to the Roman Empire. Though not directly connected with the crusades, Edward I's expulsion of the Jews from England in 1290 deserves mention, both from the standpoint of anxieties towards infidels that the expulsion illustrates, but also from the perspective of self-identification against an internal, alien community.[55] Finally, in terms of cultural developments that characterize the period of *Richard*'s textual production, I mention again the transformation of Richard from a crusading hero — an Angevin prince — into a legendary hero of the English nation.[56]

These developments — geographic boundedness, self-identification through language and culture, conflict against territorially and culturally distinct groups, as well as the transformation of a king into a national symbol — are all frequently cited in discussions of the emergence of the English nation.[57] While the term "nation" can be applied inaccurately in a medieval context, our subject is not the English nation but its emergence, its beginnings as an "imagined community." As Benedict Anderson himself states, "If nation-states are widely conceded to be 'new' and 'historical,' the nations to which they give political expression always loom out of an immemorial past."[58] Over the course of its centuries-long production, the romance of *Richard Coer de Lyon* both witnesses and fashions this "immemorial

[52] See the discussions in Gillingham, "Foundations," p. 54 and Clanchy, *England and Its Rulers*, p. 252, both noted by Heng, *Empire*, pp. 66 and 336n6.

[53] Heng, *Empire*, pp. 106, 355n69, citing Fisher, "Language Policy," p. 1169.

[54] See Heng's work in *Empire of Magic* on crusader cannibalism's impact upon medieval romance, not to mention the cannibalism in *RCL*.

[55] See Heng's discussion of English monarchs' control, persecution, and conversion of Jews in the context of prevalent themes in *RCL*, (*Empire*, pp. 78–91).

[56] See the quotation from Higden's *Polycrhronicon*, cited at note 22 above.

[57] See, for example, Ambrisco's discussion of *RCL*'s protonationalism in "Cannibalism," pp. 511–16; and Heng, *Empire*, pp. 98–99 and 150.

[58] Anderson, *Imagined Communities*, p. 11.

past."[59] Instead of projecting crusading ideals onto a Carolingian history, a distortion of the *chansons de geste*, the English poem projects the emergence of nationalistic discourses into the Third Crusade, a distortion that creates the past out of which the nation looms.

For Geraldine Heng, the romance form proves most productive in negotiating this past that figures in the emergence of England. As she states:

> Hitherto, the *chronicle* has been assumed to be the principal medieval literary genre in which a country's identity is addressed or contemplated in narrative, just as the *epic* has been assumed to address the collective ethnic identity of tribes, the *chanson de geste* to address relations between monarchs and retainers-in-chief, and romance to address the concerns preoccupying chivalric communities. My discussion . . . shows how romance, by virtue of its popularity, special dispensations, and overarchingly wide address to a variety of domestic constituencies, uniquely subserves nationalist momentum, and nationalist requirements, in the projection of a national community and its future.[60]

The *a* version of *Richard* should not be viewed as a chivalric romance, a subgenre that expresses the ideology of an elite, transnational class whose loyalties "exceed the merely local or national." It is best viewed as a popular romance, the subtype in which "the impetus toward nation formation can be most readily read." Popular romance maintains the freedom to blend fantasy with history and the ability "to transform crisis into celebration and triumphalism," characteristics that lend to this form a "special serviceability for nationalist discourse."[61] As Heng and others demonstrate, *Richard* repeatedly transforms crisis into celebration and triumph. This process begins, appropriately enough, with the king.

Richard was an unlikely candidate for becoming a symbol of the nation, a national hero. While his crusading exploits garnered him considerable fame, they did not render him an English hero. To begin, he spoke no English, and though he reigned for ten years — from 1189 to 1199 — he spent a mere ten months in England. To pay for his crusade and for his ransom, he was notorious for taxing his subjects and for selling offices. As a contemporary chronicler reports, King Richard joked that he would have sold London itself had he been able to find a buyer.[62] Installing haughty, distrusted foreigners into vital offices, for example, William Longchamp as both chancellor and bishop of Ely, won him no friends. Criticized by his subjects for his fiscal policies, the clergy condemned his moral failings, which may have included homosexuality, a grave sin in the eyes of the medieval church.[63]

---

[59] See Ambrisco, "Cannibalism," especially p. 499. "This most medieval of romances, whose creation richly exemplifies medieval textual culture and literary production at work, can be read only as a sedimented repository of cultural patterns, investments, and obsessions that were deemed important enough to be inscribed, and reinscribed, over a span of centuries—witnessed through the hands and intelligences that compiled its dual textual traditions—and not as the inspired autographic production of a single authorial genius, anonymous or attested by signature" (Heng, *Empire*, p. 67).

[60] Heng, *Empire*, p. 7.

[61] Heng, *Empire*, pp. 73, 67.

[62] Richard of Devizes, *Chronicon*, p. 9. See also Ambrisco's discussion of Richard's Angevin agenda ("Cannibalism," p. 511).

[63] Suspicion of Richard's homosexuality is predicated upon disapproving comments noted by Roger of Howden: A hermit reportedly admonished Richard to "[r]emember the destruction of

And though his achievements in the Holy Land were formidable, he did not take Jerusalem, a primary goal of the crusade.[64] Given these details, Richard's preeminent stature as a national, English hero is remarkable.

Richard both registers and participates in this transformation. The first distortion that the *a* version performs is to substitute a demon mother from the East in place of Richard's real mother, Eleanor of Aquitaine, a maneuver that accomplishes a number of functions. First, it removes the dominant, historical mother. Not only French, Eleanor of Aquitaine may have constituted a feminizing and sodomitical influence upon Richard, whose youth she supervised in her Angevin court.[65] This de-feminization of Richard continues through other romance transformations/accretions. His uncharacteristic and uncourtly rudeness to the minstrel that leads to his imprisonment, for example, contradicts Richard's love of song, not to mention his abilities as a minstrel. The story of how the minstrel, Blondel, found the imprisoned Richard in Germany, is perhaps the most famous example that links the historical king to this courtly pursuit; but the romance *Richard* excises this effete French quality from Richard.[66] In its place, *Richard* provides the hero with masculine exploits — his affair with Margery, his unchivalric exchange of blows, and his indomitable aggression in eating the lion's heart — all displaying a relentlessly aggressive, male energy.

For Alan Ambrisco, the substitution, part of the poem's effacement of Richard's French heritage, provides a rationale for the king's barbarity; this trait paradoxically manifests his "Englishness" against the French, who are not portrayed as cannibals.[67] Following Heng, Suzanne Akbari argues that the name of Cassodorien's father, "Corbaryng," alludes to "Corbarans," the name that *La Chanson d'Antioche* gave to the historical Kerbogha, the Atabeg of Mosul.[68] From this relation, Akbari argues that Richard, through his mother, "lays claim to both supernatural powers and legitimate descent from the former Saracen rulers of Antioch and its region."[69] This eastern origin also affects his appetite and health. Since unnatural food made him sick (lines 3046–47), "his cure can be found only in food that is 'sete [wholesome] / To hys body,' that is, Saracen flesh."[70] This assimilation of Saracen flesh in a performance that Akbari, among others, likens to a Eucharistic rite, "give[s] rise to a reformulated English identity in which all his followers can partake"; these followers, like Richard, thus become English.[71] For Nicola McDonald, Richard's demonic origins motivate his crusade and his cannibalism, acts that "exorcise" his infernal blood and assure his Christian identity.[72]

Sodom and abstain from illicit acts," for if he did not, God would punish him (*Chronica*, 3:74; cited by Finlayson, "'*Richard Coer de Lyon*,'" p. 168). See also Heng, *Empire*, pp. 91–98.

[64] For discussions of the Third Crusade's failure to take Jerusalem, see Heng, *Empire*, p. 351n57; and Tolan, *Sons of Ishmael*, pp. 85–91.

[65] Heng, *Empire*, p. 97.

[66] See, e.g., Boyle, *Troubadour's Song*.

[67] Ambrisco, "Cannibalism," p. 499.

[68] Heng, *Empire*, p.343n29; Akbari, "Hunger," pp. 200–01.

[69] Akbari, "Hunger," p. 201.

[70] Akbari, "Hunger," p. 210.

[71] Akbari, "Hunger," p. 199.

[72] McDonald, "Eating People," p. 141.

Just as the romance magically disposes of Richard's French mother and heritage, it marvelously dispatches the French tongue to near oblivion.[73] After all, "scarcely one in a hundred [men now] understands French,"[74] as the narrator asserts in a move characterized as both populist and nationalistic: "Lewede men cune Frensch non, / Among an hondryd unnethis on" (lines 23–24). And while it is not surprising that a shared language would form part of a collective identity, the vitality with which *Richard* uses the English vernacular to promote a collective agenda and to attenuate Richard's shortcomings is remarkable. For example, in various confrontations, Richard's enemies — Cypriot, Griffon, and French — insult the English by calling them "taylardes," and "tayled dogges," a reference to the legend that Augustine, while attempting to convert the English, caused unbelievers to sprout tails.[75] As Heng so deftly elucidates, *Richard* maneuvers this insult in a variety of directions. The tailed English are at once super-phallic, deviant, and demonic. To cite one of the more memorable barrages from the French and the Griffons: "Go home, dogges, with your tayle; / For all your boost and your orguyle, / Men shall threste in your cuyle! [Men shall thrust (shove) vigorously up your rump]" (lines 1830–32). Recalling the cloud of sodomy that followed the historical Richard, Heng observes that this insult joins a legend about Englishmen who sprout tails to reports of the king's sexual deviance. The romance, though, transforms the insult into a joke that gives the English a common name, a common identity; thus, *Richard* turns crisis into a national celebration.[76]

A similar blending of history and fantasy applies to the presentation of other leaders, most notably, Philip II Augustus, king of France; and Saladin, the formidable Muslim military leader and Sultan of Egypt, Damascus, and Aleppo. With Philip, the romance uses historical details — his treachery with Tancred (lines 1677–2036) and his early departure from the crusade (lines 5911–28) — to diminish the French monarch and to present him as Richard's enemy.[77] But the romance also manufactures incidents that disparage Philip and the French: for example, Philip's repeated demonstrations of greed and military ineptitude, notably, his leniency and taking of ransom — against Richard's advice — during the siege of Taburette (lines 3866–3926); Richard's demeaning advice to Philip on good

---

[73] Only the angels in *RCL* speak French, and this is especially so in the first half of the poem: see lines 3012 and 3749–50. In the second half, the language of the angels shifts entirely to English: lines 5550–73 and 6945–62.

[74] Turville-Petre, *England the Nation*, p. 122.

[75] Broughton, citing among other sources William of Malmesbury, *Gesta Pontificum* in *Legends of Richard I*, pp. 93–97.

[76] Heng, *Empire*, p. 94. In similar fashion, the romance unites the island's disparate histories through the use of symbols. Richard's battle ax exemplifies this point: "Kynge Rycharde, I understonde, / Or he wente out of Englonde, / Let hym make an axe for the nones, / To breke therwith the Sarasyns bones" (lines 2209–12). Wielded by Anglo-Saxon warriors, Normans, and Anglo-Normans, this weapon unites antagonistic military and political lines. In the hands of a thoroughly English king, the weapon now indicates the combination of the English and the Anglo-Norman. While Richard's ax may appear to be an odd, unchivalric weapon for a king, he is reported to have used one during the crusades: see the Explanatory Note to lines 2209–11. And *RCL* is a popular romance: for the king to use a weapon not associated with the nobility is a populist move (Heng, *Empire*, p. 101; Akbari, "Hunger," p. 203).

[77] See the Explanatory Notes to lines 1668–2040, 1679, and 5895–5928.

kingship (lines 3772–97); and the narrator's insulting characterization of the French as "arwe and feynte" (lines 3849–65). Among comments upon *Richard*'s blatant, anti-French bias, Finlayson argues that the work displays the "English nationalist feeling at the period of the compilation of the Auchinleck MS., circa 1330, on the eve of Edward III's long-lasting war with France." Citing Edward III's efforts to unite a realm divided by the deposition of Edward II, Ambrisco suggests that the "task of healing political divisions was accomplished, at least in part, by identifying France as a common enemy against which all England should devote its considerable energies."[78] While the historical record proved no obstacle to redactors' desires to vilify Philip and the French, such was not the case with Saladin.

Before discussing Saladin's presentation, it will first be useful to summarize the trajectory of his reputation in the medieval West. As John V. Tolan demonstrates:

> [E]uropeans [first] reacted to Salâh al-Dîn's victory at Hattin and his capture of Jerusalem by painting him as a scourge of the Lord, an instrument of Divine punishment for Christian sins. Second . . . narrative and artistic portrayals of the Third Crusade portray the sultan as a valorous adversary, a shrewd and humane ruler, and in every way a match for his Christian foes. Finally . . . [in] a series of legends from the thirteenth century to the fifteenth . . . European authors increasingly portray Saladin as the epitome of knighthood.[79]

Noting that the West more frequently praised than demonized the sultan, Tolan mentions Dante's tribute in the *Inferno* (4:129), where the poet exalts Saladin by placing him with Virgil and other virtuous pagans in the limbo of hell's first circle. Such high regard reflects the sultan's reputation for generosity, humanity, and religious tolerance.[80] In this regard, the contrast between the Frankish capture of Jerusalem during the First Crusade and Saladin's conquest in 1187 is illuminating. The Franks, who killed every inhabitant they met — men, women, and children — waded in the blood of their victims. When Saladin took Jerusalem, not a single person was injured nor building looted, and, what is more, he even freed the Christian prisoners. His humanity, generosity and of course military acumen may explain why Western texts induct the sultan into French and even Christian models of chivalry. For example, in the poem *Ordene de chevalerie* Saladin agrees to free a prisoner, Hugh of Tiberias, if Hugh would dub him according to the Frankish ritual.[81] The resulting manifestation of Saladin as a Frankish knight epitomizes chivalry as an aristocratic, international order. *Richard Coer de Lyon*, though, paints quite a different picture of the sultan.

A key element in this presentation is the duel between Richard and Saladin, perhaps the most famous scene in *Richard* (lines 5479–5794). This confrontation which, *chanson* style, pits Christian against Muslim leader, held a particular resonance for medieval audiences; but

---

[78] Finlayson, "'*Richard, Coer de Lyon*,'" p. 171; Ambrisco, "Cannibalism," p. 512. See also Heng, "Romance of England," pp. 150–60; McDonald, "Eating People," p. 129; and Akbari, "Hunger," pp. 203–04.

[79] Tolan, *Sons of Ishmael*, pp. 81–82. Tolan's superb treatment includes a discussion of the various motivations for the West's different portrayals of Saladin. For example, by representing Saladin as a divine scourge of sinful Christians, Pope Gregory VIII diminishes Saladin's role (*Sons of Ishmael*, pp. 77–100).

[80] Tolan, *Sons of Ishmael*, pp. 79–80.

[81] Runciman, *History of the Crusades*, 1:286; 2:466; and Tolan, *Sons of Ishmael*, pp. 85, 96.

unlike the duel between Charlemagne and Baligant in *The Song of Roland*, one a chivalric Christian, the other a chivalric Saracen (lines 3560–3624), the encounter in *Richard*, distorting history, represents Saladin as an ignoble, treacherous villain. The episode begins when messengers present Richard with both a challenge and the offer of a gift horse. Saladin challenges Richard to a combat that will determine "Whether is of more power, / Jhesu or Jubyter?" (lines 5499–5500). Richard accepts the challenge as well as the sultan's gift of a horse, unaware that a necromancer had conjured two demon steeds, a mare for Saladin and a colt for Richard. When the mare neighed, the colt would return to suckle his mother, thus exposing Richard to Saladin's blade. Warning Richard of the ruse, an angel, among other things, admonishes Richard to "Ryde upon hym in Goddes name" (line 5563), advice that Richard follows to the letter, and apparently with good reason: "[I]f a fiend commissioned for an evil purpose was commanded in the name of the Trinity by the person whom he was sent to afflict, to become his servant, and turn his powers against his sender, he was compelled to obey."[82] Then, in a combat whose frequent representation in a variety of medieval contexts demonstrates its popularity, Richard wounds and unhorses Saladin, thus proving Richard's and Christianity's superiority to the sultan and Islam with its black arts.

In this denigration of Saladin, *Richard* may warp an historical incident to express anxiety about Richard's close ties to his mother. While chronicles report that Saladin and Safadin, out of generosity and respect, each sent magnificent horses to Richard, another account holds that Saif al-Din sent a dangerously restive horse to Richard.[83] In addition to these analogues, another historical detail must be noted: during the crusades, mares were the preferred war horse for Muslims.[84] Making proper use of the power of God's names over demons, "[t]his . . . story of the mother-and-son horses seamlessly works a nugget of historical fact — a horse gift from the historical Saladin or his brother to the historical Richard — into a fabulous artifice that at once describes concern at the control that mothers have over the male military animal, and exemplifies the vanishing of history into romance within a single, memorably witty event."[85]

In addition to presenting Saladin as a *chanson* villain, *Richard* also casts him as an Old Testament Jewish warrior. For example, when his emissaries return and recount their experience of Richard's cannibalism as well as his threats, Saladin reacts by rending his garments, a traditional gesture of mourning for Jews:

In al thy land, chyld, ne wyve, *woman*
But slee alle that he may fynde,
And sethe the flesch and with teeth grynde: *boil*
Hungyr schal hem nevere eyle! *never afflict them*
Into Yngelond wole he nought seyle
Tyl he have maad al playn werk!" *smooth as finished stone (level, flat)*

[82] "On Good and Bad Fairies," p. 17. See lines 5587–99 — and related Explanatory Note — for Richard's forceful and repeated articulation of God's names in subduing the demon steed.

[83] See the Explanatory Note to line 5502.

[84] Gillmor, "Horses," p. 274.

[85] Heng, *Empire*, pp. 97–98.

His clothis off gold unto his scherk — *undergarment*
Saladyn began torase for yre (lines 3650–57).[86] — *to tear from anger*

Another allusion provides an even more forceful presentation of Saladin as a Jew. After Richard's heroic relief of Jaffa, Saladin sends two messengers who advise Richard to return home or face annihilation by the Sultan's superior forces (lines 6882–6910). Having no intention of leaving, Richard offers a colorful response:

And though I were but my selfe alone,
I would abyde them everychone; — *face them [Saladin's forces] in combat*
And yf the dogge wyll come to me,
My pollaxe shall his bane be!
And saye that I hym defye — *challenge (declare war on)*
And all his cursed company in fere. — *together*
Go now and saye to hym thus:
The curse have he of swete Jhesus! (lines 6923–30)

Richard's curse invokes the parable of the barren fig tree: "And in the morning, returning into the city, he [Jesus] was hungry. And seeing a certain fig tree by the way side, he came to it and found nothing on it. And he saith to it: 'May no fruit grow on thee henceforward forever.' And immediately the fig tree withered away" (Matthew 21:18–19). As medieval theologians repeatedly compared the Jews to this barren fig tree, Richard's curse inflects Saladin with a Jewish identity.[87] And so these presentations of Saladin as a Jewish warrior — rending his garments, cursed as a barren tree — accords with Heng's argument that *Richard* depicts Muslims as virtual Jews, as "in the calumny of well poisoning" (lines 2747–56), to cite one example she mentions.[88] Painting Saladin as a Jewish warrior certainly diverges from other crusading poems that present the archetypal Western monarch, Charlemagne, as an Old Testament warrior. This divergence, I will argue later, forms part of the poem's typological program of substituting the English for the Jews — and the Franks — as God's chosen people.

The most notable and peculiar transformation in *Richard*, is, of course, the presentation of an historical king as a cannibal. As Ambrisco and others note, the cannibalism, though troubling, is perhaps less disturbing than the romance's celebration of the king's barbarous diet. The poem's trajectory is quite unlike that of the Middle English romance *Sir Gowther*. While Richard and Sir Gowther have similar demonic origins, only the latter expresses true penance in the end. In her comprehensive examination of the relation between cannibalism and medieval romance, Heng describes both the trauma that reports of crusader cannibalism inflicted upon the Christian West and the ways in which this trauma was processed in medieval romance. As she observes, the atrocity of Christian cannibalism during the First Crusade traumatized the West for a number of reasons, some of which are less than obvious. First, she and others note that the West conceived of cannibals in part as a monstrous, peripheral other, a monstrous race encountered in the Wonders of the East

[86] For the rending of garments as a sign of Jewish mourning, see, e.g., Genesis 37:34; Leviticus 10:6; and 2 Kings 3:31.

[87] Whitman, "The Body and the Struggle," p. 53.

[88] Heng, *Empire*, p. 79.

genre, for example.[89] Furthermore, the mode of cannibalism with which the West was familiar, the rite of the Eucharist, held a fundamental relation to a Christian identity that was crafted in part upon a regimen of eating and fasting; thus, patterns and types of consumption manifested the Christian community. And, of course, the First Crusade was a sacred expedition concerned not only with regaining the holy places but also with the salvation of the crusaders' souls. Instead of ingesting the Eucharist, though, some crusaders ate "the dead bodies of an infernal race—a race, moreover, whose practices and physical presence had been described, by Pope Urban II and the chroniclers, as polluting the holy places of Jerusalem."[90] That the trauma experienced by Christians from such contagion was profound is demonstrated by the cannibalism in *Richard*, which documents the West's persistent memory of crusader cannibalism. As Heng demonstrates, though, this trauma, for which the West did not at first "find an adequate discursive voicing," became in *Richard* a channel for nationalistic discourse.[91]

Heng finds that medieval discourses begin to form national communities at the same time that they help to create races.[92] In this regard, recall Richard's reaction upon seeing the "swine's head" that he had eaten: "Hys swarte vys whenne the kyng seeth, / Hys blake berd and hys whyte teeth, / Hou hys lyppys grennyd wyde: / "What devyl is this?" the kyng cryde" (lines 3211–14). This scene, as Heng observes, "triumphantly stages the horror of the head, its color difference, and its inhuman, devilish nature." With the second instance in *Richard*, where Richard performs cannibalism in order to intimidate Saladin and his emissaries, Richard states that no food is as nourishing to a Christian Englishman as is Saracen flesh: "Ther is no flesch so norysshaunt, / Unto an Ynglyssche Crysten man . . . / As is the flessh of a Saryzyne!" (lines 3548–49, 3552). In this aggressive formulation that scholars connect to the Eucharist, Richard defines Englishness through the consumption of Saracen flesh. What is more, Richard threatens to "swallow up lineages and sweep away succession, consuming the future itself, in world domination."[93] It is an understatement, then, to say that *Richard* transforms the cultural trauma of crusader cannibalism into a triumph. As Heng argues, Richard's cannibalism becomes both a trope for figuring conquest and domination and a racializing discourse based upon color and religion that is productive of national identity.

In her wide-ranging study, *Cannibalism in High Medieval Literature*, Heather Blurton adds to this discussion. Though *Richard* is hardly the focus of her work, Blurton addresses Richard's appetite in relation to the prevalence of cannibalism by Saracens — actual or imagined — in the *chanson de geste* tradition. To be sure, *chansons de geste* frequently depict or suggest cannibalism by Saracens.[94] As Blurton argues:

---

[89] See, e.g., Blurton, *Cannibalism*, pp. 5–6; and Tattersall, "Anthropophagi," pp. 240–41.

[90] Heng, Empire, pp. 26–27.

[91] Heng, *Empire*, p. 29.

[92] Heng, *Empire*, p. 71.

[93] Heng, *Empire*, pp. 64, 75. See, in addition, her argument that this healing cannibalism alludes to the story of Brian and Cadwallo in Geoffrey of Monmouth's *Historia*, and so represents the emergence of a discourse of cannibalism in medieval romance.

[94] Arguing that "[t]he representation of Saracens as cannibals is systemic in the genre of *chansons de geste*," Blurton cites the following texts: *Le Roman de Toute Chevalerie*, *La Chanson d'Antioche*, *La*

> This romance [*Richard*] picks up on the strategic potential of cannibalism that texts like Guibert's and *La Chanson d'Antioche* suggest. Yet, whereas in their inscription of crusader cannibalism Guibert of Nogent and *La Chanson d'Antioche* deal anxiously with an event that threatens to disrupt the narrative means of representing Christendom, *Richard Coer de Lyon* tells the story of crusader cannibalism precisely because it disrupts these representations. *Richard Coer de Lyon* appropriates the cannibal imagery of the *chanson de geste* tradition—both of literal Saracen cannibals and of the metaphorical threat of territorial incorporation—and inverts it in order to invert the ideology of *chanson de geste*. . . . This reworking of generic form becomes the basis for the romance's politics of asserting a model of English dominance in a post-crusading Europe.[95]

As another approach, I would emphasize two comparisons: the similarities between *Richard* and narratives in the First Crusade Cycle, and the typological resonances between this poem and other crusade narratives. These comparisons accomplish two functions: they provide another motive for Richard's cannibalism, a feature of the work that troubles many readers; and by means of a typological framework, they make the extreme Christian violence that characterizes *Richard* more comprehensible. Consider, for example, Richard's divinely sanctioned slaughter of the Muslim hostages at Acre:

> They were brought out of the toun,
> Save twenty he heeld to raunsoun.
> They were led into the place ful evene; *all the way*
> There they herden an aungell of hevene,
> That seyde, "Seygnyours, tues, tues, *Lords, kill, kill*
> Spares hem nought — behedith these!"
> Kyng Richard herde the aungelys voys,
> And thankyd God and the Holy Croys.
> There were they behedyd hastelyke,
> And casten into a foul dyke (lines 3745–54).

This representation of an historical event should be understood within both biblical and historical patterns. I suggest that this atrocity recalls the Christian massacre of Jerusalem's inhabitants in the First Crusade, a massacre of unspeakable savagery. Just as the Franks laid siege to Jerusalem, so too Richard besieged Acre. As Jay Rubenstein notes: "Bartolph of Nangis appeals to Old Testament precedent (3 Kings 15) to explain the massacre in Jerusalem. The Franks, he says, did not wish to be like Saul, who had spared Agag against God's orders to destroy all of the Amalekites."[96] As Rubenstein argues, such manipulations, not to mention the Franks' historical presence in the Holy Land, become part of a *translatio*: replacing the Jews, the Franks become God's new chosen people:

> These associative leaps recur in a general way in the chronicles, where we learn that the Franks are the new Chosen People fighting for the spiritual Jerusalem as well as for its more

---

Conquête de Jerusalem, *La Chanson de Guillame*, *Aliscans*, *Floovant*, *Huon de Bordeaux*, and *La Prise d'Orange* (*Cannibalism*, pp. 107–08).

[95] Blurton, *Cannibalism*, pp. 120–21.

[96] Rubenstein, "Cannibals and Crusaders," p. 546n100, citing *Gesta Francorum Iherusalem expugnantium*, 35.513. Compare I Kings 15.

> mundane, earthly counterpart. . . . In the historians' minds, the Franks competed in every sense with the ancient Jews and fulfilled their destiny more completely. It seems unlikely that, when faced with new stories of cannibalism, these same historians would not have thought of those famous incidents from Josephus's narrative and from the books of Kings.[97]

The violence in *Richard*, the cannibalism, even the representation of scarcity at Acre follow a typological pattern as the English replace the Franks as God's chosen people.[98] This point brings us to *La Chanson d'Antioche* and its distancing of crusader cannibalism by confining it to the degenerate group known as the Tarfurs. With the lapse of a few years, "later in the twelfth century, at home in Europe, with the creation of increasingly sophisticated central governments and with the simultaneous crafting of refined, humane, and courtly sentiments, such behavior [cannibalism] looked aberrational and in need of explanation or repression."[99] In the later crucible of popular romance, though, the result is quite different. The movement away from a chivalric code enables the exaltation of cannibalism in the militant person of the king. The typological resonances of Richard's cannibalism and other acts reveal that he, standing for all Englishmen, replaces the Franks as the English become *populi Dei.*

One other comparison to the First Crusade Cycle, a cycle that includes *La Chanson d'Antioche*, needs to be made. Like *Richard*, this crusade cycle concerns an historical, crusading hero, Godfrey of Bouillon. The cyclic form encouraged prefiguration of the crusade hero by his ancestors' exploits and some of these prefigurations were, like the demon mother episode in this poem, quite fantastic.[100] Godfrey's later greatness, for example, is ordained by his marvelous ancestry which is recounted in *Le Chevalier au Cygne*, *The Knight of the Swan*, a story with a number of Middle English analogues.[101] And, as Robert L. Chapman notes, Richard's demon mother constitutes a fairy mistress of the "Swan Maiden type."[102] I would suggest, then, that the redactors of *Richard* modeled their revisions upon this French Crusade Cycle, the demon mother episode prefiguring Richard's later typological cannibalism.[103] And so a series of episodes deemed unhistorical and generically anomalous may follow a biblical, historiographical pattern as well as a French literary model.

---

[97] Rubenstein, "Cannibals and Crusaders," pp. 547–48.

[98] See Rubenstein's observation that chronicles of the First Crusade followed an Old Testament strategy for documenting the severity of a famine: listing the prices of food ("Cannibals and Crusaders," p. 549n100). This strategy is seen in *RCL* in lines 2837–65: see the Explanatory Note that accompanies these lines and the note to line 3428.

[99] Rubenstein, "Cannibals and Crusaders," p. 551.

[100] Trotter, *Medieval French Literature*, p. 108.

[101] For a discussion of Middle English versions of *Knight of the Swan*, see Hibbard, *Mediæval Romance*, pp. 239–52. For a brief discussion of this legend in *chason de geste* and in romance, see Nelson, "Swan Knight."

[102] Chapman, "Demon Queen," p. 393.

[103] See McDonald's analysis of the connections between Richard's demon mother, his crusade, and his cannibalism ("Eating People," pp. 141–42).

REPRESENTING AND MODIFYING THE TEXT

Richard Coer de Lyon's textual situation is challenging: seven manuscripts and two printings are extant, but no text served as the source for another. The enormous variety between these texts has led scholars to recognize that this work exists in multiple versions.[104] It must be noted, then, that the present edition, by no means definitive, offers the *a* version of *Richard*. In part, the extent of recent critical interest in *a*'s fabulous interpolations justifies editing this version. In addition, no complete text of *b* is extant. The choice of which manuscript or printing to use as a base manuscript, though, proved difficult. I first chose W, Wynkyn de Worde's 1509 printing, as my base manuscript because it offered the only complete text of *a* — C and B are each missing a number of leaves — and because it had never been edited. The dialect of B, which Brunner describes as a "Scots-North English light revision of the romance," damages the meter with fill words, among other issues; thus, B constitutes an anomalous text.[105] But I soon became disenchanted with the language and versification of W in comparison to that of C, a text I found to be much richer. My edition, therefore, is based upon C and, like Brunner's, uses W to complete lacunae.

On the one hand, the disadvantages to my choice are not inconsequential. With missing and defective leaves, C does not offer a complete text.[106] And Brunner has produced a similar, composite edition (albeit in turn-of-the-century, Austrian-inflected German). Also, C includes some tiresome, "unhistorical" adventures not found in W.[107] On the other hand, Brunner's edition is out of print and hard to find, and so a new edition of *Richard* "is long overdue."[108] Though not a critical edition, my Textual Notes, which document emendations and significant differences between the versions, are substantial, as are the Explanatory Notes. In many respects, then, this edition brings Brunner's 1913 work up to date.

It is also important to add that my approach to editing is not the same as Brunner's. My emendations, for example, are often more conservative. I emend C in the case of clear error and when C diverges from readings common to W and to B; on occasion, I emend C when a reading is attested in both versions. I am also less prone to emend for metrical reasons. Except in the case of clear error, my emendations attempt to use an attested reading: I try to avoid producing a line that does not exist in some text of *Richard*. Orthography has been modernized in accordance with the conventions of the series: the letters *i/j* and *u/v* are emended to follow modern usage; *th* replaces thorn; and yogh is represented by *y*, *gh*, or *g*. Numbers and common abbreviations, the ampersand, for example, and suspension marks have been expanded silently. Capitalization and some breaks between passages are editorial. In general, though, the breaks between passages are those found in C or in W.

---

[104] The romance *Bevis of Hampton* offers a much-studied parallel to *RCL*'s complex textual history and multiple versions. For a discussion, see the introduction to *Bevis of Hampton*, ed. Herzman, Drake, and Salisbury, pp. 187–89 and accompanying references.

[105] Brunner, *Löwenherz*, p. 5.

[106] Gaps in C include the following: lines 228–448, 679–796, 1737–2468, and 6850–6972.

[107] See note 18 above.

[108] McDonald, "Eating People," p. 146n18.

Though of immense popularity to medieval audiences, *Richard* suffered a long period of critical neglect, even disparagement.[109] Over the last decade, though, both scholarly interest in the poem and critical assessments of its value have changed considerably. Indeed, the very qualities that caused scholars to marginalize the work — its militant, violent crusading ethos, virulent nationalism, and its demonic and cannibalistic "accretions" — now prove especially meaningful to scholars. As the work of such scholars as Ambrisco, Heng, Akbari, McDonald, Blurton, and Cordery among others attests, *Richard* is a coherent text worthy of vigorous analysis. It is hoped that this edition will add to this renewed interest in this "most medieval" of popular romances.[110]

[109] For negative critical assessments of *RCL*, see note 38 above; for similar, though less damning judgments of *Bevis*, see Barron, *English Medieval Romance*, pp. 217, 233, cited in *Bevis of Hampton*, p. 197.

[110] Heng, *Empire*, p. 67.

Richard Coer de Lyon

Hic incipit vita Ricardi Regis primi	*Here begins the life of King Richard I*
Lord Jhesu, kyng of glorye,	*(see note)*
Whyche grace and vyctorye	*What [remarkable]*
Thou sente to Kyng Rychard,	
That nevere was founde coward!	
It is ful good to here in jeste	*hear in tales (storied exploits)*
Of his prowess and hys conqueste.	
Fele romaunces men maken newe,	*Many; compose*
Of goode knyghtes, stronge and trewe.	
Of here dedys men rede romaunce,	*their*
Both in Engeland and in Franse:	
Of Rowelond and of Olyver,	*Roland*
And of every doseper;	*every [one of the] twelve peers (see note)*
Of Alisaundre and Charlemayn,	
Of Kyng Arthour and of Gawayn,	
How they were knyghtes goode and curteys;	*courteous*
Of Turpyn and Oger Daneys.	*Turpin; Ogier the Dane (see note)*
Of Troy men rede in ryme,	
What werre ther was in olde tyme;	*war*
Of Ector and of Achylles,	*Hector*
What folk they slowe in that pres.	*killled in that struggle (battle)*
In Frenssche bookys this rym is wrought,	*verse narrative*
Lewede men ne knowe it nought.	*Uneducated*
Lewede men cune Frensch non,	*men do not know any French*
Among an hondryd unnethis on;	*scarcely one*
And nevertheless, with glad chere,	
Fele of hem that wolde here	*Many of them who would hear*
Noble jestes, I undyrstande,	*stories*
Of doughty knyghtes of Yngelonde.	*valiant*
Therfore now I wole yow rede	*tell*
Of a kyng doughty in dede.	
Kyng Rychard, the werryour beste	
That men fynde in ony jeste.	
Now alle that here this talkyng,	*hear; tale*
God geve hem alle good endyng!	*end of life*

Lordynges, herkenes before	*hearken to an earlier time*
How Kyng Rychard was gete and bore.	*conceived*
Hys fadyr hyghte Kyng Henry.	*was named; (see note)*
In hys tyme, sykyrly,	*certainly*
Als I fynde in my sawe,	*As; account*
Seynt Thomas was islawe	*slain*
At Cauntyrbury at the awter stone.	*altar slab*
There manye myraclys are idon.	*Where; performed*
When he was twenty wyntyr olde,	*(Henry); years*
He was a kyng swythe bolde.	*extremely*
He wolde no wyf, I understonde,	*wanted*
With gret tresore though he here fonde.	*Though he found her with great treasure*
Nevyrtheles hys barouns hym redde	*counseled him*
That he grauntyd a wyf to wedde.	*That he should consent to wed a woman*
Hastely, he sente hys sondes	*envoys*
Into manye diverse londes:	
The feyreste wymman that wore on lyf,	*fairest woman alive*
Men schold brynge hym to wyf.	*marry*
Messangeres were redy dyght,	*promptly prepared*
To schippe they wente that ylke nyght.	*same*
Anon the sayl up thay drowgh;	*At once; drew*
The wynd hem servyd wel inowgh.	*enough*
Whenne they come on mydde the see,	*in the middle of*
No wynd onethe hadden hee.	*scarcely had they*
Therfore hem was swythe woo.	*sorely distressed*
Another schip they countryd thoo,	*encountered then*
Swylk on ne seygh they nevere non.	*Such a one saw they never not one*
Al it was whyt of ruel bon,	*All of it was white as narwhal tusks*
And every nayl with gold begrave.	*engraved*
Of pure gold was the stave.	*prow*
Here mast was yvory.	
Of samyte the sayl, wytterly,	*rich silk cloth, utterly*
Here ropes were of Tuely sylk,	*silk from Toulouse*
Al so whyte as ony mylk,	*As white*
That noble schyp al with oute,	*in outward appearance*
With clothis of gold spred aboute,	
And here loof and here wyndas,	*spar; winch (see note)*
Of asure, forsothe it was!	*lapus lazuli, truly*
In that schyp ther were idyght,	*arranged*
Knyghtes and laydyys of mekyl myght;	*much power (wealth)*
And a lady therinne was,	
Bryght as the sunne thorwgh the glas.	*Fair*
Here men aborde gunne to stande,	*Their; at the side of the ship*
And sesyd that other to here hande,	*seized*
And prayde hem for to dwelle,	*entreated them to remain*
And here counsayl for to telle.	*their plan*
And they grauntyd with alle skylle,	*And they consented with all tact*

For to telle al at here wylle. *their*
"Swoo wyde landes we have went, *Such vast; traveled*
For Kyng Henry us has sent
For to seke hym a qwene,
The fayreste that myghte founde bene."
Up ros a kyng off a chayere,
With that word they spoke there.
The chayer was charbocle ston: *carbuncle stone*
Swylk on ne sawgh they nevere non; *Such one saw*
And two dukes hym besyde,
Noble men and mekyl of pryde, *great*
And welcomed the messangers ylkone. *each one*
Into that schyp they gunne gone, *went*
Thrytty knyghtes, withouten lye, *Thirty*
For sothe, was in that cumpanye!
Into that ryche schyp they went,
As messangeres that weren isent.
Knyghtes and ladyes come hem aghen, *came toward them*
Sevene score and moo, I wene, *believe*
Welcomyd hem alle at on wurd. *in unison*
They sette tresteles and layde a bord. *placed a board [on them]*
Cloth of sylk theron was sprad,
And the kyng hym selven bad *requested*
That hys doughtyr were forth fette, *fetched*
And in a chayer before hym sette.
Trumpes begonne for to blowe,
Sche was fet forth in a throwe, *brought forth quickly*
With twenty knyghtes here aboute,
And moo of ladyes that were stoute, *more; noble*
Alle they gunne knele here twoo, *did kneel to her*
And aske here what she wolde han doo. *wished to have done*
They eeten and drank and maden hem glade, *pleased themselves*
As the kyng hym self hem bade.
Whenne they hadde nygh ieete, *nearly [finished] eating*
Aventures to speke they nought forgete. *Marvelous tales*
The kyng hem tolde in hys resoun, *account (tale)*
It com hym thorwgh a vysyoun: *came to him*
In hys land that he cam froo,
Into Yngelond for to goo,
And hys doughtyr that was so dere,
For to wende bothe in fere. *to travel; together*
"In this manere we have us dyght, *prepared ourselves*
Into that lond to wende ryght." *travel straight*
Thenne answeryd a messanger,
Hys name was callyd Bernager:
"Forthere wole we seke nought,
To my lord sche schal be brought.

When he with eyen schal sen, *eyes shall see*
Fol wel payed wole he ben." *satisfied*
The wynd aros out of the northeste,
And servede hem right with the beste.
At the Tour they gunne arryve, *Tower [of London] (see note)*
To londe the knyghtes wente belyve. *disembark; promptly*
The messangeres the kyng have told
Of that lady, fayre and bold, *noble*
Ther he lay in the Tour, *Where*
Of that lady whyt so flour. *as flower*
Kyng Henry gan hym sone dyght, *did soon prepare himself*
With erl, baroun, and manye a knyght,
Agayn the lady for to wende, *Toward; walk (proceed)*
For he was curteys and hende. *courteous and noble*
The damysele on londe was led,
And clothis of gold before here spred,
And here fadyr here beforn *before her*
With a coroun of gold icorn. *pure gold*
The messangers by ylke a syde, *on every side*
And menstralles with mekyl pryde. *great splendor (see note)*
Kyng Henry lyghte in hyyng, *descended in haste*
And grette fayre that uncouth kyng. *greeted graciously; unknown (strange)*
And that fayre lady alsoo:
"Welcome be ye me alle too."
To Westemenstre they wente in fere, *together*
Lordynges and ladyys that ther were.
Trumpes begonne for to blowe,
To mete they wente in a throwe. *To eat; in a short time*
Knyghtes served there good spede, *great abundance*
Of what to telle it is no nede.
And aftyr mete, in hyyng *food, in haste*
Spak Kyng Henry, oure kyng,
To the kyng that sat in same: *same [place]*
"Leve sere, what is thy name?" *Dear*
"My name," he sayde, "is Corbaryng.
Of Antyoche I am kyng."
And tolde hym in hys resoun, *account*
He cam thedyr thorwgh a vysyoun.
"Forsothe, sere, I telle thee,
I hadde elles brought more meyné *troops (retainers)*
Manye moo, withouten fayle,
And moo schyppys with vytayle." *victuals*
Thenne askyd he that lady bryght,
"What hyghtest you, my swete wyght?" *are you named; creature*
"Cassodorien, withouten lesyng." *lying*
Thus answeryd sche the kyng.
"Damysele," he seyde, "bryght and schene, *fair and beautiful*

Wylt thou dwelle and be my qwene?” *remain*
Sche answeryd with wordys stylle, *meek*
“Sere, I am at my faderys wylle.” *under; control*
Here fadyr grauntyd thenne ful sone, *consented right away*
Al hys wyl scholde be done,
Hastely that she were wedde
As qwene unto kynges bedde.
And prayed hym for hys curtesy,
It moste be don prevyly. *without pomp (discreetly)*

The spousyng was idon that nyght; *wedding*
Theratte daunsyd many a knyght.
Mekyl joye was hem among.
A preest on morwe the messe song; *in the morning sang the mass*
Beforn the elevacyoun, *elevation [of the host] (see note)*
The qwene fel in swowne adon.
The folk wondryd and were adrad. *frightened*
Into a chambyr sche was lad,
Sche seyde, “For I am thus ishent: *disgraced (injured)*
I dar nevere see no sacrement.”
Here fadyr on morwe took hys leve;
No lengere wolde he there beleve. *remain*
The kyng dwellyd with hys qwene;
Chyldren they hadden hem bytwene,
Twoo knaves and a mayde, *(see note)*
Forsothe, as the book us sayde.
Rychard hyghte the fyrste, iwis, *was named*
Of whom this romaunce imakyd is. *composed (written)*
Jhon that other forsothe was.
The thrydde, hys sustyr, Topyas.
Thus they dwellyd in fere *together*
To the fyftenthe yere.
On a day before the Rode, *Cross*
The kyng at hys masse stode. *celebrated mass*
There com an erl of gret pousté *power (authority)*
“Sere,” he sayde, “hou may this be *Sire (Sir)*
That my lady, youre wyf, the qwene,
The sacrement ne dar nought sene? *dare not witness*
Geve us leve to don here dwelle, *to make her remain*
Fro that begynnes the gospelle *From [the time]*
Tyl the messe be sungge and sayd,
And you schalt se a queynte brayd.” *an unusual occurrence*
The kyng grauntyd with good wylle, *consented*
To holden here with strengthe stylle.
“Neyther for wele, neyther for woo, *prosperity; woe*
Let here nought out fro kyrke goo.” *church*
And whene the belle began to ryng,

The preest scholde make the sakeryng *consecration of bread and wine*
Out of the kyrke sche wolde away. *wished to leave*
The erl, "For Gode," sayde "nay.
Lady, you schalt here abyde
For ony thyng that may betyde." *In spite of; happen*
Sche took here doughtyr in here hond,
And Johan her sone she wolde not wonde, *forsake (abandon)*
Out of the rofe she gan her dyght, *took herself*
Openly, before all theyr syght.
Johan fell frome her in that stonde, *moment*
And brake his thygh on the grounde;
And with her doughter she fled her waye,
That never after she was isey. *seen*
The kynge wondred of that thynge,
That she made suche an endynge.
For love that he was served so, *rewarded*
Wolde he never after come there ne go.
He let ordeyne after his endynge, *death*
His sone, Rycharde, to be kynge.
Crowned after Kynge Harry, *(see note)*
Thus was Rycharde, sykerly, *truly (indeed)*
That was in his fifteenth yere.
He was a man of grete powere.
Dedes of armes he gave hym to, *devoted himself*
As falleth for kynges and knyghtes to do. *As is appropriate*
He waxed so stronge and so wyght, *brave*
Ayenst hym had no man no myght.
In every stede he toke honoure, *place; received homage (allegiance)*
As a noble kynge and conqueroure. *victor*

The fyrst yere that he was kynge,
At Salysbury he made a justynge, *arranged a tournament*
And commaunded every man to be there,
Bothe with shelde and with spere.
Erles and barons, everychone, *every one*
At home ne dwelled never one, *not one*
On forfeyture on lyfe and londe: *On penalty of losing*
For nothynge that they ne wonde. *Not for anything should they be absent*
This was cryed, I understond, *announced*
Thorughout all Englonde.
All was for to loke and se,
The knyghtes that best myght be.
There they came all at his wyll,
His commaundement to fulfyll.
The partyes were sonder set, *set apart*
Togyder they ran without let. *without delay*
Kynge Rycharde gan hym dysguyse

In a full stronge queyntyse. — *heavy armor*
He came out of a valaye
For to se of theyr playe, — *martial play*
As a knyght aventurous. — *knight errant*
His atyre was orgulous; — *arrogantly splendid*
All togyder cole blacke
Was hys horse, without lacke. — *without flaw*
Upon his creste a raven stode — *(see note)*
That yaned as he were wode, — *gaped; mad*
And aboute his necke a bell,
Wherfore the reason I shall you tell.
The kynde of the raven is — *disposition*
In travayll for to be, iwis.
Sygnyfyaunce of the bell,
With holy chyrche to dwell, — *remain*
And them to noy and to greve — *to harm and to harass*
That be not in the ryght byleve. — *faith*
He bare a shafte that was grete and stronge.
It was fourtene fote longe,
And it was grete and stoute:
One and twenty inches aboute.
The fyrst knyght that he there mette,
Full egerly he hym grette — *struck*
With a dente amyd the shelde. — *blow in the middle of*
His horse he bare downe in the felde, — *overthrew*
And the knyght fell to grounde,
Full nye deed in that stounde. — *moment*
The next that he mette thare,
A grete stroke he hym bare. — *thrust*
His gorgere with his cornell tho, — *His gorget with his lance point then*
His necke he brake there a two.
His horse and he fell to grounde,
And dyed bothe in that stounde. — *moment*
Kynge Rycharde harde gan hove and abyde, — *close by did linger and wait*
Yf ony mo wolde to hym ryde.
Trumpettes began for to blowe,
Knyghtes justed in that rowe, — *company*
Another knyght, hardy and good,
Sate on a stede rede as blode.
He dyde hym arme and well dyght, — *arrayed himself well*
In all that longed to suche a knyght. — *was appropriate*
A shafte he toke, grete and longe,
That was so hevy and stronge,
And sayd he wolde to hym ryde,
Yf he durste hym abyde. — *dared to wait for him*
Trumpettes began to blowe than;
Therby wyste many a man — *knew*

That they sholde juste mere, *utterly*
The noble knyghtes that there were.
Kynge Rycharde of hym was ware,
And a spere to hym he bare,
And encountred hym in the felde;
He bare awaye halfe his shelde, *knocked*
His pusen therwith gan gone, *gorget (throat armor); did go*
And also his brandellet bone, *shoulder armor*
His vyser and his gorgere.
Hym repented that he came there! *He regretted*
Kynge Rycharde hoved and behelde, *lingered*
And thought to rest hym in the felde,
Yf there were other knyght or swayne *retainer*
That wolde more ryde hym agayne. *also*
He sawe there wolde come none;
On his waye he gan forth gone
Into a wode out of theyr syght,
And in another tyre he hym dyght. *attire; dressed*
Upon a stede rede as blode,
With all the tyre that on hym stode, *trappings*
Horse and shelde, armure and man,
That no man sholde knowe hym than.
Upon his creste a rede hounde:
The tayle henge to the grounde.
That was sygnyfycacyon
The hethen folke to brynge downe,
Them to slee for Goddes love,
And Crysten men to brynge above.
Styll he hoved and bode thore; *lingered; waited there*
To them he thought to ryde more. *Against them*
He rode the thronge all aboute,
He helde within and withoute. *observed*
A baron he sawe hym besyde;
Towarde hym he gan ryde.
To a squyer he toke his spere: *entrusted*
To hym he wolde it not bere *Against him [Richard]*
Forth he toke a mansell, *mace*
A stroke he thought to be set well
On his helme that was so stronge. *helmet*
Of that dente the fyre out spronge. *blow*
The baron tourned hym asyde,
And sayd, "Felowe, forth thou ryde,
With thy peres go and playe! *peers*
Come no more here, I thee praye,
And sykerly, yf thou do, *assuredly*
Thou shalte have a knocke or two."
Kynge Rycharde wondred in his thought

That he set his stroke at nought,
And came agayne by another waye,
And thought to make a better paye. *reprisal*
In his styrope up he stode,
And smote to hym with irefull mode. *against him; mood*
He set his stroke on his yron hat,
But that other in his sadell sat.
Hastely, without wordes mo,
His mase he toke in his honde tho *then*
That was made of yotyn bras. *cast (molded)*
He wondred who that it was,
Such a stroke he hym lente,
That Rycharde feet out of his steropes wente.
For plate, ne for acketton,[1]
For hawberke, ne for campeson,
Suche a stroke he never had none ore *before*
That dyde him halfe so moche sore.
Full swythe awaye he gan ryde, *Very swiftly*
Out of the prees there besyde.
To hym selfe he sayd tho: *then*
"Of suche strokes kepe I no mo!" *receive*
He wente adowne to a well,
And with his helme dranke his fell, *fill*
And he watred his stede also.

In the thyrde atyre he let hym do,[2]
All his atyre whyte as mylke.
His croper was of sylke. *crupper*
Upon his shulder a crosse rede,
That betokeneth Goddes dede *death (service; heroic achievement)*
With his enemyes for to fyght,
To wynne the Crosse, if that he myght. *(see note)*
Upon his heed a dove whyte, *(see note)*
Sygnyfycacyon of the Holy Spyryte,
To be bolde to wynne the pryse,
And dystroye Goddes enemyes.

To the Kynge Rycharde gan hym dyght *Against; did betake himself*
Than another noble knyght. *Then*
Fouke Doly was his name. *(see note)*
The kynge hym loved for his fame.
To hym a stroke he dyght, *delivered*
Well to paye with all his myght. *to repay (strike)*
He smote hym on his bassenet, *helmet*

[1] Lines 375–76: *In spite of armor, in spite of padded garment / In spite of mail shirt, in spite of the quilted jacket*

[2] *In the third attire (equipment) he placed (put on) himself*

A grete dente without let. *delay*
It foundred to his cheke bone. *penetrated*
Syr Fouke bad hym forth gone,
That he no lenger abyde,
In aventure yf ony stroke betyde. *On the chance that any blow should befall [him]*
The kynge sawe he felte no sore,
And thought to gyve hym more,
And another stroke he hym brayde. *dealt him*
His mase upon his heed he layde;
With good wyll that stroke he set.
The baron thought he wolde hym let, *stop*
And with his hevy mase of stele,
There he gave the kynge his dele *portion*
That his helme all torove, *So that; shattered*
And he over his sadell drove,
And his steropes he forbare. *relinquished*
Such a stroke had he never are. *before*
He was so astonyed of that dente, *stunned*
That nye he had his lyfe lente, *lost*
And for that stroke that hym was gyven,
He ne wyst whether it was daye or even. *did not know*
Tho he recovered of his swowe, *When; swoon*
To his palays he hym drowe. *travelled*
  Than he commaunded hastely
Herodes for to make crye, *Heralds*
And every man for to wende *travel*
Home to his owne frende. *comrade (ally)*
The kynge anone a messengere *at once*
Full prevely he sente there *Very discreetly*
To Syr Thomas of Multon
That was a noble baron,
And to Syr Fouke Doly,
That they come to hym on hye: *at once*
"Let them not dwell in no manere. *delay*
Bydde them come bothe in fere." *Ask; together*
The messengere therwith wente, *in response*
And sayd the kynge after them sente,
Swythe for to come hym to, *Promptly*
Without delaye that it be do. *be done*
The knyghtes hyed and were blythe. *travelled quickly; joyful*
To the kynge they wente swythe, *quickly*
And hendly they hym grette, *courteously*
And he them toke and by hym sette, *received them*
And sayd to them wordes free: *kind*
"Welcome be ye now to me!"
In eythyr hond he took on, *one*
In to a chaumbyr he bad hem gon. *them*

Quod Rychard, "Leve frendes twey, *Said; Dear; two*
Tel me the sothe, I yow prey,
Of these joustes, paramours, *dear friends*
What knyght was he that rod best cours? *charge (passage at arms)*
And whiche coulde best his crafte, *who knew*
For to demene well his shafte, *use*
With dentes for to fell his foos?
Whiche of them wan the loos, *prize*
And who the styfeste tymbyr brak?"
Quod Multoun, "On in atyr blak *One*
Com preckande ovyr the falewe feld; *galloping*
Alle that was there tho hym beheeld, *then*
Hou he rod as he were wood. *mad*
Aroume he hovyd and withstood. *At a distance he waited and held fast*
On hys crest sat a raven swart, *dark (black)*
And he ne heeld with neyther part. *did not support either side*
A schafte he bar, styff and strong,
Of fourtene foote it was long,
On and tweynty ynches aboute. *One*
He askyd at al the route, *of all the company*
Yf ony durste come and prove *dared; try*
A cours, for hys lemannes love, *lover's*
With a knyght aunterous now here. *knight-errant*
A yonge knyght, a strong bachelere,
He hente a schaft and stede bystrod, *seized; mounted*
And to the knyght aunterous he rod.
The aunterous with hym mette,
Swylke a strok on his scheld he sette *Such*
That hors and man overthrewe; *fell down*
But there was no man that hym knewe.
Trumpys blewe, herowdes gred, *heralds; cried*
And alle othere of hym dred *feared*
To jouste with hym eft with launse. *again*
Enauntyr hym tydde swylk a chaunce. *Lest such a fate should happen to him*
An hardy knyght, stout and savage, *bold*
Hente a schaft with gret rage. *Seized; fierceness*
'Now he has on of oure felde! *one of ours; felled*
Wurthe we nevre for men telde, *We shall never be judged to be men*
Sith he hath don us this despyte, *insult*
Yif he agayn passe quyte, *unharmed*
That he ne have fyrste a knok!' *Unless*
He prykyd forth out of the flok, *galloped; troop*
With a long schaft, stout and quarrey. *sturdy*
In myd the cours thenne mette they;
The aventurous smote his shelde amyddde,
A wonders case our knyght betydde.
The aunterous felde hym with yre, *errant knight; fury*

Doun off his stede and brak hys swyre. *neck*
The thrydde knyght to speke bygan:
"This is a devyl and no man
That our folke felles and sleth! *Who*
Tyde me lyf, or tyde me deth, *Let me live, or let me die*
I shal mete hym yf I may!"
The aunterous with gret deray, *ferocity*
So harde to oure knyght he droff, *drove (hit)*
Hys shelde in twoo peses roff. *split*
Hys schuldre with hys schafte he brak,
And bar hym over hys hors bak,
That he fel doun and brak hys arme.
He ne dede hym no more harme!
The aunterous tho turnyd agayn, *then*
And hovyd stylle for to seyn *remained*
Who durste jouste with hym more. *dared*
Of hym they were adred ful sore, *extremely*
That non durste jouste with hym eft, *afterwards*
Lest he hadde hem here lyf bereft; *Lest he should deprive them of their lives*
And whenne he seygh ther com no moo, *saw*
He rod agayn ther he com froo.

Aftyr the blak, another come;
Alle the folk good kep nome. *paid close attention*
Hys hors and al hys atyr was red;
Hym semyd weel to ben a qued. *He seemed genuinely to be a devil*
A red hound on hys helme above.
He comme to seke and to prove
Yif ony jouste with hym dar.
Whenne non wolde he was war
With schaft to hym make chalenge,
He rod doun ryght be the renge. *ring*
The devyl hym honge where he be! *Let the devil*
I not what, devyl, him eylid at me![1]
Hys schaft a squyer he betook, *entrusted to*
And behelde me with grymly look, *fierce*
And smot me soo with hys mase,
Ne hadde be Jhesu Crystys grace, *Had it not been for Jesus Christ's grace*
My swyre hadde gon in twey. *neck*
I bad hym ryden forth hys wey,
Dele with fooles as hymself was.
Agayn he com be anothir pas,
And gaf me a wel werse than that, *a much worse blow*
But stylle in my sadyl I sat.
Tho seyde many a modyr sone,

[1] *I know not what, the devil, he had against me*

'Allas, Ser Thomas of Multone!
That he is smete with unskyl!' — *smote wrongfully*
My mase I hente with good wyl, — *seized readily*
I smot hym that alle folk it seyn. — *so that*
Doun off hys hors almost he fleygh, — *flew*
Whenne I hym hadde a stroke iset, — *struck*
And wolde have blyssyd hym bet, — *struck him better*
No moo strokes wolde he abyde; — *wait for*
Awey swythe thenne gan he ryde." — *quickly*
Whenne Multoun hadde hys tale told,
Fouk Doyly, a baroun bold,
Seyde to the Kyng Rychard:
"The thrydde ther come aftyrward
In atyr whyt as snowgh.
Ther byheeld hym heyghe and lowgh.
In hys scheeld a croys red as blod; — *cross*
A whyte culvere on hys helme stod, — *dove*
He hovyd and beheeld us yerne, — *tarried; keenly*
Yif ther was ony knyght so sterne,
So hardy man and strong of bones,
That durste jouste with hym ones.
Ther was non so stoute ne gryme, — *nor fierce*
That durste jouste thoo with hym.
Doun by the renge he yede doun faste, — *went*
To me he com ryght at the laste.
Iwis, Sere kyng," quod Sere Fouke, — *Certainly*
"I wene that knyght was a pouke. — *I believed that knight was a devil (evil spirit)*
With hys mase on my basynet,
With hys ryght hand a dynt he set,
With wraththe strong and egre mayn, — *rage; fierce strength*
That nygh al stonyd was my brayn. — *dazed*
I spak to hym at wurdes fewe:
'Ryde now forth, you wode schrewe, — *mad rogue (devil)*
And pleye with hem that is thy pere.
Yif you come eft in this manere, — *a second time*
For to be wys I schal thee teche.'
Eft he gan more cunteke seche, — *A second time he sought to engage in more combat*
A werre strok he gaf me yette, — *more severe; anyway*
And with my mase I hym grette. — *greeted*
Bothe hys styropes he forles; — *lost*
And stonyd he rod out of the pres,
And agayn undyr wode bowgh."
Kyng Rychard sat fol stylle and lowgh, — *laughed*
And sayde, "Frendys, sykyrly,
Takes noght to greef, for it was I, — *Do not take offense*
Whenne ye were gaderyd alle in fere, — *all together*
Aunterous I com in this manere,

Who so was strengest yow to asaye, *to test*
And who cowde best strokes paye.
Lordyngs," he sayde, "wete ye nought *know you not*
What I have ordeynyd in thought? *decided*
The Holy Lond to wende too, *to travel*
We three withoute knyghtes moo,
Al in palmeres gyse, *pilgrims'*
The Holy Lond for to devyse. *inspect*
To me, I wole that ye be swore, *wish; be sworn*
No man to wete that now is bore, *To inform no man who now is born*
Neyther for wele, ne for woo,
Tyl that we comen and goo."
They grauntyd hym hys askyng *request*
Wythouten more a gaynsayyng, *objection*
With hym to lyve and to dye,
And lette nought for love ne eye. *delay; fear*
On the book they layde here hand,
To that forwarde for to stand; *agreement be bound*
And kyste hem thenne alle three,
Trewe sworn for to bee. *(see t-note)*
Trumpes blewe and gan to cry, *began to resound*
To mete wente they hastyly, *meal*
And on the twentythe day at ende,
They were redy for to wende
With pyke and with sclavyn, *With spiked staff and pilgrim's cloak*
As palmers weren in paynym. *As pilgrims wear in heathen lands*

Now they dyghten hem ful yare, *prepared themselves thoroughly*
These three knyghtes for to fare. *travel*
They setten up sayl, the wynd was good:
They saylyd over the salte flood
Into Flaundrys, I you saye, *Flanders*
Rychard and hys feres twaye. *two companions*
Forth they wente with glad chere,
Thorwgh manye landes, fer and nere,
Tyl they come to Braundys, *Brindisi*
That is a coost of mekyl prys. *shore (region) of great excellence (renown)*
A noble schyp they founde thare,
Into Cyprys redy to fare. *Cyprus*
The seyl was reysyd, the schyp was strong,
And in the see they were long,
And at the laste, I undyrstande,
At Famagos they come to lande. *Famagusta*
There they dwellyd fourty dawes, *days*
For to lerne landes lawes; *customs*

And sethen deden hem on the see[1]
Toward Acres, that ceté, — *Acre*
And so forth to Massedoyne, — *Macedonia*
And to the ceté of Babyloyne, — *Cairo*
And fro thennes to Cesare; — *Caesarea*
Of Nynyve they were ware, — *Nineveh*
And to the cyté of Jerusalem,
And to the cyté of Bedlem, — *Bethlehem*
And to the cyté of Sudan Turry, — *Sidon-Tyre (?)*
And eke alsoo to Ebedy, — *Ebren (?)*
And to the Castel Orglyous, — *Castle of Pride*
And to the cyté, Aperyous, — *Piraeus*
To Jaffe and to Safrane, — *Jaffa; Safoire (?)*
To Taboret and Archane. — *Tiberias (?); Archas*
Thus, they vysytyd the Holy Land,
How they myghten wynne it to here hand;
And seththen homward they hem dyght, — *afterward; betook themselves*
To Yngelond with al here myght.
  Whenne they hadde passyd the Grykys se, — *Greek sea*
In Alemayne the palmeres thre, — *Germany*
Letten or they myghten goo, — *Lingered before they were able to depart*
That turnyd hem to mekyl woo! — *brought them*
I schal yow telle that be here,
Herkenes alle in what manere!

  A goos they dyghte to her dynere, — *prepared; their*
In a taverne there they were.
Kyng Rychard the fyr bet, — *kindled*
Thomas to the spyte hym set, — *spit*
Fouk Doyly tempryd the woos, — *mixed the sauce*
Dere aboughte they that goos! — *Dearly*
Whenne thay hadde drunken wel afyn, — *thoroughly*
A mynstralle com there in,
And sayde, "Goode men, wyttyrly — *Good men, indeed*
Wole ye have ony mynstryalsy?" — *music (singing)*
Rychard bad that he scholde goo,
That turnyd hym to mekyl woo!
The mynstralle took in mynde, — *took into his memory*
And sayde, "Ye are men unkynde,
And yif I may, ye schall forthynk, — *regret*
Ye gaf me neyther mete ne drynk!
For gentylmen scholden bede — *offer*
To mynstrall that abouten yede — *travel about*
Of here mete, wyn, and ale:

[1] *And afterward they betook themselves on the sea*

For los ryses of mynstrale.”[1]
He was Ynglysch and well hem knewe,
Be speche and syghte, hyde and hewe. *skin and complexion*
Forthe he wente in that tyde *time*
To a castell there besyde,
And tolde the kynge all and some, *one and all*
That thre men were to the cyté come,
Strong men, bolde and fere; *proud (fierce)*
In the worlde is not theyr pere. *peer (equal)*
Kynge Rycharde of Englonde was the one man,
Fouke Doly was that other than,
The thyrde, Thomas of Multon,
Noble knyghtes of renowne.
In palmers wede they be dyght *clothing; dressed*
That no man sholde knowe them ryght. *truly*
To hym sayd the kynge, “Iwys, *Indeed*
That thou haste tolde, yf it sothe is, *What*
Thou shalte have thy warysowne, *reward*
And chose thy selfe a ryche towne.”
The kynge commaunded hys knyghtes
To arme them in all myghtes:
“And go and take them all thre,
And swythe brynge them to me!”
Forth wente the knyghtes in fere,
And toke the palmers at theyr dynere.
They were brought before the kynge,
And he asked them in hyenge: *in haste*
“Palmers,” he sayd, “Whens be ye?”
“Of Englonde,” they sayd, “we be.”
“What hyght thou, falowe?” sayd the kynge. *What are you called*
“Rycharde,” he sayd, without lesynge.
“What hyght thou?” he said to the elder man.
“Fouke Doly,” he answered than.
“And what thou,” he sayd, “gray here?”
“Thomas of Multon,” he sayd there.
The kynge asked them all thre,
What they dyde in his countré:
“I saye you, without lyes, *truly*
Ye seme well to be spyes!
Ye have sene my londe up and downe,
I trowe ye thynke me some treasowne.[2]
For as moche as thou, Syr kynge,
And thy barons, without lesynge,

[1] *For fame rises from musical entertainment (the song of minstrels)*

[2] *I believe you are plotting for me some treason*

Seme not to be thus dyght,	*thus [as a king and nobles] dressed*
Therfore, ye shall with law and ryght,	
Ben put in a stonge pryson,	
For ye thynke to do me treason."	
Kynge Rycharde sayd, "So mote I thee,	*As I may prosper*
Thou dooth unryght, thynketh me,	*an illegal act, it seems to me*
Palmers that gone by the waye,	
Them to pryson, nyght or daye.	
Syr kynge, for thy courtesy,	
Do us palmers no vylony!	
For His love that we have sought,	
Let us go and greve us nought,	
For aventures that may betyde	*In the event that hazards may happen*
In straunge londes where thou ryde.	
The kynge commaunded anone,	
Into pryson them to done.	
The porter, I understonde,	*gatekeeper (guard)*
Toke Rycharde by the honde,	
And his felawes with hym tyte.	*quickly*
Lenger had they no respyte,	*consideration*
Tyll that other daye at pryme,	
The kynges sone came in evyll tyme.	*happened upon an unlucky time*
Wardrewe was his name:	
He was a knyght of grete fame.	
He was grete, stronge, and fere;	*fierce (proud)*
In that londe was not his pere.	
"Porter," he sayd, "I praye thee,	
Thy prysoners lette me see!"	
The porter sayd, "All at your wyll,	
Erly or late, loude or styll."	*under all circumstances*
He brought them forth, all thre,	
Rycharde formest tho came he,	*first then came*
Wardrewe spake to hym than:	
"Arte thou Rycharde, the stronge man,	
As men saye in eche londe?	
Darste thou stonde a buffet of my honde?	*Dare you; blow*
And to morowe I gyve thee leve	
Suche another me to gyve?"	
Anone, Kynge Rycharde	
Graunted to that forwarde.	*agreement*
The kynges sone, fyers and proute,	*proud and haughty (valiant and noble)*
Gave Rycharde an eere cloute:	*a box on the ear*
The fyre out of his eyen spronge.	*eyes*
Rycharde thought he dyde hym wronge	
And sware his othe by Saynt Martyn:	
"Tomorowe, I shall paye myn!"	
Thy kynges sone with good wyll,	

Badde they sholde have theyr fyll,
Bothe of drynke and eke of mete,
The best that they wolde ete,
That he myght not awyte — *That he might not blame*
For feblenes his dente to smyte; — *On account of feebleness his blow to strike*
And in to bedde be brought to reste,
To quyte his that he be preste. — *repay; ready*
The kynges sone was curtese, — *courteous*
That nyght he made hym well at ease.
On the morowe whan it was daye,
Rycharde rose, as I you saye.
Waxe he toke, clere and bryght,
And sone a fyre he hym dyght, — *prepared*
And wexed his hondes by the fyre,
Overthwarde and endlonge, be you sure, — *Crosswise and lengthwise*
A strawes brede thycke and more, — *breadth*
For he thought to smyte sore — *grievously*
With his honde he hath tyght, — *prepared*
To make the payne that he hath hyght. — *punishment; vowed*
The kynges sone came in than
To holde forwarde as a trewe man, — *To keep the agreement*
And before Rycharde he stode,
And spake to hym with irefull mode: — *fiercely*
"Smyte," he sayd, "with thy myght,
As thow art a stalworth knyght,
And yf I stope or felde,[1]
Kepe me never to bere shelde."
Under his cheke Richarde his honde layde,
He that it sawe the sothe sayd,
Flesshe and skynne awaye he droughe,
That he fell downe in a swoughe. — *swoon*
In twoo he brak hys cheke bon:
He fel doun ded as ony ston.
A knyght sterte to the kyng, — *rushed*
And tolde hym this tydyng,
That Rychard has hys sone islon. — *slain*
"Allas!" he sayde, "now have I non!"
With that worde, he fyl to grounde
As man that was in woo ibounde. — *overcome by woe*
He swownyd for sorwe at here feet, — *their*
Knyghtes took hym up ful skeet, — *very quickly*
And sayde, "Sere, let be that thought,
Now it is don, it helpes nought."
The kyng spak thenne an hy — *in a loud voice*

---

[1] Lines 791–92: *And if I should slump (bend) forward or move away, / Prevent me from ever bearing a shield*

To the knyght that stood hym by:
"Tel me swythe of this caas,
In what manere he ded was." *died*
Stylle thay stood, everylkon, *every one*
For sorwe ther myghte hym telle non.
With that noyse ther come the qwene.
"Allas!" sche sayde, "Hou may this bene?
Why is this sorwe and this fare? *behavior*
Who has brought yow alle in care?"
"Dame," he sayde, "wost thou nought *"Lady," he said, "don't you know*
Thy fayre sone to dethe is brought!
Syththen that I was born to man, *Since*
Swylke sorwe hadde I nevere nan! *Never had I not any such sorrow*
Alle my joye is turnyd to woo,
For sorwe I wole myselven sloo!" *slay*
Whenne the qwene undyrstood,
For sorwe, sertys, sche wax nygh wood. *nearly became mad*
Her kerchers she drewe and heer also, *scarves (kerchiefs); tore*
"Alas," she sayd, "what shall I do?"
Sche qahchyd here self in the vysage, *scratched; face*
As a wymman that was in a rage.
The fase fomyd al on blood, *gushed with*
Sche rente the robe that sche in stood,
Wrong here handes that sche was born: *Wrung*
"In what manere is my sone ilorn?" *lost*
The kyng sayde, "I telle thee,
The knyght here standes, he tolde it me.
Now tel thee sothe," quod the kyng than,
"In what manere this dede began;
And but thou the sothe seye, *Unless*
An evele deth schalt thou deye."
The knyght callyd the jayler,
And bad he scholde stonde ner
To bere wytnesse of that sawe, *statement (report)*
In what maner that he was slawe.
The jayler sayde, "Yystyrday at pryme,
Youre sone com in evyl tyme
To the presoun dore to me. *prison*
The palmeres he wolde see,
And I fette hem forth, anon. *brought them*
The formeste Rychard gan gon. *did go*
Wardrewe askeyd withouten let *without delay*
Yif he durste stonde hym a buffet,
And he wolde hym another stande,
As he was trewe knyght in lande,
And Rychard sayde, 'Be this lyght,
Smyt on, sere, and doo thy myght!' *do your utmost*

Wardrewe so Rychard smette, *smote*
That wel nygh he ovyrsette: *prevailed*
'Rychard,' he sayde, 'now bydde I thee,
To morwe another now geve thou me.'
They departyd in this wyse.
At morwen Rychard gan aryse, *morning*
And youre sone, anon he come,
And Rychard agayn hym the way nome, *took the position against him*
As comenaunt was betwen hem tway. *covenant*
Rychard hym smot, forsothe to say,
Evene in twoo hys cheke bon. *Completely*
He fyl doun ded as ony ston.
As I am sworn unto yow here,
Thus it was, and in this manere."
The kyng sayde with egre wylle: *angrily*
"In presoun they schal leve stylle, *prison; remain yet*
And fetters upon theyr fete feste
For the dedes that aren unwrest. *depraved (wicked)*
That he has my sone islawe, *Since*
He schal dye be ryght lawe." *in accord with the law*
The porter yede, als he was sent, *went as*
To don hys lordys comaundement.
That day eete they no meete,
Ne no drynk myghte they gete.

The kyngys doughtyr lay in here bour, *chamber*
With here maydenys of honour:
Margery here name hyght; *was called*
Sche lovede Rychard with al here myght.
At the mydday, before the noone, *ninth canonical hour (3:00 pm)*
To the presoun sche wente soone, *without delay*
And with here maydenes three.
"Jayler," sche sayde, "let me see
Thy presouns now, hastyly!" *prisoners*
"Blethely," he sayde, "sykyrly." *Happily; surely*
Forth he fette Rychard anon ryght;
Fayre he grette that lady bryght, *fair (beautiful)*
And sayde to here with herte free, *gladly*
"What is thy wylle, lady, with me?"
Whenne sche sawgh hym with eyen twoo,
Here love sche caste upon hym thoo. *gave to him*
And sayde, "Rycharde, save God above,
Of alle thyng, most I thee love!"
"Allas!" he sayde in that stounde, *then*
"With wrong am I brought to grounde! *taken (captured)*
What myghte my love doo to thee? *accomplish for you*
A pore presoun, as thou may see. *prisoner*

This is that othir day igon, — *second*
That meete ne drynk ne hadde I non!"
The lady hadde of hym pyté,
And sayde it scholde amendyd bee.
Sche commaunded the jaylere,
Meete and drynk to fette hym there;
"And the yryns from hym take, — *irons (shackles)*
I comaunde thee for my sake.
And aftyr soper, in the evenyng,
To my chaumbyr, thou hym bryng
In the atyr of a squyer: — *Dressed as a squire*
My self thenne schal kepe hym ther. — *guard (confine)*
Be Jhesu Cryst and Seynt Symoun,
Thou schalt have thy warysoun!" — *reward for service*
At even the porter forgat it nought,
To here chaumbyr Richard was brought.
With that lady he dwellyd stylle, — *remained secretly*
And played with here al hys fylle — *heart's desire*
Tyl the sevenyght day, sykyrly, — *Until the same day a week later*
He yede and com fol prevyly. — *He went and came in complete secrecy*
He was aspyyd of a knyght,
That to here chaumbyr he com o nyght.
Prevyly, he tolde the kyng
Forleyn was hys doughtyr yyng. — *Seduced; young*
The kyng askyd ful soone,
"Who thenne, hath that dede idone?"
"Rychard," he sayde, "that tretour! — *(see note)*
He has don this dyshonour.
Sere, be my Crystyndam, — *Christian faith*
I sawgh whenne he yede and cam."

The kyng in herte sykyd sore, — *moaned (sighed) deeply*
To hym thenne spak he no more,
But swythe, withouten fayle,
He sente aftyr hys counsayle, — *council*
Erlys, barouns, and wyse clerkes,
To telle of these wooful werkes.
The messangers gunne forth gon, — *went forth*
Hys counsaylleres, they comen anon.
By that it was the fourtenthe day,
The counsaylers comen, as I yow say.
Al with on they gretten the kyng, — *All as one*
The sothe to saye withouten lesyng. — *without lying*
"Lordynges," he sayde, "welcome alle!"
They wente hem forth into an halle,
Among hem the kyng hym set. — *himself sat*
And sayde to hem, withouten let, — *without delay*

"Why I have aftyr you sent,
To geve a traytour jugement
That has don me gret tresoun:
Kyng Rychard is in my presoun."
Alle he tolde hem in hys sawe,   *report (speech)*
Hou he hadde hys sone islawe,
And hys doughtyr also forlayn: *seduced*
"That he were ded I were ful fayn!   *well pleased (satisfied)*
But now it is ordeynyd soo,   *commanded (decreed)*
Men schal no kyng to deth doo."
To hym spak a bold baroun:
"Hou com Kyng Rychard in presoun?   *came*
He is halden so noble a kyng,   *regarded*
To hym dar no man doo no thyng."
The kyng hym tolde in all wyse,   *in every particular*
Hou he fond hym in dysgyse,
And with hym othere twoo barouns,
Noble men of gret renouns.   *reputations*
"I took him thorwgh suspeccyoun,   *suspicion*
In this manere to my presoun."
He took leve at hem ylkone,   *each one*
Into a chaumbyr he bad hem gone
For to take here counsayle,
What hem myghte best avayle.   *best help them*
In here speche they dwellyd thare   *remained*
Thre dayes and sumdel mare.   *somewhat more*
And stryvenn faste als they were wode,   *quarrelled*
With grete erroure and egere mode;   *confusion and angrily*
Some wolde have hym adawe   *put to death*
And some sayde it was no lawe.   *against the law*
In this manere, for here jangelyng,   *because of their quarrelling*
They myghte acorde for no thyng.   *agree*
The wyseste sayde, "Verrament   *Assuredly*
We can hym geve no jugement."   *decision (punishment)*
Thus answeryd they the kyng,
Sertaynly, withouten lesyng.
A knyght spak swythe to the kyng: *right away*
"Sere, greve yow no thyng.
Sere Eldryd, for sothe, iwis,   *truly, indeed*
He can telle what best is,
For he is wys man of red,   *judgment (counsel)*
Manye has he don to ded."   *death*
The kyng bad, withouten lette,   *ordered, without delay*
That he were before hym fette.
He was brought before the kyng;
He askyd hym in hys sayyng:
"Canst thou telle me in ony manere,

Of Kyng Rychard that I vengyd were?" *Upon King Rychard that I might be avenged*
He answeryd with herte free: *willingly*
"Theron I moot avysyd be
Ye weten weel, it is no lawe,
A kyng to hange and to drawe. *hang; disembowel and dismember*
Ye schal doo be my resoun; *act by my counsel*
Hastely takes youre lyoun, *(see note)*
And withhaldes hym hys meete, *withhold*
Three dayes that he nought eete,
And Rycharde into chaumbyr ye doo, *bring*
And lete the lyoun wende hym too. *go to him*
In this manere he schal be slawe.
Thenne dost thou nought agayn the lawe. *nothing*
The lyoun schal hym there sloo;
Thenne art thou wroken of thy foo." *avenged upon*
The mayde aspyyd that resoun, *proceeding; (see note)*
That he scholde dye thorwgh tresoun.
And aftyr hym sone sche sente,
To warne hym of that jugemente.
When he to the chaumbyr com than, *came then*
"Welcome," sche sayde, "my lemman. *lover*
My lord has ordeynyd thee thorwgh red, *sentenced (judged); council*
The thrydde day to be don to ded.
Into a chaumbyr thou shalt be doo, *brought*
A lyoun schal be late thee too, *turned loose upon you*
That is forhongryd swythe sore; *starving very severely*
Thanne wot I wel thou levyste no more! *will live*
But, leve lemman," thenne sayde sche, *dear love*
"To nyght we wole of lande flee, *flee from the kingdom*
With golde and sylver, and gret tresore,
Inowgh to have for evre more!"
Rychard sayde, "I undyrstande
That were agayn the lawe of land,
Away to wende withouten leve: *permission (see note)*
The kyng ne wole I nought so greve.
Of the lyoun, ne geve I nought, *I pay no heed*
Hym to sle now have I thought.
Be pryme on the thrydde day, *second canonical hour (6:00 am)*
I geve thee hys herte to pray." *as plunder*
Kevercheves he askyd of sylk, *Kerchiefs (scarves)*
Fourty, whyte as ony mylk: *(see note)*
"To the presoun thou hem bryng,
A lytyl before the evenyng."
Whenne it to the tyme cam,
The wey to the presoun the mayden nam, *took*
And with here a noble knyght.
Here soper was ful wel idyght. *Their; prepared*

Rychard bad hys twoo feres,
Come to hym to here soperes,
"And thou, sere Porter, alsoo.
The lady comaundes thee thertoo."
That nyght they were glad inowgh,
And sythen to the chaumbyr they drowgh; — *afterward; withdrew*
But Rychard and that swete wyght, — *creature*
Dwellyd togedere al that nyght.
At morwen whenne it was day,
Rychard here preyde to wende here way. — *Richard pleaded with her to depart*
"Nay, " sche sayde, "be God above,
I schal dye here for thy love!
Ryght now here I wole abyde,
Though me scholde the deth betyde. — *Though death should be my fate*
Sertes, henne wole I nought wende: — *from this place; (see note)*
I shall take the grace that god wyll sende."
Rychard sayde, "Lady free, — *noble*
But yif thou wende swythe fro me, — *Unless*
Thou schalt greve me so sore — *anger me so severely*
That I schal nevere love thee more."
Ther agayn sche sayde, "Nay!
Lemman, have now good day.
God that deyde upon the tree,
Save thee yyf hys wyll bee!"
The kevercheves he took on honde,
Abouten hys arme he hem wonde. — *wrapped*
He thoughte with that ylke wyle, — *very device (strategy)*
To sloo the lyoun with sum gyle, — *guile*
And seyngle in a kertyl he stood, — *without armor in a cloak*
Abood the lyoun, fers and wood. — *Waited; mad*

With that com the jaylere,
And othere twoo with hym in fere,
And the lyoun hem among.
Hys pawes were bothe sharpe and long.
The chambre dore thay hafe undo,
And inn the lyoun lete hym to.
Rychard cryyd, "Help, Jhesu!"
The lyoun made a gret venu, — *attack*
And wolde have hym al torent; — *torn him all to pieces*
Kyng Rychard thenne besyde he glent, — *moved quickly to the side*
Upon the brest the lyoun he spurnyd, — *kicked*
That al aboute the lyoun turnyd.
The lyoun was hungry and megre, — *enfeebled*
He beute hys tayl for to be egre, — *beat*
Faste aboute on the wowes. — *walls*
Abrod he spredde alle hys powes,

And roynyd lowde and gapyd wyde. *roared*
Kyng Rychard bethoughte hym that tyde,
What it was best, and to hym sterte. *rushed*
In at hys throte hys arme he gerte, *cast*
Rente out the herte with hys hand, *Tore*
Lungges and lyvere, and al that he fand. *found*
The lyoun fel ded to the grounde.
Rychard hadde neyther wemme ne wounde. *injury*
He knelyd doun in that place,
And thankyd God of hys grace
That hym kepte fro schame and harme.
He took the herte, al so warme, *indeed (very)*
And broughte it into the halle
Before the kyng and hys men alle.
The kyng at meete sat on des *dais*
With dukes and erles, prowde in pres. *splendid in the throng*
The saler on the table stood. *saltcellar*
Rychard prest out al the blood,
And wette the herte in the salt; *dipped*
The kyng and alle hys men behalt, *beheld*
Wythouten bred the herte he eet.
The kyng wonderyd and sayde skeet: *quickly*
"Iwis, as I undyrstonde can, *Certainly*
This is a devyl, and no man,
That has my stronge lyoun slawe, *slain*
The herte out of hys body drawe,
And has it eeten with good wylle. *readily*
He may be callyed, be ryght skylle, *for good reason*
Kyng icrystenyd of most renoun, *Christian*
Stronge Rychard, Coer de Lyoun!"

Now of this lete we bee,
And of the kyng speke we.
In care and mournyng he ledes hys lyf,
And often he calles hymself caytyf, *wretch*
Bannes the tyme that he was born, *Curses*
For hys sone that was forlorn, *lost*
And hys doughtyr that was bylayn, *seduced*
And hys lyoun that was soo slayn. *in the way described*
Erlys and barouns come hym too,
And hys qwene dede alsoo,
And askyd hym what hym was. *was the matter with him*
"Ye weten weel," he seyde, "my caas, *know*
And why I leve in strong dolour;
For Rychard, the strounge traytour, *grievous (fierce)*
Has me wrought so mekyl woo.
I may hym nought to dethe doo;

Thefore, I wole for hys sake,
Raunsum for hys body take.
For my doughtyr that he has schent — *dishonored (ruined)*
Agayn the staat of sacrement, — *state of being married*
Of every kyrke that preest in syng, — *church*
Messe is sayd, or belle in ryng,
There twoo chalyses inne be,
That on schal be brought to me; — *one*
And yyf ther bee moo than thoo, — *those*
The halvyndel schal come me too. — *half*
Whenne I am servyd of that fee,
Thenne schal Rychard delyveryd bee."
And my doughter for her outrage
Shall forgoo her herytage.
"Thus," he sayde, "it schal be doo."
The barouns grauntyd weel thereto. — *assented heartily*
Kyng Rychard they aftyr sente,
For to here that ordeynemente. — *decision*
  Kyng Rychard com in to the halle,
And grette the kyng and hys men alle.
Thenne sayde the kyng: "Verrayment,
We have lokyd thorwgh jugement, — *ordained through decree*
That thou shalt paye raunsoun,
For thee and thy twoo baroun.
Of every kyrke in thy land,
Thou schalt doo me come to hand,[1]
There twoo chalys inne bee, — *Where*
That on schal be brought to mee;
And yyf there be moo then thoo,
The halvyndel schal come me too.
Thorwghout thy land, wete it weel, — *know it well*
I wole have the halvyndel. — *half*
Whenne thou hast thus maad thy pay,
I geve thee leve to wende thy way,
And my doughtyr alsoo with thee,
That I yow nevere with eyen see." — *So that*
Kyng Rychard sayde, "As thou has told, — *spoken*
To that forewarde I me hold." — *To that agreement I hold myself*
Kyng Rychard, curteys and hende, — *noble*
Seyde, "Who wole for me wende
To Engeland to my chaunceler
That my raunsoun be payde her? — *So that; here*
And who so dos it, withouten fayle,
I schal aquyte hym weel his travayle." — *I shall repay him well [for] his effort*
Up ther stood an hende knyght: — *noble*

[1] *You shall cause to come into my hand (possession)*

"The message I wole doo ful ryght." *in full*
Kyng Rychard dede a lettre wryte, *compose*
A noble clerk it gan adyte, *did write it*
And made therinne mensyoun,
More and lesse of the raunsoun. *Altogether*
"Gretes weel, as I yow say, *Greet well*
Bothe myn erchebysschopys tway, *two archbishops*
And so ye doo the chaunceler,
To serve the lettre in alle maner.
In no manere thee lette fayle;
Sykyrly, it schal hem avayle." *help them*
Hys seel theron he has set;
The knyght it takes withouten let. *without delay*
Dyghtes hym and made hym yare *Prepares himself; ready*
Over the see for to fare.
Whenne he was theron ibrought, *into that place [England] brought*
To gon hys way forgat he nought;
To London he hyyd hym anon. *hurried at once*
There he fond hem everylkon.
He took the lettrys, as I yow say,
To the erchebysschopys tway,
And bad hem faste don it rede:
It is don for mekyl nede.
The chaunceler the wex tobrak, *broke apart the [seal's] wax*
Sone he wyste what to spak. *knew what to say*
The lettre was rede among hem alle,
What therofe scholde befalle, *occur*
Hou Kyng Rychard with tresoun,
In Alemayne dwelles for raunsoun.
The kynges sone he has slayn,
And also hys doughtyr he hath forlayn,
And alsoo slayn hys lyoun:
Alle these harmes he hath don.
They beden clerkys forth to wende *directed; to travel*
To every kyrke, fer and hende, *far and near*
Hastely, that it were sped, *Hastily, so that it would be accomplished*
And the tresore to hym led. *taken (brought)*
"Messanger," thenne sayden hee, *[the chancellor]*
"Thou schalt dwelle, and have with thee, *linger (remain)*
Fyve bysschopys to ryde thee by,
And fyve barouns, sykyrly, *assuredly*
And othere folk inowe with thee. *enough*
In us ne schal no fawte bee. *On account of us no neglect in duty will be*
Of every kyrke, lesse and more, *smaller and greater*
They gaderyd up al the tresore,
And over the see thenne are they went, *have departed*
For to make the fayre present.

Whenne they comen the cyté too,
The ryche kyng they gretten thoo, *then*
And sayden as they were bethought: *as they planned (were resolved)*
"Sere, thy raunsoun is here brought,
Takes it al to youre wyl. *to your satisfaction*
Lat goo these men as it is skyl." *right (fitting)*
Sayde the kyng, "I geve hem leve.
I ne schal hem no more greve."
He took hys doughtyr by the hand,
And bad here swythe devoyde his land. *leave*
The qwene sawgh what scholde falle, *happen*
Here doughtyr sche gan to chaumbyr calle,
And sayde, "Thou schalt dwelle with me,
Tyl kyng Rychard sende aftyr thee,
As a kyng dos aftyr hys qwene;
So I rede that it schal bene." *So I counsel*

Kyng Rychard and hys feres twoo
Took here leve and gunne to goo *started to go*
Home agayn unto Yngelonde.
Thankyd be Jhesu Crystys sonde, *grace*
They come to Londoun, that cyté.
Hys erles and hys barouns free, *noble*
They thankyd God, al so blyve *happy*
That they seygh here lord on lyve. *alive*
Hys twoo feres wenten home,
Here frendes were glad of here come. *arrival*
Bathid here bodyys that were sore,
For the travayle that they hadde before.
Thus, they dwellyd half a yer,
Among here frendes of gret power,
Tyl they were stalworth to fond. *to be found strong*
The kyng comaundyd thorwgh the lond,
At London to make a parlement.[1]
Non withstonde his comaundement, *None refused (resisted)*
As they wolden saven here lyf,
And here chyldren and here wyf.
To Londoun to hys somoun, *at his summons*
Come erl, bysschop, and baroun,
Abbotes, pryours, knyghtes, squyers,
Burgeyses and manye bachelers,
Serjauntes and every freholdande, *sergeants; freeholder*
The kynges heste to undyrstande. *command*
Befor that tyme a gret cuntré,
That was beyonde the Grykkyssche see, *Greek Sea*

[1] *At London to convene (summon) an assembly*

Acres, Surry, and fele landes, *Acre; Syria; many*
Were in Crystene mennes handes,
And the croys that Cryst was on ded, *killed upon*
That boughte us alle fro the qued; *redeemed; devil*
And al the cuntree of Bethleem,
And the toun of Jerusalem,
Of Nazareth and of Jerycho,
And al Galylee alsoo.
Ylke palmere and ylke pylgryme,
That wolde thedyr goo that tyme,
Myghte passe with good entent, *will*
Withouten ransoun and ony rent,
Other of sylvyr or of golde, *Either*
To every plase that he wolde. *wished*
Fond he no man hym to myssay, *slander (insult)*
Ne with evele hondes on hym to lay.
Of Surry land, the Duke Myloun, *Syria; (see note)*
Was lord that stounde, a wol bold baroun. *at that time; a very*
Mawgré the Sawdon that lond he heeld, *Against the Sultan*
And weryd it weel with spere and scheeld. *protected*
He and the doughty Erl Renaud,
Wel often gaf hym wol hard assaut, *very hard assault*
And wol often in playn batayle,
They slowe knyghtes and gret putayle *many foot soldiers (infantry)*
Of Sarezynys that mysbelevyd: *held a false religious belief*
The Sawdon was sore agrevyd. *Sultan; grievously troubled*
Lystenes of a tresoun strong *vile*
Of the Eerl Roys, that was hem among;
To whom Myloun tryste mekyl, *had much faith in*
And he was traytour fals and fykyl. *deceitful*
The Sawdon stylly to hym sente, *secretly*
And behyghte hym land and rente, *promised*
The Crystene hoost to betrayen. *army*
Whanne he hadde wunne hem, for to payen *conquered them*
Of gold many a thousand pounde,
The eerl grauntyd hym that stounde. *gave his consent at that time*
Another traytour, Markes Feraunt,
He wyste alsoo of that comenaunt. *knew; agreement (plot)*
He hadde part of the gold the eerl took,
And aftyrward Crystyndom he forsook.
Thus thorwgh tresoun of the Eerl Roys,
Surry was lorn and the Holy Croys. *lost*
The Duke Renaud was hewen smale, *hewn to bits*
Al to pesys, so says oure tale.
The Duke Myloun was geven hys lyf,
And fleygh out of lande with hys wyf, *flew*
— He was was heyr of Surry lande, *heir of Syria*

Kyng Bawdewynys sone, I undyrstande —
That no man wyste nevere siththe, *knew afterward*
Where he be come, ne in what kiththe: *country (region)*
So that this los and this pyté, *loss; sorrow (distress)*
Sprong out thorwgh al Crystyanté. *Became known*

An holy pope that hyghte Urban, *was named; (see note)*
Sente to eche a Crystene man, *each [leader]*
And asoylyd hem of here synne. *absolved them*
And gaf hem paradys to wynne, *to earn*
Alle that wolde thedyr gon, *to that place*
To wreke Jhesu of his foon. *avenge; foes*
The kyng of France, withouten fayle,
Thedyr he wente with gret vytayle, *provisions*
The duke of Bloys, the duke of Burgoyne, *Burgundy*
The duke of Ostrych, and the duke of Cessoyne, *Austria; Soissons*
And the Emperour of Alemayne, *Germany*
And the goode knyghtes of Bretayne, *Brittany*
The eerl of Flaunders, the eerl of Coloyne,
The eerl of Artays, the eerl of Boloyne. *Artois*
Mekyl folk wente thedyr before, *Many*
That nygh hadde here lyf forlore,
In gret hete and hongyr hard,
As ye may here aftyrward.

In hervest, aftyr the nativité,
Kyng Richard, with gret solempnyté,
At Westemynstyr heeld a ryal feste *royal feast*
With bysschop, eerl, baron honeste, *noble*
Abbotes, knyghtes, swaynes strong. *soldiers below the rank of knight*
And aftyr mete, hem among
The kyng stood up and gan to sayn:
"My leve frendes, I wole yow prayn,
Beth in pes, lystenes my tale,
Erlys, barouns, grete and smale,
Bysschop, Abbot, lewyd and lerde, *the unletttered and the learned*
Al Crystyndom may ben aferde! *fearful*
The pope, Urban, has to us sent
Hys bulle and hys comaundement:
How the Sawdon has fyght begunne,
The toun of Acres he has wunne
Thorwgh the Eerl Roys and hys trehcherye,
And al the kyngdom of Surrye. *Syria*
Jerusalem and the Croys is lorn, *Cross*
And Bethleem, there Jhesu Cryst was born, *where*
The Crystene knyghtes ben hangyd and drawe;
The Sarezynys have hem now islawe,

Crystene men, children, wyf, and grome. *women, and young men*
Wherefore the lord, the pope of Rome,
Is agrevyd and anoyyd
That Crystyndom is thus destroyyd.
Ilke Crystene kyng he sendes bode, *Each; word*
And byddes, in the name of Gode, *requests*
To wende thedyr with gret hoost, *travel; army*
For to felle the Sarezynys bost. *to overcome; pride*
Wherefore my self, I have mente, *intended*
To wende thedyr, with swerdes dent *with sword's blow*
Wynne the Croys, and gete los. *fame*
Now frendes, what is youre purpos? *intention*
Wole ye wende? Says ye or nay!"
Erles and barouns and all they
Sayden: "We ben at on accord: *one*
To wende with thee, Rychard, oure lord."
Quod the kyng, "Frendes, gromercy! *Said; many thanks*
It is oure honour: lystenes why!
Wendes and grauntes the pope hys bon,[1]
As other Crystene kynges have don.
The kyng of Fraunce is wente forth.
I rede est, west, south, and north, *I counsel (exhort)*
In Yngelonde that we do crye, *announce*
And maken a playn croyserye." *summon a true crusade*
Mekyl folk that the croys have nomen, *take the cross*
To Kyng Rychard they were comen
On hors and foote, wel aparaylyd. *equipped*
Twoo hondryd schyppys ben wel vitailid, *stocked*
With flour, hawberks, swerdys, and knyvys;
Thrittene schyppys i-laden with hyvys *hives; (see note)*
Of bees, of tymbyr, grete schydys and long *great shides (planks)*
He leet make a tour ful strong[2]
That queynteyly engynours made, *engineers skillfully made*
Therwith three schyppys were wel lade. *supplied*
Another schyp was laden yet, *in addition*
With an engine hyghte robynet. *named*
That was Rychardys o mangenel, *one (only) mangonel*
And all the takyl that therto fel. *equipment*
Whenne they ware dyght al yare, *thoroughly prepared*
Out of havene for to fare, *harbor*
Jhesu hem sente wynd ful good,
To bere hem over the salte flood.
Kyng Rychard sayde to hys schipmen: *sailors*
"Frendes, doth as I yow ken, *instruct*

---

[1] *Agree (Set out) and grant the pope his request*

[2] *He ordered a very strong tower to be made*

And maystyr Aleyn Trenchemere,
Whether ye come fer or nere,
And ye meten be the see stronde, — *shore*
Schyppys of ony other londe,
Tho Crystene men, of lyf and leme[1]
Looke no goodes ye hem beneme;
And yyf ye ony Sarezynys mete,
Loke on lyve that ye non lete! — *See to it that you let none live*
Catayl, dromoun, and galeye, — *(see note)*
Al I yow geve unto youre preye; — *as your booty*
But at the cyté of Marchylé, — *Marseille*
There, ye moot abyde awhile; — *must*
Be cable and ankyr for to ryde, — *By*
Me and myn hoost for to abyde.
For I and my knyghtes of mayn — *household (retinue)*
Wole hastily wende thorwgh Alemayn — *Germany*
To speke with Modard, the kyng,
To wete why and for what thyng — *To find out*
That he me in presoun heelde;
But he my tresore agayn yelde — *Unless*
That he of me took with falshede,
I schal quyten hym hys mede." — *pay him his due*

Thus Kyng Rychard, as ye may here,
Bycome Goddys owne palmere — *pilgrim*
Agayns Goddys wythirhynys. — *enemies*
The erchebysschop, Sere Bawdewynys,
Before wente with knyghtys fyn
Be Braundys and be Constantyn, — *Brindisi; Constantinople*
And al ther last thenne aftyrward — *finally*
Thenne come the doughty Kyng Rychard.
Three hoostes Kyng Richard gan make — *armies (divisions) appointed*
Into hethenesse, for Goddys sake: — *[To go] into heathen territory*
In the forme warde hym self wolde be, — *vanguard*
With hardy men of gret pousté, — *strength*
That other ledes Fouke Doyly, — *second*
Thomas, the thrydde, sykerly.
Every hoost with hym gan lede
Fourty thousande goode at nede; — *capable in time of need*
Non therinne but man of myght
That were wel provyd in werre and fyght.
Kyng Richard callyd hys justys: — *justices*
"Lokes that ye doo be my devys, — *Take care that you perform my order*
My land kepes with skele and lawe: — *reason and justice*

[1] Lines 1411–12: *Then Christian men, [upon pain] of life and limb / See to it that you do not take away goods from them*

Traytours lookes ye honge and drawe.
In my stede schal be here
The bysschop of York, my chauncelere.
I wole that ye ben at hys wylle, *command*
To wyrke aftyr ryght and skylle, *justice and fairness*
That I hereaftyr here no stryf,
As ye wole save youre owne lyf!
And in the name of God Almyght,
Ledes the pore men be ryght!"
Thertoo heeld they up here hand,
With ryght to lede al Yngeland.
Bysschopys gaf hem here benysoun, *blessing*
And prayde for hem in kyrke and toun;
And prayde Jhesu Cryst hem spede, *aid them*
In hevene to quyten hem here mede. *To give them their reward in heaven*

Now is Kyng Rychard passid the see;
Sone he delte hys hoost in thre. *divided*
For he wolde nought folk anoye,
And here goodes nought destroye,
Ne nothyng take withouten pay.
The kyng comaundyd, as I yow say,
Every hoost fro othir ten myle; *away from the other*
Thus he ordeynyd that whyle, *during that time*
In the myddyl hoost hym self to ryde,
And hys hoostes on bothe syde.
Forth they wenten withouten ensoyne, *without delay*
To the cyté of Coloyne.
The hye mayre of that cyté
Comaundyd, as I schal telle thee,
No man selle hem no fowayle, *fowl*
For no thyng that myghte avayle. *be profitable*
The styward tolde Richard, the kyng,
Sone anon of that tydyng,
That he myghte no fowayle beye,
Neyther for love, neyther for eye. *fear*
"Thus defendes Modard, the kyng, *forbids*
For he hates yow ovyr alle thyng.
Weel he woot that ye have swore *knows; sworn*
Al that ye take to paye therfore;
Ye wole take with no maystry; *force*
Therfore, he wenes, sykyrly *hopes*
That ye schal have mete non;
Thus he thynkes youre men to slon." *slay*
Kyng Richard answerid as hym thought:
"That ne schal us lette nought. *not hinder us at all*
Now styward, I warne thee, *exhort*

Bye us vessel, gret plenté, *tableware*
Dysschys, cuppys, and sawsers,
Bolles, treyes, and plateres,
Fattys, tunnes and costret, *Vats, casks, and flasks*
Makes oure mete withouten let, *Prepare our meal; hesitation (delay)*
Whether ye wole sethe or brede; *boil or roast*
And the pore men also, God yow spede, *may God aid you*
That ye fynde in the toun,
That they come at my somoun."
Whenne the mete was greythid and dyght, *meal; cooked and ready*
The kyng comaundyd to a knyght
After the mayr for to wende, *mayor*
For he is curteys and hende.
The mayr come, as I have sayde, *came*
Bord and cloth was redy layde. *Table*
Anon they were to borde sette, *table seated*
And fayr servyse before hem fette. *brought*
Kyng Rychard askyd in hyyng: *at once*
"Sere mayr, where is thy lord, the kyng?"
"Sere," he sayde, "at Gumery, *Worms*
Sykyrly, withouten ly,
And alsoo, my lady, the qwene.
The thrydde day ye schal hem sene,
And Margery, hys doughtyr free,
That of youre comyng wol glad wil be." *very glad*
They waschede as it was lawe of land, *washed; customary*
A messanger ther come rydand,
Upon a stede whyt so mylke, *as*
Hys trappys were of tuely sylk, *ornamental gear; crimson*
With fyve hondryd belles ryngande,
Wel fayr of syghte, I undirstande. *Very pleasing to see*
Doun off hys stede he lyght,
And grette Kyng Rychard fayr, I plyght: *I assure you*
"The kynges doughtyr that is so free,
Sche gretes thee weel by me.
With an hondryd knyghtes and moo, *more*
Sche comes ar thou to bedde goo." *before*
Kyng Rychard answeryd in hyyng: *at once*
"Welcome," he sayde, "ovyr alle thyng!"
He made at ease the messangere, *comfortable*
With glad semblaunt and merye chere,
And gaf hym a cloth of golde,
For he was to hym leef iholde. *held dear*
They come to hym that ylke nyght, *very*
The knyghtes and the lady bryght.
Whenne Kyng Rychard myghte here see,
"Welcome, lemman," sayde hee.

Ayther of hem othir gan kysse, *Each of them*
And made mekyl joye and blysse.
Thenne they dwellyd tyl it were day,
At morwen they wenten in here way. *on their way*
At mydday, before the noon, *ninth canonical hour (3 pm)*
They comen to a cyté boon, *good city*
The name was callyd Marburette.
There the kyng hym wolde lette. *insisted that he would remain*
Hys marschal swythe come hym too: *swiftly came to him*
"Sere," he sayde, "Hou schole we doo? *proceed*
Swylk fowayle as we boughte yistyrday? *[With] Such fowl*
For no catel gete I may." *livestock*
Rychard answereyd with herte free: *generous*
"Of froyt here is gret plenté, *fruit (crops)*
Fyggys, and raysyns in frayel, *Figs; basket*
And notes may serve us fol wel, *nuts*
And wex sumdel caste thertoo, *And throw a little wax in there*
Talwgh and grese menge alsoo; *Tallow; mix in*
And thus ye may oure mete make,
Seththen ye mowe non other take." *Since*
There they dwellyd al that nyght;
On the morwe to wenden they have ityght *resolved to travel*
To the cyté of Carpentras.
There Kyng Modard hymself in was.
Further thenne myghte he fle hym nought; *might he not retreat*
Thorwgh the land he hadde hym sought.
Kyng Rychard hys hostel gan take, *took his lodging*
There he gan hys ferste wrake *to avenge his cruelty*
With gret wrong agayn the ryght,
For the goos that he hadde dyght. *prepared*
Kyng Modard wot Rychard is come, *knows*
Weel he wenes to be nome, *expects to be taken*
And in presoun ay to bee, *always*
"But yyf my doughtyr helpe me!" *Unless*
Sche come to hym there he sat:
"What now, fadyr, hou is that?"
"Sertes, doughtyr, I gete blame; *will suffer disgrace*
But yif thou helpe, I goo to schame!"
"Sertes, sere," sche sayde than,
"As I am gentyl womman,
Yyf ye wole be mylde of mood,
Kyng Rychard wole do yow but good.
But grauntes hym with good wylle, *grant to him*
That he wil aske, and fulfylle, *That which*
And dos yow al in hys mercy, *And put yourself completely at his mercy*
Ye schole be kyssyd, be oure ledy!
Ye that have ben soo wrothe, *angry*

Ful fayre accordyd ye schal be bothe, *reconciled*
And eke, alsoo my lady, the qwene, *likewise*
Goode frendes thenne schole ye bene."
Sche took here fadyr and with hym yede, *went*
To Kyng Rychard, as I yow rede. *as I tell you*
And alsoo erles and barouns moo,
And syxty knyghtes withouten thoo. *in addition, then*
Kyng Richard sawth hou that he come,
The way agayns hym he gan nom. *toward; did take*
Kyng Modard on knees hym sette,
There Kyng Richard ful fayre he grette,
And sayde, "Sere, I am at thy wille." *under your control*
Sayde Rychard, "I wole nought but skylle.[1]
With so thou yelde agayn my tresore, *Provided that*
I schal thee love for everemore,
Love thee and be thy frende."
Quod Kyng Modard, "My sone hende,
I wole ye swere upon a book,
Redy is it I of thee took:
Redy is al thy tresore,
Yyf thou wylt have it and mekyl more,
I schal thee geve, my pes to make." *peace (reconciliation)*
Kyng Rychard gan hym in armes take,
And kyste hym ful fele sythe: *very many times*
They were frendes and made hem blythe.
That ylke day Kyng Modard
Eet, iwis, with Kyng Rychard.

And aftyr mete, sone and swythe,
Kyng Rychard spak with wordis blythe
To the kyng that sat hym by:
"Welcome be thou, sykyrly!
Sere, of thy love, I praye thee, *for your love, I beseech you*
Of thyn help to wende with me *travel*
To hethynnesse, withouten fayle, *heathen territory*
For Goddes love to geve batayle."
The kyng grauntyd al in grith, *friendship*
Al hys land-folk to wende hym with, *his countrymen*
"And myself to wende theretoo."
"Nay," quod Rychard, "I wole nought soo,
Thou art to old to beker in fyght, *contend*
But I pray thee that thou me dyght *render me*
An hondryd knyghtes, styff to stande, *stalwart*
And the beste in al thy lande;

[1] *Said Richard, "I desire nothing but that which is fitting"*

And of vytayle, redy bon, — *all prepared*
For al a yer that it be don, — *For an entire year*
And squyers that falles hem too." — *are joined to them*
The kyng grauntyd to be soo.
"Another thyng I schall thee geve
That may thee helpe whyl that thou leve: — *live*
Twoo ryche rynges of gold, — *splendid (powerful)*
The stones thereinne be fol bold. — *[magically] unthwartable*
Hennes to the lond of Ynde, — *From here; India*
Betere thenne schalt thou non fynde; — *than*
For who soo has that on ston, — *one stone*
Watyr ne schal hym drenche non. — *drown*
That othir ston, who so it bere,
Fyr ne schal hym nevere dere. — *injure*
"Sere," quod Rychard, "graunt mercy!" — *many thanks*
Hys knyghtes weren dyght al redy,
Serjauntes of armes and squyers, — *(see note)*
Stedes chargyd and destrers, — *Horses loaded; warhorses*
With armure and othir vytayle; — *provisions*
Kyng Richard wente with hys parayle, — *war equipment*
To Marcyle they gunne ryde, — *Marseille*
And hys hoostes on bothe syde.
Fouk Doyly, Thomas of Multoun,
Duke, eerl, and many baroun.
Rychardys maystyr, Roberd of Leycester, — *(see note)*
In al Yngelond was non his betere;
And alsoo Robert Tourneham:
Gret Ynglys peple with hym cam. — *High ranking*
Al redy they founde there here flete,
Chargyd with armure, drynk, and mete. — *Loaded; food*
They schyppyd armes, man and stede,
And stoor here folk al with to fede. — *And provisions to feed all their people*
They schyppyd al be the see stronde, — *boarded; shore*
To wende into the Holy Londe.
The wynd was bothe good and kene, — *strong*
And drof hem ovyr to Messene. — *Messina*
Before the gates of the Gryffouns, — *Greeks (see note)*
Kyng Rychard pyghte hys pavylouns. — *pitched*
The kyng of Fraunce there he founde, — *[Philip II]*
In pavylouns quarre and rounde; — *square*
Eyther of hem kyste othir,
And becomen sworen brothir,
To wenden into the Holy Londe,
To wreke Jhesu, I undyrstonde. — *To avenge*

A tresoun thoughte the kyng of Fraunce,
To doo Kyng Richard, withouten destaunce. — *without delay*

To Kyng Tanker he sente a wryt,[1] *(see note)*
That turnyd hym sythen to lytyl wyt;
That Kyng Richard, with strengthe of hand,
Wolde hym dryve out of hys land.
Tanker kyng of Poyl was, *Apulia*
For this wryt he sayde, "Allas!"
He sente anon a messanger
To hys sone that hyghte Roger, *was named*
That was kyng in Sesyle land. *Sicily*
He scholde come unto hys hand;
And also aftyr hys barouns,
Erles and lordes of renouns,
And whenne they were icome, ylkon, *each one*
The kyng sayde to hem anon,
And sayde hym hou the kyng of Fraunce, *told him [Roger]*
Warnyd hym of a dystaunse. *trouble*
Hou Kyng Richard was come fro ferre, *from far away*
With gret strengthe on hym to werre. *against him*
Kyng Roger spak fyrst above, *called for silence by*
And smot pes with hys glove: *And striking with his glove*
"Mercy, my fadyr, at this tyme,
Kyng Richard is a pylgryme,
Croysyd into the Holy Lande; *Having become a crusader into the Holy Land*
That wryt lyes, I undyrstande. *I believe*
I dar for Kyng Rychard swere *would swear on behalf of*
For hym ne tydes yow nevere dere; *Because of him harm never befalls you*
But sendes to hym a messangere,
That he come unto yow here;
He wil come to yow ful fawe, *very gladly*
And that he thynkes he wil beknawe."[2]
The kyng was payyd of that counsayle, *well pleased*
And sente aftyr hym, saunt fayle. *without fail*
At morwen he com to hym, iwis,
Into the ryche cyté of Rys. *Riace (Reggio)*
He fond Tanker in hys halle,
Among hys erlys and barouns alle.
Eyther othir grette ful fayre,
With mylde wurdes and debonayre. *and gracious*
Thenne sayde Tankar to Kyng Richard:
"Loo, Sere kyng, be Seynt Leonard,
Me it is idon to wyt *It comes to pass for me to learn*
Of frendes be a fol good wryt, *by a legitimate document*
That thou art comen with gret powere,

---

[1] Lines 1679–80: *To King Tancred he sent a letter (document) / That afterward limited his reasoning*

[2] *And what he thinks (plans) he will acknowledge*

Me to bereve my landes here. *deprive*
Thou were fayrere to be a pylgrym *more esteemed*
For to sloo many a paynym, *In order*
Thenne for to greve a Cristene kyng
That nevere mysdede thee no thyng!" *(see note)*
Kyng Richard wax al aschamyd, *became*
And of hys wurdes sore agramyd, *bitterly vexed*
And sayde, "Tanker, thou art mysthought *think wrongly*
To have on me swylke a thought, *such*
And swylke a rage upon me bere,
That I thee scholde with tresoun dere, *injure*
And swylke a tresoun to me sopos. *suspect*
Upon my flesch I bere the cros!
I wole dwelle but a day;
Tomorwe I wole wende my way.
And I praye thee, Syr Tanker Kynge,
Procure me none evyll thynge; *Bring upon me no harmful thing*
For many men weneth to greve other, *hope to injure*
And on his heed falleth the fother; *burden*
For who so wayteth me despyte, *does me injury*
Hymselfe shall nought passe quyte." *not go unharmed*
"Syr," quod Tanker, "Be not wrothe for this.
Lo, here the letter forsothe, iwys, *Behold*
That the kynge of Fraunce me sente
That other daye in presente." *in this place*
Kynge Rycharde sawe and understode
The kynge of Fraunce wolde hym no gode. *intended*
Kynge Rycharde and Kynge Tanker kyste,
And were frendes with the beste
That myght be in ony londe,
Iloved be Jhesu Crystes sonde! *Praised be Jesus Christ's ordering of events*
Kynge Rycharde wente agayne well styll, *very peaceably*
And suffred the Frensshe kynges wyll.
He undyde his tresore,
And bought hym bestes to his store. *beasts for his stores*
He let bothe salte and slene *He gave up both salted and slain*
Thre thousande of oxen and kene, *livestock (cows)*
Swyne and shepe, so many also
No man coude tell tho. *count at that time*
Whete and benys twenty thowsande
Quarters he boughte als that I fynde;
And of fysshe, foules and venyson,
I ne can nought account in ryght reason.
The kynge of Fraunce, without wene, *doubt*
Lay in the cyté of Messene,
And Kynge Rycharde without the wall, *outside*
Under the house of the Hospytall. *(see note)*

The Englysshe men wente into the chepynge, *market*
And ofte hente harde knockynge. *received hard blows*
The Frensshe and the Gryffons downeryghtes *outright*
Slewe there our Englyssche knyghtes.
Kynge Rycharde herde of that dystaunce, *conflict*
And playned to the kynge of Fraunce,
And he answered he helde no wardes, *guards (keepers)*
Of the Englysshe taylardes. *Of the tailed Englishmen (see note)*
"Chase thy Gryffons, yf thou myght, *Greeks*
For of my men geteth thou no ryght." *justice*
Quod Kynge Rycharde: "Syth it is so, *Since*
I wote well what I have to do.
I shall me of them so awreke *I shall myself so avenge them*
That all the worlde therof shall speke."
Crystmasse is a tyme full honeste. *worthy of respect*
Kynge Rycharde it honoured with grete feste. *celebration*
All his erles and barons
Were set in theyr pavylyons,
And served with grete plenté
Of mete and drynke and eche deynté. *delicacy*
Than came there a knyght in grete haste;
Unneth he myght drawe his blaste. *Barely might he drawe his breath*
He fell on knees, and thus he sayd:
"Mercy, Rycharde, for Mary mayde! *maid Mary*
With the Frensshe men and the Gryffownes,
My brother lyeth slayne in the townes,
And with hym lyeth slayne fyftene
Of thy knyghtes, good and kene. *brave*
This daye and yesterdaye, I tolde arowe *counted one by one*
That syxe and thyrty they had islowe!
Faste lesseth your Englysshe hepe![1]
Good Syr, take good kepe,
Awreke us, syr, manly, *Avenge*
Or we shall hastely
Flee peryll, I understonde,
And tourne agayne to Englonde."
Kynge Rycharde was wrothe and eger of mode, *furious; fierce of mood*
And began to stare as he were wode. *mad*
The table with his fote he smote,
That it wente on the erth fote-hote *immediately*
And swore he wolde be awreked in haste. *speedily*
He wolde not wende for Crystes faste. *not set out because of Christ's fast*
The hygh daye of Crystmasse
They gan them arme, more and lasse. *the greater and the smaller (everyone)*

[1] *Quickly your English military strength diminishes*

Before wente Kynge Rycharde,
The erle of Salysbury afterwarde
That was called by that daye
Syr Wyllyam, the Longe Spaye. *Longsword*
The erle of Leysestre, the erle of Herdforde,
Full comly folowed they theyr lorde, *splendidly*
Erles, barons, and squyers,
Bowmen and arblasteres, *crossbowmen*
With Kynge Rycharde they gan reke *went quickly*
Of Frensshe and Gryffons to be awreke. *Upon; to be avenged*
The folke of that cyté aspyed rathe *quickly*
That Englysshemen wolde do them skathe. *harm*
They shette hastely the gate
With barres that they found therate,
And swythe they ranne on the wall
And shotte with bowe and spryngall *catapult*
And called our men, saunce fayle, *without fail*
"Go home, dogges, with your tayle;
For all your boost and your orguyle, *pride*
Men shall threste in your cuyle!"[1]
Thus they mysdyde and myssayde; *mistreated; slandered*
All that daye kynge Rycharde they trayde. *vexed*
Our kynge that daye for no nede *on no account*
In baytayll myght nothynge spede. *achieve*
On nyght, Kynge Rycharde and his barons
Wente to theyr pavylyouns.
Who that slepte or who that woke
That nyght Kynge Rycharde no rest toke.
On the morowe, he ofsente his counseyllers *sent for*
Of the portes, the mayster maryners.
"Lordynges," he sayd, "ye ben with me: *you are*
Your counseyll ought for to be pryvé. *secret*
All we sholde us venge fonde *We should all strive to avenge ourselves*
With queyntyse and with strength of honde, *With strategy*
Of Frensshe and of Gryffons,
That have dyspysed our nacyons. *insulted our people*
I have a castell, I understonde,
Is made of tembre of Englonde, *timber*
With syxe stages full of tourelles *six stories; turrets*
Well flourysshed with cornelles; *decorated; embrasures (openings for weapons)*
Therin I and many a knyght
Ayenst the Frensshe shall take the fyght.
That castell shall have a surnownne: *distinguishing name*
It shall hyght the mate-gryffon.[2] *(see note)*

[1] *Men shall thrust (shove) vigorously up your rump*

[2] *It shall be called the mate-gryphon (kill-Greek)*

Maryners, arme your shyppes,
And holde up well your manshippes. *And raise up (maintain) your spirits*
By the water-halfe ye them assayle, *by the water side*
And we wyll by londe, saunce fayle.
For joye come never to me
Tyll I of them awreked be!"
Therto men myght here crye,
"Helpe God and Saynt Mary!"
The maryners gan to hye *travelled quickly*
Bothe with shyppe and with galye,
With ore, sprete, and sayle also, *pole*
Towarde them they gan go.
The knyghtes framed the tre castyll *siege tower*
Before the cyté upon an hyll.
All this sawe the kynge of Fraunce,
And sayde: "Have ye no doutaunce *fear*
Of all these Englysshe cowardes,
For they ne be but mosardes. *wretches (dolts)*
But reyse up your mangenell, *raise; catapult*
And caste to theyr tre castell,
And shote to them with arblast,
The tayled dogges for to agast." *terrify*
Now harken of Rycharde, our kynge,
How he let bere in the dawnynge, *How he caused to bear in the dawning*
Targes and hurdis his folke all *Shields and bulwarks*
Ryght before the cyté wall.
His hoost he let at ones crye, *He ordered at once his army to cry*
Men myght it here in the skye:
"Now let come the Frensshe mosardes, *dolts*
And gyve batayll to the taylardes!" *tailed ones*
The Frensshe men them armed all,
And ranne in hast upon the wall; *speedily*
And began the Englysshe for to assayle.
There began a stronge batayle:
The Englysshe shotte with arblast and bowe, *crossbow and bow*
Frensshe and Gryffons felde and slowe. *dropped (wounded) and slew*
The galeys came unto the cyté,
And had nygh wonne entré,
They hade so myned under the wall,
That many Gryffons gan downe fall.
With hoked arowes, and eke quarelles, *crossbow bolts*
Felde them out of the tourelles, *dropped*
And brake bothe legges and armes,
And eke theyr neckes: it was none harmes! *no loss*
The Frensshe men came to the stoure *conflict*
And caste wylde fyre out of the toure;
Wherwith, I wote, forsothe, iwys, *With which, I know, truly, indeed*

They brente and slewe many Englysshe, *burnt*
And the Englysshe men defended them wele *themselves well*
With good swerdes of browne stele *shining (polished) steel*
And slewe of them so grete chepes, *so great a number*
That there laye moche folke on hepes;
And at the londe gate, Kyng Rycharde
Helde his assawte lyke harde. *Performed; equally*
And so manly he toke one, *took command*
He lefte of his men never one. *He abandoned of his men not one*
He loked besyde and sawe hove *raised up (hoisted)*
A knyght that tolde hym with a glove. *beckoned*
Kynge Rycharde come and he hym tolde
Tales in Englysshe, stoute and bolde. *Claims (assertions)*
"A lorde," he sayd, "I aspye now right
A thynge that maketh myn herte lyght. *valiant*
Here," he sayd, "is a gate one,
That hath warde ryght none. *guard*
The folke is gone to the water toure,
For to do them theyr socoure, *give assistance*
And there we may, without dente, *dint (blow)*
Entre in now, verament." *truly*
Blythe therof was kynge Rycharde,
Stoutly he wente thederwarde.
Many a knyght, doughty of dede,
After hym prycked upon theyr stede.
Kynge Rycharde entred without drede;
Hym folowed full grete felawrede. *armed troop*
His baner upon the wall he pulte; *placed*
Many a Gryffon it byhulte. *beheld it*
As greyhoundes stryken out of lese, *rush released from a leash*
Kyng Rycharde threste amonge the prese. *struck; press [of combat]*
Seven chaynes with his good swerde,
Our kynge forcarfe amydwarde *cut in two midway*
That were drawen for grete doute, *for great fear*
Within the gates and without.
Porcules and gates up he wan, *Portcullis; pulled*
And lette come in every man.
Men myghte se by strete and lane,
Frensshe and Gryffons tholed schame; *suffered*
And some to hous ran in haste,
Dores and wyndowes barred faste;
Oure Englissh with grete levours *crowbars*
Breke hem up with grete vigours. *strength (resolve)*
All that they founde ayenst them stonde
Passed thorugh dethes honde.
They brake cofers and toke tresoure: *coffers (chests)*
Golde and sylver and covertoure, *quilt (garment)*

Jewelles, stones, and spycery, *spices as merchandise*
All that they founde in tresoury.
There was none of Englysshe blode
That he ne had as moche gode *goods (wealth)*
As they wolde drawe or bere *tow*
To shyppe or to pavylyons, I swere;
And ever cryed Kynge Rycharde: *And again and again*
"Slee downe every Frensshe cowarde
And ken them in bataylles *teach*
That ye have no tayles!"
The kynge of Fraunce came pryckynge *galloping*
Ayenst Rycharde, our kynge, *Toward*
And fell on knees downe of his hors
And bad mercy, for Goddes corps, *body*
For the crowne and for the love *crown [of thorns]*
Of Jhesu Cryste, kynge above,
And for the vyage and for the crose, *journey (crusade)*
He should be in gree, and take lose; *agreement; the honor*
And he wolde one hande take,
They sholde amende all the wrake *injury*
They that had hym or his
Ony thynge done amys.
Kynge Rycharde had grete pyté
Of the kynge of Fraunce that sat on knee,
And lyght downe, so sayth the boke,
And in his armes up hym toke
And said it sholde be peas styll, *peaceful from this time forward*
And yelde the towne all to hys wyll *[Richard would] yield*
And bad hym nought greve hym tho, *then*
Though he venged hym of his fo *avenged himself*
That had his good knyghtes quelde, *killed*
And eke on hym despyte itelde. *disparaged him*
The kynge of Fraunce gan to preche *speak*
And bad Rycharde be his soules leche, *physician*
And the tresoure yelde agayne than *relinquish back then*
That he had take of every man,
And elles he ne myght, in Goddes paye, *might not be able, with God's approval*
To Jherusalem take the waye.
Kynge Rycharde sayde, "With alle thy tresoure *[French and Greek] treasure*
They myght nought amende the dyshonoure
And that they have me done amys; *wrong*
And Syr, also thou dyde amys
Whan thou sentest to Tanker, the kynge,
To appayre me with thy lesynge. *slander; lying*
We have to Jherusalem the waye sworne.
Who breketh our pylgrymage, he is forlorne, *violates (interferes with); is damned*

Or he that maketh ony medlaye *quarrel*
Betwene us two in this way."
Whan abbated was that dystaunce, *that disagreement (strife) was ended*
There came two justyces of Fraunce
Upon two stedes ryde,
And kynge Rycharde they gan chyde.
That one was hyght Margaryte,
That other Syr Hewe Impetyte.
Swythe sore they hym trayde, *Very harshly they vexed him*
Cleped hym taylarde and hym myssayde. *Called him tailed one and slandered him*
Kynge Rycharde helde a tronchon tewe, *tough (strong) truncheon*
And to them two he hym drewe. *took himself*
Margaryte he gave a dente than *then*
Above the eye upon the pan. *head*
The skull brake with that dente;
The ryght eye flewe out quytemente, *quickly*
And he fell downe deed in haste.
Hewe of Impetyte was agaste,
And prycked away without fayle,
And Rycharde was soone at his tayle. *rear*
And gave hym a stroke on the molde *the top of the head*
That deed he thought be he sholde.
Ternes and quernes he gave hym there *Triples and quadruples*
And sayd, "Syr, thus thou shalte lere *learn*
To myssaye thy overhedlynge. *slander your superior*
Go playne now to your Frensshe kynge!" *complain*
An archebysshop came full soone;
He fell on knees and badde a bone. *pleaded for a favor*
Of Kynge Richarde he asked mercy
That he wolde ther sesy, *cease*
And there no more harme do,
For Goddes love, the people to.
Kynge Rycharde graunted hym then, *gave his consent*
And drewe to pavylyon all his men.
To this daye men may here speke
How the Englysshe were there awreke. *avenged*
All the whyle that they were there,
They myght well bye theyr chafere; *goods*
There was none so hardy a man
That one evyll worde spake gan. *did speak*

Kynge Rycharde in peas and reste,
Fro Crystmasse, the hygh feste,
Dwelléd there tyll after the Lente
And than on his waye he wente. *(see note)*
In Marche moneth the kynge of Fraunce
Wente to shyppe without dystaunce. *without delay*

Whan he was gone, soone afterwarde
Came the doughty Kynge Rycharde.
Forth towarde Acrys wende he wolde *travel*
With moche store of sylver and golde. *(see note)*
Foure shyppes were charged, I fande, *loaded; I found (discovered)*
Towarde Cyprys, all saylande,
Charged with tresour every dell, *completely*
And soone a sorowfull caas there fell. *event*
A grete tempest arose sodaynly
That lasted fyve dayes, sykerly. *truly*
It brake theyr maste and theyr ore
And theyr takell, less and more, *rigging*
Anker, bowe spret and rother, *bowsprit and rudder*
Ropes, cordes, one and other;
And were in poynt to synke adowne
As they came ayenst the Lymosowne. *toward; Limassol (a port in Cyprus)*
The thre shyppes, ryght anone, *immediately*
All tobrake ayenst the stone. *broke apart*
All to peces they totare; *broke apart*
Unnethe the folke saved ware. *With difficulty*
The ferde schippe behynde duellede: *fourth*
Unnethes the maryners it helde; *restrained it*
And that schippe lefte righte in the depe,
That the folkes one the lande myghte wepe;
For the Gryffons, with sharpe wordes,
Some with axes and some with swerdes,
Grete slaughter of our Englysshe maked,
And spoyled the quycke all naked. *stripped the living*
Syxtene hondred they brought of lyve, *killed*
And into pryson, hondredes fyve,
And also naked syxty score,
As they were of theyr moders bore.
Of the shyppes brekynge they were blythe.
The Justyces of Cyprys ran full swythe *swift*
And drewe up cofers manyfolde *And hauled up coffers in large numbers*
Full of sylver and of golde,
Dysshes, cuppes, broches, and rynges,
Cuppes of golde, and ryche thynges.
No man by south ne by north,
Ne coulde account what it was worth;
And all was borne, that tresour, *carried*
Wheder that wolde the emperour. *To whatever place the emperor wished*
The thyrde daye afterwarde,
The wynde came dryvynge Kynge Rycharde
With all his grete navyes, *ships*
And his saylynge galyes,
To a shyppe that stode in depe.

The gentylmen therin dyde wepe,
And whan they sawe Rycharde, the kynge,
Theyr wepynge tourned all to laughynge.
They welcomed hym with worshyppes, *with respect (high honor)*
And tolde hym the brekynge of theyr shyppes,
And the robbery of his tresoure,
And all that other dyshonoure.
Than waxed Kynge Rycharde full wrothe,
And he swore a full grete othe
By Jhesu Cryste, our savyoure:
It sholde abye the emperoure. *cost; dearly*
He cleped Syr Steven and Wyllyam,
And also Roberte of Turnam,
Thre gentyll barons of Englonde,
Wyse of speche, doughty of honde:
"Now go and saye to the emperoure
That he yelde agayne my tresoure,
Or I swere by Saynt Denys,
I wyll have thre syth double of his; *three times double*
And yelde my men out of pryson,
And for the deed paye raunson,
Or hastely I hym warne,
I wyll worke hym a harme
Bothe with spere and with launce.
Anone I shall take vengaunce!"
The messengers anone forth wente,
To do theyr lordes commaundement,
And hendly sayd theyr message. *courteously*
The emperoure began to rage,
He grunte his tethe and faste blewe, *gnashed his teeth; breathed fast*
A knyfe after Syr Roberte he threwe.
He blente awaye with a lepe, *moved away suddenly*
And it flewe in a dore a span depe! *hand's breadth*
And syth he cryed, as uncourteys: *And afterwards; just as rudely*
"Out, taylardes, of my paleys! *palace*
Now go, and saye your tayled kynge
That I owe hym no thynge!
I am full gladde of his lore, *loss*
I wyll hym yelde none other answore,
And he shall fynde me to morowe,
At the haven to do hym sorowe, *harbor*
And werke hym as moche wrake *destruction*
As his men that I have take."
The messengers wente out full swythe, *very quickly*
Of theyr ascapynge they were blythe.
The emperours stewarde, with honoure,
Sayde thus unto the emperoure:

“Syr,” he sayd, “thou hast unryght! *you are wrong*
Thou haddest almoost slayne a knyght
That is messenger unto a kynge,
The best under the sonne shynynge.
Thou hast thy selfe tresoure enoghe.
Yelde hym his tresour or thou getis grete woghe; *injury*
For he is crossed and pylgrym, *taken the cross*
And all his men that ben with hym.
Lette hym do his pylgrymage,
And kepe thy selfe frome domage.” *harm*
The eyen twynkled of the emperoure
And smyled as an evyll traytoure.
His knyfe he drewe out of his shethe
Therwith to do the stewarde scathe, *injury*
And called hym, without fayle,
And seid he wolde tellene hym a consaile. *a secret matter*
The stewarde on knees hym set a downe
With the emperour for to rowne, *to converse*
And the emperour of evyll truste *faithless emperor*
Carved of his nose by the gruste *off; gristle*
And sayd, “Traytour, thefe, stewarde,
Go playne to Englysshe taylarde! *complain*
And yf he come on my londe,
I shall hym do such a shonde — *dishonor*
Hym and all his men quycke slayne — *Him and all his living men slay*
But he in haste tourne agayne!” *Unless; turn back*
  The stewarde his nose hente *seized*
— Iwys, his vysage was ishente — *face was ruined*
Quyckely out of the castell ran:
Leve he ne toke of no man! *Permission*
The messengers mercy he cryed,
For Maryes love in that tyde,
They sholde tell to theyr lorde
Of the dyshonour, ende and worde: *beginning and end*
“And haste you agayne to londe,
And I shall sese into your honde *yield*
The keyes of every toure
That oweth that fals emperoure; *That that false emperor possesses*
And I shall brynge hym this nyght
The emperours doughter bryght
And also an hondred knyghtes,
Stoute in batayll, stronge in fyghtes,
Ayenst that fals emperoure
That hath done us this dyshonoure.”
  The messengers them hyed harde *hastened*
Tyll they came to Kynge Rycharde.
They founde kynge Richarde playe

At the chesse in his galaye. — *chess*
The erle of Rychemonde with hym played,
And Rycharde wan all that he layed. — *wagered*
The messengers tolde all the dyshonour
That them dyde the emperour; — *That the emperor did to them*
And the despyte he dyde his stewarde — *injury (humiliation)*
In despyte of kynge Rycharde — *In order to spite*
And the stewarde presentynge
His byhest and his helpynge. — *pledge; assistance*
Than answered Kynge Rycharde,
In dede lyon, in thought, lybarde: — *leopard (see note)*
"Of your sawes, I am blythe! — *words*
Anone set us to londe swythe!"
  A grete crye arose fote-hote: — *suddenly*
Out was shotte many a bote. — *bolt of a crossbow*
The bowe men and eke the arblasters
Armed them at all aventers — *Armed themselves for every possibility*
And shotte quarelles, and eke flone — *arrows*
As thycke as the hayle stone.
The folke of the countré gan renne — *fled*
And were fayne to voyde and flenne. — *eager to depart and flee*
The barons and good knyghtes
After came anone ryghtes
With theyr lorde, Kynge Rycharde,
That never was founde no cowarde.

  Kynge Rycharde, I understonde, — *(see note)*
Or he wente out of Englonde, — *Before*
Let hym make an axe for the nones,[1]
To breke therwith the Sarasyns bones.
The heed was wrought ryght wele:
Therin was twenty pounde of stele;
And whan he came into Cyprys londe,
The axe he toke in his honde.
All that he hytte he all tofrapped. — *beat all to pieces*
The Gryffons a waye faste rapped; — *hurried*
Nevertheles, many one he cleved, — *split apart*
And theyr unthonkes therby leved! — *thereby their resentment ended*
And the pryson whan he came to
With his axe he smote ryght tho — *right then*
Dores, berres, and iren chaynes, — *bars*
And delyvered his men out of paynes. — *imprisonment*
He let them all delyver cloth; — *commanded; clothing*
For theyr despyte he was wroth — *humiliation*

---

[1] *Had himself an axe made for the occasion*

And swore by Jhesu, our savyoure,
He sholde abye, that fals emperoure. *be punished*
All the bourgeyses of the towne, *citizens (freemen)*
Kynge Rycharde let slee without raunsowne. *ordered slain*
Theyr tresour and theyr jewells
He sesyde als his owne catells. *as his own property (treasure)*
Tydynges came to the emperour,
Kynge Rycharde was in Lymasour *Limassol (a port in Cyprus)*
And had his burgeyses to deth ido. *put to death*
No wonder though hym were wo! *No wonder if he were grieved*
He sente anone, without fayle,
After all his counsayle,
That they came to hym on hye *at once*
To wreke hym of his enemye. *avenge*
His hoost was come by mydnyght,
And redy on the morowe for to fyght.
Herken now of the stewarde!
He came at nyght to Kynge Rycharde,
And the emperours doughter hym with.
She grette Kynge Rycharde in pease and gryth. *in amity and accord*
He fell on knees and gan to wepe
And sayd, "Kynge Rycharde, God thee kepe!"
The stewarde sayd, "I am shente for thee! *disfigured (shamed); on account of*
Gentyll lorde, awreke thou me!
The emperours doughter bryght, *fair (beautiful)*
I thee betake, gentyll knyght, *I deliver to you*
The keyes also I betake thee here
Of every castell in his powere.
An hondred knyghtes I you behyght, *promised*
Lo them here, redy in all ryght. *Behold; prepared in the best manner*
That shall you lede and socoure *aid in battle*
Ayenst that fals emperoure!
Thou shalte be bothe lorde and syre,
Or to morowe of his empyre, *Before*
And swete syr, without fayle,
Yet thee behoveth my counsayle. *Still you need my counsel*
I shall thee lede by a coost *coast (shore)*
Pryvely upon his hoost.
In his pavylyon ye shall hym take;
Than thynke upon thee moche wrake *consider for yourself what great injury*
That he hath done thee or this! *before this*
Though ye hym slee, no force it is!" *it does not matter*
Moche thanked Kynge Rycharde *King Richard greatly thanked*
Of the counseyll the stewarde,
And swore by God, our savyoure,
His nose sholde be bought well soure. *be avenged very fully*

Ten hondred stedes, good and sure, *sturdy*
Kynge Rycharde let araye in trappure. *directed to be equipped in armor*
On everyche lepte an Englysshe knyght,
Stowte in armes and stronge in fighte,
And as the stewarde, applyght, *in faith*
Ladde them by the mone lyght
So nygh the emperours pavylyoune,
Of the trompis he herde the sowne —
It was before the dawynynge —
The stewarde sayd to Rycharde, the kynge:
"Lette se, Rycharde, assayle yerne *Look here, Richard, forcefully assail*
The pavylyon with the golden herne. *heron*
Therin lyeth the emperour.
Awreke thou this dyshonour!"
Than was Rycharde as fresshe to fyght
As ever was foule to the flyght.
He prycked forth upon his stede,
Hym folowed full grete ferrede. *troop*
His axe he helde in honde idrawe; *drawn*
Many Gryffons he hath islawe.
The waytes of that hoost that dyde aspye *watchmen*
And full loude began they for to crye:
"As armes lordynges, alle and some: *To arms*
We bene betrayed and inome! *are betrayed and captured*
In an evyll tyme our emperour
Robbed Kynge Rycharde of his tresour,
For he is here amonge us
And sleeth downe-ryght, by Jhesus!" *outright*
The Englysshe knyghtes, for the nones,
All tohewed the Gryffons bodyes and bones. *Cut all to pieces*
They smote the cordes and felled downe *brought down*
Of many a ryche pavylyowne;
And ever cryed squyer and knyght: *again and again*
"Smyte! Lay on! Slee downe-ryght! *Do battle! Inflict blows! Slay outright!*
Yelde the tresour ayenwarde *back again*
That ye toke from Kynge Rycharde!
Ye ben worthy to have suche mede, *requital (reward)*
With many woundes to lye and blede!"
In the emperours pavylyon, Kynge Rycharde
Alyght, so dyde the stewarde; *Dismounted*
And the emperour was fledde awaye
Hymselfe alone, or it was daye: *before*
Flowen was that fals coward. *Fled*
Narowe hym sought Kynge Rycharde. *Fiercely*
He fande his clothis and his tresoure,
Bot he was fled, that vile traytoure.
Longe or the daye began to dawe,

Twenty thousande Gryffons were islawe.
Of sylke, sendell, and syclaton[1]
Was the emperours pavylyon:
In the worlde never non syche, *never [was] any such thing*
Ne by moche thynge so ryche. *Not so rich by a considerable extent*
Kynge Rycharde wan the grete worshyp, *gained the great honor*
And bad they sholde be lad to shyp: *brought*
Such at Acrys was there none founde,
Pavylyons of so moche mounde. *excellence*
Cuppes of golde, grete and smale,
He wan there without tale. *without number*
Many cofers small and grete *chests*
He founde there full ibete. *precisely decorated*
Two stedes founde the Kynge Rycharde,
That one hyght Favell and that other Lyarde. *(see note)*
In the worlde was not theyr pere,
Dromedary nor destrere, *Camel; war-horse*
Stede rabyte, ne camayle, *Arabian steed*
That ran so swyfte, without fayle.
For a thousande pounde itolde *counted out*
Sholde not that one be solde.
All that his men before had lore, *lost*
Seven double they had therfore. *Sevenfold; in return*
  Tydynges to the emperour was come
That his doughter was inome, *taken*
And how that his hygh stewarde
Her had delyvered to Kynge Rycharde.
By that he wyst well, iwys. *he knew, certainly*
That he had done amys.
Two messengers he clyped anone, *called at once*
And bad them to Kynge Rycharde gone,
"And saye your emperour and your kynge,
That I hym sende Goddes gretynge.
Homage by yere I wyll hym gyve and yelde
And all my londe I wyll of hym helde, *hold from him*
So that he wyll, for charyté, *On condition that*
In peas hereafter let me be."
  The messengers anone forth wente
And sayd theyr lordes commaundemente.
Kynge Rycharde answered therto:
"I graunte well that it be so.
Goth and seithe your emperour
That he dyde grete dyshonour
Whan he robbed pylgrymes

[1] *Of silk, sendal, and silk fabric woven with gold*

That were goynge to the paynymes.
Let hym yelde me my tresour, every dele,
Yf he wyll be my specyele, *retainer*
And also saye your emperour
That he amende that dyshonour
That he dyde to his stewarde
In despyte of Kynge Rycharde;
And that he come erly tomorowe
And crye me mercy with sorowe, *beg me for pardon; remorse*
Homage by yere me to bere, *acknowledge*
And elles, by my crowne I swere, *Or else*
He shall not have a fote of londe
Never more out of my honde."
 The messengers by one accorde
Tolde this the emperour, theyr lorde.
Than the emperour was full wo *very distressed*
That he this dyde sholde do. *deed*
To Kynge Rycharde he came on the morowe;
In his herte he had moche sorowe.
He fell on knees, so sayth the boke,
Kynge Rycharde by bothe the fete he toke
And cryed mercy with good entent, *will*
And he forgave hym his maltalent. *hostility (ill will)*
Fewté he dyde hym, and homage, *Fealty*
Before all his baronage.
That daye they were at one accorde,
And in same dyde ete at one borde; *in the same [place]; ate; table*
In grete solace and moche playe,
Togyder they were all that daye,
And whan it drew towarde the eve,
The emperour toke his leve
And wente towarde his hostell: *lodging*
In herte hym was nothynge well.
He helde hymslelfe a foule cowarde
That he dyde homage to Kynge Rycharde,
And thought how he hym awreke myght. *might avenge himself*
Forth he rode anone ryght
To a cyté that hyght Bonevent. *Buffavento*
He came by daye, verament. *in truth*
There he founde many a grete syre, *lord*
The rychest men of his empyre.
To them playned the emperour
Of the shame and of the dyshonour
That hym dyde Kynge Rycharde
Thorugh the helpe of his stewarde.
Up there stode a noble barowne,
Ryche of castell and of towne, *Mighty*

The stewardes eme he was, *uncle*
That the emperour had shente his fas. *mutilated*
"Syr," he sayd, "thou arte mystaught; *misinformed*
Thou arte all aboute naught. *concerned with nothing*
Without encheson and jugement *grounds for conviction and verdict*
Thy good stewarde thou haste ishent *shamed*
That sholde, as he well couthe, *Who would, as he well knew*
Us have holpe and saved nouthe! *now*
Thorugh thy wyll malycyous,
Ryght so thou woldest serve us; *Just so*
And I saye the wordes bolde:
With suche a lorde kepe I not holde *I will not maintain service*
To fyght ayenst Rycharde, the kynge,
The best under the sonne shynynge.
Ne none of all my baronage, *Neither*
Ne shall thee never do homage." *Nor*
  All the other sayd at one worde *in unison*
That Rycharde was theyr kynde lorde,
And the emperour, for his vylanye,
Was well worthy for to dy.
The emperour sawe and understode
His barons wolde hym no gode: *wished him*
To another towne he wente and helde hym thare. *remained*
In his herte he had moche care.
That same tyme the hygh stewarde
Counseylled with Kynge Rycharde.
He sayd that hym forthought sore *it grieved him keenly*
That the emperour was so forlore. *dishonored*
They sought hym in all wyse, *ways*
And founde hym in the cyté of Pyse.
And certaynly, Kynge Rycharde
Wolde not loke to hym warde; *not endeavor to protect him*
For he had broken his treuth. *his oath of fealty*
Of hym had he no reuth, *pity*
But let a sergeaunt hym bynde
His hondes soone hym behynde,
And caste hym into a galey,
And ledde hym into Surrey, *Syria*
And swore by Hym that made mone and sterre,
Ayenst the Sarasynes he sholde lerne to werre.
  Whan all this warre abated was, *ended*
Kynge Rycharde set that londe in peas.
The Erle of Leycestre, full truly,
Thorugh counseyll of his barony,
He made hym stewarde of that londe, *governor (see note)*
To kepe his realme to his honde; *(see t-note)*
Grete feest they helde afterwarde.

His shyppes let dyght Kynge Rycharde: *ordered his ships prepared*
Forth towarde Acrys he wolde
With moche store of sylver and golde,
With two hondred shyppes, I fynde, *I read*
Saylynge forwarde with the wynde,
And afterwarde fyfty galyes *behind*
For to warde his navyes. *protect his fleet*
And as the doughty Kynge Rycharde
Came saylynge to Acrys warde *stronghold (direction)*
And had sayled with wynde at wyll,
Ten dayes fayre and styll, *free of storms (quiet)*
The unleventhe day thay saylyd in tempest. *eleventh*
That nyght ne day hadde they no rest.
And as they were in gret aventure, *jeopardy*
They sawgh a drowmound out of mesure. *an immense dromond (ship)*
The drowmound was so hevy fraughte *loaded*
That unethe myghte it sayle aught. *with difficulty; at all*
It was toward the Sarezynys *on the way to*
Chargyd with corn and with wynys, *Loaded with grain; wine*
With wylde fyre and other vytayle. *provisions; (see note)*
  Kyng Richard saygh the drowmound, saun faile;
He callyd in haste Aleyn Trenchemer,
And bad hym to wende hem neer, *to sail them near*
And aske whens that they ware *from what place*
And what they hadden in chaffare. *in goods (merchandise)*
Aleyn quyk and men inowe *enough*
To that drowmound begunne to rowe,
And askyd with whom that they ware,
And what they hadden in chaffare.
Anon stood up here latymer *their translator*
And answeryd Aleyn Trenchemer:
"With the kyng of Fraunce, saun faile;
Fro Poyl we brynge this vytaile. *Apulia*
A monith we haven leyen in the see,
Toward Acres wolde wee."
"Wynde up sayl," quod Aleyn swythe,
"And sayle we forth with wyndes lythe!" *light*
"Nay! be Seynt Thomas of Ynde, *(see note)*
Us moste nedes come behynde! *It is very necessary for us to come behind*
For we ben so hevy fraught, *loaded*
Unethis may we saylen aught." *Hardly may we sail by any means*
Thenne sayde Alayn sone anon:
"I here of yow speke but on. *one*
Let stande up alle in fere, *together*
That we now myghte moo here *So that; hear more*
And knowe youre tungge aftyr than; *your language; after that*
For we wole nought leve oo man." *For we will not believe one man*

"Sertes," quod the latymere, *interpreter*
"With no moo men spekys thou here.
They were this nyght in tempeste;
They lyggen alle and take here reste." *lie at ease*
"Sertes," sayde thenne goode Aleyn,
"To Kyng Rychard I wole seyn,
That ye aren alle Sarezynes,
Chargyed with cornes and with wynes!" *grain*
The Sarezynes sterten up al preste, *ready*
And sayden, "Felawe, goo doo thy beste!
For Kyng Richard and hys galyes,
We wolde nought geve twoo flyes!"
Tho Trenchemer gan rowen hard,
Tyl he come to Kyng Richard,
And swor to hym be Seynt Jhon,
That they were Sarezynes everylkon. *every single one*
Thenne sayde oure kyng of renoun
That hyghte Richard Coer de Lyoun: *was named*
"Of youre sawes, I am blythe; *Of your words; happy*
Lat see arme you now swythe! *Let us see you arm quickly*
Stere thou my galye, Trenchemer,
I wole asaye that pawtener. *test; scoundrel*
With myn ax I schal hem frape; *strike them*
Ther schal no Sarezyn me ascape!"
Als tyte hys ax was to hym brought; *Right away*
Hys othir armure forgat he nought.
To hym comen maryners inowe. *enough*
Kyng Richard bad hem faste rowe:
"Rowes on faste! Who that is feynt, *timid (lacking in courage)*
In evel water moot he be dreynt!" *may he be drowned*
They roweden harde and sunggen thertoo
With "hevelow" and "rummeloo." *[sailors' cries]*

The galeye wente alsoo fast, *just as quickly*
As quarel dos of the arweblast; *As does a bolt out of the crossbow*
And as the drowmund come with the wynde,
A large quarter out behynde *A large piece from the rear*
The galey rente with the bronde *tore; beak*
Into the see, I undyrstonde.
Thenne were the Sarezynys armyd wel
Bothe in yryn and in steel;
And stood on borde and foughten hard *onboard*
Agayn the doughty Kyng Richard;
And Kyng Richard and his knyghtes
Slowen the Sarezynes doun ryghtes,
And as they gunne to wyrke hem woo *inflict misery upon them*
Evere there stood up moo and moo, *more and more*

And rappyd hem on, for the nones, *rained blows on them, indeed*
Sterne strokes with harde stones
Out of the topcastel an hygh, *on high*
That Richard was nevere his deth so nygh.
Thenne comen sevene galyes behynde
To that drowmound quyk saylynde,
And stood on borde, baroun and knyght,
To helpe Kyng Richard for to fyght.
A strong batayle there began,
Betwene the hethene men and tham, *them*
With swerdes, speres, dartes kene,
Arwes and quarelles fleygh between *arrows from crossbows*
Also thykke, withouten stynt, *Just as; ceasing*
As hayl aftyr thondyr dynt. *hail; a thunder clap*
And in the bykyr that was so hard, *battle*
Into the drowmound come Kyng Richard.
Whenne he was comen in on haste,
He dressyd hys bak unto the maste. *placed his back against*
With his ax that he ovyrraughte, *whom he reached*
Hastely hys deth he caughte. *he received*
Some he hytte on the bacyn *basinet (helmet)*
That he clef hym to the chyn. *So that; cleaved*
And some to the gyrdyl-stede, *the waist*
And some unto the schyppes brede. *ship's plank*
Some in the hals so hytte hee *the neck*
That hed and helme fleygh into the see. *flew*
For non armour withstood hys ax,
No more than a knyf dos in the wax.
The Sarezynes, as I yow telle,
Sayden he was a devyl of helle;
And ovyr the bord lopen thay *jumped overboard*
And drownyd hem in the see that day. *drowned themselves*
Syxtene hundryd be aqueled, *killed*
Save thrytty Sarezynes the kyng leet held, *ordered to be held*
That they scholden bere wytnes *So that*
Of this batayle at Acres.
The kyng fond in the drowmound, saun fayle,
Mekyl stor and gret vytayle, *Abundant provisions; stocks of food*
Many barel ful of fyr Gregeys, *Greek fire*
And many a thousand bowe Turkeys. *Turkish bows*
Hokyd arewes and quarelles. *Barbed arrowheads*
They fond there ful manye barelles
Of whete and wyn gret plenté,
Gold and sylver, and ylke deynté. *every delicacy*
Of tresour, he hadde nought half the mounde *riches*
That in the drowmounde was ifound;
For it drownyd in the flood, *the sea*

Ar half unchargyd were that good. *Before half that property was unloaded*
Avaunsyd was al Crystyanté;
For hadde the drowmound ipassed the see,
And comen to Acres fro Kyng Richard,
An hondryd wyntyr aftyrward,
For alle Crystene men undyr sunne,
Hadde nought Acres ben iwunne! *Acre would not have been regained*
Thus Kyng Richard wan the drowmound,
Thorwgh Goddes help and Seynt Edmound.

Kyng Richard aftyr anon ryght *immediately*
Toward Acres gan hym dyght; *went (betook himself)*
And as he saylyd toward Surrye, *Syria*
He was warnyd of a spye, *by a spy*
Hou the folk of the hethene lawe
A gret cheyne hadden idrawe
Ovyr the havene of Acres fers, *Across the harbor of great Acre*
And was festnyd to twoo pelers *fastened to two pillars*
That no schyp ne scholde in wynne: *gain entry*
Ne they nought out that were withinne.
Therfore, sevene yer and more,
Alle Crystene kynges leyen thore, *remained there*
And with gret hongyr suffryd payne
For lettyng of that ylke chayne. *On account of the hindrance of that very chain*
Kyng Richard herde that tydynge,
For joye his herte began to sprynge.
And swor and sayde in hys thought, *to himself*
That ylke chayne scholde helpe hem nought.
A swythe strong galey he took
And Trenchemer, so says the book,
Steryd the galey ryght fol evene *directly*
Ryght in the myddes of the havene.
Were the maryners saughte or wrothe, *Whether the mariners were at peace or angry*
He made hem saylle and rowe bothe.
The galey yede as swyfte,
As ony foule by the lyfte, *air*
And Kyng Richard that was so good,
With hys ax in foreschyp stood; *front of the ship*
And whan he came to the chayne,
With his axe he smote it atwayne,
That alle the barouns, verrayment, *So that; truly*
Sayden it was a noble dent, *stroke*
And for joye of this dede,
The cuppes faste abouten yede, *went*
With good wyn, pyement and clarré, *spiced wine; clary*
And sayllyd toward Acres cyté.
Kyng Richard out of hys galye

Caste wylde fyre into the skye,
And fyr Gregeys into the see,
As al on fyre weren hee. — *As if; they [sea and sky]*
Trumpes yeden in hys galeye, — *sang*
Men myghten it here into the skye,
Taboures and hornes Sarezyneys. — *Military drums and Saracen horns*
The see brente al of fyr Gregeys.

Gunnes he hadde on wondyr wyse,[1]
Magneles of gret queyntyse, — *ingenuity*
Arweblast, bowe, and with gynne, — *skill*
The Holy Lond for to wynne.
Ovyr al othere wyttyrly, — *Surpassing all others skillfully (clearly)*
A melle he made of gret maystry,[2]
In myddes a schyp for to stande
Swylke on sawgh nevere man in lande. — *Such a one never saw man in the world*
Foure sayles were thertoo,
Yelew and grene, rede and bloo,
With canevas layd wel al aboute, — *canvas*
Ful schyr withinne and eke withoute, — *Very bright*
Al within ful of feer — *fire*
Of torches maad with wex ful cleer;
Ovyrtwart and endelang, — *Crosswise; lengthwise*
With strenges of wyr the stones hang, — *strings of wire; hung*
Stones that deden nevere note: — *never performed work*
Grounde they nevere whete no grote, — *wheat nor hulled grain*
But rubbyd als they were wood. — *as; mad*
Out of the eye ran red blood — *eye (hole in a millstone)*
Before the trowgh ther stood on, — *trough (grain hopper in a mill); one*
Al in blood he was begon, — *covered*
And hornes grete upon hys hede:
Sarezynes therof hadden grete drede.
For it was within the nyght
They were agrysed of that syght, — *frightened*
For the rubbyyng of the stones,
They wende it hadde ben mennes bones. — *believed*
And sayd he was the devyll of hell,
That was come them to quell.
A lytyl before the lyght of day,
Clenly they were don away. — *Thoroughly; driven away*

Kyng Rychard aftyr that mervayle,
Wente to the lond, saun fayle.
The kyng of Fraunce agayn hym come, — *toward*

---

[1] *He had miraculous siege engines [that hurled missiles]*

[2] *A mill he made from special skill (of great strength)*

And in hys armes he hym nome, *took him [Richard]*
And kyste hym with gret honour,
And so dede many an emperour.
Alle the kynges of Crystyanté
That there hadden longe tyme ibee, *been*
And leyn there sevene yer in dolour, *remained; suffering*
Resseyvyd Kyng Richard with honour.
The archebysschop of Pyse *Pisa*
Dede Kyng Richard his servyse, *Pledged; service (feudal allegiance)*
And ledden hym, as ye may see,
Into a pavyloun in pryvyté,
And tolde hym a doolful tale *sorrowful*
Of schrewede aventures, manye and fale: *Of deadly deeds; hard (dangerous)*
"Kynge Richard," he sayde, "now here!
This sege has lastyd sevene yere.
It may nought fro thee be holde, *defended*
Mekyl sorwe have we tholde! *suffered*
For we ne hadde no castel
That us of ony warde fel, *That allotted to us any protection*
But a wyde dyke and a depe
We made withinne us for to kepe
With barbycanes, for the nones, *barbicans (outer fortifications)*
Heyghe wrought of harde stones. *Made high*
And whenne that oure dyke was made, *moat (defensive ditch)*
Saladyn the Sawdon was glade,
And come on us with gret route, *company*
And besette us al aboute,
And with hym Markes Manferaunt, *Marquis (Conrad of) Montferrat*
That leves on Mahoun and Termagaunt.[1]
He was a Crystene kyng sumwhyle; *formerly*
He dos us schame and moche gyle *deceit*
Thenne the Sawdon and al hys hoost. *Than*
Fadyr and Sone and Holy Gost,
Graunte hym grace of worldis schame, *public disapproval*
Markys Feraunt be hys name!
Oure ferst bataylle, sykyrly,
Was ful strong and ful deedly,
Weel foughten oure Crystene knyghtes,
And slowen the Sarezynes doun ryghtes.
Oure Crystene hadden the maystry; *victory*
The Sarezynes flowen with woo and cry. *fled*
We slowe of hem manye thoo, *then*
And they of us manye alsoo;
And I schal telle thorwgh what cas *what fate*
It fyl to many a man, allas! *Happened*

[1] *Who believes in Muhammad and Termagaunt (fictitious deity)*

As we dede Sarezynys to dede, — *put; to death*
Befel that a noble stede — *It happened*
Outrayyd fro a paynym. — *Dashed out*
Oure Crystene men faste folewyd hym.
The Sarezynes seyghen that they come, — *saw*
And fleygh asyde, alle and some. — *And moved swiflty*
And come on us with gret fyght, — *came; fighting power*
And slowgh many a Crystene doun right,
That there we loste ar we it wyste, — *before we knew it*
The beste bodyes undyr Cryste.
The Erl of Ferrers of Yngeland,
Ther was no doughtyere man of hand; — *armed might*
And the Emperour of Alemayne, — *Germany*
And Janyn, the Eerl of Playn Spayne.
Onlevene thousand of oure meyné — *Eleven thousand; army*
There were slayn withouten pyté!
  Therofe was the Sawdon glade,
On morwen a newe sawt he made. — *assault*
He leet taken alle the cors — *He ordered all the corpses [to be] taken*
Of the men and of the hors,
And caste into the watyr of oure welle
Us to poysoun and to quelle; — *kill*
Dede he nevere a wers dede
To Crystene men for no nede. — *on no account*
Thorwgh that poysoun and that brethe, — *stench*
Fourty thousand toke theyr dethe.
  Sone aftyr newe yer, is nought to hyde, — *[there] is nothing to conceal*
The thrydde caas us gan betyde. — *The third predicament afflicted us*
A schyp come saylande in the see — *sailing*
Chargyd with whete gret plenté, — *Loaded abundantly with wheat*
With wylde fyr and armes bryght,
To helpe the Sarezynes for to fyght.
The Crystene token to red, saun fayle, — *agreed*
They wolde the schyp for to assayle,
And so they dede to oure damage!
The wynd blew with gret rage;
The Sarezynes drowgh up here sayl,
And ovyrsayleyd oure folk, saun fayl, — *overwhelmed our folk*
That there were lost syxty score — *So that; sixty score (twelve hundred)*
Of the beste bodyes that weren bore! — *were born*
This was the begynnyng of oure care — *grief (hardship)*
That we have had this sevene yare,
And yit, sere kyng, thou schalt here more
That has grevyd us ful sore.

  On Seynt Jamys even, verrayment, — *eve (24 July)*
The Sarezynes out of Acres went,

Weel a myle us besyde,	*Fully a mile*
And pyght up pavylouns round and wyde,	*pitched (set)*
And sojournyd there a long whyle,	
And alle it was us to begyle.	
Oure Crystene men that were wyght,	*brave*
Erl, baroun, squyer, and knyght,	
Seyghen the Sarezynes have ryhchesse,	*Saw; riches*
And we of alle good dystresse,	*And we of all prosperity [have] scarcity*
And thoughte to wynne to oure pray	*booty*
Of that tresore and that noblay.	*wealth*
Fyfty thousynd hem armyd weel,	*armed themselves fully*
Bothe in yren and in steel,	
And wenten forth to batayllyng.	*combat*
The Sarezynes sawgh here comyng,	*their*
And flowen asyde swythe faste,	*moved aside very fast*
And oure men comen aftyr in haste,	
And gunnen to ryde swythe gret raundoun	*with great speed*
Tyl they come to here pavyloun.	
They founde therinne no ferede:	*armed troop*
They wende they hadde ben flowen for drede.	*believed; put to flight*
They founden there whyt bred and wynes,	
Gold, sylvyr and bawdekynes:	*Oriental silk cloths (brocade)*
Vessel of sylvyr, coupes of golde,	
More thenne they take scholde.	*could take*
Some stood and some sat doun,	
And eet and drank gret foysoun;	*great abundance*
And aftyr mete the pavylouns newe,	
With there swerdes doun thay hewe,	
And chargyd hors with vytayle,	*loaded; provisions (food)*
As nyse men scholde, saun fayle!	*As foolish*
Gold and sylvyr in males they pytte,	*in bags; shoved*
And with here gerdeles they hem knytte.	*their belts they fastened them*
Whenne that ylke man hadde his charge,	*each man had his cargo (burden)*
Home they wolden, withouten targe.	*delay*
The Sarezynes seygh wel here wendyng	*their movement*
And comen aftyr faste flyngyng:	*came fast rushing*
At schorte wurdes, a gret route,	*In short; a great crowd*
And besette oure hoost aboute.	*surrounded our army*
There here males doun they caste,	*bags*
Agayn the Sarezynes they foughten faste;	
And there were lost thousandes fyftene,	
Noble men, hardy and kene.	
This caas grevyd us so sore	
That we wende have ben forlore;	*considered ourselves to be lost*
And God Almyghty, hevene kyng,	*Unless*
Sente us sone socouryng.	*assistance*
The doughty eerl of Champayne,	*(see note)*

And goode knyghtes of Bretayne,
And Randulf, the Glamvyles. *(see note)*
And Jhon the Neel and hys brother Myles, *(see note)*
And Bawdewyne, a clerk ful mery, *Baldwin*
The Erchebysschop of Cauntyrbery,
And with hym come hys nevewe, *nephew*
A baroun of gret vertewe,
Huberd Gawter of Yngelande, *(see note)*
Agayn the Sarezynes for to stande;
And manye knyghtes of Hongry, *Hungary*
And mekyl othir chevalry. *nobles*
Thenne heeld we strong bataylle,
But an hard caas us fel, saun faylle. *situation befell us*

At Myghhylmasse, it moste be told, *Michaelmas [29 September]*
The wedyr gan to wexe cold.
Than fel bothe rayn and hayl
And snowgh fyve foote deep, saun fayle.
Thondyr, lyghtnyng, wedyr towgh, *severe*
For hungyr oure folk it slowgh;[1]
For hungyr we loste, and colde wyndes,
Of our folk sixty thousyndes!
Thenne oure goode hors we slowe,
Dede sethe and eete the guttys towe. *Did boil and eat the tough guts*
The flesch was delyd with deynté: *divided with dignity*
Therofe had no man plenté.
Al to peses we carf the hede,
And on the coles we gan it brede, *coals; cooked*
In watyr we boylyd the blood:
That us thoughte was mete ful good! *food*
A quarter of whete men us solde
For syxty pound of floryns tolde! *florins; counted out*
For fourty pound men solde an oxe,
Though it were byt lytyl woxe. *grown*
A swyn for an hundryd floryn,
A goos for half mark of gold fyn, *pure gold*
And for an hen, to syke thynges, *two*
Men gaf of penyes, fyftene schillinges,
For an hen ay, penyes unlevene, *hen's egg; eleven*
And for a pere, syxe or sevene, *pear*
And for an appyl, penyes sexe;
And thus began oure folk unwexe, *to decline*
And dyede for hungyr and for woo. *misery*
The ryche men token to rede thoo *agreed then*
A ryche dole for to dyghte *A rich share (portion) to allot*

[1] *Through hunger, our folk it [the weather] slew*

To barouns and to pore knyghte.
Twelve penyes men gaf to everyche, *everyone*
And syxe to othere that were nought ryche,
And foure to the smale wyghtes; *common men*
Thus, the ryche here dole dyghtes.
Therwith the more and lasse, *persons of higher and of lower station*
Boughte hem flesch of hors and asse. *bought themselves; donkey*
They myghte have non othir thyng,
For whyt tourneys, ne for sterlyng. *Not for French or English currency*
I have thee told, sere kyng, here
Of oure men al the lere, *story*
And the damage of Acres hoost.
But blessyd be the Holy Goost,
And Marye that bar Jhesus,
That thou art comen among us!
Thorwgh thyn help we hopen snelle *swiftly*
The Sarezynes hoost doun to felle!"
Kyng Richard wepte with hys eyen bothe,
And thus he sayde to hym, forsothe: *after that*
"Sere bysschop, bydde thou for us, *plead*
That myght me sende swete Jhesus, *So that sweet Jesus might dispatch me*
Hys foos alle to destroye, *foes*
That they no more us anoye!"
Kyng Richard took leve and leep on stede, *leaped onto*
And pryckyd out of that felawred. *rode; body of knights*
He rod aboute the clos dyke *around the moat*
Toward Acres, sykyrlyke,
Tyl he come to the hospytale *came*
Of Seynt John, as I fynde in tale. *in [the] narrative*
There leet he pyghte hys pavyloun, *There he ordered his pavilion to be pitched*
And arerede hys mate-gryffoun, *And erected (raised) his mate-gryphon*
That was a tree castell ful fyne *siege tower very fine*
To assaute with many Sarezyn,
That he myghte into Acres seen.
He hadde thryttene shyppes full of been. *bees*
Whenne the castel was framyd wel. *well constructed*
They sette therinne a magnel, *mangonel*
And commandyd hys men belyve, *without delay*
To brynge up many a bee-hyve,
And beet on tabours and trumpes to blowe, *drums*
And made a sawt al in a throwe.[1]
Kyng Richard into Acres cyté
Leet keste the hyves gret plenté. *Ordered the hives cast in great number*
It was hoot in the someres tyde.
The bees bursten out on every side

[1] *And make an assault all in a short space of time*

That were anoyyd and ful of grame; *anger*
They dede the Sarezynes ful gret schame,
For they hem stungge in the vysage, *face*
That alle they gunne for to rage,
And hydde hem in a deep selere, *cellar*
That non of hem durste come nere;
And sayden kyng Richard was ful fel, *very crafty (fierce)*
Whenne hys flyes byten so wel!
  Anothir gyn Kyng Richard upsette, *engine; erected*
That was callyd Robynette,
A strong gyn for the nones,
And caste into Acres harde stones.
Kyng Richard, the conquerour,
Callyd in haste hys mynour, *miner (see note)*
And bad hym myne up to the tour
That is callyd Maudyt Colour.
And swoor hys oth be Seynt Symoun, *oath*
But yif it were ibrought a doun *unless*
Be noon the uttermeste wal, *By; outermost*
He scholde hym hewe to peses smal.
The mynours gunne to myne faste;
The gynours ben and stones cast. *bees*
The Sarezynes hem armyd alle,
And runne anon unto the walle. *immediately*
In whyte schetys they gunne hem wryen, *sheets; took cover*
For the bytyng of hys flyen, *flying insects*
And sayde, "This man dos us strong pyne, *pain (injury)*
Whenne he wole bothe throwe and myne.
We sawe nevere kyng so begynne:
It is gret doute he schal us wynne![1]
Kyng Richard stood in his mate-griffoun,
And sawgh here dedes in the toun:
And whedyrwardes the Sarazenes flowen, *In whatever direction; fled*
Archers seygh and to hem drowen, *Archers saw and to them drew (shot)*
And arweblasters with quarell smerte,
Thorwgh legges and armes, hed and herte.
The Frenssche men with gret noblay, *nobleness*
Halp to myne that ylke day
That outemeste wal was doun caste, *So that*
And many a Sarezyn slayn in haste.
That day Kyng Richard spedde so thor *triumphed so there*
That he was holden a conqueror: *considered*
For betere he spedde that day or noon *before*
Then the othre in the sevene yer hadde don.

[1] *There is reason to fear that he will defeat us*

The Sarezynys myghten nought doure: *endure*
They flowen into the heyghe toure, *high*
And lyghten torches abouten the wal,
Men myghte it sen ovyr al. *[So that]*
The torchys caste a gret lyght
That betokenyd a newe fyght
That was comen fro Yngelonde,
Where thorwgh they myghte nought withstonde,[1]
But yf Saladyn, the Sawdan, *Unless*
Come to helpe with many a man.
Saladyn was ten myle thenne, *thence (from that place)*
And seygh the torches lyghtly brenne. *saw; burn radiantly*
They gaderede here folk togedere,
As thykke as rayn falles in wedere. *adverse weather*
They assemblyd on a playn
Besyde Acres, on a mountayn.
Syxty thousand footmen, I fynde,
Knehches of hay he made hem bynde, *Bunches*
To goo before hastelyke
To fylle ful the Crystene dyke.
Soo they have taken here red, *So they have agreed*
To doo the Crystene men to ded.
Aftyr comen barouns and knyghtes,
An hundryd thousand stronge in fyghtes.
Be ordre they comen in here maners,[2]
Of red sendel were here baners, *sendal (costly fabric)*
With thre gryffouns depayntyd weel, *(see note)*
And of asure a fayr bendel. *azure; ornamental band*
Sone theraftyr come rydande as fele *as many*
Of bolde barouns by gentyl stele. *with noble armor*
Here gonfanouns and here penseles, *Their pennons; company standards*
Were weel wrought of grene sendeles, *sendal (linen)*
And on everylkon, a dragoun
As he faught with a lyoun.
The fyrste were rede, and thyse were grene.
Thenne come the thrydde bataylle bedene: *battalion all together*
Fyve and syxty thousand knyghtes,
In ynde armyd to all ryghtes.[3] *(see t-note)*
Aftyr come, whyte as the snow,
Fyfty thousand in a rowe.
Ther among was Sere Saladyn,
And hys nevewe, Myrayn-Momelyn. *(see note)*
Here baner whyt, withouten fable, *without lie*

[1] *For which reason, they might not hold out*

[2] *According to rank, they came following their custom*

[3] *In ynde [fabric dyed with indigo], armed in the best manner*

With thre Sarezynes hedes of sable — *black (see note)*
That were schapen noble and large;
Of balayn, bothe scheeld and targe. — *whalebone (baleen); light shield*
No man cowde telle the route: — *count; host of soldiers*
They besette the Crystene al aboute.
The footmen kast in knehches of hay — *bunches; (see note)*
To make the horsmen in redy way,
And fylde the dyke ful upryghte,
That al the hoost entre in myghte.
The Sarezynys hadden entry negh, — *nearly*
But God Almyghty thertoo segh. — *Yet; saw*
The cry aros into the Crystene hoost,
"Susé seynours, has armes tost![1] — *(see note)*
But we have the betere socour, — *Unless; [spiritual] assistance*
We beth forlore be Seynt Savour!" — *lost; [we swear] by Christ*
Thoo myghte men see many wyght man, — *many [a] brave man*
Hasteyly to hys armes ran
And wenten quykly to the dyke,
And defendyd hem hastelyke. — *defended themselves*
There was many gentyl heved — *head*
Quykly fro the body weved; — *severed*
Scheldes, many schorn in twoo,
And many stede stykyd alsoo. — *stabbed*
And many a knyghte loste his armys,
And many a stede drewe theyr tharmes, — *dragged their entrails*
And manye a doughty man, saun faylle,
There was slayn in that batayIle.
Kyng Richard was syke thoo, — *ill then*
Al Crystyndom to mekyl woo! — *[was brought] into great woe*
He myghte hym nought of hys bed stere, — *stir (move)*
Though his pavyloun hadde ben on fere. — *Even if; fire*
Therfore the kyng of Fraunce leet crye
Among the Crystene cumpanye
That no man scholde, for dedes doute, — *for death's fear*
Passe the clos dyke withoute; — *Pass beyond the moat on the outer side*
But holde them all within
That the Sarasynes sholde them not wyn; — *So that; defeat them*
And thoo that were in icomen — *And those that had come in*
Of the Saryzynes that were inomen, — *that were captured*
Fol hastyly were they don to dede: — *put to death*
For them yede no raunsoun to mede! — *no ransom did any good as fee*

Why Kyng Richard so syke lay
The resoun I yow telle may:
For the travaylle of the see — *exertion of the journey*

[1] *Onwards, lords, all to arms at once!*

And strong eyr of that cuntree,
And unkynde cold and hete, *unnatural (unwholesome)*
And mete and drynk that is nought sete *wholesome*
To hys body that he there fonde,
As he dede here in Yngelonde.
Rychard bad hys men seche *search*
For some wys clerk and sertayn leche, *trustworthy physician*
Crystyn othir Sarezyn *or*
For to loken hys uryn. *examine*
And every man sayde hys avys, *opinion*
But ther was no man so wys
That myghte don his sorwe sese, *make; cease*
Ne of hys paynes hym relese. *Or*
Sory were the folk Englysch,
For here lorde laye in grete anguysch; *such anguish*
So was the Crystene hoost eke,
For Rychard lay so sore seke.
On knees prayden the Cristene hoost,
To the Fadyr, and Sone, and Holy Goost,
Be nyght and day with good entent: *will (spiritual attitude)*
"Geve Kyng Richard amendement!" *recovery (relief)*
For love of his modyr dere,
Here Sone grauntyd her prayere. *their*
Thorwgh hys grace and his vertu,
He turnyd out of hys agu. *acute fever*
To mete hadde he no savour, *He had no appetite for food*
To wyn, ne watyr, ne no lycour,
But aftyr pork he was alongyd; *was craving*
But though his men scholde be hongyd,
They ne myghte in that cuntree,
For gold, ne sylver, ne no moné,
No pork fynde, take, ne gete,
That Kyng Richard myghte ought of eete. *by any means*

An old knyght was with Richard Kyng;
Whenne he wyste of that tydyng, *report*
That the kynges maners were swyche, *conditions; such*
To the styward he spak, prevylyche:
"Oure lord kyng sore is syke, iwis, *indeed*
Aftyr pork he alongyd is; *is craving*
And ye may non fynde to selle. *for sale*
No man be hardy hym so to telle! *Let no man have the audacity to tell him so*
Yif ye dede, he myghte deye!
Yow behoves to don als I schal seye, *You need to do as I shall say*
That he wete nought of that. *So that; know nothing*
Takes a Sarezyn, yonge and fat;
In haste that the thef be slayn, *Make sure the wretch be slain in haste*

Openyd, and hys hyde of flayn, *skin flayed*
And soden ful hastyly, *boiled very quickly*
With powdyr and with spysory, *seasoning; spices*
And with saffron of good colour.
Whenne the kyng feles therof savour, *smells the odor*
Out of agu, yif he be went, *Out of his fever, if he is passed*
He schal have thertoo good talent. *appetite*
Whenne he has a good tast,
And eeten weel a good repast,
And soupyd of the broweys a sope, *And drunk of the broth (stew) a mouthful*
Slept aftyr, and swet a drope, *sweat a drop*
Thorwgh Goddes myght and my counsayl,
Sone he schal be fresch and hayl." *vigorous; healthy*
  The sothe to saye at wyrdes fewe,
Slayn and soden was the hethene schrewe; *boiled; rogue (devil)*
Before the kyng it was forth brought.
Quod hys men: "Lord, we have pork sought: *gone and gotten*
Etes and soupes of the broweys swote. *Eat and drink of the sweet broth*
Thorwgh grace of God it schal be youre boote." *remedy*
Before Kyng Rychard karf a knyghte; *carved*
He eet fastere than he kerve myghte.
The kyng eet the flesch and gnew the bones, *gnawed*
And drank wel aftyr, for the nones;
And whenne he hadde eeten inowgh,
Hys folk hem turnyd away and lowgh. *turned themselves; laugh*
He lay stylle and drowgh in hys arme, *drew*
Hys chaumbyrlayn hym wappyd warme. *wrapped*
He lay, and slepte, and swette a stounde *a while*
And become hool and sounde.
Kyng Richard cladde hym and aros, *dressed himself*
And walkyd abouten in the clos; *enclosed area*
To alle folk he hym schewyd, *showed himself*
Glad was bothe leryd and lewyd, *the learned; the unlettered*
And thankyd Jhesu and Marye *(see note)*
That he was out of his maladye.
  The Sarezynes spedde day and nyght *hastened*
The dyke to wynne with here myght.
The barbycanes they felden a doun *outer fortifications*
And had nygh entred an in icome.
Whenne Kyng Richard therof herde,
As a wood man he spak and ferde: *mad man; behaved*
"Armes me in myn armure,
For love of Cryst, oure creature! *creator*
To fyghte I have gret delyte
With houndes that wil us do despyte.
Now I me fynde hool and lyght. *I find myself healthy; relieved of illness*
This day schal I prove my myght

Yif I be strong as I was wone, — *accustomed to be*
And yif I strokes dele cone, — *am able to deliver strokes*
As I was wunt in Yngeland. — *accustomed*
Have I myn ax in myn hand,
Al that I mete schal me fele, — *I shall vanquish*
And swylk dole I schal hem dele — *torment; deliver to them*
That evere for love of here Mahoun, — *Muhammad*
They schole have here warysoun." — *reward*
He was armyd to alle ryghtes, — *fittingly*
And hys footemen, squyers and knyghtes,
And the Crystene alle bedene. — *Christians all together*
Wondyr was that hoost to sene!
The sothe to say, and nought to hele, — *truth; conceal*
The hethene were twoo so fele. — *twice as many*

Before wente his Templers, — *(see note)*
His Gascoynes and his Ospytalers;
Oure kyng among the Sarezynes ryt — *rode*
And some to the sadyl he slyt. — *split*
A kyng he hytte above the scheeld,
That hed and helm fleygh into the feeld.
Another he has a strok ibrought,
That al hys armure halp hym nought.
Into the sadyl he clef the ferthe:, — *cleaved (split) the fourth*
Al that he smot it fleygh to the erthe. — *flew*
Blythe was the Crystene felawrede — *company*
Of Kyng Richard and of hys dede;
For non armour withstood hys ax
No more than a knyf dos in the wax.
Whenne the Sawdon seygh hym so strong,
He sayde the devyl was hem among;
For Kyng Richard ryght doun slowgh.
With al hys hoost he hym withdrowgh,
And fleygh quyk with hys barounnage — *fled*
Into a toun men calles Gage.
But sertes, al the rerewarde — *rear guard*
Was islayn with Kyng Rycharde. — *by King Richard*
The Sarezynys that in Acres ware, — *were*
Were anoyyd and ful of care — *troubled*
Whenne they seyghen the Sawdon flee,
And Kyng Richard dounryght slee. — *slay [Saracens] outright*
Thus al the day tyl it was nyght,
They and the Crystene heeld the fyght.
At even whenne the sunne was set,
Every man drowgh to hys recet. — *shelter*
The Crystene, bothe pore and ryche,
Wente withinne the clos dyche

To reste, for they were wery.
Kyng Richard leet make a cry, *command*
Trusty folk that nyght the paleys to kepe, *guard*
Whyl that othere lay and slepe.
The Sarezynys that were withouten,
Of Kyng Richard so sore hem douten, *were so afraid of King Richard*
For he hadde the prys iwunne. *victory*
Away thay ryden and swythe runne, *swiftly*
That nyght to fle and to hyde,
That non of hem durste hym abyde *dared to permit him (wait for him)*
The mountenaunce of ten myle. *time needed to travel ten miles*
When Kyng Richard hadde restyd a whyle,
A knyght hys armes gan unlace.
Hym to counforte and solace,
Hym was brought a sop in wyn: *morsel of bread [dipped]*
"The hed of that ylke swyn *same*
That I of eet," — the cook he bad, —
"For feble I am, feynt and mad. *giddy*
Of myn evyl now I am fere; *Of my sickness I am now afraid*
Serve me therwith at my sopere!"
Quod the cook, "That hed I ne have."
Thenne sayde the kyng, "So God me save,
But I see the hed of that swyn, *Unless*
For sothe, thou schalt lese thyn!"
The cook seygh non othir may bee, *discerned that he had no other choice*
He fette the hed and leet hym see. *brought*
He fel on knees and made a cry,
"Loo, here the hed, my lord, mercy!" *(see note)*
Hys swarte vys whenne the kyng seeth, *When the king sees his swarthy (black) face*
Hys blake berd and hys whyte teeth,
Hou hys lyppys grennyd wyde:
"What devyl is this?" the kyng cryde,
And gan to lawghe as he were wood.
"What? Is Sarezynys flesch thus good,
And nevere erst I nought wyste? *And never before did I know it*
By Goddys deth and Hys upryste, *resurrection*
Schole we nevere dye for defawte *for lack [of food]*
Whyl we may in any assawte *As long as*
Slee Sarezynys, the flesch mowe taken, *[we] may take the flesh*
Sethen and roste hem and doo hem baken, *Boil*
Gnawen here flesche to the bones.
Now I have it provyd ones, *tested; once*
For hungyr, ar I be woo, *before; wretched*
I and my folk schole eete moo!"
On the morwe, withouten fayle,
The cyté they gunne for to assayle. *did assail*
The Sarezynes myght nought endour;

They fledde into the heyghe tour,
And cryeden trewes and parlement — *called for a true parley*
To Kyng Richard that was so gent, — *high born (noble)*
And alsoo to the kyng of Fraunce,
And bad mercy without dystaunse. — *delay*
Anon stood up here latymer, — *translator*
And cryede lowde with voys cler:
"Heris," he sayde, "gentyl lordynges," — *Hear*
I yow brynge goode tydynges
That Saladyn yow sent by me.
He wole that Acres yolden bee — *He wishes that Acre be yielded*
And Jerusalem into youre hand,
And of Surry, all the land
To flum Jordan, the water clere, — *the river Jordan*
For ten thousand besauntes be yere; — *bezants (gold coins)*
And yif that ye wole noght soo,
Ye schole have pes for everemoo,
So that ye make kyng of Surry — *Provided that*
Markes Feraunt, of gret maystry; — *power (status, skill)*
For he is strengeste man, iwis,
Of Crystyndom and of Hethenys."
  Thenne answeryd Kyng Richard:
"Thou lyes," he sayde, "fyle coward! — *vile*
In ylke gaderyng and in ylke a pres, — *In this gathering and in every battle (army)*
Markes is fals traytour and les. — *faithless*
He has whytyd Saladynys hand — *whitened [with silver, i.e., bribed]*
To be kyng of Surrye-land,
And, be the King in Trynyté, — *by*
That traytour schal it nevere bee!
He was Crystene be my fadyr day, — *in my father's time (reign)*
And siththen he has renayyd his lay — *after that; forsaken his religion*
And is becomen a Sarezyn:
That God geve hym wol evele fyn![1]
He is wurs than an hound!
He robbyd syxty thousand pound
Out of the Hospytelers hand
That my fadyr sente into this land,
That was callyd Kyng Henry,
Crystene men to governy. — *to protect*
I hote hym goo out of this hoost,[2]
For I swere be the Holy Gost
And be Marye that bar Jhesus:
Fynde I that traytour among us,

[1] *For that, may God may give him a wholly wretched end*

[2] *I command him [the Marquis] to come out of his army*

Other be nyght, other be dawe, — *Either by; or by*
With wylde hors he schal be drawe." — *(see note)*
Thenne answeryd the kyng of Fraunce
To Kyng Richard withoute destaunce: — *without delay*
"A sufre, sere, bele amys, — *Be patient, Sire, good friend*
Thou hast wrong, sere, be Seynt Denys, — *You act unjustly*
That thou thretyst that markis — *threaten; marquis*
That thee nevere yit dede amis.
Yif he have ony thyng don ylle,
He schal amende it at thy wylle.
I am hys borwgh: Loo, here the glove! — *guarantor (see note)*
Tak it, leve sere, for my love!"
"Nay," quod kyng Richard, "be God, my Lord,
Ne schal I nevere with hym acord! — *become reconciled*
Ne hadde nevere be lost Acres toun, — *(see note)*
Ne hadde ben thorwgh hys tresoun. — *had it not been*
Yif he yelde agayn my faderis tresour,
And Jerusalem with gret honour, — *dignity (reverence)*
Thenne my wraththe I hym forgeve,
And nevere ellys whyl that I leve." — *more*
Kyng Phylyp was woo therfore, — *distressed*
But he durste speke no more:
For evere he dredde of dentys hard — *feared hard blows*
To underfonge of Kynge Richard; — *to be subjected to from*
And whenne the latymer herde this,
That kynge myght not be Syr Markys,
"Heres," he sayde, "goode lordynges,
I yow brynge othir tydynges,
That mekyl more is to youre wylle: — *much more; satisfaction*
That oure folk may passe stylle, — *in peace*
With lyf and leme, hand and arme, — *limb*
Without dente and without harme,
And we wole yelde yow this toun,
And the holy croys with gret renoun, — *(see note)*
And syxty thousand presons, thertoo, — *captives*
And an hundrid thousand besauntes and moo, — *bezants*
And have ye schole alsoo herinne
Ryche tresore and mekyl wynne, — *booty*
Helmes and hawberks, syxty thousynde, — *coats of mail*
And other ryhchesse ye may fynde;
Whete inowgh and othir tresore,
To al youre hoost sevene yer and more,
And yif ye wole nought this fonge, — *not accept this*
We may kepe yow out ful longe,
And evere to fynde on of oures — *one*
For to slen ten of youres.
For we have herinnne, withouten fable,

Syxty thousand men defensable; *armed men (capable of fighting)*
And we praye, for the love of God,
That ye wolden taken oure bode. *offer*
Takes the tresore, more and lasse,
And lat us quyt awey passe!" *And allow us to get completely away*
Thenne answeryd Kyng Richard:
"In myn half, I graunte thee forward, *grant to you the agreement (see note)*
So that ye lete us in come, *Provided*
It schal be don, al and some." *entirely*
They leten hem in come anon,
They token hem into hostage ylkon, *every one*
And into presoun put them thore.
Olde and yonge, lesse and mare,
Moste non out of Acres toun *None must leave out of Acre*
Tyl that payde were here raunsoun,
And the Holy Croys therwith,
Ar they moste have pes or grith.[1]
There was founde catel strong *livestock*
That was delyd the knyghtes among. *divided up*
Cuntek was at the in-coming; *Controversy; entering*
The best tresore hadde Richard, oure kyng.
Crystene presouns in Acres toun, *captives*
He gaf hem clothis gret foysoun, *[in] great abundance*
Mete and drynk and armes bryghte, *Nourishment; shining arms*
And made hem fel for to fyghte, *keen*
And took hem into hys partyes *armies*
To venge God of hys enemyes. *(see note)*

Kyng Richard in Acres hadde nome *had captured in Acre*
Of Sarezynys that were thedir icome,
That were hys strengeste enemys, *greatest*
Hardy knyghtes and of most prys, *of most nobility*
Of hethenesse chef lordynges, *Of heathendom's lords of highest rank*
Prynces, dukes sones, and kynges,
Amyrallys and many sawdan: *Emirs*
Here names nought telle I can;
In presoun they lay bounden faste.
To the Sawdon they sente in haste:
"We bere so manye grete cheynes,
And there men do us so grete peynes,
That we may neyther sytte ne lye;
But ye us out of presoun bye, *Unless you liberate (free) us from prison*
And with raunsoun us helpe and borwe, *free (rescue)*
We schole dye or the thrydde morwe." *before the third day*

[1] *Before they might have peace or law and order*

The ryche Sawdon was woo therfore;
Prynces, eerles, weel twoo score,
Amyrall, sawdon, and many lord,
Seyden: "We rede make acord *counsel; an agreement*
With Kyng Richard that is so stoute,
For to delyvere oure chyldren oute,
That they ne be hongyd, ne todrawe. *dismembered*
Of tresore Kyng Richard wole be fawe, *joyful (fain)*
That oure chyldren may come hom hayl. *So that; healthy*
Charges mules and hors, be oure counsayl, *Pack mules*
Of brende gold and of bawdekyn, *pure (refined); rich cloth (brocade)*
For oure heyres to make fyn. *heirs; payment*
Men saye Englyssche love weel gyfte."
Of gold, weel twenty mennys lyfte, *nearly twenty men's loads*
Were layd on mule and rabyte, *Arabian horse*
Ten eerles alle clad in samyte,
Alle olde, hore, and nought yungge, *gray-haired*
That were weel avysy of tungge, *well learned of language*
To Kyng Richard the tresore broughte.
On knees of grace hym besoughte:
"Our Sawdon sendith thee this tresore,
And wole be thy frend ever more,
For the prisouns that thou dest neme. *the captives; seized*
Let hem goo with lyf and leme!
Out of prisoun that thou hem lete, *May you let them out of prison*
That no man hem slee ne bete; *So that; nor beat them*
For alle they are doughty vassales,
Kynges sones and amyrales.
At this tyme the beste doande *the most valiant ones*
That be in alle Sarezyn lande,
And oure hoost most trustes too. *And most trustworthy to our army*
Saladyn loves hem wel alsoo;
Lese non of hem he wolde,
Nought for a thousand pound of golde."
Kyng Richard spak with wurdys mylde,
"The gold to take God me schylde: *God prevents me*
Among yow partes every charge. *divide every cargo*
I brought in schyppes and in barge,
More gold and sylvyr with me
Then has youre lord and swylke three. *three others such as him*
To hys tresore have I no nede;
But, for my love, I yow bede *request*
To mete with me that ye dwelle, *That you remain to dine with me*
And aftyrward I schal yow telle,
Thorwgh counsayl, I schal yow answere
What bode ye schal youre lord bere." *message (offer)*

They grauntyd hym with good wylle, *consented to him*
Kyng Rychard callyd hys marchal stylle, *marshal; privately; (see note)*
And in counsayl took hym alone:
"I schal thee telle what thou schalt don,
Pryvely, goo thou to the presoun; *Secretly*
The Sarezynys of most renoun,
That be comen of the ryhcheste kynne,
Pryvely slee hem therynne;
And ar the hedes off thou smyte, *before*
Looke every mannys name thou wryte, *See to it that you write every man's name*
Upon a scrowe of parchemyn. *scroll of parchment*
And bere the hedes to the kechyn, *kitchen*
And in a cawdroun thou hem caste, *cauldron*
And bydde the cook sethe hem faste. *boil them well*
And loke that he the her off stryppe *removes the hair*
Of hed, of berd, and eke of lyppe.
Whenne we scholde sytte and eete,
Loke that ye nought forgete *See to it*
To serve hem herewith in this manere:
Lay every hed on a platere;
Bryng it hoot forth al in thyn hand, *hot*
Upward hys vys, the teeth grennand *face; grinning*
And loke that they be nought rowe. *raw (uncooked)*
Hys name faste above hys browe, *fix*
What he hyghte and of what kyn born. *was named*
An hoot hed bryng me beforn;
As I were weel apayde withal, *As if I were completely well satisfied*
Faste therof ete I shall,
As it were a tendyr chyke, *chicken*
To se hou the othere wyl lyke."
The styward, so says the jeste, *story*
Anon dede the kynges byheste. *commandment*
At noon, "a laver," the waytes blewe,[1]
The messangerys nought ne knewe *knew not at all*
Rychardis lawe ne hys custome.
Sayde the kyng, "Frendes, ye are welcome!"
To hem he was cumpanyable. *genial*
They were set a syde-table, *at a table apart*
Salt was set on, but no bred, *set out (placed)*
Ne watyr, ne wyn, whyt ne red.
The Sarezynes saten and gunne to stare,
And thoughten, "Allas, hou schal we fare?"
Kyng Richard was set on des *dais (raised platform)*
With dukes and eerles, prowde in pres. *noble among the crowd*

[1] *At noon, "to the washbasin" the guards blew [a trumpet]*

Fro kechene com the fyrste cours,
With pypes and trumpes and tabours.
The styward took ryght good yeme *paid great heed*
To serve Kyng Richard to queme, *properly (at his pleasure)*
Lest aftyr mete hym tydde harm. *harm should befall him*
A Sarezynys hed, also warme,
He broughte oure kyng — was it nought leued! *unlettered*
His name was wreten in hys forheved! *on his forehead*
The messaungerys were servyd soo, *in this way*
Evere an hed betwyxe twoo.
In the forehed wreten hys name:
Therof they had all grame! *From that they received every sorrow (rage)*
What they were whenne they seyen, *When they saw who they were*
The teres ran out of here eyen; *eyes*
And whenne they the lettre redde,
To be slayn ful sore they dredde. *violently (cruelly)*

Kyng Richard hys eyen on hem threwe,
Hou they begunne to chaunge here hewe.
Fore here frendes they syghyd sore, *deeply*
That they hadde lost forevere more.
Of here kynde blood they were. *kindred*
Thenne they myghte weel forbere *abstain*
For to pleye and for to leyghe! *laugh*
Non of hem wolde hys mes neyghe, *dish draw near*
Ne therof eeten on morsel. *one*
The kyng sat and beheeld fol wel.
The knyght that scholde the kyng serve,
With a scharp knyf the hed gan kerve.
Kyng Richard eet with herte good: *with great enjoyment*
The Sarezynes wenden he hadde be wood. *believed; had gone mad*
Every man sat stylle and pokyd othir;
They sayden, "This is the develys brothir
That sles oure men and thus hem eetes!"
Kyng Richard thoo nought forgetes; *forgets nothing*
Abouten hym gan loke ful yerne *very intently*
With wrathful semblaunt and eyen sterne. *countenance*
The messangers thoo he bad: *then; requested*
"For my love bes alle glad, *may you be*
And lokes ye be weel at eese! *And see to it you be well at ease*
Why kerve ye nought off youre mese, *food*
And eetes faste as I doo? *vigorously*
Tel me why ye louren soo?" *look so dejected (frightened)*
They seten stylle and sore quook; *trembled severely*
They durste neyther speke ne look.
In the erthe they wolde have crope, *crawled*
To be slayn fol weel they hope; *fully expected*

There was non answeryd a word.
Quod Kyng Richard: “Beres fro the bord
The mete that ye before hem sette,
And other mete before hem fette.” *bring*
Men broughten bred, withouten bost, *without arrogance (meekly)*
Venysoun, cranes, and good rost,
Pyment, clarré, and drynkes lythe. *Spiced wine, clary; pleasant*
Kyng Richard bad hem alle be blythe.
Was non of hem that eete lyste,[1]
Kyng Richard here thoughte wel wyste, *knew*
And sayde: “Frendes, beth nought squoymous, *squeamish*
This is the maner of myn hous,
To be servyd ferst, God it woot, *God knows it*
With a Sarezynys hede al hoot;
But youre maner, I ne knewe!
As I am kyng, Crysten and trewe,
Ye schole be therof sertayn,
In saf condyt to wende agayn; *In safe-conduct to return again*
For I ne wolde, for no thyng,
That wurd of me in the world scholde spryng,
That I were so vylayne of maners *ill-bred of manners (ill-mannered)*
For to mysdoo messangeres.” *harm*
Whenne they hadde eeten, the cloth was folde, *tablecloth*
Kyng Richard gan hem to beholde:
On knees they askyd leve to gon,
But of hem alle was ther nought on *not even one*
That in message was thedyr come, *But that on a mission came there*
That hym hadde levere have ben at home,[2]
With wyf, frendes, and here kynde, *kindred (kinfolk)*
Thenne al the good that was in Ynde! *wealth*
Kyng Rychard spak to an old man:
“Wendes hom and tell thy Sowdan, *Travel*
Hys malycoly that he abate, *So that he lessen his sorrow*
And says that ye come to late. *came*
To slowghly was youre terme igesseyd,[3]
Or ye come the flesch was dressyd *Before; prepared*
That men scholden serve with me
Thus at noon and my meyné. *household (retinue)*
Say hym it schal hym nought avayle
Though he forbarre oure vytayle, *block our food supplies*
Brede, wyne, flesshe, fysshe and kunger, *conger eel*
Of us non schal dye for hungyr,

[1] *There were none of them who cared to eat*

[2] *Who would not have preferred to have been at home*

[3] *The time [goal estimated] allowed was too long*

Whyle that we may wenden to fyght, — *go*
And slee the Sarezynes dounryght, — *outright*
Wassche the flesche and roste the hede.
With oo Sarwzyn I may wel fede, — *one; fully feed*
Wel a nyne or a ten, — *No less than*
Of my goode, Crystene men."
Kyng Richard sayd: "I you waraunt,
Ther is no flesch so norysshaunt, — *nourishing*
Unto an Ynglyssche Crysten man,
Partryk, plover, heroun, ne swan, — *Partridge*
Cow, ne oxe, scheep, ne swyn,
  As is the flessh of a Saryzyne!
There he is fat and therto tendre,
And my men are lene and sclendre.
Whyl any Sarezyn quyk bee — *As long as; be alive*
Lyvande now in this cuntree, — *Living*
For mete wole we nothyng care:
Aboute faste we schole fare, — *stoutly (vigorously); proceed*
And every day we schole eete
Al so manye as we may gete. — *Just as*
To Yngelond wole we nought gon, — *go*
Tyl they be eeten, everylkon." — *every single one*
  The messangerys agayn hom tournyd,
Before the lord they comen and mournyd. — *mourned*
The eldeste tolde the Sawdan
Kyng Richard was a noble man, — *mighty*
And sayde, "Lord, I thee werne, — *assure you*
In this world is non so sterne! — *fierce*
On knees we tolde hym oure tale,
But us ne gaynyd no gale. — *But talking did not benefit us*
Of thy gold wolde he non;
He swor he hadde betere won
Of ryche tresore thenne hast thou.
To us he sayde, 'I geve it yow,
Tresore of sylvyr, gold, and palle, — *fine cloth*
Deles it among yow alle.' — *Divide*
To mete he bad us abyde, — *dinner; stay*
We were set at bord hym besyde, — *table*
That stood Rychardes table negh;
But non of us before hym segh, — *before himself saw*
No bred brought forth, whyt ne sour, — *leavened*
But salt, and non othir lycour. — *drink*
What mes fyrst before hym come, — *dish (course of food)*
Weel I beheld, good keep I nome, — *paid close attention*
A knyght broughte fro the kechyn
An hed soden of a Sarezyn! — *boiled head*
Withouten her, on a plater brode, — *hair*

Hys name beforn hys hed-schode, — *crown of head*
Was iwreten aboven hys yghe. — *eye*
Me standes non awe for to lye, — *I have no fear so as to lie*
Whos hed it was, my feres aske, — *companions ask*
It was the Sawdones sone of Damaske! — *sultan of Damascus's son*
At borde as we sate in fere, — *together*
We were servyd in this manere:
Evere an hed betwen tweye. — *two*
For sorwe we wende for to deye! — *expected to die (see t-note)*
Ther come before my felaw and me
The kynges sone of Nynyve.
Hys of Perce hym that sat me by; — *His [the king's son] of Persia*
The thrydde, hys of Samary; — *Samaria*
The ferthe, hys of Egypte:
Thoo ylkon of us hys eyen wypte![1]
The fyfthe, hys of Auffryke, — *Africa*
For sorwe thoo we gan to syke, — *then; to sigh*
Us thoughte oure herte barst ryght insundyr! — *burst apart immediately*
Lord, yit thou myght here a wundyr.
Before the kyng a knyght in haste,
Karf off the hed, and he eet faste. — *Carved from; ate vigorously*
With teeth he gnew the flesch ful harde, — *gnawed*
As a wood lyoun he farde, — *mad; carried on*
With hys eyen stepe and grym, — *glaring and fierce*
He spak and we behelde hym.
For drede we wende for to sterve. — *expected to die*
He bad us that we scholde kerve
Oure mes and eeten as he dede.
To Mahoun we boden oure bede, — *Muhammad; offered our prayer*
Fro deth that he be oure waraunt! — *protector*
He segh oos make soure semblaunt, — *saw us make an agonized (fearful) expression*
For drede hou we begunne to quake!
Oure mes he bad hys men uptake, — *take up our course*
And othir mete thoo us fette, — *food then to go and get*
Hoot whyte bred before us sette,
Gees, swannes, cranes, venysoun,
And other wylde foul gret foysoun, — *abundance*
Whyte wyn and red, pyment and clarré,
And sayde: 'Ye be welcome to me.
Bes blythe, yif it be youre wylle;
Dos gladly and lykes nought ylle, — *do not be displeased*
For I knew nought nothyng youre gyse. — *custom*
In my court, this is the servyse: — *provision of food (sequence of dishes)*
Be servyd ferst, I and myn hynys, — *household*
With hedes hote of Sarezynys.'

[1] *Thereupon each one of us wiped (dried) his eyes*

Of hym and hys we stoden swylk eye, *stood in such terror*
For drede and dool we wende to deye. *From fear and grief we expected to die*
Non of us eet morsel of bred,
Ne drank of wyn, whyt ne red,
Ne eete of flesche, baken ne brede, *baked or roasted*
So sory were we thenne for drede. *distressed*
Aftyr mete we gunne take leve,
He spak to us wordes breve: *few words*
'Ye schole gon in saf coundyte. *safe conduct*
No man schal do yow dysspyte.' *injury*
He sente thee certayn answere:
Or that we myghte come there, *Before*
Men of ryhcheste kyn were slawe, *slain*
He geves ryght nought though thou withdrawe[1]
And hyde stor al fro hys hoost. *provisions*
He says, and hys men make boost:
He schal nought lete on lyve *spare one life*
In al thy land, chyld, ne wyve, *woman*
But slee alle that he may fynde,
And sethe the flesch and with teeth grynde: *boil*
Hungyr schal hem nevere eyle! *never afflict them*
Into Yngelond wole he nought seyle
Tyl he have maad al playn werk!" *smooth as finished stone (level, flat)*
 His clothis of gold unto his scherk *undergarment (see note)*
Saladyn began torase for yre. *to tear from anger*
Kynges, prynces, and many a syre *lord*
Seyden allas that they hadden lorn
Here gentyl heyres of here bodies born, *Their noble heirs*
That were so wyghte men and stronge. *valiant*
"Weylaway!" they sayden, "We leve to longe. *live*
Herde we nevere swylke mervayle!
It is a devyl, withouten fayle. *(see t-note)*
Allas, this werre was begunne!
Now Richard has Acres wunne.
He has ment, yif he may go forth *planned; advance*
To wynne est, west, south, and north,
And ete oure chyldren and us!
Lord Saladyn, we rede thus: *advise*
Sende to hym, and beseke hym eft, *Dispatch [a mission] and beg him once more*
For hem that ben on lyve left. *remain alive*
Lete hem goo, yif so he wolde,
Geve hym, siththe he wole no golde, *since he desires no gold*
Goode males, for the nones, *bags, for the occasion*
Ful of ryche, precyouse stones,
Chargyd in harneys and in coffre. *Loaded in saddle packs and treasure chests*

---

[1] *He cares not at all though you carry off*

Soo that he wole, thou hym profere, *you proffer to him*
To lete Jhesu and Mary, *To forsake*
To geve hym land a gret party *a great deal*
That he be in pes, and lete the werre. *So that; give up (abandon); war*
For he is comen from so ferre,
Wylt thou noghte that he his travayle lese.
Graunte hym come hym self and chese *choose*
The landes that hym thynkith best,
And make hym Sawdon heyest
Aftyr thyself, and ryhcheste kyng; *most powerful*
Conferme it hym and hys ospryng. *Ratify it [by charter] to him and his offspring*
Yif he be payed so to doo,
Swythe in pes he come thee to. *Quickly in peace that he arrives and departs*
Thowgh he have thy folk ischent, *killed*
Thou schalt forgeve thy maltalent. *ill will*
As thy brothir love hym and kysse,
And he schal thee teche and wysse *teach; guide*
In werre to ben bold and wys,
Of al the world to wynne the prys. *preeminence (distinction)*
And so shall ye leve and be frendes
With joye to your lyves endes."

Saladyn by hys serjauntes *sergeants (officers)*
Sende Kyng Richard these presauntes, *Sent*
And besoughte hym of hys men *begged him for*
That he hadde in hostage then,
And yif he wolde Jhesu forsake,
And Mahowne to lord take, *Muhammad*
Of Surrye he wolde make hym kyng,
And of Egipte, that ryche thyng,
Of Darras, and of Babyloyne, *Dara(?) (a fortress on the Persian front)*
Of Arabye and of Cessoyne, *Cesson (Kesoun) (a bishropic east of Edessa)*
Of Affryk, and of Bogye, *the Buqaia(?)*
And of the lond of Alysaundrye,
Of grete Grece, and of Tyre,
And of many a ryche empyre,
And make hym he wolde Sawdoun anon
Of al Ynde unto Preter Jhon."[1]
Kyng Richard answeryd the messangeres:
"Fy upon yow losyngeres, *Fie upon you rascals*
On yow and Saladyn, youre lorde!
The devyl hange yow be a corde!
Gos and says to Saladyn
That he make to morwe fyn *make payment*
For alle hys dogges in hostage,

[1] *Of all of India as far as [the lands of] Prester John (central Asia)*

Or they schole dye in evyl rage!	
And yif I mowe leve a fewe yere,	*might live*
Of alle the landes ye have nempnid here,	*mentioned*
I schal hym lete nought half foote	*leave (allow) him*
So God do my soule boote!	*help my soul; (see t-note)*
I wolde nought lese my lordes love	
For al the londes under heven above.	
And but I have the croys to morwe,	*Unless*
They schole dye with mekyl sorwe."	
They answered at the frome,	*at once*
They nyste where the croys was become.	*knew not; (see note)*
Quod Kyng Rychard: "Siththen it is soo,	
I wot weel what I have to doo.	*know*
Youre Sawdon is nought so slye,	*crafty*
So queyntyly to blere myn yghe."	*In this way cunningly to hoodwink me*
He callyd his knyghtes sone anon,	
And bad hem into Acres gon,	*commanded them to go*
"And taken Sarezynes syxty thousandes	*(see note)*
And knytte behynde hem here handes,	*secure their hands behind them*
And ledes hem out of the cyté,	
And hedes hem withouten pyté	*behead*
And so schal I telle Saladyn	*answer*
To pray me leve on Appolyn!"	*believe in Apollo*
They were brought out of the toun,	
Save twenty he heeld to raunsoun.	
They were led into the place ful evene;	*all the way*
There they herden an aungell of hevene,	*(see note)*
That seyde, "Seygnyours, tues, tues,	*Lords, kill, kill*
Spares hem nought — behedith these!"	
Kyng Richard herde the aungelys voys,	
And thankyd God and the Holy Croys.	
There were they behedyd hastelyke,	
And casten into a foul dyke;	
Thus Kyng Richard wan Acrys.	
God geve hys soule moche blys!	
Hys doughty dedes, who so wyl lere,	*learn*
Herkenes now, and ye mowe here.	
Merye is in the tyme of May	*(see note)*
Whenne foules synge in here lay.	*song*
Floures on appyl trees and perye,	*pear*
Smale foules synge merye,	
Ladyes strowen here boures	*bestrew; chambers*
With rede roses and lylye floures.	
Gret joye is in frith and lake,	*woodland meadow*
Beste and bryd plays with his make.	*mate*
The damyseles lede daunse;	

Knyghtes playe with scheld and launse
In joustes and turnementes they ryde,
Many a caas hem betyde, *predicament*
Many chaunces and strokes hard!
So befel to Kyng Richard,
Kyng Richard Phelyp to feste bad; *invited*
Aftyr mete, thoo they were glad,
Rychard gaf gyftes gret wones, *in great abundance*
Gold and sylvyr and precyouse stones;
To herawdes and to dysours, *heralds; minstrels*
To tabourrers and to trumpours *drummers*
Hors and robes to bere his los; *his praise*
Thorwgh here cry his renoun ros,
Hou he was curteys and free. *generous*
Ful noble was that ensemblé! *gathering*
Kyng Richard gaf castelles and tounnes
To hys eerlys and to barounnes,
To have therinne here sustenaunce. *support*
Kyng Richard bad the kyng of Fraunce:
"Geve of thy gold and of thy purchase *gain*
To erl, baroun, knyght and serjaunt of mace!
Frely aquyte thou hem here travaylle; *Generously reward them their service*
They swonke for thee in bataylle. *toiled*
Yif thou have eft with hym to done, *If you have dealings with him again*
They wole be the gladdere eftsone *the next time*
To helpe thee at thy nede."
Kyng Phelyp took therof non hede,
But layde thertoo a def eere *deaf*
And gaf hym ryght non answere: *absolutely no*
Kyng Richardes wordes he took in vayn.
Richard began unto hym sayn:
"Among us be pes and acord;
Graced be Jhesu Cryst, oure Lord,
That gaf us myght this toun to wynne!
To ryde forth lat us begynne
Saladyn the Sawdon to anoye
And fonde hym for to destroye. *seek*
Yif he scounfyte us in bekyr, *defeat; in battle*
Yif nede be, we mowe be sekyr, *must be secure*
Yif God us have lyf ischape, *If God ordains us to have life*
And we may hedyr ascape, *to this place [Acre] escape*
And come quyk withinne the walle,
For Saladyn and hys folk alle, *From*
And the gates be weel ischet, *fastened*
We be sekyr of strong recet." *sure of strong shelter*
Kyng Richard gan Phelyp to telle:
"I rede we here no lengere dwelle.

Ryde we forth the cuntré to seche,
And Phelyp, doo as I thee teche.
Myn hoost I schal parte on three, — *army; divide in three*
And Kyng Phelyp, tak thy meyné, — *troops*
Departe hem in hostes tweye, — *Divide; two armies*
And looke thou doo as I thee seye.
Toun, cytee, and castel, yif thou wynne,
Slee alle the folk that be therinne.
In Goddes name, I thee forbede,
For gold, sylvyr, ne for no mede, — *not under any inducement*
That they may profere and geven, — *offer*
Ryche ne pore, lat non leven, — *let none live*
Hosebonde ne wyf, mayde ne grome, — *young man*
But yif he wole take Crystyndome!" — *receive Christianity*
Phelyp the wurdes undyrstood.
Anon he gan to chaunge mood
That kyng Richard at hys devys, — *Because King Richard in his judgment*
Sette hym and hese at so lytyl prys.[1]
Phelyp to hym was cumpanyable; — *genial*
He gan to glose and make fable, — *He used fair words and told untruths*
And thankyd hym with glad semblaunt, — *bearing*
And sayde, "Brothir, I thee graunt,
To doo as thou sayst, sekyrly,
For thou art wysere man than I,
And of werre canst wel more." — *know considerably more*
Netheles, he was agrevyd sore.
For drede, he and hys men so dede
As Kyng Richard hadde hem bede, — *asked them*
In aventure that he hente knokkes. — *In fear that he would receive blows*
Hys men he delyd in twoo flokkes; — *squadrons*
Richard, with hys hoost, wente hys way,
And fro hym to wynne pray. — *booty*
With love they departyd asundyr,
But now ye may here a wundyr.
Frenssche men arn arwe and feynte, — *are timid and weak*
And Sarezynys be war and queynte, — *shrewd and crafty*
And of here dedes engynous; — *military actions ingenious*
The Frenssche men ben covaytous. — *greedy*
Whenne they sytten at the taverne,
There they ben stoute and sterne, — *brave and daring*
Bostfyl wurdes for to crake, — *speak*
And of here dedes, yelpyng to make. — *boasting*
Lytyl wurth they are and misprowde; — *haughty (arrogant)*
Fyghte they cunne with wurdes lowde, — *are able*
And telle no man is here pere; — *proclaim; equal*

[1] *Appraised him and his [people] at such little value*

But whene they comen to the mystere, — *time of peril (show-down)*
And see men begynne strokes dele, — *deliver*
Anon they gynne to turne here hele,
And gynne to drawe in here hornes[1]
As a snayl among the thornes.
Slake a bore of here boost! — *Scare off a boar by their boast*
  Kyng Phelyp anon with hys hoost,
A strong cyté he besette — *besieged*
That was callyd Taburette. — *Mount Tabor*
With hys hoost he layde it aboute; — *surrounded it*
The Sarezynes myghte neyther in ne oute,
Lest they scholden be tohewe. — *cut to pieces*
On the walles armyd they hem schewe, — *are seen*
Out of toureles and of kyrnelles, — *turrets; embrasures*
Sette up baners and penselles, — *standards*
And manly gan hem to defende. — *themselves*
There to dye the Frenssche wende. — *expected*
Trumpes lowde for bost they blowe,
But durste they neyther schete ne throwe — *shoot*
With bowe, slynge ne arweblast
To make the Sarezynes with agast; — *terrified*
Ne the cyté for to assayle.
But of the toun the chef amyrayle, — *chief emir*
Hys name was callyd Terryabaute:
"Lord, ar thou geve us assaute, — *before*
Alle the folk of this toun
Profere hem to knele a doun, — *Offer; kneel themselves*
And rewefully with oo cry, — *one*
To seke thee myldely of mercy;
And the toun they wolen unto thee yelde,
And alle the goodes that they welde. — *possess*
Man, wumman, every Sarezyn,
Grauntith thee with herte fyn — *true*
Every man to paye a besaunt. — *bezant*
Sere, on swylk a comenaunt, — *covenant*
That thou graunte that they crave: — *request*
Here lyves and lemes for to have, — *limbs*
Bestes, catel, and tresore,
And that they wole for everemore
Of thyn heyres holden this toun." — *For your heirs*
Phelyp of hem took raunsoun:
For mede he sparede hys foon. — *For reward; foes*
Thus with hem he was at on, — *in agreement*
And bad hys folk, up lyf and leme, — *upon life and limb*
No good fro hem to beneme, — *goods; take away*

[1] *And begin to pull in their horns (reduce their ardor)*

Meete ne drynk, catel ne cloth.
Alle they sworen hym hool oth *solemn*
To ben hys men that were there;
And hys baner they uprere *raise up*
On a schaft in the heyeste tour
With flour delys of gold and asour. *fleur-de-lis; azure*
  Thoo they hadde this iwunne, *Though*
To breke sege thenne they begunne. *To end the siege*
They chargyd in waynes and in cartes, *They loaded in wagons*
Swerdes and speres, scheeldes and dartes.
Kyng, eerles, barouns, knyghtes and squyers,
Ryden ryally on trappyd destrers, *Rode regally on well-equipped steeds*
The foote men yeden on here feete; *went*
Ryght soo they helden the heyghe strete, *Just so they followed the main road*
That they turne nought, ne outraye. *nor became disorderly*
They trumpyd, and here baners dysplaye
Of sylk, sendel, and many a fane: *standard (flag)*
Ful ryghte way wenten to Archane. *Arqah (Arka, Archas?)*
Phelyp of hem took raunsoun,
Ryght as he dede at the othir toun,
And leet hem leve forth in pes, *depart out*
But for the lesse, the more he les. *Except for the poor, the rich he set free*

  Kyng Richard with hys hoost gan ryde,
And wente be anothir syde, *way*
With many an eerl and baroun
Iborn of Ynglyssche nacyoun:
All hardy men and stronge of bones,
And weel armyd for the nones.
They seten on stedes, goode and stronge,
Many Gascoyn was hem among,
And so ther were of Lumbardy,
Wol goode knyghtes, and hardy, *Nobly (doughty)*
And folk off the coost of Alemayn, *Germany*
And hys eme, Henry of Chaumpayn, *nephew*
And hys maystyr, Robert of Leycetere,
Among hem alle was non hys betere.
Fouk Doyly and Thomas Multone
That evere yit was here wone *custom*
In fyght fyrst for to bede, *request*
To helpe here kyng weel to spede. *prosper well*
Off the coost of Braundys with hym nam, *From; took*
A noble baroun that hyghte Bertram, *was named*
And hys clergy, and hys freres, *monks (comrades)*
And Templeres, and hys Hospytaleres.
The numbre was by ryght assent *mutual agreement*
Of hors-men an hondryd thousend,

And of foote men, swylke ten, *ten times as many*
Garscoynes, Lumbardes, and Englyssche men.
Al becoveryd were feeldes and pleynes
With knyghtes, footmen and with sweynes. *soldiers below the rank of knight*
Kyng Richard hovyd and beheeld, *waited*
And devysyd hys hoost in the feeld, *arrayed (made ready)*
And to hys hoost he sayde thus:
"Folk inowe we have with us. *enough*
I rede we departe hem in three, *advise; divide them*
That on part schal wende with me; *one*
That othir, certayn for alle cas, *certainly, in all events*
Schal lede of Multoun, Sere Thomas,
And Fouke Doyly schal lede the thrydde.
On lyf and leme, now I yow bydde, *On [penalty of]; command*
Toun, cyté, castel, yif that ye wynne,
Spares non that is therinne.
Sleys hem alle and takes here good;
But yif they graunte with mylde mood *Unless; consent*
To be baptyzed in fount-ston: *baptismal font*
Elles on lyve loke ye lete non!" *Otherwise, see to it that you let none live*

Kyng Rychard with hys cumpany
Wenten to Sudan Turry; *Sidon and/or Tyre?*
Thomas, a knyght engynous, *skillful*
Wente with hys hoost to Orglyous;
And Sere Fouke, the Doyly,
Wente to the cyté of Ebedy.
Every man belayde hys toun aboute. *encircled*
No Sarazyn durste come withoute,
For the sege was so strong and hard.
But speke we now of Kyng Richard
That Sudan Turry has belayd. *besieged*
The Sarezynes at the fyrste brayd, *assault*
Here brygges wounden up in haste,
And here gates barryd faste;
Hem to defende they gunne asaye. *To defend themselves they strove*
Kyng Richard hys baner leet dysplaye.
Whenne Sarezynys saygh it arerde,
Of hym they were sore aferde; *raised*
For drede they begunne to quake.
Here wardayn has hys counsayl take; *warden (governor)*
He was callyd Grandary. *Great Honor*
In the cyté, he leet make a cry:
Ilke a man that myghte armes bere, *Any man*
Goo to the wal the toun to were. *defend*
The Sarezynes armyd forth lepe
Upon the walles the toun to kepe, *guard*

Stout in touret and in hurdys. *hurdles (palisades)*
Richard bente an arweblast of vys, *drew back an arbalest*
And schotte it to a tour ful evene, *fully all the way*
And it smot thorwgh Sarezynes sevene. *pierced through*
Ded fyl the dogges vyle, *fell*
But lystenes of a queynte gyle! *heed; strategem*
Kyng Richard leet hys folk apparayle, *make preparations*
On that on half the toun to assayle. *other side of*
The toun folk drowgh to that on syde, *one*
Kyng Richard sente of hys men that tyde,
On heyghe laddres for to gon in
That weren iwrought of queynte gyn. *of clever invention*
With yrene hokes, goode and stronge,
On the walles they gunne hem honge.
Sevene men myghten gon in on brede; *across*
Thus men ovyr the walles yede, *went*
Three thousande or the Sarezynes wende, *before; knew*
So they gan the toun defende.
The Crystene comen in or they weten; *before; knew*
They schotten to hem and harde smeten, *hastened; struck*
Gret peple of hem doun felle, *Many*
But thoo the cunstable herde telle *But when; constable*
That the Crystene were in comen,
Ten thousand he has i-nomen; *taken*
The othere, he leet kepe the toun. *guard*
"For these," he sayde, "gos no raunsoun.
Thar hem no mercy crave! *Of these let them not beg mercy*
Kyng Richard schal hem nevere save;
Anon-ryght they schole deye!" *Immediately*
  Whenne Kyng Richard herde hem so seye,
For scorn he gan to lawghe schrylle, *In scorn*
And bad hys men be of good wylle,
"And prove we this toun to wynne, *strive*
Rescue this folk that be withinne."
The Sarezynes kydden here myght *exercised their power*
The Crystene to sle doun-ryght *outright*
That were comen ovyr the walle.
Oure folk togedere heeld hem alle; *pressed them hard in battle*
Arwes and quarelles to hem drowen: *Arrows and bolts shot at them*
Alle that thay hytten anon thay slowen.
With egre mayn gaf hem bekyr. *With fierce strength attacked them*
Of good help for they were sekyr *certain*
Of Kyng Richard that was withouten. *From*
Oure Crystene men ran abouten,
And some to the gates they sterte, *hastened*
Alle that they founden thorwgh they gerte. *stabbed*
And threwen hem out of the tour,

And cryeden: "Sere kyng, do us socour! — *help us*
Savely thou schalt in come, — *In safety*
In lytyl whyle, it schal be nome!" — *taken*
Thus they gunne Kyng Richard grete,
And the brygges doun thay lete, — *lowered*
And setten the gates up on brode. — *wide open*
Kyng Richard was the fyrste that in rode.
And next hym, Roberd Touneham, — *immediately after*
Robert of Leycetre and Sere Bertram.
These reden in the vawmewarde; — *rode; vanguard*
To slee the houndes, non ne sparde. — *nor spared any*
Kyng Richard, hys ax in hond he hente, — *took*
And payde Sarezynys here rente! — *rent (tribute)*
Swylke levery he hem delte, — *Such blows*
Al that he hytte, anon they swelte. — *Whoever; immediately they perished*
They slowe every Sarezyn,
And took the temple of Appolyn.
They felden it doun and brende Mahoun; — *burned*
And al the tresore of the toun
He gaf to knyght, squyer and knave,
Al so mekyl as they wolde have. — *as much*
Sarezynes none on lyve he lafte;
But in a tour on an hygh schafte,
Kyng Richard sette up hys baner,
And wan the toun on this maner.

Now beth in pes, lystenes apas! — *listen closely*
I schal yow telle of Sere Thomas,
The noble baroun of Multone,
That lay with many a modyr sone[1]
At Orglyous, a strong castel.
Lystenes now what chaunce befel!
The Sarezynes for felonye,
Soone senten out a spyye
That hadde ben Crystene in hys youthe.
Many an evyl wrenche he couthe! — *trick; knew*
He come to Thomas and thus sayde,
And thoughte to have hym betrayde:
"Sere, I am a Crystene man.
I brak presoun and out I wan. — *escaped*
Truste ryght wel to my speche.
Yif thou wylt doo as I thee teche,
Thou schalt wynne hem in a whyle.
In al the toun ther is no gyle; — *treachery*

[1] *Who was encamped with many a mother's son (man)*

The sothe to thee, I am beknowe." *known*
Quod Thomas: "Byndes hym in a throwe! *quickly*
Al is les that the thef saith; *lies; thief*
He is at the Sarezynes faith. *under*
He was sent us to beswyke. *deceive*
Hys comyng schal hym evele lyke; *His arrival shall distress him*
Therfore, he schal anon dyen.
So schal men teche hym to lyen!
And hys eeren in twoo slyttes, *ears; split open*
And to hys feet a strong roop knyttes,
And hanges hym up tyl he dye."
Quod the renay: "Mercy I crye! *apostate*
To no vyle deeth ye me dooth!
Al that I can, I schal seye soth. *know (am able)*
Yif ye me fynde in falshede,
Other in wurd, other in dede, *Either in word*
That ye mowe evere see or wryten, *confirm*
Anon myn hed ye ofsmyten! *cut off*
I was sent to betraye yow;
I schal yow telle: herkenes how!
Before the gate is a brygge —
Lestnes weel what I schall sygge — *say*
Undyr the brygge ther is a swyke *trap*
Coverde clos, joynande queyntelyke,[1]
And undyrnethe is an hasp *fastening*
Schet with a stapyl and a clasp; *Closed*
And in that hasp a pyn is pylt. *pin; placed*
Thou myght bewar, yif thou wylt —
Me were wol loth that thou mystydde — *fare badly*
Though thou and thy folk were in the mydde, *If*
And the pyn smeten out were, *knocked out*
Doun ye scholden fallen there
In a pyt syxty fadme deep; *fathoms*
Therfore, bewar and tak good keep.
At the passyng ovyr the trappe,
Many on has had ful evyl happe. *Many a person*
Be peays it closes togedere aghen; *By [counter]weight*
Where it is no man may seen." *(see t-note)*
"Now, Sarezyn, anon me rede, *at once advise me*
Hou we schole doo at this nede?" *peril*
"Thou has horsmen and putaylle; *footsoldiers*
Er thanne thou the toun assaylle, *Before the time*
Ye have with yow goode engynes,
Swylke knowen but fewe Sarezynes. *Such [machinery]*

[1] *Covered so as to conceal [it] (tightly), joined together ingeniously*

A mangenel thou doo arere, *machine for hurling stones*
And soo thou schalt hem weel afere. *terrify*
Into the toun thou slynge a ston grete,
And also, swythe thou me lete *swiftly*
Passe into the toun aghen;
And also soone thou schalt seen
The toun they schole yelde soone;
But I bydde thee a bone: *request; favor*
Yif I doo thee wynne this toun,
That thou geve me my warysoun." *reward*
Quod Thomas: "Thertoo I graunte."
They departyd with that comenaunte. *agreement*
The engyne was bent and set al preste; *made all ready*
A gret ston into the toun was keste.
They slowe men and houses doun bare *bore (thrust) down*
Or ony man of hem was ware. *Before*
"We be ded! Help, Mahoun!" they cryede;
In every syde, away they hyede *hurried*
To hyden hem for woo and drede.
The renay into the toun yede *apostate (traitor); went*
And sayde to the wardayn, Orgayl:
"We be dede, withouten fayl!
He that the ston to yow threwe,
Al youre tresoun fol wel he knew:
How youre brygges gos insundyr, *bridges*
And al the tresoun that is therundyr,
And hou it gos aghen be peys. *works by a counterweight*
Bes war, barounnes and burgeys!
It helpes yow nought youre gates to schette
Hym and hys men out for to lette. *shut out*
Yif ye fyghte and yow defende,
Moo stones he wole yow sende,
Schende yow and the toun doun bete. *To defeat*
Stondynge hous wil he non lete; *allow*
It is betere let hym in stylle *peaceably (meekly)*
Than hereinne that he yow spylle; *lay waste (kill)*
Thenne we may be trust to leve." *expect to survive*
But whenne he hadde this counseil geve, *Hardly had he this counsel given*
As he hem redde, they deden anon. *advised; at once*
"Mercy, Thomas!" they cryeden echon.
"Have here the keyes of this cyté;
Doo therwith what thy wylle bee,
Yif soo thou graunte us oure lyves, *If as a result*
And oure chyldren, and our wyves."
Thomas of Multoun the keyes fong, *seized*
And another ston inslong *cast*
To Sere Mahouns habitacle, *dwelling (settlement)*

And smot out a gret pynacle. *knocked down; turret*
Out com the warden, Orgayl,
And an hundryd knyghts in his parayle: *clothing (attire)*
Barfoot, ungyrt, withouten hood. *not wearing armor*
"Mercy, Thomas! Spylle nought oure blood!
Tak thee alle the goodes that we have.
With that thou wylt oure lyves save, *spare*
Lat us passe awey al nakyd."
"Brekes the brygge," quod Thomas, "that ye han makyd,
And lyme and ston throwes in the pyt, *mortar*
Or, be Jhesu that in hevene syt,
Alle therinne, ye schole brenne, *burn*
That non schal goo, ne out renne,
Of yow alle, pore ne ryche,
But yif ye fylle weel the dyche *Unless*
To the banke, al in a resse, *at once*
That we anon may faste in presse." *enter*
The amyral therof was blythe,
And brak the brygges al soo swythe,
And lym and ston keste in the pytte.
Anon it was feld and fordytte *filled up; covered*
Up to the banke, maad al playn *flat*
In lengthe and brede, ful trust, certayn *completely sound, indeed*
That twenty men, othir besyde,
On armyd stedes myghten inryde,
Withoute drede have entree;
Thus, they come to that cytee.
The toun folk comen, alle and some, *one and all*
And fayre hym they gunne welcome, *graciously*
Cryede mercy with lowde stevene. *voice*
Agayn on Crystene man they were sevene *one*
In that cyté of Sarezynes.
Gold and sylvyr and bawdekynes *precious silks (brocades)*
To Sere Thomas anon they profere,
And with good wyl to hym ofere
Landes, houses, and tresore,
Of hym to holde for evere more.

Before Thomas com the renay, *apostate*
"Mercy, Lord, thynk, I thee pray,
For this toun what thou me hyghte *promised*
As thou were a gentyl knyghte.
No more wole I that thou me geve,
But mete and drynk whyl that I leve.

For wollewarde on my bare feet,[1]
I schal walken in snowgh and sleet,
Me to amende of my synne,
The joye of hevene for to wynne!"
To a preest, he schroof hym clene. *absolved him fully*
The comenaunt that was hem betwene, *covenant*
Thomas grauntyd with good wylle;
Thus with hym he lefte stylle, *treated peaceably (left alone)*
In werre and pes whan he gan wende,
Evere unto hys lyves ende.

Lordyngs, heres to my pleynte! *listen; charge (grievance)*
Ye schal here of a tresoun queynte,
Hou the Sarezynes have bespoken *spoken out*
Of Crystene men to ben awroken; *Upon; avenged*
Hou the amyral hem redde: *advised*
"Whenne the Crystene be to bedde,
And they ben in here fyrste sleepe,
We schole come armyd, on an hepe. *together (as a group)*
On schal dwelle the clos withinne, *One shall remain within the stronghold*
The gate to unschette and unpynne,
And stylly to unschette the lok. *secretly*
We schole come prevyly in a flok, *troop*
And slee Thomas of Multone,
And with hym, every modyr sone
That he has with hym brought."
Therof Sere Thomas wyste right nought.
They soden flesch, rost and brede, *boiled; roasted and fried*
And to the soper faste they yede.
Plenté ther was of bred and wyn,
Pyment, clarry, good and fyn:
Of cranes, swannes, and venysoun,
Partryhches, plovers, and heroun,
Of larkes, and smale volatyle. *bird*
The Sarezynes, al for a gyle, *crafty trick*
Of strengeste wyn gaf hem to drynke.
They were wery, and lest weel wynke; *very much wanted sleep*
They slepte faste, and gunne to route. *snore*
The Sarezynes, they were alle withoute,
And comen armyd to the gate.
The renay stood redy therate.
They knokkede on the wyket; *small door (window)*
He leet it stande stylle ischet,

[1] Lines 4221–23: *By wearing woolen clothing next to my skin, / And by walking on my bare feet in snow and sleet / To atone for my sins*

And tolde Thomas that he herde, *what*
Al togeder hou it ferde. *how things went*
Sere Thomas no bost gan make;
Anon hys folk he gan to awake.
"For Goddys love," he hem bed,
Dyghte yow tyt or ye ben ded!" *Prepare yourselves quickly*
They styrten up and were afrayde
For that he hadde to hem sayde. *On account of what*
They armyd hem swythe yerne, *very quickly*
And wenten out by a posterne *side door*
Er thenne the Sarezynys wyste;
That whyle they hovyd and gunne to presten, *waited and gathered together*
With strengthe wolde in have wunnen,
The Crystene to the gatys runnen,
And schetten faste with the kaye.
By that began to sprynge the daye.
Bowe and arweblast the Cristene bente, *crossbow*
Thorwghout every stret they wente,
And schotten arwes and quarel;
Many Sarezyn ded doun fel. *dead*
They ne lefte, be way ne hous, *by street or*
No man levande in Orglyous, *living*
Burgeys, ne wyf, ne children ying. *young*
  Whenne they had maad this rekenyng, *settled this account*
He gaf hys men, withouten othis, *assuredly*
All the tresore and the clothis,
Sylvyr and gold, every grot, *every bit*
Every man hadden hys lot.
Ther was non soo lytyl page
That ne hadde to hys wage
Of gold and sylvyr and gret tresore
To be ryche for everemore.
Thomas leet, or he wente then, *released; before he departed*
Out of presoun the Crystene men,
Every pylgrym and palmere,
Gaf hem rente and hous there, *income*
With hem stabled the toun aghen; *brought order to; again*
Who so com ther myghte weel seen,
In ylke an hygh chef touret, *on high*
Kyng Richardes armes were upset. *raised*

  Lordynges, now ye have herd
Of these townes, hou it ferd;
Hou kyng Richard with hys maystry *power*
Wan the toun of Sudan Turry;
Orglyous wan Thomas Multone, *Thomas Multon defeated Orglyous*
And slowgh every modyr sone.

Of Ebedy we schal speke,
That faste now hath here gate steke, *securely; locked up*
Whenne Fouke Doyly it bylay,
That entre in nought he may.
The cyté was strong and stoute;
Sevene myle it was aboute.
Thrytty pryse toures be tale, *splendid towers by count*
In every tour, a cheef amyrale.
Folk of armes, by ryght ascent,
Numbre ther were fyfty thousend.
With other smal putayle *foot soldiers*
That there come in to the batayle,
That ne cowde no man acounte
To how manye they wolde amounte.
Sere Fouke broughte goode engynes,
Swylke knewe but fewe Sarezynes.
In every half he leet hem arere, *On every side*
His enemyes a newe play to lere. *game to teach*
A mangenel he leet bende,
To the prys-tour a ston gan sende; *great tower*
That ston whanne it out fleygh,
The Sarezynes that it seygh,
"Allas!" they cryeden, and hadden wondyr,
"It routes as it were a thondyr!" *resounds*
On the tour the ston so hytte,
That twenty feet awey it smytte. *brought destruction*
To another a ston he threwe,
For to make hem game newe.
Al that on syde he smot away,
And slowgh dogges of fals fay. *faith*
They beet doun the toures all
In the toun and on the walle.
A prys tour stood ovyr the gate;
He bente hys engyne and threwe therate
A gret ston that harde drof, *struck*
That the tour al torof, *broke into pieces*
The barre, and the hurdys, *barrier; bulwark (palisade)*
The gate barst, and the portecolys. *portcullis*
Therto he gaf anothir strook
To breke the bemes alle of ook, *oak*
And slowgh the folk that therinne stood.
The othere fledden, and were nygh wood,
And sayden it was the develys dent.
"Allas, Mahoun! What has he ment,
This Ynglyssche dogge that hyghte Fouke?
He is no man: he is a pouke *fiend*
That out of helle is istole! *came stealthily*

An evyl deth moot he thole	*may he suffer*
For us beseges faste.	*By*
Yif he moo stones to us caste,	
Al this toun wole be doun bete.	
Stondande hous wole he non lete!"	*permit*
Sere Fouke gan hym apparaylle,	*prepare himself*
With his folk the toun to assaylle.	
Or he the toun with strengthe wan,	
There was slayn many a man!	
The toun dykes on every syde,	*moats*
They were depe and ful wyde.	
Ful of grut no man myghte swymme,	*mud*
The wal stood faste upon the brymme.	*brink*
Betwen hem myghte no man stande.	
The archers al of this lande	
Schotten in with arewes smale;	
The toun folk ne gaf no tale.	*paid no attention*
The Sarezynes wenten up on the walles,	
And schotten with areweblast and spryngalles,	*catapults*
And with quarelles they gunne hem stonye.	*did inflict pain on them*
Of oure folk, they slowen monye:	
Envenymyd here takyl was.	*Poisoned their weapons (arrows) were*
But whenne Fouke Doyly seygh that caas,	
That hys men scholde be slawe,	
He bad hem to withdrawe:	
"And brynges trees, and manye a bowgh."	*branch*
To don hys wylle folk come inowgh.	
Crystene men maden hem a targe	*shield*
Of dores and of wyndowes large.	
Some caughten a bord and some an hach,	*gate*
And broughten to tymbyr, and thach,	*thatch*
And grete schydes, and the wode,	*beams; the wood*
And slunge it into the mode,	*mud*
And the thach above theron,	
That Crystene men myghte on gon	
To the wal, and stonde sekyr,	*safely*
And hand be hand to geve bekyr:	*battle*
A sory beverage there was browen!	*Great harm was there inflicted (see note)*
Quarellys and arweys thykke flowen;	
The Ynglyssche slowen that they oftoke.	*apprehended*
Durste no man over the walles loke,	
That the Crystene hem ovyrthrewe.	*Lest; cast them down (destroy)*
And wylde fyr ovyr the walles they blewe:	
Many an hous, anon ryght,	
Bycome upon a fayr lyght,	*Became thereafter a fair (bright) light*
Many a lane and many a strete.	
The Sarezynes, thoo, for hete,	*fire (heat)*

Drowgh out godes, and faste gan flye:
"Allas!" and "Help!" lowde gan they crye.
The Ynglyssche men herden the cry,
They were stronge and wel hardy;
To wynne the toun weel they wende. *expected*
They withinne weel hem defende. *defended themselves well*
Though it were soo that on doun falle, *one*
Another styrte upon the walle *jumped*
In the stede there he stood, *place*
And weryd it weel with herte good. *defended well*

Among the toun folk was no game; *mirth*
To counseyl they gaderyd hem insame. *gathered themselves all together*
Thenne sayde the chef amyrale:
"Lordynges, lystnes to my tale! *speech (argument)*
This sege is gret, thys fyr is stronge;
Thus may we nought dure longe.
To slen us they have gret desyre,
They have set oure toun afyre!
Pes of hym tydes us no graunt, *It happens to us that he will not grant peace*
But it be at swylke a comenaunt *Unless*
That we oure god, Mahoun, forsake, *Muhammad*
And Crystyndom undyrtake,
And trowe in Jhesu and Mary.
Despyt it wore, and velony[1]
That we scholde leve on fals lay! *believe; false religion*
So arme hym, every man that may,
That strong is wepene for to bere,
And fonde we this toun to were! *strive; to defend*
Of hoost, we have swylke ten *Of the army; ten times*
As he has of Crystene men
To fyghte with us now hedyr brought. *hither*
Bes bold and doutes hym ryght nought! *fear him not at all*
Betere it is that we outrenne *engage [in battle]*
Thenne as wrehches in hous to brenne,
And frye in oure owne gres! *burn up; grease*
Englyssche be feynte and herteles: *faint and cowardly*
Of mete and drynk they have defawte. *lack*
We scholen hem slee alle in asawte, *assault*
And fellen hem alle in the feelde.
Hangyd be he that this toun yelde
To Crystene men whyl he may leve!"
But whenne he hadde this counseyl geve,
Every man hys armes on keste, *threw on*

[1] *Disobedience (shame) it were, and villainy (wickedness)*

And to hym they come alle preste; *ready*
For to fyghte they were ful fel. *very spirited (fierce)*
To here temple they wente ful snell; *very swiftly*
Ylke a man armyd in hys queyntyse, *battle trappings*
And made there here sacrefyse
To Mahoun and to Jubiterre,
That he hem helpe in here werre:
"We hadde nevere nede or now, *before*
And here we make hym oure avow:
The prys this day yif that we wynne, *victory*
That we schole nevere blynne *cease*
For to fyghte with Crystene schrewe
Tyl that they ben al tohewe." *slain*
In foure partyes they delte here route, *army*
And at the foure gates they issuyd oute.

The fyrste hoost Sere Arcade ledde,
All aboute on brede they spredde. *far and wide*
Sere Cudary ledde that othir,
And with hym, Orphias, hys brothir.
The thrydde hoost with hym gan lede
Sere Materbe, wyght in wede; *valiant in armor*
Sere Gargoyle ledde the ferthe.
There they rede, al the erthe *Where they rode*
Undyr the hors feet it quook. *shook*
Sere Fouke beheeld and gan to look.
Here folk were rengyd in that playn, *arrayed*
Foure score thousand, for sothe to sayn,
Of footmen, knyghtes, and squyers,
And of lordes with baners.
Ther were syxty amyrales,
The soth to say, in sertayn tales. *tallies*
On stedes weel trappyd, armyd they ryden,
Redy batayle to abyden. *await*

Sere Fouke gan hys folk ordeyne, *put in order*
As they scholden hem demeyne. *conduct themselves*
Formeste he sette hys arweblasteres,
And aftyr that, hys gode archeres,
And aftyr, hys staff slyngeres, *[soldiers armed with] staff and slings*
And othere with scheeldes and with speres.
He devysyd the ferthe part *arrayed (made ready)*
With swerd and ax, knyf and dart.
The men of armes com al the last.
Quod Fouke: "Seres, beth nought agast, *afraid*
Though that they ben moo than wee!"
They blyssyd hem and fel on kne: *blessed themselves*

"Fadyr, and Sone, and Holy Gost,"
Quod Fouke, "Kepe the Crystene hoost! — *Guard*
Mary milde oure erande bede! — *deliver our own message*
Thy Chyld us helpe at our nede,
And kepe oure honour, we thee preye!
Prest we ben for thee to deye, — *Prepared*
And for Hys love that deyde on roode!"
  The Sarezynes with egre mode,
Here wepenes begunne for to grype.
They trumpyd anon and gunne to pype.
To fyghte the Crystene were ful swyft;
Ylke a lord hys baner gan uplyft,
Of kynde armes of hys owen,[1]
That his men scholde hym knowen,
And to folewe hym that tyde
In the bataylle where they gan ryde.
Sarazynes comen with gret wylle
When the Crystene myghte drawe hem tylle. — *Until; reach them*
To schete the arweblasteres hem dresse, — *shoot; took up position*
And the archeres to hem gesse. — *aimed at them; (see t-note)*
Sere Fouke leet sette up a standard
With armes of the Kyng Richard.
Whenne the Sarezynes it sen,
They wende Richard hadde there iben. — *believed*
Among hem alle in bataylle thore,
Of hym they were adred ful sore.
Knyghtes and amyralles prowde,
"Kylles doun ryght," they cryeden lowde. — *outright*
"Brynges the cyté out of cares!
Hangyd be he that hys foo spares!"
  Sere Archade took a gret launse,
And come prykande with bobaunce. — *pride (fierceness)*
To Fouke Doyly he gan it bere, — *did it bear*
And with anothir, Fouke mette hym there.
Ryght in pleyn cours in the feelde, — *full charge*
He hytte hym upon the scheelde.
Ryght thorwghout the herte it karff:
The mysbelevyd paynym starff. — *unbelieving heathen died*
  With bost come Sere Cudary — *Violently*
Agayn a Crystene knyght hardy.
With a fawchoun he gan hym smyte; — *falchion*
Sekyrly, it wolde weel byte.
In the nekke he hytte hym withal, — *indeed*
That the hed trendelyd off as a bal. — *rolled down*

[1] *Consisting of his own hereditary coat of arms*

On a rabyte com Orphias, *Arabian steed*
For bost he prekyd a gret pas. *Through pride; galloped at great speed*
A gret fawchoun in hand he bar:
"Come fyght with me now hoo that dar!" *who*
Sir John Doyly, Sir Foukes nevew,
A yonge knyghte of gret vertew,
In hande he took a spere long:
The schafte that was bothe styfe and strong,
And on hys scheeld, he smot hym soo
That it cleved evenen in twoo,
And slewe hym there sekyrly,
And sayde, "Dogge, there thou ly
And reste thee there tyl domysday,
For thou art payyd of thy pay!" *wages*
Togedere whenne the hoostes mete,
The archers myghten no more schete.
Men of armes, the swerdes out breyden, *brandished*
Balles out of hoodes soone ther pleyden.
Swylke strokes they hem geven,
That helme and bacynet al toreven, *shattered*
That on the schuldre fel the brayn;
The Crystene men slowen hem with mayn. *vigor*
The foote folk and sympyl knaves,
In hande they henten ful goode staves.
Ther was no Sarezyn in that flok
That, yif that he hadde had a knok *Who*
With a staff wel iset
On helm other on bacynet,
That he ne yede doun, saun fayle, *went down*
Off hys hors top over taylle. *head over heels*
Sone withinne a lytyl stounde,
The moste party yede to grounde. *part fell*
The lordes saygh hou that they spedde; *fared*
Anon hastyly they fledde:
Into the toun they wolde agayn.
Sere Fouke and hys men therof were fayn *eager*
The paas to kepe and to lette; *road; guard; hinder movement*
On every half they hem withsette, *side; blocked them*
That non of hem ne myghte ascape.
The Crystene on hem gan faste to frape. *strike*
Whenne the foot folk weren islawe,
Grete lordynges doun they drawe
Of stedes and rabytes trappyd; *From; Arabian horses caparisoned*
Anon here hedes were of clappyd. *struck off*
That Jhesu hem helpyd it was wel sene;
The Sarezynes weren islayn alle clene,
Strypyd hem nakyd to the serke; *shirt*

But whene they hadde maad al pleyn werk, *unornamented*
Sere Fouk, that noble man and wyse,
With trumpes he leet blowe the prys. *sound the call [that the game is taken]*
No man woulde tho dogges berye: *bury*
Crystene men resten and maden hem merye.
Of good wyn ylke man drank a draught,
And whenne that they herte hadde caughte,[1]
Colyd hem, and keveryd here state,
Anon they broken the toun gate.
Syre Fouk with his men inrode,
No Sarezyn there hym abode. *waited for him*
Every Sarezyn that they mette,
With swyche wessayl they hem grette *toast [of death] (see note)*
For the love of here Mahoun,
That by the schuldre they schoof the croun. *shaved off the head*
The footemen come behynde,
And slowgh alle that they myghte fynde.
Man, wumman, al yede to swerde, *went*
Bothe in hous and eke in yerde.
The Crystene men the fyr gan quenche;
There was more good than man myghte thenche *goods; think*
Of sylvyr and gold in that cyté,
The Crystene men hadde gret plenté.
Ful curteysely seyde Sere Fouke,
"Every man hys wynnyng brouke *keep*
Amonges yow alle to dele and dyghte." *distribute*
For good was no nede to fyghte. *goods*
Crystene men Sere Fouke lete, *Sir Fouke caused Christian men*
In every lane and every strete,
To take keep and to wake, *observe; remain awake*
By nyght and day warde to make, *watch*
For to save weel afyn *defend completely*
Fro the Sawdon Saladyn.
On the toun wal, on every corner,
He leet sette up a baner
Upon schaft brode dysplayde,
With Kyng Richardes armes portrayde,
In sygne, to bere record *to show (to testify)*
That Kyng Richard was here ovyrlord.

Whenne he hadde stabelyd the toun, *brought order to*
With hys hoost he wente boun *armed (prepared)*
To Orglyous to Sere Thomas.

[1] Lines: 4588–89: *And when they had regained their heart (courage) / Refreshed themselves, and recovered their health*

Forth they wenten a gret pas
To Kyng Rychard to Sudan Turry,
And he hem took and sette hym by. *placed him beside*
Every man tolde other is chaunce. *his exploits*
To hem come the kyng of Fraunce.
Unto Acres they gan turne,
Aftyr swynk there to sojurne, *After toil in battle there to lodge*
To dwelle and reste hem a stounde,
To hele hem that hadde gret wounde.
Upon a day aftyrward,
Kyng Phelyp eet with kyng Richard,
Dukes, eerles, and barouns,
Men of Fraunce of most renouns;
With hem alle, the knyghtes free
That they broughten fro beyunde the see.
Thomas of Multone, Fouke Doyly,
Erles and barouns, sekyrly,
Of Yngelond, Gascoyne, and of Spayne, *Gascony*
Of Lumbardy, Gyan, and Alemayne. *Aquitaine; Germany*
Trumpes blewen, tabours dasschen, *roll*
Mete was greythid, they gunne to wasschen. *Food; prepared*
They were set doun at a table,
And weel iservyd, withouten fable,
To here talent of flesch and fysch, *appetite*
Frenssche men, Lumbardes, Gascoynes, Ynglysch.
Of ryche wyn ther was plenté,
Pyment and ryche clarré.
Aftyr mete the cloth was drawe;
Of here comynge, Rychard was fawe. *joyful*

Aftyr mete they maden game;
They begynne to speke insame. *together*
Quod kyng Richard: "Every man telle
Hou he has don, hou hym befelle.
Whoo has ben in most dystresse,
And who has don the moste prowesse."
Quod Rychard: "I myself wan Sudan Turry,
Of the folk hadde I no mercy.
Alle tha that ther wore, I and myn hoost slowgh, *All those*
And wunne therinne tresore inowgh;
Crystene men therinne wone." *remain*
Thomas gan hys dedes mone: *did speak of his deeds*
"And I wan Castel Orglyous;
Maydyn and grome, hosebonde and spous, *boys (youth)*
Myn hoost slowgh, and non ovyrhaf, *spared*
Al the tresore that hem I gaf."
Thoo tolde Fouke Doyly: *Then spoke*

"And I wan the cyté of Ebedy,
Gaynyd hem no mercy to crye: *To cry mercy availed them not*
What scholde dogges doo but dye?
Al the flok hoppyd hedeles! *were beheaded*
In this manere I made pes:
Destroyyd alle hethene blood.
To Crystene men al the good
I gaf that I therinne fond,
And stablyd it into Crystene hond." *settled*
Quod Phelyp: "And I dede nought soo, *did*
Taburet and Archane I wente too.
The folk come of bothe cytees, *came out of*
Cryde mercy, and fylle on knees.
For every hed I took raunsoun;
They yolde to me every toun, *yielded*
And up thay sette my baner:
We weren at on in this maner. *thus in unison*
To sloo men was me nevere leeff."[1]
  Kyng Richard took it to greff, *took it amiss*
And on hym gan to loke rowe: *angrily (violently)*
"Cursyd be he that thy werk alowe!
Thou were weel wurthy mawgrý to have, *to be reproached*
Sarezynes that thou woldyst save!
For to graunte hem lyf for mede,
Thou dost God a gret falshede! *wickedness*
Thou hast don us gret schame:
Thou were wurthy to have blame!
Alle swylke werkes I refuse,
And thou, sere kyng, yif thou it use, *permit it*
Thou dedyst nought as I thee bad!
Yif thou be eft in fyght bestad, *again beset in fight*
Thou schalt fynde hem, everylkon,
They schole ben thy moste foon. *chief enemies*
Yif thou haddyst hem alle slayn,
Thenne myghtyst thou have ben fayn,
And wunnen al the good therinne.
Now is it eft newe to begynne, *it is once again a new undertaking*
And that thyself now schalt sen."
Quod Phelyp: "I wole wende aghen
For to prove yif it be soth.
Whether the folk me gyle doth, *If; deceive me*
Be aboute me to anoye, *Strive to offend me*
I schal hem brenne, sloo, and stroye!
They schole nevere have grith!" *mercy*

[1] *To slay men was to me never acceptable (pleasing)*

Quod Richard: "Yif I wende thee with,
The betere hap thee may betyde." *fortune*
On morwen they begunne to ryde
With here hoost to Taburet.
The folk withinne the gatys schet;
They callyd, "Phelyp, feynte coward!
False wrehche, thou broke foreward! *agreement*
Thou gaf us lyf for raunsoun.
Thee tydes no more of this toun *This town is obliged to you no more*
Henne to the worldes ende!" *From now*
Quod Kyng Rychard: "Phelyp, tak in mende *take in mind*
I sayde thee soth — now may thou wete!" *know*
Anon hys baner doun they smete, *knocked*
And brak it up in gret despyt, *defiance*
Twoo peces brak it also tyt, *To; right away*
And out into the dyke it throwen,
And setten up on of here owen, *one*
And bad hym: "Now doo thy beste!"
Quod Richard: "Frendes, haves no reste!
This toun assayle we now swythe.
Every man hys strengthe kythe *exercise (exert)*
On these dogges to ben wroken!" *be avenged*
Whenne kyng Richard thus hadde spoken,
The Crystene men gunne make a scryke. *battle cry*
Anon they wunne ovyr the dyke.
The folk on the walles above
To defende faste they prove, *strove*
In al that they may and cunne.[1]
Stones and stokkes they threwen dounne; *timbers*
Summe of the Crystene they herte. *hurt*
For drede, archeres abak they sterte. *backed away*
The Sarezynys they gunne grete: *did challenge (attack)*
Arwys, qwarellys, thykke they schete,
And slowen that they ovyrtoke. *reached*
Ovyr the walles durste no man loke.
The Crystene the walles undyrmyn.
Quod Richard: "I schal nevere syne *commit a sin; again*
Sytte on grounde, drynke, ne eeten,
Tyl I have this toun igeten." *Until; conquered*
In the dyke the wal ovyrthrewe; *overturned*
The hoost wan in, and on hem hewe *proceeded in*
With swerdes, axes, and kene knyves,
And slowen men, chyldren, and wyves. *women*
The hoost wolde no lengere be thare;

[1] *In all [ways] that they were able and knew*

Toward Archane gunne they fare.
The folk of the toun the gatys schet,
Kyng Phelyp out for to let, *leave*
And sayden: "Coward, goo thy way!
Here hast thou lost thy pray. *booty (prize)*
Thou gaf us lyf for tresore:
Of this toun tydes thee no more. *you get nothing else*
Al at ones thy pay thou grepe; *All at once you obtained your payment*
Here hast thou lost thy lordschepe.
Thou art a fals, faynt wrehche!
Hangyd be he that of thee rehche! *that cares for (heeds) you*
Al that thou may doo us, thou doo!"
For that they despysyd hym soo,[1]
Kyng Richard swoor and was agrevyd:
"The Sarezynnes therinne that misbelevyd, *hold false beliefs*
Schal non of hem be savyd quykke!" *None of them shall save their lives*
Arwes, quarelles flowen thykke;
The Crystene men the gates brente,
They broke the walles, and in they wente.
The Sarezynes fledden, awey gunne fyken, *retreated quickly*
The Crystene folwen, slen, and styken, *followed, slew, and stabbed*
And gaf alle here folk here bane; *death*
Thus Kyng Phelyp wan Archane.

Quod Richard: "Phelyp, tak to thee
The goodes of ayther cyté;
Thus thou myghtyst have don or this. *before this*
Certes, Phelyp, thou art nought wys.
Thee be forgeven the fyrste gylt: *transgression*
Thou may bewar, yif that thou wylt.
Now be we frendes bothe,
But, sykyrly, we schole be wrothe,
Swylke folyes, yif thou haunte, *engage in such folly (impudence)*
Sarezynys lyf, yif thou graunte.
Bewar, though thou gold coveyte:
In this land, do us no dysseyte! *deceit*
Yif thou be eft founden with gyle *again; falseness (deceit)*
Wherethorwgh we fallen in peryle, *Through which we should come into peril*
Be thee chyld in oure lady barme, *Were you a child on our lady's breast*
Goo schalt thou nought withouten harme!
Of gold schalt thou have thy fylle!"
He gan to moorne, and heeld hym stylle; *He was troubled and remained silent*
He glouryd, and gan to syke, *glowered; sighed*
With Kyng Richard gan hym evyl lyke, *With King Richard he became upset*

[1] *Because they disparaged him to such an extent*

For wordes he gan to hym deyl. *uttered*
Kyng Richard gan hym to counseyl:
"Be trewe, doo as I thee teche.
Goo we forth this cuntré to seche, *invade*
To sloo oure foos and wynne the croys!"
Kyng Phelyp withouten noys *without quarrel*
Sayde: "In me schal be no delay
To helpe thertoo, that I may."
Kyng Richard and Phelyp with here hoost
Wenten forth be the see coost.
Ageynes hem comen here naveye, *Toward*
Cogges, drowmoundes, many galeye,
Barges, schoutes, crayeres fele
That were chargyd with all wele, *wealth (goods)*
With armure, and with othir vytaylle,
That nothyng in the hoost scholde fayle. *be lacking*

It was before Seynt James tyde, *25 July*
Whenne foules begunne merye to chyde, *twitter*
Kynge Richard turnde his ost to pas
Toward the cyté of Cayphas, *Haifa*
Evere forth be the maryn, *sea-coast*
By the rever of Chalyn.
Saladyn it herde telle
And come flyngande aftyr snelle, *rushing; quickly*
With syxty thousand Sarezynes kene,
And thoughte to doo Crystene men tene; *harm*
And ovyrtooke the rerewarde, *rear guard*
And begunne to bekyr harde.
Hastely swerdes they drowen,
And many a Crystene man they slowen.
Unarmyd was the rerewarde,
They fledde in haste to Kyng Richarde.
Whenne Kyng Richard wyste this, *learned*
The Sawdon slowgh hys men iwis,
On Favel of Cypre he sat, falewe, *brownish yellow [colored horse]*
Also swyft as ony swalewe. *Just as; swallow*
In this world at grete nede
Was nevere founde a better stede. *place*
Hys baner anon was unfolde;
The Sarezynes anon it gan beholde.
Thoo that myght the baner see, *Those who*
Alle they gunne for to flee.
Kyng Richard aftyr hem gan ryde,
And they withturnyd hem that tyde, *And they turned around at that time*
And smot togedere with swylke raundoun *so much speed (violence)*
As yif al the world scholde fall doun.

Kyng Richard before smot *struck first (in front)*
With hys ax that byttyrly boot; *slashed (bit)*
He them tohewed and tocarfe: *cut (dismembered); cut to pieces*
Manye undyr his hand gan sterve. *died*
Never was man in erthe ryght
That better with hem gon fyght,
And manye Crystene, I telle yow sekyr,
Hente here deth in that bekyr *Received*
Thorwgh a carte that was Hubertes Gawtyr, *On account of; cart*
That was set al in a myr. *all fixed; mire (bog)*
For Saladynes sones theder came
And the harneys them bename. *fighting gear (armor and weapons) they seized*
The cartere les his hand ryght; *lost*
There was slayn many a knyght.
For the harneys kepyd fourty, *fighting gear protected*
And therof were islayn thrytty.
Kyng Richard hyyd thedyr with thate; *hastened; on account of that*
  Yet almoost he came to late!
In honde he helde his axe good, *bore*
Many Sarezyn he leet blood! *he bled (wounded)*
Ther was non armure, varrayment, *armor, truly*
So good that myghte withstande his dent. *stroke*
And the Longe Spay that tyde, *[William] Longespée*
Layde on be every syde, *Delivered blows*
That doun it wente al that he smot
With hys fawchoun that byttyr bot; *fiercely struck (bit)*
And the batayle was dotous, *uncertain*
And to his folk wol perylous, *very*
For the hete was so strong,
And the dust ros hem among,
And forstoppyd the Crystene onde, *smothered; breathing (life)*
That they fylle ded upon the sonde.
Moo dyede for hete, at schorte wurdes, *in short*
Thenne for dent of spere or swordes. *Than by*
Kyng Richard was al most ateynt, *overcome*
And in the pouder nygh adreynt. *dust; suffocated*
On hys knees he gan doun falle,
Help to Jhesu he gan calle,
For love of His modyr, Mary;
And as I fynde in hys story,
He seygh come Seynt George, the knyght, *(see note)*
Upon a stede, good and lyght, *swift (nimble)*
In armes whyte as the flour
With a croys of red colour. *cross*
Al that he mette in that stounde, *place*
Horse and man he felde to grounde,
And the wynd gan wexe lythe; *grew gentle*

Sterne strokes they gynne to kythe. *delivered*
Whenne Kyng Richard seygh that syght,
In herte he was glad and lyght, *brave*
And egyrly, withouen fayle,
The Sarezynes he gan assayle.
Bertram Braundys, the goode Lumbard,
Robert Tourneham, and Kyng Richard,
Alle that agayn hem gan dryve, *against them charged*
Soone they refte hem of here lyve. *released them*
The Sarezynes fledden to recet *refuge*
To the mount of Nazareth, withoute let. *without delay*
They were so hyyd at the spore, *hurried; spur (at full speed)*
That mekyl of here folk was lore.
Kyng Richard wente a gret pas *at great speed*
Toward the cyté of Cayphas, *Haifa*
And thankyd Jhesu, Kyng of glorye,
And Marye, his modyr, of that victorie.
Alle they maden gret solas *rejoiced greatly*
For the wynnyng of Cayphas.

At morwen, kyng Richard leet crye
Among hys hoost that they scholde hye *hurry*
Ever more forth be the maryn *Henceforth onward by the coast*
To the cyté of Palestyn. *(see note)*
There here pavylouns they telte, *pitched*
And al to longe there they dwelte,
For to abyde here vytayle *await; provisions*
That comen by watyr, saun fayle.
Certes, that was the werste dwellyng
That evere dwellyd Richard, oure kyng!
That whyle the Sawdon Saladyn, *During that time*
Sente many a Sarezyn
To bete adoun manye castelles, *raze (level)*
Cytees, tounes, and tourelles.
Fyrst they bete doun the castele
That was callyd Myrabele;
And aftyr the castel Calaphyne
That was ful of good engyne.
Of Sessarye they fellyd the wal, *Caesarea*
And the tour of Arsour al. *Arsuf*
Jaffe castel they bete adoun, *Jaffa; razed*
And the goode castel Touroun. *Castle Toron (Le Toron des Chevaliers)*
Castel Pylgrym they felden there, *Castle Pilgrim (Chateau Pelerin)*
And the goode castel La Fere;
The castel of Seynt George Dereyn, *St. George LaBane (the defender)*
They felde doun and made al pleyn,
The walles they felde of Jerusalem,

And eke the walles of Bedlem, *Bethlehem*
Maydenes castel they lete stande,
And the castel of Aukes land. *Perverse Land? (see note)*
Be that coost were no moo leten, *spared*
But they were feld and doun beten; *razed*
And this he dede withouten lette, *without interruption*
For Richard scholde have no recette. *In order that; refuge*
Whenne he hadde thus idoo,
Kyng Richard he sente untoo,
And seyde he wolde the nexte morwe
Mete hym in the feld with sorwe, *anger*
And with a launce to hym ryde,
Yif that he durste hym abyde. *dared face him*
Undyr the forest of Arsour,
He wolde asaye hys valour. *test*
Kyng Richard made it nought towgh, *not difficult*
But for that tydyng faste he lowgh,
Hee leet crye in hys hoost
In the name of the Holy Gost
That they scholden, with vygour, *resolve (determination)*
That nyght reste before Arsour,
And dyghten hem al redy than,
At morwen to fyghte with the Sawdan.
On Seynt Marye even, the natyvyté,
This ylke bataylle scholde be. *very*
Many was the hethene man
With Saladyn that come than:
Of Inde, of Perse, of Babyloyne,
Of Arabye and of Cessoyne, *Cesson (Kesoun)*
Of Aufryk and of Bogye, *North Africa; the Buqaia(?)*
Of al the lond of Alysaundrye,
Of grete Grece and of Tyre,
And of many another empire;
Of moo landes than ony can telle,
Save He that made hevene and helle.
That nyght was Kyng Richard before Arsour,
Undyr the forest of Lysour.
With hym ther were of Yngeland
Wyse knyghtes, doughty of hand; *strong of hand*
Manye Frensche folk and Templers,
Gascoynes and Hospytaleres,
Of Provynce, a fayr cumpanye, *Provence; sizable (excellent)*
Of Poyle and of Lumbardye, *Apulia*
Of Gene, of Sesyle, and of Tuskayn; *Genoa; Sicily; Tuscany*
There was many a doughty man
Of Ostrych and of Alemayn *Austria; Germany*
That weel cowde fyghte in the playn.

Of Crystene knyghtes that were hende *nearby*
The fayreste hoost to the worldes ende.
And ye schal here as it is wrete, *written*
Hou the batayle was ismete. *fought*

Saladyn come be a mountayn,
And ovyrspradde hyl and playn,
Syxty thousand sayde the spye,
Was in the fyrste cumpanye,
With longe speres on heye stedes.
Of gold and asure were here wedes. *battle gear*
Syxty thousynd comen aftyrward
Of Sarezynes stoute and hard,
With many a pensel of sykelatoun, *(see note)*
And of sendel grene and broun, *sendal*
Almost come fyve and fyfty thousinde
With Saladyn that comen behynde;
They comen alle stylle nought fer behende, *continually*
Here armure ferde al as it brende. *Their armor appeared as if it burned*
Thre thousand Turkes comen at the laste,
With bowe Turkeys and arweblaste.
A thousand taboures and yit moo, *drums; even more*
Alle at ones they smeten thoo: *struck then*
Al the erthe donyd hem undyr. *resounded*
There myght men see a syghte of wundir.
Now speke we of Richard, oure kyng,
Hou he com to batayle with hys gyng. *troop*
He was armyd in splentes of steel, *plates*
And sat upon his hors, Favel.
Weel hym lovede baroun and knyght, *Well baron and knight loved him*
For he cowde weel araye a fyght! *prepare a fight*
The fyrste batayle to the Templeres
He gaf, and to the Hospytaleres,
And bad hem goo in Goddes name,
The feend to schentschepe and to schame. *confound*
Jakes Deneys and Jhon de Neles,
Before they wenten in that pres. *In front*
In this world thenne were there
No betere knyghtes thenne they were.
Forth they prekyd, as I fynde, *rode; read*
With knyghtes fully twenty thousynde,
And the Sarezynes they mette,
With grymly launse they hem grette. *deadly*
Many Sarezyn hadden here fyn, *their end*
And wenten to Mahoun and Appolyn; *Muhammad and Apollo*
And tho that caughten deth of oure, *And those of ours who received death*
Wenten to Cryst, oure Saveoure.

Jakes Deneys was a noble knyght;
To slee paynymys he ded hys myght. *did all he could*
He prekyd before his folk to rathe *to provoke*
With hys twoo sones, and that was scathe, *was a pity*
Thre thousand Turkes comen with boost, *arrogance (threats)*
Betwen Jakes and hys hoost,
That non help myghte come hym too,
For no thynge that they cowde doo.
Ne he ne myghte hym withdrawe,
For the folk of hethene lawe. *On account of*
It was gret scathe, by Jhesu Cryste; *misfortune*
Kyng Richard therof nought ne wyste, *nothing knew*
For he was yit al behynde
To ordeyne othir twenty thousynde *make ready*
Thoo scholde the Duke of Burgoyne *Whom*
Lede, and the Eerl of Boloyne.
These comen and deden here devers *duty*
Agayn the hethene pawteners; *scoundrels*
And Jakes and hys sones twoo
Almost weren islayn thoo. *then*
He layde on every syde ryght,
And steryd hym as noble knyght. *conducted himself*
Twenty he slowgh, and ayther sone ten *each son*
Of the vyle, hethene men.
And nyne sethyn hys hors was felde, *And nine after*
And evere he coveryd hym with his schelde.
He had non help of Templere,
Ne of non othir Hospytalere.
Nevertheles doughtely he faught:
The Sarazynes yet felde hym naught.
He layde on with his sworde,
And evere he sayde, "Jhesu, Lord,
I schal dye for Thy love:
Resseyve my soule to hevene above!"
The Sarezynes layde on with mace
And al tofrusschyd hym in the place, *crushed him*
Hym and hys sones bothe;
Therfore Kyng Richard was ful wrothe.
Whenne Kyng Richard wyste this,
That ded was Jakes Denys,
"Allas!" he sayde, "that is wronge!
Behynde I dwellyd al to longe!"
He smot Favel with spores of golde,
Sewe hym that sewe wolde! *Follow after him who would follow*
A launse in hys hand he heelde;
He smot an amyral in the scheelde.
The dynt smot thorwgh the hethene herte:

I undyrstande it gan hym smerte! — *did cause him pain*
Kyng Richard hys honde withdrowgh:
With that launse a kyng he slowgh.
So he dede an amyrayle,
And fyve dukes withouten fayle.
With that ylke launse selve — *very same lance*
Kyng Richard slowgh kynges twelve.
The thryttenethe to the chyn he kerff; — *pierced*
The launse barste, the Sarezyn sterff. — *died*
Hys ax on his fore arsoun hyng: — *front saddlebow; hung*
Anon it took Richard, oure kyng.
On he hytte on the schuldyr bon — *One*
And karf hym to the sadyl anon!
And of som he pared so the croune
That helme and hed fel adoun!
Non armure iwrought with hand
Myghte Kyng Richardes ax withstande.
Of my tale bes nought awundryd: — *astonished*
The Frenssche says he slowgh an hundrid, — *(see note)*
Whereof is maad this Ynglyssche sawe, — *narrative (history, poem)*
Or he reste hym ony thrawe. — *rested hymself; at all*
Hym folewyd many an Ynglyssche knyght,
That egyrly halp hym for to fyght,
And layden on as they were woode
Tyl valeys runnen al on bloode.
The Sarezynes sayden in here pavylouns, — *said*
The Crystene ferden as wylde lyouns; — *behaved*
And that Rycharde with theyr folke fares
As hende grehoundes do with hares.
Upon here steedes, manly they lepen;
Swerdes and speres, manly the grepen.
Manye man there slowgh othir;
Many a Sarezyn loste there his brothir,
And manye of the hethene houndes, — *(see note)*
With here teeth gnowgh on the groundes. — *bit the dust (died)*
Be the blood upon the gras,
Men myghte see where Richard was!
Brayn and blood he schadde inowgh;
Many an hors hys guttes drowgh. — *dragged his guts*
There was a manye an empty sadyl, — *empty*
That it bewepte the chyld in the cradyl. — *So that the child in the cradle mourned it*
He thoughte rescue Jakes Denayn,
And ar he come, he was islayn.
For he and hys sones anon
Were tofrusschyd, flesch and bon. — *crushed*
He ledde hym to hys pavyloun, — *betook himself to his [Saladin's?]*
In despyt of here god Mahoun. — *In defiance of their god, Mahoun*

Thoo delte Richard on ylke a syde, *[blows] on every side*
The Sarezynes durste no lengere abyde.
Syxe thousand and sevene score,
At onys he drof hym before *once*
Up agayn an hygh cleve. *cliff*
They fledde as deer that hadde ben dreve; *driven*
And for the drede of Kyng Richard,
Off the clyff they fell dounward,
And al tobarste, hors and men, *burst apart*
That nevere non com to lyve than. *after*
That seygh the Sawdon, Saladyn:
He was ful sekyr hys lyf to tyn. *certain; lose*
He lefte hys pavylouns and hys tente,
And fledde away verramente.
Whenne Kyng Richard seygh hym fleande, *fleeing*
He sewyd aftyr, faste flyngande. *followed; galloping*
To sloo the Sawdon was hys thought,
But, for he myghte hym overtake nought, *since*
Of a footman a bowe he took,
He drowgh an arwe up to the hook, *barb*
And sente it to the Sawdon anon,
And smot hym thorwgh schuldyr bon;
Thus, the Sawdon with dolour,
Fledde fro the batayle of Arsour.
Syxty thousand there were slawe,
Sarezynys of hethene lawe,
And of Crystene but ten score:
Blyssyd be Jhesu Cryst, therfore!
   Kyng Richard took the pavylouns
Of cendeles and of sykelatouns.
They were schape of casteles,
Of gold and sylvyr were the penseles. *pennons*
Manye were the noble geste *splendid narrative; (see note)*
Theron were wryten of wylde beste:
Tygrys, dragouns, leouns, lupard,
Al this wan the kyng Richard.
Bounden coffres and grete males
He hadde there withouten tales. *without number*
Of tresore they hadde so mekyl wone, *much seized*
They wyste nowher where here goodes to done. *their plunder to store*
   Kyng Richard wente with honour,
Into the cyté of Arsour,
And rested hym there all nyght,
And thanked Jhesu ful of myght.
On the morowe Kynge Rycharde arose;
Hys dedes were riche and his los. *admirable; praise*
Of Naples he callyd Sere Gawter

That was his maystyr Hospitaler.
He bad hym take with hym knyghtes,
Stronge in armes, stoute in fyghtes,
And agayn to the feelde tee *go*
There the batayle hadde ibee, *Where*
And lede Jakes, the noble baroun,
Into Jerusalem toun,
And berye his body there in erthe,
For he was man that was wel werthe.
Al was don withoute cheste, *strife*
Hastyly Kyng Richardes heste. *command*
Thus, Kyng Richard wan Arsour,
God graunte hys soule mekyl honour!

At morwen he sente to the kyng of Fraunce,
And sayde to hym withoute bobaunce: *arrogance*
"Wende we to Nynyvé *Nineveh*
That is a swythe strong cyté.
For hadde we that toun iwunne,
Thenne were oure game fayre begunne. *auspiciously*
Hadde we that and Massedoyne, *Macedonia*
We scholde wende to Babyloyne. *Egypt*
Thenne myghte we safly ryde
An hundryd myle by ylke a syde." *in every direction*
Richard and Phylyp in Arsour lay.
A messanger thenne come to say
That the Sarezynes wolde abyde *stand their ground (halt)*
And in batayle to hem ryde.
In the pleyn Odok, sothe to seye,
There they wele leve or deye.
Kyng Richard hem answerid anon: *immediately*
"I schal yow telle, be Seynt Jhon!
And I wiste what day it wore, *If I knew what day [the battle] would be*
I scholde mete with hym thore!" *then*
The messanger sayde, by his lay, *law*
That it scholde be on the sevenyght day. *seventh*
That tyme come, as he telde,
The Sarezynes comen into the feelde
With syxty thousand and weel moo. *considerably more*
Kyng Richard come ageynes hem thoo.
Hys hoost he delte in foure manere, *divided in four ways*
As they sayde that ther were:
Fouke Doyly be that on syde; *one*
Thomas be that othir to abyde,
Kyng Phelyp, the thrydde part,
And the forthe, Kynge Richard.

Thus they besette hem withoute[1]
The Sarezynes that were bolde and stoute.
In every hoost Crystene men,
Sarezynes baners outputte then. *Then raised Saracen banners*
The Sarezynes wenden thenne anon, *believed then*
They hadde ben Sarezynes, everylkon.
Soone so Richard seygh this, *As soon as*
That the Sarezynys hoost beclosyd is, *surrounded*
His owne baner was soone arerde.
Thenne were the Sarezynes sore aferde,
And abaschyd hem in a thowe. *And became afraid in a moment*
The Crystene gan the baner to knowe, *recognized*
They smeten on in that stounde, *battled on*
And slowgh many an hethyn hounde.
Kyng Richard upon Favel gan ryde,
And slowgh dounryght on ylke a syde, *on every side*
And alle his folk dede alsoo,
Alle foure hostes layden too,
Many Sarezyn they schente. *killed*
Allas, an hoost from hem wente;
By the kyngys syde of Fraunce,
The hoost passyd by a chaunce, *by a favorable circumstance*
Into Nynyvé agayn thoo;
Therfore was kyng Richard woo.
The Sarezynys that they founde thore,
They yeden to dethe, lesse and more, *suffered death; the poor and the rich*
The numbre that there to dethe yede, *went*
Fyftene thousand as I yow rede. *recount to you*
  Kyng Richard wente with his meyné *army*
Toward the cyté of Nynyvé.
Kyng Phelyp wente hym by *travelled with him*
With a gret hoost, sykyrly,
Tyl they come to Nynyvé,
And tylde here pavylouns besyde the cyté. *pitched*
Kyng Richard on morwen whenne it was day,
To armes he comaundyd alle that may,
And hastyly, withoue pytee,
To assayle that cyté
With arweblast and with other gynne, *siege machine*
Yif they myghte the cyté wynne.
Alle the folk withouten chydyng, *quarrelling*
Deden Kyng Richardys byddyng.
The gynours mangeneles bente, *operators of siege engines drew back*
And stones to the cyté they sente.
Harde stones in they threwe:

[1] *Thus they arranged themselves in front of*

The Sarezynes that wel knewe!
Arweblast of vys with quarel, *bolt*
With staff slynges that smyte wel, *slings attached to staffs*
With trepeiettes they slungen alsoo, *trebuchet*
That wroughte hem fol mekyl woo,
And blew wylde fyr in trumpes of gynne, *tubes of clever design*
To mekyl sorewe to hem withinne. *great agony (grief)*

Now seygh the Sarezynes, ylkone,
That they scholde to deth gone.
A messanger anon they sente;
To Kyng Richard forth he wente.
And prayed, yif hys wille be,
Of batayle betwen thre.
Three of hem, and three of hys,
Whether of hem that wynne the prys *victory*
And who that haves the heyere hand *victory*
Have the cyté and al here land,
And have it for evere more.
Kyng Richard grauntyd hem thore, *agreed; then*
And bad hem come hastyly.
The messanger wente in on hy, *on high*
And sayde to the amyrayle,
That Kyng Richard, withouten faylle,
Weel armyd with spere and scheelde,
Wolde mete hem in the feelde,
And with hym othere twoo barouns,
Noble men of gret renouns,
For to fyghte with swylke three
As ye wole sende of this cytee.
Thenne on rabytes were they dyght,[1]
Three amyralles, bolde and wyght. *valiant*
Here names I schal yow telle anon,
What they hyghten, everylkon. *were named*
Sere Archolyn in fyrst rod,
Coudyrbras hovyd and abode, *lingered and waited*
Sere Galabre hovyd stylle *remained motionless*
To see who wolde ryde hym tylle. *ride towards him*
Kyng Richard, the noble knyght,
Agayn Sere Archolyn hym dyght. *readied himself*
They smete togedere dyntys sare, *painful blows*
He ne schal kevere nevere mare! *recover ever again*
And he gaf Richard a sory flat *painful blow*
That foundryd bacynet and hat.[2]

---

[1] *Then on Arabian horses they were placed (made ready)*

[2] *That knocked to the ground his unvisored helmet*

Kyng Richard was agrevyd sore — *greatly annoyed*
For the strok that he hadde thore.
King Richard took his ax ful strong,
And on the Sarezyn fast he dong — *vigorously dealt blows*
On the helm above the crown:
He clef hym to the sadyl arsoun. — *saddlebow*
Hys lyf, for sothe, nought longe leste, — *lasted not at all long*
For Kyng Richard was his preeste.
Sere Cowderbras forth gan ryde;
Sere Thomas thoughte hym to abyde. — *combat*
They reden togedere, as we rede,
That bothe to the erthe they yede.
Up they styrten in that stounde,
And smeten togedere with grym wounde. — *fierce blow*
They foughten ful sore with fawchouns kene; — *sharp daggers*
Strong batayle was hem bytwene.
Cowderbras, for felonye, — *ruthlessness*
Smot Sere Thomas, withouten lye,
On hys spawdeler of his scheelde, — *shoulder-armor; away from his shield*
That it fleygh into the feelde. — *fell*
Thomas was agrevyd sore,
And thoughte to anoye hym more.
He took to hys mase of bras — *grasped*
That fayleyd hym nevere in no cas,
And gaf hym a sory wefe — *painful blow*
That his helme al toclefe. — *helmet split in two*
And al tobrosyd his herne panne; — *And completely shattered his brainpan*
Kyd he was a doughty manne. — *Made known; [Thomas]*
Out of hys sadyl he hym glente, — *betook himself*
And with the rabyte forth he wente. — *departed*

Sere Galabre hovyd stylle — *remained still*
To see who wolde ryde hym tylle. — *towards him*
He nyste whethir hym was most gayn[1]
For to fyghte or turne agayn. — *turn back*
Sere Fouke Doyly weel it say: — *saw*
Loth hym were he scapyd away. — *He did not wish for him to escape*
To hym he prekyd upon a stede, — *galloped*
Agayn hym that othir yede. — *went*
With egyr ire togedere rode — *fierce fury*
That eyther stede to grounde glode, — *fell*
And brak here nekkes in that stounde,
That they lay ded upon the grounde.
Here speres scheveryd in the feeldes, — *shattered*
So eythir hytte othir in the scheeldes. — *So greatly*

[1] *He knew not whether it was most advantageous*

Eyther gaf othir strokes felle: *fierce*
Dere they gunne here lyves selle.[1]
Galabre was stout and wyght, *valiant*
That Fouke ne myghte hym hytte nought ryght,
But at the laste he gaf hym on *one*
That he brak his schuldre bon
And hys on arme thertoo: *next to it*
Thenne was hys fyghtyng doo. *done*
On knees he fyl doun and cryde: "Creaunt, *I submit (surrender); (see note)*
For Mahoun and Termagaunt!" *For the sake of*
But Sere Fouke wolde nought soo:
The hed he smot the body froo.
The lordynges of that cyté *[Nineveh]*
Agayn hem comen and fellen on kne, *Before him came and kneeled*
And the keyes with hem they broughte.
Of mercy Kyng Richard besoughte: *begged King Richard for mercy*
Yif he wolde save here lyff,
They wolde be crystenyd, man and wyff, *woman*
And wenden with hym, withouten fayle, *go to fight*
In the brest of every bataylle, *front*
And of hym, holden that cyté.
Kyng Richard grauntyd with herte free. *agreed willingly*
A bysschop he leet come anon,
And dede hem crystene, everylkon,
Lytyl, mekyl, lasse and more,
In that tyme crystynyd wore.
Kyng Richard a whyle there lefte stylle; *remained quietly*
The comounners servyd hym at wylle.
Of alle that he with hym broughte,
Betere myghte thay serve hym noughte.
The chef Sawdon of Hethenysse *Muslim territory*
To Babyloyne was flowen, iwisse. *had fled*
His counseyl he ofsente that tyme, *sent for*
There semblyd many a bold paynyme. *assembled*
Syxty thousand there were telde *counted*
Of gylte spores in the feelde, *gilded spurs (knights)*
Withouten footmen and putayle *foot soldiers*
That ther come in to batayle.
As he sayde that was the spye
That tolde the folk on bothe partye, *counted; sides*
Twoo hundryd thousand of hethene men
To batayle hadde the Sawden.
Lystnys lordes, yungge and olde,
For His love that Judas solde.
The men that love treweth and ryght,

[1] *For a great price did they barter their lives*

Evere he sendes hem strengthe and myght:
That was there ful weel sene. *very well seen*
Oure Crystene hoost, withoute wene, *without doubt*
Was, as we in booke fynde,
No more but foure score thousynde. *than eighty thousand*
Kyng Richard thrytty thousand ladde,
For Phelyp and hys men were badde. *worthless*
Fyfty thousand hadde hee, *[Saladin]*
By that on syde of that cytee *one*
That kepte withinne Sarezynes stoute:
Was non so bold to passen oute,
And Kyng Richard on that othir syde lay, *While*
On batayll redy every daye
With mangenels and with spryngeles,
With manye arewes and quarelles.
Was no Sarezyn so stoute
Ovyr the walles to loken oute.
The cyté was so ful strong withinne,
That no man myghte unto hem wynne. *make [his] way to them*
Oure stronge engynes, for the nones,
Broken here walles with harde stones,
Here gatys and here barbycan. *fortified gate or bridge*
Be ye sekyr, the hethene man *Be assured*
Gaf the encountre hard and strong *Waged the combat*
That manye a man was slayn among.
For hadde Phelyp trewe bee *honorable*
At that sege of that cytee,
Hadde ther non iscapyd than, *then*
Hethene kyng, ne Sawdan,
That they ne hadde be slayn dounryght: *Who would not; killed outright*
For Kyng Richard ever upon the nyght, *at all times*
Whenne the sunne was gon to reste,
With hys hoost he wolde be prest, *ready*
Gaf the bataylle hard and smerte, *swiftly*
That no paynym myghte withsterte, *mount resistence*
And slowgh hem doun gret plenté,
And wylde fyr caste in to the cytee.
The Sarazynes defendyd hem faste *strongly*
With bowe Turkeys and arweblaste.
Hard fyght was hem bytwene:
So sayde thay that it sene.
Quarellys, arwes, al so thykke flye *flew as thick*
As it were thondyr in the skye, *a thunderstorm*
And wylde fyr the folk to brenne. *burn*
A counsayl took the hethene menne *A decision made*
To fyghte with hem in the feelde: *against them*
They wolde nought the cyté yelde.

Of Kyng Richard myghte they nought spede *From; succeed*
To take trewes for no mede. *no (any) price*
"For no thyng," sayde Richard than,
"Tyl I have slawe the Sawdan,
And brend that is in the cytee!" *burned those who are*
The latemere tho turnyd aghee *translator; then turned back*
To that other syde of the toun,
And cryeden "Trewes!" with gret soun
To the false kyng of Fraunce;
And he hem grauntyd with a myschaunse *ill fortune*
For a porcyoun of golde.

Ellys hadde the toun ben yolde, *surrendered*
And the Sarezynes islayn;
But the Sowdan was full fayne, *very joyful*
And alle here folk on Richard felle, *descended upon (engaged with)*
For that othir syde was stylle.
Kyng Richard wende that Phelip foughte, *hoped*
And he and hys men dede ryght noughte, *And yet he [Philip]; nothing*
But maden hem merye al that nyghte,
And were traytours in that fyghte.
He lovyd nought crownes for to crake,
But doo tresoun and tresore take.
  Tho Kyng Phelyp to Richard sende,
Hou he myght him no lenger defende:
For hungyr, he and his men alsoo
Moste breke sege and goo. *must end the siege*
Woo was kyng Richard than,
And sayde, "Traytour, false man!
For covaytyse of tresour
He dos hymself gret dyshonour
That he schal Sarezynys respyt gyve.
It is harme that swylke men lyve!"
He brekes sege and gynnes to withdrawe:
Thenne were the Sarezynes wundyr fawe; *happy*
Gret joye made hem among,
Carollyd, trumpyd, and merye song. *Danced; merrily*

  The nexte day aftyr than,
Messangeres comen fro the Sawdan,
And grette Richard in fayr manere,
And sayden: "Sere, yif thy wyl were,
My lord, the Sawdon to thee sente,
Yif thou wylt graunte in presente: *If you will permit, at present*
Thou art strong in flesch and bones,
And he doughty for the nones,
Thou doost hym gret harme, he says,

And destroyyst hys countrays,
Slees hys men and eetes among. *slay and eat his men*
Al that thou werres, it is with wrong. *wage war on; wickedly*
Thou cravyst herytage in this lande, *sovereignty*
And he dos thee weel to undyrstande
That thou hast thertoo no ryght!
Thou sayst thy God is ful of myght:
Wylt thou graunte with spere and scheelde,
To deraye the ryght in the felde, *vindicate; claim*
With helme, hawberk, and brondes bryght, *swords*
On stronge stedes, goode and lyght, *swift*
Whether is of more power, *Which*
Jhesu or Jubyter?
And he sente thee to say this: *dispatched you*
Yif thou wylt have an hors of his? *(see note)*
In all the landes there thou hast gon,
Swylk on say thou nevere non! *Such [a] one you never saw not one*
Fauvel of Cypre, ne Lyard of prys, *of great value*
Are nought at nede as that he is;[1]
And yif thou wylt, this selve day, *same*
It schal be brought thee to asay." *test*
Quod kyng Richard: "Thou sayst weel!
Swylke an hors, be Seynt Mychel,
I wolde have to ryden upon,
For myn are wery and forgon; *all exhausted*
And I schal, for my Lordes love,
That syttes heyghe in hevene above,
And hys owne hors be good, *Even if*
With a spere schede hys blood. *[Saladin's]*
Yif that he wole graunte and holde *promise and perform*
In this manere that thou hast tolde,
As I moste, God my soule yelde, *release*
I schal hym meten in the feelde.
Bydde hym sende that hors to me;
I schal asaye what that he bee. *I shall ascertain what sort that he be*
Yif he be trusty, without fayle,
I kepe non othir into batayle." *take (desire)*
The messanger thenne hom wente,
And tolde the Sawdon in presente, *at once*
Hou Kyng Richard wolde hym mete;
The ryche Sawdon also skete, *fierce*
A noble clerk he sente fore then,
A maystyr nigromacien. *necromancer*
That conjuryd, as I yow telle,
Thorwgh the feendes craft of helle,

[1] *Are useless in time of peril compared to what he is*

Twoo stronge feendes of the eyr
In lyknesse of twoo stedes feyr,
Lyke bothe of hewe and here. — *Both of like color and hair*
As thay sayde that were there,
Nevere was ther sen non slyke. — *none such*
That on was a mere lyke, — *like a mare*
That other, a colt, a noble stede.
Where he were in ony nede, — *in any trouble*
Was nevere kyng ne knyght so bolde
That whenne the dame neyghe wolde, — *mother*
Scholde hym holde agayn his wylle,[1] — *constrain him (the horse)*
That he ne wolde renne here tylle, — *run towards her*
And knele adoun and souke hys dame: — *suckle his mother*
That whyle the Sawdon with schame — *At that time*
Scholde Kyng Richard soone aquelle. — *kill*
   Al thus an aungyl gan hym telle
That come to hym aftyr mydnyght,
And sayde: "Awake thou, Goddes knyght!
My Lord dos thee to undyrstande
That thee schal come an horse to hande. — *A horse shall be made available to you*
Fayre he is, of body pyghte, — *well built*
To betraye thee yif the Sawdon myghte.
On hym to ryde have thou no drede:
He schal thee helpe at thy nede.
Purveye a tree, styf and strong, — *Obtain*
Though it be fourty foote long,
And trusse it ovyrthwert his mane: — *And fasten it crosswise over his mane*
Alle that he metes schal have his bane; — *destruction (death)*
With that tree he schal doun felle. — *vanquish*
It is a feend as I thee telle.
Ryde upon hym in Goddes name,
For he may doo thee no schame. — *cause you*
Tak a brydyl," the aungyl seyde,
"And mak it fast upon hys hede,
And be the brydyl in his mouth,
Thou schalt turne hym north and south.
He schal thee serve al to thy wylle,
When the Sawdon rydes thee tylle. — *at you*
Have here a spere hed of steel:
He has non armure iwrought soo weel
That it ne wole perce be thou bolde!" — *you may be sure*
But whenne he hadde thus itolde,
Agayn to hevene he is wente. — *departed*
   At morwen hys hors was to hym sente.
Kyng Richard of the horse was blythe,

[1] *Would be able to constrain him against his will*

And dyghte hym a sadyl al soo swythe. — *prepared himself*
Both his arsouns weren of yren, — *saddlebows*
For they scholde be stronge and dyren. — *lasting*
With a cheyne they gyrde hym faste.[1]
The brydyl upon his hed he caste
As the aungyl hadde hym taught.
Twoo goode hokes forgat he naught — *not*
In hys arsoun he sette before. — *On his saddelbow he placed*
With wax he stoppyd his eeres thore,
And sayde, "Be the aposteles twelve, — *(see note)*
Though thou be the devyl hym selve,
Thou schalt me serve at this nede!
He that on the Roode gan blede,
And sufryd grymly woundes fyve, — *(see note)*
And siththen ros from deth to lyve, — *after that*
And boughte mankynde out of helle,
And siththen the fendes pousté gan felle,[2]
And aftyr steygh up into hevene, — *ascended*
Now God, for his names sevene,
That is on God in trynité,
In his name, I comaunde thee — *the horse*
That thou serve me at wylle!" — *at my command*
He schook his hed and stood ful stylle. — *[The horse]*

At morwe, as soone as it was lyght,
And Kyng Richard was thus dyght, — *rigged (prepared)*
Syxe Sawdones with gret route — *a large company*
Of the cytee comen oute,
And bataylld hem on a ryver. — *lined up in formation*
With brode scheeldes and helmes cler. — *gleaming*
That day was told, withoute lesynges, — *counted*
Of sawdons and of hethene kynges,
An hondryd and yit wel moo, — *even considerably more*
The leste brought with hym thoo — *least [powerful]*
Twenty thousand and yit ten. — *in addition ten*
Agayn on of oure Crystene men, — *one*
There were a doseyn, be the leste: — *at least*
As men myghten se in here foreste
Of Sarezynes, so ferde the hoost: — *appeared*
Weel a ten myle of a coost! — *a side*
They made scheltroun and batayle byde; — *battle formation; awaited*
Messangerys betwen gan ryde
To Kynge Phelyp and to Kyng Richard,
Yif they wolde holde foreward — *keep the pledge*

[1] *With a chain they fastened the saddle girth upon him (the horse) securely*

[2] *And afterward the devil's power overwhelmed*

That they made the day before.
The Sarezynes ful redy wore:
Three hundryd thousand and moo ther bee.
Kyng Richard lokyd and gan to see,
As snowgh lygges on the mountaynes, *lies*
Behelyd were hylles and playnes *Covered*
With hawberkes bryghte and helmes clere.
Of trumpes and of taboure re,
To here the noyse it was wundyr.
As though the world above and undyr
Sholde falle, so ferde the soun.
Oure Crystene men make hem boun. *ready*
Kyng Richard hem no thyng ne dradde, *feared them not at all*
To his men, "Has armes!" he gradde. *"To arms!"; called out*
And sayde, "Felawes, for love of the roode,
Looke ye ben of coumfort good! *See that you are of good comfort*
And yif we gete the prys this day, *prize (victory)*
Of hethenesse al the nobelay *All the valor of the Muslim world*
For evere more we have wunne. *will have conquered*
For He that made mone and sunne,
Be oure help and oure myght!
Beholdes hou my self schal fyghte
With spere, swerd, ax of steel,
But I this day note hem weel, *Unless; use*
Evermore fro henne forward *from this time*
Holdes me a feynt coward
But every Crystene man and page, *But rather*
Have this nyght unto his wage *for his effort*
An hed of a Sarezyn
Thorwgh Goddes help and alsoo myn!
Swylk werk I schal among hem make *Such*
Of tho that I may ovyrtake,
That fro this to domysday, *Doomsday*
They schole speke of my pay!" *reprisal*
Oure Crystene men ben armyd weel,
Bothe in yryn and in steel.
The kyng of Fraunce with his batayle *battalion*
Is redy the Sarezynes to asayle.
Above the Sarezynes they ryden, *rode*
And scheltroun pyghten and batayle abyden,[1]
And forstoppyd the lande wayes: *blocked; routes*
They myghte nought flee into the cuntrayes, *the open country*
Ne no socour to hem come, *Nor any help*
But yif they were slayn or nome! *Unless; captured*
The Frenssche gunne blowe bost and make *bragged loudly and pretended*

[1] *And set up in formation and awaited battle*

To sloo Sarezynes and crownes crake, *heads split*
But in jeste as it is tolde, *chronicle*
Non of hem was so bolde
For to breke the Sarezynes scheltrome *battle formation*
Tyl kyng Richard hym self come.
Now sewyd Richard with his hoost, *went*
And closyd hem in be anothir coost, *encircled; side*
Betwyxen hem and the cyté,
That no Sarezyn myghte flee.
Thenne hadde Richard hoostes three:
That on gaf asawt to the cytee, *one assaulted*
The othere twoo with hym he ladde.
To bryngen hym his hors he badde *requested*
That the Sawdon hadde hym sent.
He sayde, "With hys owne present
I schal hym mete longe or nyght." *before*
To lepe to horse tho was he dyght;
Into the sadyl or he leep,
Of manye thynges he took keep.
Hym lakkyd nought but he it hadde;
Hys men hym broughte al that he badde.
A quarry tree of fourty foote, *sturdy*
Before his sadyl anon dede hote *did command*
Faste that men scholde it brase, *Securely; fasten*
That it fayleyd for no case: *failed for no reason*
So they dede with hookes of yren *They did so*
And good rynges that wolde duren. *links*
Other festnynge non ther was *binding*
Then yryne cheynes for alle cas,
And they were iwrought ful weel.
Bothe in gerthes and in peytrel, *upon girths; breastplate*
A queyntyse of the kynges owen, *An ornament*
Upon hys horse was ithrowen. *put*
Before hys arsoun, his ax of steel, *saddlebow*
By that other syde, his masuel. *mace*
Hymself was richely begoo *ornamented*
From the crest unto the too. *top of the helmet; toe*
He was armyd wondyr weel,
And al with plates of good steel,
And ther above an hawberk;
A schaft wrought of trusty werk; *lance*
On hys schuldre a scheeld of steel
With three lupardes wrought ful weel. *leopards; fashioned*
An helme he hadde of ryche entayle; *lavish ornamentation*
Trysty and trewe his ventayle.
On his crest a douve whyte,
Sygnificacyoun of the Holy Speryte.

Upon a croys the douve stood,
Of gold wrought riche and good.
God hymself, Marye, and Jhon,
As he was nayleyd the roode upon,
In signe of hym for whom he faught.
The spere hed forgat he naught:
Upon his spere he wolde it have,
Goddes hyghe name theron was grave. *engraved*

Now herkenes what oth they swore
Ar they to the batayle wore. *Before*
Yif it were soo that Richard myghte
Sloo the Sawdon in feeld with fyghte,
Hee and alle hese scholde gon *his [men]*
At here wylle everylkon
Into the cyté of Babyloyne *Cairo*
And the kyngdome of Massedoyne *Macedonia*
He scholde have undyr his hand;
And yif the Sawdon of that land
Myghte sloo Richard in that feeld,
With sweerd or spere undyr scheeld,
That Crystene men scholden goo *Those*
Out of that land for everemoo,
And Sarezynes haven here wylle in wolde. *have their will far and wide*
Quod Kyng Richard: "Therto, I holde,
Thertoo, my glove, as I am knyght!"
They ben armyd and weel adyght; *well equipped*
Kyng Richard into the sadyl leep.
Whoo that wolde therof took keep,
To se that syghte was ful fayr.
The stedes ran ryght with gret ayr, *straight; vigor*
Al so harde as they myghte dure. *as hard; endure*
Aftyr here feet sprong the fure. *fire*
Tabours beten and trumpes blowe.
There myghte men see in a throwe *moment*
How Kyng Richard, the noble man,
Encountryd with the Sawdan,
That cheef was told of Damas. *was held to be from Damascus*
Hys trust upon his mere was. *(see note)*
Therfore, as the book telles,
Hys crouper heeng al ful of belles *crupper*
And hys peytrel and his arsoun: *breastplate*
Three myle myghten men here the soun!
The mere gan nyghe, here belles to ryng, *neigh*
For gret pryde, withouten lesyng.
A brod fawchoun to hym he bar;
For he thoughte that he wolde thar

Have slayn Kyng Richard with tresoun — *deceitfulness*
Whenne his horse hadde knelyd doun
As a colt that scholde souke; — *suckle*
And he was war of that pouke. — *But; evil spirit*
Hys eeres with wex were stoppyd faste,
Therfore was Richard nought agaste. — *fearful*
He strok the feend that undyr hym yede,
And gaf the Sawdon a dynt of dede. — *heroic blow*
In hys blasoun, verrayment, — *On his shield, truly*
Was ipayntyd a serpent.
With the spere that Richard heeld,
He bar hym thorwgh undyr the scheeld.[1]
None of hys armes myghte laste:
Brydyl and paytrel al tobraste; — *breastplate [for a horse]; broke all apart*
Hys gerth and hys styropes alsoo;
The mere to the grounde gan goo. — *went*
Mawgrý hym, he garte hym stoupe[2]
Bakward ovyr his meres croupe, — *hindquarters*
His feet toward the fyrmamente;
Behynde the Sawdon the spere outwente. — *At the backside of*
He leet hym lye upon the grene.
He smote the feend with spores kene; — *spurred*
In the name of the Holy Gost,
He dryves into the hethene hoost,
And also soone as he was come,
He brak asyndry the scheltrome. — *shattered; formation*
For al that evere before hym stode,[3]
Horse and man to erthe yode, — *went*
Twenty foote on every syde.
Whom that he overraughte that tyde, — *caught*
Of lyf ne was here waraunt non! — *In that place was no safeguarding of life*
Thorwghout he made hys hors to gon. — *To every part*
As bees swarmen in the hyves,
Crystene men in aftyr dryves,
Stryke thorwgh that doun they lygges,
Thorwgh the myddyl and the rygges. — *backs*
   Whenne they of Fraunce wysten — *knew*
That the maystry hadde the Crysten, — *victory; Christian*
They were bolde, here herte they took, — *regained courage*
Stedes prekyd, schaftes schook.
The Kyng Phelyp with a spere,
An hethene kyng gan doun bere; — *overthrew*
And othere eerles and barouns,

[1] *He pierced him all the way through under the shield*

[2] *Despite all he could do, he was compelled to fall*

[3] *In spite of all who ever stood in front of him*

Stronge men of grete renouns,
Slowen the Sarezynes dounryght.
Of Yngelond, many a noble knyght
Wroughte weel there that day. *Performed*
Of Salysbury, that Longespay
To grounde he feelde with his brond *sword*
Alle that he before hym fond.
Next Kyng Richard evere he was, *Nearest to*
And the noble baroun, Sere Thomas,
Fouk Doyly, Robert Leycetre:
In Crystenedom, ther were non betre.
Where that ony of hem come,
They sparyd neyther lord ne grome, *retainer (youth)*
That they ne dreven alle adoun. *Lest they not strike all down*
That Sarezynes that weren withinne the toun, *Those*
For gret sorwe that they sen,
They wepte with bothe here eyen,
And "Mercy!" lowde thenne they cryde.
They wolden kaste up the gates wyde,
And lete hem at here wyl in come.
The Crystene have the cyté nome.
Anon hastely withalle, *at that time*
They setten baners upon the walle,
The kynges armes of Yngelande.
Whenne Saladyn gan undyrstande
That the cyté yolden was,
He gan to crye, "Allas, allas!
The prys of hethenesse is done,[1]
And gan to flee also soone,
And fayn alle thoo that myghte. *happy [were]*
And Kyng Richard, that noble knyghte,
Whenne he seygh the Sawdon fleygh,
"Abyde, coward!" he cryede on heygh, *Stay; in loud voice*
"And I schal thee proven fals,
And thy cursede goddes als."
Kyng Richard dryves aftyr fast;
The Sawdon was ful sore agast.
A gret wode before hym he sees,
Thedyr in wol faste he flees.
Kyng Richard neyghyd the wode nere, *drew close to the wood*
He doutyd for encumbrere: *was fearful because of encumbrance*
He myghte nought in for his tree.
His horse agayn soone tournyd hee
And mette with an hethene kyng.
He took his ax out of the ryng,

[1] *The nobility (pre-eminence) of the Muslim lands is finished*

And hytte hym on hygh upon the crest
And clef hym doun unto the brest.
Anothir he raughte upon the scheeld *struck*
That helme and hed fleygh into the feeld.
Syxe he slowgh of hethene kynges,
To telle the sothe in alle thynges.
  In the jeste, as we fynde,
That moo than syxty thousynde
Of empty stedes aboute yede, *wandered*
Up to the feetlakkes in the bloode, *fetlocks*
Astray they yeden with grete pride;
The man that wolde myght ryde.
The batayle laste tyl it was nyght,
But whenne thay weren islayn dounryght *outright*
The Sarezynes that they myghte ovyrtake,
Gret joye gan the Crystene make,
Knelyd and thankyd God of hevene,
Wurschepyd hym and hys names sevene.
On bothe sydes were folk slawe.
The numbre of the Crystene lawe
That lay ded in the feelde,
To God they gunne the soules yelde:
There were slawen hundredes three;
Of Sarezynes was ther more plenté,
Syxty thousand and yit moo.
Loo, swylke grace God sente thoo!
  The Crystene to the cyté gon;
Of gold and sylvyr and precyous ston,
They founde inowgh, withouten fayle,
Mete and drynk and othir vytayle. *provisions*
At morwen whenne Kyng Richard aros,
Hys dedes were noble, and his los. *fame*
Sarezynes before hym came,
And askyd hym Crystyndame. *And requested of him the Christian faith*
There were crystenyd, as I fynde,
More than fourty thousynde.
Kyrkes they maden of Crystene lawe, *Churches*
And here Mawmettes leet doun drawe.[1]
And that wolden nought Crystene become, *those*
Richard leet slen hem, alle and some. *Richard commanded that they be slain*
They departyd the grete tresour *divided*
Among the Crystene with honour,
Erl, baroun, knyght, and knave,
As mekyl as they wolde have.

[1] *And caused their Muhammad's [idols] to be smashed*

There they sojournyd fourtene nyght.
On a day they have hem dyght:
Toward Jerusalem gunne they ryde.
Kyng Phelyp spak a wurd of pryde:
"Kyng Richard, lystene to me,
Jerusalem, that ryche cyté,
Though thou it wynne, it schal be myn."
"Be God," quod Richard, "and Seynt Austyn, *St. Augustine*
And as God doo my soule boote, *help my soul*
Of my wynnyng noghte half a foote
Thou ne schalt have of no lande!
I doo thee weel to undyrstande!
And yif thou wylt have it," he seyde then,
"Goo and gete it with thy men!
Myn offeryng," quod Richard, "loo it here, *see it here*
I wyl come the cyté no nere!"
An arweblast of vys he bente,
A floryng to the cyté he sente *florin (a gold coin)*
That was in signifyaunce *was a sign*
Of Jhesu Crystys honouraunce.
For yre become syke the kyng of Fraunce;
The leche sayde withouten dotaunce, *physician; doubt*
That he myghte nought hool ben *be healthy*
But he to Fraunce wolde tourne ayen. *Unless*
The kyng hys counsayl undyrstood
And sayd it was trewe and good.
His schyppes he leet dyghte, more and lesse, *ordered made ready*
And wente home at Alhalewe-messe. *the festival of All Saints*
King Richard on hym gan crye, *King Richard cried out against him*
And sayde he dede gret velonye
To wende hom for maladye
Out of the lond of Surrye
To don were Goddes servyse, *Until God's service was finished*
For lyf or deth in ony wyse.
The kyng of Fraunce wolde hym nought here,
But departyd in this manere;
And aftyr that partyng, for sothe,
Evere yit they were wrothe. *Ever from that time*

Kyng Richard withouten bost,
To Jaffe wente with his hoost.
The kynges pavyloun fair and fyne,
He leete tylde in on gardyn. *He caused to be pitched in a garden*
Othere lordes gan aboute sprede,
Here pavyloun in a fayr mede.
Kyng Richard with hys meyné alle, *retinue*
Of the cyté leet make the walle,

That nevere was non in Sarezyneys *in Saracen territory*
So strong wrought and of gret ryhcheys. *of great opulence; (see t-note)*
That castel was strong and ryche,
In the world was non it lyche.
Theder myght come by the see,
Of every good gret plenté.
He made here warde of noble knyghtes, *guard*
Stoute in armes, stronge in fyghtes.
Inowe men myghte wende aboute, *Enough; roam about*
Manye mile withouten doute.
Kyng Richard dwellyd with honure
Tyl that Jaffe was maad al sure. *secure; (see t-note)*

Fro thennes to Chaloyn they wente, *Ascalon*
And fond the walles al torente. *destroyed*
Large and fayr was that cyté:
Kyng Richard therof hadde pyté.
He besoughte the lordes alle,
Of the cyté to make the walle;
And the lordes, everylkon,
Grauntyd hym hys askyng anon,
Save the Duke of Ostryke: *Austria*
Kyng Richard he thoughte to beswyke. *deceive*
Kyng Richard gan to travayle *worked*
Aboute the walles, saunfayle,
So they dede, on and othir. *So they did, one and another*
Fadyr and sone, eme and brothir *uncle (nephew)*
Made morter and layde ston
With here myght, everylkon.
Every kyng and emperere,
Bare stones or mortere,
Save the duke; ful of prede, *pride*
He ne wolde hem helpe for no nede. *reason*

On a day, Kyng Richard hym mette,
And hendely the kyng hym grette, *graciously*
And bad hym, for hys curteysye,
Make of the walles hys partye; *share*
And he answeryd in this manere:
"My fadyr nas masoun ne carpentere, *was not*
And though youre walles scholde al toschake, *break apart*
I schal nevere helpe hem to make!"
Kyng Richard pykkyd gret errour; *became greatly enraged*
Wraththe dede hym chaunge colour. *Anger made him*
The duke with hys foot he smot
Agayn the brest, God it wot, *God knows it*
That on a ston he ovyrthrewe. *fell*

It was evyl don, be Seynt Mathewe! *unluckily done*
"Fy! a debles, vyle coward! *Fie a devil*
In helle be thou hangyd hard!
Goo quykly out of oure hoost!
Curs hast thou of the Holy Goost!
By the sydes of swete Jhesus,
Fynde I thee, traytour among us,
Ovyr this ylke dayes thre,
My self schal thy bane bee.
Traytour, we travayle day and nyght,
In werre, in wakyng, and in fyght, *maintaining a watch*
And thou lys as a vyl glotoun, *parasite*
And restes in thy pavyloun,
And drynkes the wyn, good and strong,
And slepes al the nyght long.
I schal breke thy banere
And slynge it into the revere!" *hurl*
Home wente the duke ful wroth,
Hys owne lyf hym wax loth. *His own life grew unpleasant to him*
Of that despyte, he was unblythe *insult; unhappy*
And trussyd hys harneys al so swythe, *loaded; armor and weapons*
And swor by Jhesu in Trynyté,
And he myghte evere his tyme see, *If*
Of Richard scholde he be so awreke *avenged*
That al the world scholde therof speke.
He heeld hym al to weel foreward: *He kept the pledge all too well*
In helle moot he be hangyd hard! *may*
For thorwgh hys tresoun and trehcherye,
And thorwgh the waytyng of hys aspye, *covert watch; spying*
Kyng Richard he dede gret schame
That turnyd al Yngelond to grame. *grief*
A lytyl lengere hadde he most *been permitted to*
Have levyd, for the Holy Gost,
Ovyr kyng, duke, and emperour,
He hadde be lord and conquerour.
Al Crystyanté and al Paynym *Heathendom*
Scholde have holden undyr hym.
The Duke of Ostrych hyyd hym faste
Away with his meyné in haste.
With hym the duke of Burgoyne,
The folk of Fraunce and the eerl of Boloyne.
Kyng Richard brak the dukes baner,
And keste it into the rever,
And cryyd on hym with voys ful stepe, *against him; loud*
"Home, schrewe! Coward! and slepe!
Come no more in no wyse,
Nevere eft in Goddes servyse!" *again*

The duke awey prekyd thenne. — *galloped away*
For yre his herte began to brenne. — *burn*
Kyng Richard lefte with hys Englys,
Tuskaynes, Lumbardes, Gascoynes, iwis,
Scottes, Yrysch, folk of Bretayne,
Gennayes, Bascles, and of Spayne, — *Genoese; Basques*
And made the wal day and nyght
Tyl it were maad strong, aplyght. — *in faith*
  Than Kynge Rycharde with grete pyne — *When*
Had made the walles of Chalyne, — *Ascalon*
All his hoost with hym he taas, — *takes*
And wente forth a grete paas.
The fyrst nyght in the name of Marye,
He laye at a towne that hyght Famelye. — *Famiya(?)(a Syrian town)*
On the morowe he let hym arme wele
Bothe in yryn and in steel;
Be the maryn forth he wente — *sea-coast*
To Albary, a castel gente — *splendid*
That was a castel of Sarezynesse — *of Heathendom*
Ful of stor and gret ryhchesse: — *provisions*
Bothe fat flesch and lene,
Whete and ooten, pesen and bene. — *oats; peas*
Kyng Richard it wan, and sojournyd there
Thre monethis al plenere; — *Three months in full*
And sente spyes every wayes — *every direction*
For to aspye the cuntrayes. — *countryside*

  Of castel Daroun, Kyng Richard herde — *(see note)*
Al togedere hou it ferde.
Al was it ful of Sarezynes
That were Goddes wytherwynes. — *adversaries*
Kyng Richard hyyd thedyr faste,
The Sarezynes for to make agaste.
So longe he wente by hys journay,
He come thedyr be Seynt James day. — *25 July*
He besegyd castel Daroun
To take the castel and the toun.
The castel was maad of swylke ston
That they doutyd sawt ryght non. — *did not fear an assault*
Aboute the castel was a dyke:
They hadde nevere isen non slyke — *never seen such*
The Sarezynes cryyd in here langage:
"Crystene houndes of evyl rage!
But ye wenden swythe home, — *Unless; travel*
Here have ye fet youre dome!" — *received your condemnation*
Whenne Kyng Richard herde that cry,
He swor hys oth be Seynte Mary,

The Sarezynes scholde be hangyd alle,
Or swylke a cas hem scholde befalle. — *Before; such a fate*
The Crystene asaylyd and they defendyd:
Many quarel out they sendyd.
Al that day and al that nyght,
They and the Crystene heeld the fyght.
The Crystene sen thay myghte nought spede; — *attain success*
Kyng Richard took an othir rede. — *course of action*
Kyng Richard garte alle the Englys, — *caused*
Schere ryssthys in the marys — *To cut rushes in the marshes*
To fylle the dykes of Daroun,
To take the castel and the toun.
Twoo grete gynnes for the nones, — *machines*
Kynge Richard sente for to caste stones.
By water they were ibrought anon;
The mate gryffoun was that on — *one*
That was set upon an hel — *hill*
To breke doun tour and castel.
That othir hyghte Robynet,
That on an othir hyl was set.
Kyng Richard keste a mangenel — *placed*
That threw to an other tourel. — *turret*
Kyng Richard dede the ryssches faste
Bynden, and into the dyke caste,
And al playne the dykes made. — *level*
The Sarezynes therof hadde no drade, — *fear*
For wylde fyr theron they caste,
The ryssches be comen on fyre in haste, — *rushes*
And brenden ryght to the grounde,
Ryght withinne a lytyl stounde. — *a short time*
Of oure Crystene, many an hundryd
Were therof gretly awundryd. — *astonished*
The mangeneles threw alway, — *continually*
And brak the walles nyght and day.
The robynet and the mate gryffoun,
Al that they hytte wente adoun,
So that withinne a lytyl stounde,
The outemeste wal was layde to grounde, — *outermost*
And fyllyd ful the grete dyke,
And oure men entryd hastelyke.
Tho oure Crystene men myghten wel — *Then*
Entren into Dareyn Castel.
The eerl of Leyceterre, Sere Roberd,
The treweste knyght in myddylerd, — *on this earth*
He was the fyrste, withoute fayle,
That Daroun Castel gan assayle. — *did attack*

Up he lyfte hys banere,
And smot upon hys destrere. *spurred; war-horse*
The Sarezynes, with mysaventoure, *with misfortune*
Fledde up into the heyeste toure;
And manye of hem stoden withoute,
And foughten faste in gret doute. *stoutly; fear*
Agayn the Eerl, Sere Robard,
They gave many a dynt ful hard.
Many an helme was there ofwevyd, *struck off*
And many a bacynet was clevede. *basinet (under-helmet); split apart*
Scheeldes fele schorn in twoo;
Many stede stekyd alsoo. *stabbed*
Robert Tourneham with hys fawchoun,
There he crakyd many a croun.
The Longespay, the Eerl of Rychemeound,
Wolde spare non hethene hound.
Among hem come Kyng Richarde,
To fyghte weel no thyng he sparde.
Many on in a lytyl stounde
With his ax he felde to grounde.
Al on foote he gan fyghte.
Whenne the Sarezynes hadden syghte *saw*
Hou plenteuous was hys payment, *abundant*
Non there durste abyde hys dent. *dared wait for*
They wenten quyk, withoute fable,
And slowe here stedes in here stable, *slew*
The fayreste destreres and stedes,
That myght bere knyght in ony nedes. *difficult situations*
Whete and flour, flesche and lardere, *salted meat*
Al togedere they sette on fere. *fire*
They hadden levere to don soo *They preferred*
Thenne with here vytaylles helpe here foo.
By the brethe Richard aspyde, *smoke*
And slowgh dounright on ylke a syde
Alle that he myghte ovyrtake, *those*
None amendes must they make.
He gunne asayle the heye tour
With wyghte men of gret valour. *brave*
The Sarezynnes in the tour on hygh,
Seygh here endynge day was nygh. *Saw*
Wylde fyr swythe in haste *greatly*
Among the Crystene men they caste.
That fyr fleygh aboute so smerte *fiercely*
That manye Crystene men it herte.
They myghte nought longe suffre that thrawe; *pain*
Anon they gunnen hem withdrawe
A myle fro Daroun Castel.

They caste abrode many fyr-barel,[1]
Soone withinne a lytyl spase, *in a little while*
Thorwgh the help of Goddes grace,
The castel become on afyr al
Fro the tour to the outemeste wal.
Here houses brende and here hurdys, *burned; their hurdles*
Gret smoke ther arose, iwis.
The Sarezynes in the heyghe tour
Were in swyche strong dolour. *very great agony*
In the hete, they were almost ateynt, *overcome*
And in the smoke, nygh adreynt. *suffocated*
Ten ther cryd at on word: *in unison*
"Mercy, Kyng Richard, leve lord!
Let us goo out of this tour,
And thou schalt have gret tresour!
With lyf and leme thou lete us goo, *limb*
A thousand pound we geve thee too."
"Nay!" quod Richard, "Be Jhesu Cryst,
By hys deth and hys upryst, *resurrection*
Ye schole nevere come adoun
Tyl payed be youre raunsoun,
And yit her aftyr be at my wylle,
Whether I wole yow save or spylle, *slay*
Or elles ye schole here ryght sterve." *perish right here*
"Lord," they sayde, "we schole thee serve.
At thy wylle with us thou doo,
With that we may come thee too.
To honge or drawe, brenne or sle
Our fredome, lorde, is in thee."
Kynge Richard grauntyd than, *consented then*
And comaundyd every Crystene man
Lete the Sarezynys to borwe[2]
Tyl the sunne ros on morwe.
It was so don, as I fynde.
Kynge Rycharde let them faste bynde,
Upon a playn besyde the walle,
Kyng Richard bad lat brynge hem alle;
And he that payde a thousand pound
For hys hed myghte goo sound. *unharmed*
And that wolde so mekyl geve *And those who would so much give*
Tyl a certayn tyme, he leet hem leve; *to depart (live)*
And he that payde no raunsoun,
Als tyt the hed was stryken doun; *Right away*

---

[1] *They threw across the distance many barrels full of wild fire*

[2] *To allow the Saracens to ransom [themselves] (pledge surety)*

And thus Kyng Richard wan Daroun.
God geve us alle hys benysoun! *blessing*

Aftyr the wynnyng of Daroun,
Kyng Richard wente to another toun,
To Gatrys with fayr meyné *(see note)*
To besege that cyté.
Now herkenes hou he it wan,
And ye shall here of a doughty man,
A stout werreour and a queynte *skillful*
And nevere founden in herte feynte.
He that was lord of Gatris
Hadde ben a man of mekyl prys, *worth*
And fel to fyght ageyns hys foo; *fierce*
But that ylke tyme he was nought soo,
For he was fallen into elde, *old age*
That he myghte non armes welde.
But as he dede a fayr queyntyse, *ingenious ruse*
Herkenes now al in what wyse!
In myddes the toun upon a stage,
He leet make a marbyl ymage, *statue*
And corownyd hym as a kyng,
And bad his folk, olde and ying,
That they scholde nevere be aknowe *acknowledge (reveal)*
To Crystene man, hygh ne lowe,
That they hadde no lord of dygnyté *high rank*
But that ymage in that cyté.
Kyng Richard, the werreour kene,
There assaute he began bydene. *immediately*
Anon, his mangeneles were bente,
And stones to the cyté he sente.
The Sarezynes "Mercy!" cryede:
They wolde kaste up the gates wyde,
Yif it were Richardes wylle
That he wolde nought here peple spylle. *kill*
Kyng Richard grauntyd, withoute les, *without lie*
And they hadde entré al in pes.
Kyng Richard askyd at a word *in short order*
Of that cyté where was the lord,
And they answerde to the kyng
That they hadde non othir lordyng *ruler*
But that ymage of marbyl fyn,
And Mahoun, here god, and Appolyn. *their*
Kynge Rycharde stode, so sayth the boke,
And on the ymage he gan for to loke,
How hewge he was wrought and sterne, *massive*
And sayd to them all yerne:

"O, Sarezynes," sayde Richard, withouten fayle,
"Of youre lord I have mervayle! *I wonder greatly about your lord*
Yif I may, thorwgh my Lord so goode,
That boughte us alle upon the rode, *redeemed*
With a schaft breke his nekke asundir, *to pieces*
And ye may see that grete wundyr.
Wole ye leve alle upon my Lord?" *believe*
"Ye!" thay sayden at on word. *in unison*
Kyng Richard leet dyghte hym a schaft *a shaft made ready for himself*
Of trusty tree and kynde craft; *native skill*
And for it scholde be stronge and laste,
He leet bynde thertoo ful faste,
Foure yerdes of steel and yre; *poles; iron*
And Kyng Richard, the grete syre,
Leet sette theron a corounnal kene. *sharp spearhead*
Whenne it was redy on tosene, *to look upon*
Fauvel of Cypre was forth fette; *brought forth*
And in the sadyl he hym sette. *seated himself*
He rode the cours to the stage,
And in the face he smot the ymage.
That the hede flowe fro the body insundyr, *in two pieces*
And slowgh fyve Sarezynes therundyr.
Alle the othere seyde than
He was an aungyl and no man; *angel (devil) (see note)*
And alle becomen Crystene thore, *there*
Olde and ying, lesse and more,
And hastely, withouten lessyng,
Here olde lord they leet forth bryng *caused to be brought forth*
And tolde hys compassement. *scheming*
Kyng Richard lowgh with good entent, *cheerfully*
And gaf hym the cyté with wynne to welde, *with joy to govern*
Though he levyd Adammis elde. *Even if he lived as long as Adam did*

To Chaloyn Kyng Richard wente agayn,
Al be the maryn, soth to sayn. *by the sea-coast*
There he sojournyd fourtenyght
With many a noble and doughty knyght.
They pyght pavylyons fayre and well *set up*
To besege a strong castel
That was a lytyl besyde hym, *a little way from him*
Thre myle fro Castel Pylgrym,
With thykke walles and toures of pryde,
That was callyd Lefruyde. *(see note)*
The Sarezynes seygh the kyng come, *saw*
Weel they wende to be benome. *They very much expected to be taken*
Theyr hertes were full of wo
All by nyght awaye they flo *fled*

The gates they unschette ful yerne, *opened very quickly*
And fledden awey by a posterne. *a side gate (secret door)*
For al this wyde myddyl erde,
Durste they nought abyde Kyng Richerde. *confront*
The noble castel, verrayment,
Kyng Richard wan withoute dent. *without a blow*
Fro thennes he wente to Gybelyn;
Ther the Hospytaleres hadde wonyd in, *Where; dwelled in*
And Templeres bothe in fere, *both together*
And kepten the cyté many a yere. *held (defended)*
Whenne Bawdewyn was slayn with bronde, *sword*
Saladyn took that toun on honde. *under his control*
In that cyté was Seynt Anne ibore, *born*
That Oure Lady was of core. *Who was chosen [to bear] by Our Lady*
There they pyghte here pavyloun,
And with gret fors they wunne the toun.
And slowgh the Sarezynes all insame *all together*
That wolde nought leve in Crysteys name. *have faith in*

Thenne ther come most wykke tydyng, *distressing report*
To Quer de Lyoun, Richard, oure kyng: *Coeur*
Hou of Yngelond hys brothir Jhon,
That was the fendes flesshe and bon,
Thorwgh help of the barouns some,
The chaunceler they hadde inome, *had seized*
And wolde with maystry of hand, *dominance of armed might*
Be corownyd kyng in Yngeland
At Estyr day aftyrward.
Thenne answerde Kyng Richard:
"What devyl!" he sayde, "Hou gos this?
Telles Jhon of me no more prys,[1]
He wenes that I wil nought leve longe; *supposes; live*
Therfore, he wyl doo me wronge,
And yif he wende I were on lyve, *believed; alive*
He wolde nought with me stryve. *quarrel*
I wole me of hym so bewreke,[2]
That al the world therof schal speke!
And Jhon hym corowne at Estyr-tyde, *If*
Where wole he thenne me abyde? *face me in battle*
There is no kyng in Crystyanté,
Sertys, that schal his waraunt bee. *protector*
I ne may leve it for no nede *believe; any reason*
That Jhon, my brother, wil do this dede."

[1] *Does John count (appraise) me of no more worth*

[2] *I will avenge myself to such an extent on him*

"Yis, certes," quod the messangere,
He wyl do soo, be Seynt Rychere." *(see note)*
  Kyng Richard al this tydyng
In herte heeld but as lesyng. *lying*
Fro Gybelyn forth thenne he wente,
To Bethanye, a castel gente.
And slowgh there many an hethene man,
And the noble cyté wan.
Ther come othere messangers
That tolde Kyng Richard, stout and fers,
That Jhon, hys brothir, wolde bere
Corowne at Estren, he wolde swere.
Richard was loth withdrawe his hand *armed might*
Tyl he hadde wunne the Holy Land,
And slayn the sawdon with dynt of sword,
And avengyd Jhesu, oure Lord;
But he bethoughte hym aftyr then, *decided afterwards*
That he wolde leve there alle his men,
And with hys prevy meyné *band of retainers*
Into Yngelond thenne wolde hee,
And asesse the werre anon, *put an end to*
Betwyxe hym and hys borther Jhon,
And come agayn in hyyng, *in haste*
To fulfylle hys begynnyng. *To complete*

  And as he thoughte in hys herte, *(see note)*
A stout Sarezyn gan in sterte *rushed in*
That oughte Kyng Richard raunsoun *owed*
For the wynnyng of Daroun.
He spak to the kyng apertelyche, *openly*
Among the peple, pore and ryche:
"Sere, thou schalt aquyte me here,[1]
And alle oure other hostagere: *hostages*
Thorwgh my queyntyse and my gynne, *skill; ingenuity*
I schal doo thee gret tresore wynne. *cause*
More then an hundryd thousand pounde
Of floryns, both rede and sounde, *pure; unimpaired*
Of Saladynes cheef tresore,
And mekyl ryhchesse of here store.
Therto I laye in hostage my lyff, *To that, I pledge my life as security*
And my chyldre and my wyff:
But yif I doo thee to wynne that preye, *Unless; booty*
On evele deth do me to deye!"
Quod Richard: "Thou myscreaunt,

[1] *Sire, you will release me from my obligation here*

So as thou bylevest on Termagaunt,
Tel me now what folk it is, *company (group)*
I wene it is but al feyntys." *deceit*
"Thoo that lede the tresore, saunt fayle,
Sere, they are thre thousand chamayle, *camels*
And fyve hundryd ther are alsoo
Of asses and mules, and yit moo
That leden gold to Saladyn,
Tryyd sylvyr, and tresore fyn, *Refined*
Flour of whete and spysory, *spices*
Clothis of sylk and gold therby."
Sayde Kyng Richard: "So God thee deme, *may judge you*
Is ther mekyl peple the tresore to yeme?" *protect*
"Yé, Sere," he sayde, "ther are before
Knyghtes rydande syxty score, *riding*
And aftyrward, thousandes ten
Of swythe stronge, hethene men.
I herde hem speke in rownyng, *in whispers (private)*
They were aferyd of thee, Sere Kyng."
Quod Kyng Richard: "They schal it fynde,
Thowgh ther were syxty thousynde,
And I were but myself alone,
I wolde mete hem, everylkone.
Doo now, say me anon ryght, *tell me right now*
Where may I fynde hem this nyght?"
The Sarezyn sayde: "I thee telle
Where thou wylt abyde and dwelle. *wait and linger*
Here be southe, mylys ten, *southward*
Thou may fynde the hethene men.
There they wole resten and abyde
Tyl more folk come ther ryde."
The kyng hym graythid, and wente anon, *equipped himself*
Hys barouns aftyr, everylkon.
Al that nyght with fayr covey *company*
They rede forth by the wey.
Thenne sayde the spye to the kyng:
"Sere, make here thy restyng.
They are loggyd in this toun:
I wyl goo and aspye ther roun. *around*
Anon, I wole to hem goo,
And brewe hem a drynk of woo,
And saye to hem that Kyng Richard
Is at Jaffe to Yngeland ward.
They wole leve me with the beste, *believe me completely*
Thenne wole they gon to reste.
Thenne may thou to hem wende,
And slou hem alle faste slepende. *slay*

"Fy a debles," quod the kyng,
"God geve thee now an evyl endyng!
I am no traytour, tak thou kepe,
To sloo men whyl they slepe;
And ryght now here I wole abyde,
Tyl I see the Sarezynes come ryde.
Be cleer day upon the feeldes,
They schole see cloven helmes and scheldes.
Be they dukes, prynces, or kynges,
Here schole they make here endynges."
The Sarezyn the kyng answerde:
"Thy pere is nought in myddyl erde, *peer (equal)*
Ne non so mekyl of renoun. *Nor none so great*
Weel may thou hote Coer de Lyoun! *be named*
Therfore, I wole it nought hele, *conceal*
Ther are of Sarezynes twoo so fele *as worthy*
As thou hast folk in this cuntree,
Certaynly, I telle thee."
Quod kyng Richard: "God geve thee care! *distress*
Therfore is nought myn herte sare; *saddened*
For on of my Crystene men
Is wurth Sarezynes nyne or ten.
The moo ther be, the moo I schal sloo,
And wreke Jhesu of hys foo." *And avenge*
Forth wente the spye with then *with that*
To aspye the hethene men.
Al he spyyd here compassyng *plotting*
And tolde it Richard, oure kyng.
He gan crye, "Az armes, yare! *To arms, make ready*
Coer de Lyoun! Loo now they fare!" *Lo; go*
Anon leep Kyng Richard
Upon hys goode stede, Lyard;
And hys Ynglyssch and his Templers
Lyghtly lopen on here destrers,
And flynges into the hethene hoost, *rushes*
In the name of the Holy Goost.

As the Sarezynes with here nobelay *wealth*
To the Sawdon were in here way, *on their way*
Kyng Richard smot hem among; *struck among them*
There aros no blysseful song,
But to Termagaunt and Mahoun *(see note)*
They cryede faste, and to Plotoun.
Kyng Richard a kyng gan bere *did pierce*
Thorwgh the herte with a spere.
Aftyrward hys ax he drowgh,
And many an hethyn hound he slowgh.

Some he clevyd into the sadyl:
It bewepte the chyld al in the cradyl. *The child in the cradle grieved over it*
A kyng he clef unto the arsoun, *saddlebow*
That hym halp nought hys God, Mahoun.
Many an hethene Sarezyne
He sente there to helle pyne. *the torment of hell*
The Templers and the Hospytalers
Wunne there manye fayre destrers.
So longe they foughte, so says the story,
That Kyng Richard hadde the vyctory
Thorwgh help of hys gode knyghtys,
Stoute in armes and stronge in fyghgtes;
And manye scapyd with dedly wounde,
That ne levyd nought no stounde. *not long*
They wolde aftyr no more mete
Kyng Richard be wey ne strete.
Now may ye here the wynnyng *the booty*
That ther wan Richard, oure kyng.
Hors of prys and gret camayle, *of worth*
Fyve hundryd and ten, saun fayle.
Syxe hundryd hors of grete coursours *mighty chargers*
Chargyd al with riche tresours, *Loaded all*
That were in cofres bounden ferlye, *wonderfully*
With fyn sylvyr and gold ful trye. *refined*
Ther were thre hundryd mules and moo
That penyys and spyses boren thoo. *coins*
Ther aftyr fyftene hyndryd asse
Bar wyn and oyle, more and lasse.
And als manye with whete brede. *just as*
It was to Richard a gracyous dede! *fortunate*
When he al this tresore wan,
Home he wente to hys men than,
Into the cyté off Bethany the noble,
With that tresore and the moble. *movable goods*
He gaf the ryche and the lowe
Of his purchas good inowe. *gain; goods (wealth) enough*
He gaf hem destrers and coursours,
And delte among hem his tresours. *divided*
So Richard partyd hys purchas, *Thus (After); distributed; goods*
Of al Crystyndom belovyd he was.
Theraftyr, in a lytyl stounde,
Comen messaungerys of mekyl mounde: *great nobility*
The Bysschop of Chestyr was that on, *Chester; (see note)*
That othir, the abbot of Seynt Albon,
That brought hym lettres speciele, *(see note)*
Aselyd with the barouns sele, *Sealed*
That tolde hym his brothir, Jhon,

Wolde doo corowne hym anon, — *Would give himself the crown soon*
At the Pask, be comen dome, — *Easter, by unanimous judgment*
But he the rathir wolde come home,[1]
For the kyng of Fraunce with envye — *enmity*
Hath aryvyd in Normandye.

Quod Kyng Richard: "Be Goddes payne,
The devyl has to mekyl mayne! — *too much power*
Al here bost and here deray, — *outcry*
They schal abeye it sum day!" — *pay a high price*
And there he dwellyd tyl Halewemes, — *All Saints' Day (1 November)*
And thenne he passyd to Jaffes.
For sevene yer and yit more,
The castel he gan astore. — *stocked with provisions*
Fyftene thousand, I fynde in boke,
He lefte that cyté for to loke, — *watch over*
For to kepe weel that land
Out of Saladynys hand
Tyl he agayn come myghte
Frome Yngelond, as he had tyghte; — *intended*
And thenne he wente to Acres ward,
The doughty body, Kyng Richard.
Now of Saladyn speke we,
What dool he made and pyté, — *suffering; grief*
Whenne he wyste of that caas, — *found out*
That hys tresore robbyd was,
And for hys men that were slawe, — *slain*
He waryyd hys god, and cursyd his lawe, — *spoke impiously to*
And swor he wolde awroken be,
Myghte he evere hys tyme isee.
Soo that tyme a spye come in, — *After*
And sayde thus to Saladyn:
"Lord," he sayde, "be blythe of mode. — *happy in spirits*
For I thee brynge tydynges goode,
To thyn herte a blythe present.
Kyng Richard is to Acres went: — *gone*
For ovyr he wole to Yngelonde. — *will cross over*
For hym is come swylke a sonde — *such a message*
That Jhon, hys brother, I thee swere,
Wole elles hys corowne bere. — *Will otherwise*
Jaffes he hath stored a ryght,
With many a baroun and gentyl knyght.
Fyftene thousand, I wot ful weel,
Schal kepen wel that castel. — *defend*

[1] *Unless he [Richard] the sooner would come home*

Yif he may so weel spede,
Tyl he come from his thede. — *return; realm*
But see, Lord, withouten fayle,
Fro his body kyttes the tayle."[1]
Ofte was Saladyn wel and woo, — *happy and sorrowful*
But nevere soo glad as he was thoo. — *then*
The spye he gaf an hundrid besauntes — *bezants*
That broughte hym that presauntes, — *proposal*
And also a fayr destrere,
And a robe ifurryd with blaundenere. — *ermine?*
Thenne wolde he no lengere abyde;
He sente aboute on ylke a syde,
Upon leyme and upon lyff, — *On limb and on life*
Upon chyldryn and upon wyff,
That they come to hym belyve — *without delay*
To helpe hym out of londe dryve
Kyng Richard with hys grete tayle.
To hym come many an amyrayle,
Many a duke, and many a kyng,
And many ful gret lordyng
Of Egypte and of Arabye,
Of Capados and of Barbarye, — *Cappodocia; Barbary*
Of Europ and of Asclanoyne,
Of Ynde and of Babyloyne,
Of grete Grece and Tyre alsoo,
Of empyres and kyngdomes manye moo,
Of alle hethene land, I fynde,
Fo the Grekyssche see to grete Ynde. — *(see note)*

Charles Kyng ne Alysaundre, — *Charlemagne; Alexander the Great*
Of whom has ben so gret sclaundre, — *fame*
He hadde nevere swylke an hoost. — *so great an army*
In the cuntré ther he lay acoost, — *where; nearby*
Fyve myle it was of brede — *in breadth*
And more, I wene, so God me rede,[2]
Twenty myle it was of lengthe:
It was an hoost of gret strengthe.
To Jaffe cyté they comen skete; — *swiftly*
The Crystene men the gates dede schete.
Ther was withinne a lytyl thrawe, — *while*
On bothe half, many man slawe. — *slain*
So strong and hard was that batayle
That it ferde withouten fayle, — *proceeded (seemed)*

[1] *From his body, [you] cut the tail (cut off the source of support)*

[2] *And more, I believe, as God may guide me*

As it hadde ben fro hevene lyght, *the light of heaven*
Among the swerdes that were so bryght,
And evere the Crystene ful weel faught,
And slowen Sarezynes, but it servyd naught; *provided no benefit*
For it ferde thar, no man axen,[1]
As they out of the ground were waxen, *were growing out of the ground*
That no slaughtyr of swerdes kene *sharp*
Myghte there nothyng be sene.
  The Crystene fledde into the castel,
And kepten the gatys swyth wel. *defended the gates*
The Sarasynes the cyté nome
To theyr will and to theyr dome. *command*
Thenne began the Sarezynes
Undyr the wal to make mynes.
The Crystene men, for the nones,
Al tofrusschyd hem with stones. *Utterly crushed*
The Sarezynys yede aboute the wal,
And threwe and schotten in ovyr al;
Many a brennande, scharp quarel *burning, sharp bolt*
They schotten into Jaffe castel.
They soughten where they myghten beste
Oure Crystene men agreve meste. *most*
At the laste a gate they founde,
Nought faste schet at that stounde. *time*
There they fond strong metyng *combat*
With swerdes and speres ful grevyng. *very punishing*
To wedde they lefte a thousynd men, *They left dead*
And of the Crystene were slayn ten.
The Sarezynes, though they were stoute,
At the gate men putte hem oute.
The Sarezynes, for no nede, *on no account*
That day ne myghte they nought spede.
  At nyght be the mone cler,
The Crystene sente a messanger
To Kyng Richard to Acres cyté,
And prayde the kyng for Goddes pyté,
That he scholde to hem come
Or elles they were al inome. *captured*
They tolden hym the harde caas *circumstances*
Of the Sawdonys hoost, hou it was,
And but he come to hem anon,
They were forlorn, everylkon. *completely lost*
Kyng Richard answeryd anon ryght: *at once*
"Weel I knowe the Sawdonys fyght; *prowess*

[1] *How it turned out there, let no man ask*

He wole make a lytyl deray, *attack*
And al so tyt he wole hys way, *And right away he will [go] his way*
I nele for hym to hem wende, *I will not on account of him go to them*
But soone I wyll hem socour sende." *help*
He callyd to hym hys nevew, *nephew*
A baroun of ryght gret vertew *valor*
That hyghte Henry of Champayn,
And bad hym wende to Jaffe playn.
"Tak," he sayde, "with thee thyn hoost,
And abate the Sawdonys boost. *And diminish the Sultan's pride*
Az armys!" anon he gan crye *To arms*
Among hys hoost: they scholde hyghe *hurry*
With Sere Henry for to wende,
Jaffe to socoure and to defende
Agayn the Sawdon, Saladyn,
And many a cursyd Sarezyn.
  On morwen wente there with Sere Henry
Many a baroun and knyght hardy,
Gascoynes, Spaynardes and Lumbarde.
For the byddyng of Kyng Richard,
They wente forth be the maryn *sea-coast*
Tyl they comen to Palestyn.
Of Saladynys hoost they seye then *saw*
Al the cuntré coveryd with hethene men;
And whenne the Sawdon of hem herde,
Swythe towarde them he ferde,
And whenne the Duke Henry it wiste, *knew it*
He fledde ayen, be Jhesu Cryste, *away*
That he made no taryyng *delay*
Tyl he come to Richard, oure kyng,
And seyde he ne seygh nevere, ne herde
In al this wyde myddyl erde
Halvyn-del the peple of men, *Half the troops (forces)*
That Saladyn has be doune and den. *by hill and dale*
"No tungge," he seyde, "may hem telle: *count them*
I wene they comen out of helle." *believe*
Thenne answerde Kyng Richard:
"Fy a debles, vyle coward! *Fie on devils*
Schal I nevere, be God above,
Trustene unto Frenssche mannes love!
My men that in Jaffe beth,
They may wyte thee of theyr deth; *blame you for their death*
For thy defawte, I am adred, *failure*
My goode barouns beth harde bested. *beset (pressed)*
Now, for the love of Seynte Marye,
Schewe me quykly my galye!
Now to schyp, on and othir,

Fadyr and sone, eme and brothir, *uncle (nephew)*
Alle that evere love me,
Now to schyppe, pour charyté!" *for the sake of*
Alle that wepne bere myghte, *might bear weapon*
They wente to schyppe anon ryghte,
And wente agayn to Jaffe ward
With the noble kyng Richard.

Now herkenes to my tale soth,
Thowgh I swere yow none oth!
I wole rede romaunce non *wish to (will) read (relate)*
Of Partinope, ne of Ypomadon, *Partonope; Ipomedon (see note)*
Of Alisaunder, ne of Charlemayn,
Of Arthour, ne of Sere Gawayn,
Ne of Sere Launcelet de Lake,
Of Beffs, ne Gy, ne Sere Vrrake, *Bevis (of Hampton); Guy (of Warwick)*
Ne of Ury, ne of Octavyan, *Urré*
Ne of Hector, the stronge man,
Ne of Jason, ne of Hercules,
Ne of Eneas, ne of Achylles. *Aeneas*
I wene nevere, par ma fay, *judge (believe); by my faith (honor)*
That in the tyme of here day,
Dede ony of hem so doughty dede
Of strong batayle and gret wyghthede, *bravery*
As dede Kyng Rychard, saun fayle,
At Jaffe in that batayle,
With hys ax and hys sword:
His soule have Jhesu, oure Lord! *May Jesus, our Lord, keep his soul*
It was before the heyghe myd nyght,
The mone and the sterres schon ful bryght.
Kyng Richard unto Jaffe was come
With hys galeyes, alle and some.
They lokyd up to the castel:
They herde no pype ne flagel. *flageolet (a flute-like instrument)*
They drowgh hem nygh to the lande,
Yif they myghte undyrstande,
And they ne cowde nought aspye,
Be no voys of menstralsye, *musical instrument (music)*
That quyk man in the castel ware. *living*
Kyng Richard thenne become ful of care.
"Allas!" he sayde, "that I was born:
My goode barouns ben forlorn.
Slayn is Roberd of Leycestre
That was myn owne curteys meystre. *master (high official)*
Ylke leme of hym was wurth a knyght! *Each limb*
And Robert Tourneham that was so wyght, *valiant*
And Sere Bertram, and Sere Pypard,

In batayle that were wys and hard;
And alsoo myn other barouns,
The best in all regyouns.
They ben slayne and all totore, *destroyed*
Hou may I lengere leve therfore? *live*
Hadde I betyme comen hedyr, *early enough*
I myghte have savyd al togedyr!
Tyl I be wreken of Saladyne, *avenged*
Certys, my joye schal I tyne!" *I shall forfeit*
  Thus waylyd Kyng Richard ay *unceasingly*
Tyl it were spryng al of the day. *fully dawn of the day*
A wayte ther com in a kernel,[1]
And a pypyd a moot in a flagel.
He ne pypyd but on sythe, *but one time*
He made many an herte blythe. *joyful*
He lokyd doun and seygh the galey
Of Kyng Richard and his navey.
Schyppys and galeyes wel he knew,
Thenne a meryere note he blew,
And pypyd, "Seynyours! or suis! or sus! *Lords, arise now! Up now!*
Kyng Richard is icomen to us!"
  But whenne the Crystene herde this,
In herte they hadde gret joye, iwis, *certainly*
Erl, baroun, squyer, and knyght,
To the walles they sterten anon ryght, *rushed immediately*
And seygh Kyng Richard, here owne lord.
They cryede to hym with mylde word:
"Welcome, lord, in Goddes name!
Oure care is turnyd al to game!" *distress; joy*
Kyng Richard hadde nevere, iwis,
Halvyn-del so mekyl joye and blys. *Half so much*
"Az armes!" he cryede, "Makes yow yare!" *To arms; yourselves ready*
To hem that with hym comen ware:
"We ne have lyfe but one:
Sell we it dere, bothe flesshe and bone.
For to cleyme oure herytage,
Slee we the houndes ful of rage!
Who so doutes for here manace, *Whosoever fears because of their threat*
Have he nevere syghte of Goddys face! *May he never*
Take me myn axe in myn honde
That was made in Ingelonde.
Here armure no more I ne doute *fear*
Thenne I doo a pylche cloute! *ragged coat*

---

[1] Lines 6761–62: *A lookout came to an opening in a battlement (protective wall) / And piped a blast (note) on a flageolet (wind instrument)*

Thorwgh grace of God in Trynyté,
This day men schal the sothe isee!"
Al ther ferst on lande he leep, *First of all of them*
Of a dozeyn, he made an heep. *pile of corpses*
He gan to crye with voys ful cler,
"Where are these hethene pawtener *scoundrels*
That have the cyté of Jaffe inome?
With my pollaxe I am come
To waraunte that I have idoo,[1]
Wesseyl I schal drynke yow too!" *(see note)*
He leyde on ylke a syde ryght, *He delivered blows on every side*
And slowgh the Sarezynes, aplyghte. *in faith*
The Sarezynes fledde and were al mate, *checkmated (put to shame)*
With sorwe, they runne out of the gate. *distress (grief)*
In here herte they were so yarwe, *eager*
Alle here gates hem thoughte to narwe. *too narrow*
To the walles they fledden of the toun:
On every syde they fellen adoun.
Summe of hem broken here swere, *neck*
Legges and armes al in fere; *all together*
And ylkon cryede in this manere *each one*
As ye schal aftyrrward here:
"Malcan staran nair arbru; *(see note)*
Lor fermoir toir me moru."
This is to seye in Englys,
"The Englyssche devyl icome is;
Yif he us mete, we schal deye!
Flee we faste out of hys weye!"
Out of the toun they fledden ylkone,
That ther lefte never one, *remained not one*
But foure hyndryd or fyve *Other than*
That Richard broughte out of lyve. *of life (killed)*
At the gate he sette porters, *gatekeepers*
And stablede up hys destrers.
He leep upon his stede, Favel,
Weel armyd in yryn and in steel.
The folk hem armyd alle in fere *all together*
That out of the galeys comen were,
And manye comen out of the castel
That were armyd wundyr wel.
Kyng Richard rod out at the gate;
Twoo kynges he mette therate,
With syxty thousand Sarezynes fers, *fierce*

---

[1] Lines 6801–02: *To guarantee (provide surety) what I have to do / Wassail [a toast] I shall drink to you (I shall kill you).*

With armes bryghte and brode baners.
That on upon the hood he hytte *one; hood*
That to the sadyl he hym slytte.
That othir he hytte upon the hood,
That at the gyrdylstede it stood; *So that at the waist it came to a stop*
And hys Templers and hys barouns,
Fared ryght lyke wood lyouns, *crazed*
They slowen Sarezynes also swythe *as fast*
As gres fallith fro the sythe. *grass; scythe*
The Sarezynes seyghen no betere won *saw; choice*
But flowen awaye everylkon,
Unto Saladynes grete hoost
That fyftene myle lay acoost. *nearby*
Twoo and thrytty thousand, forsothe to say,
The Sowdan loste that same daye,
For theyr armure fared as waxe
Ayenst Kynge Rychardes axe.
Many a Sarazyne and hygh lordynge
Yelded them to Rycharde, our kynge. *themselves*
Rycharde put them in hostage tho:
There were a thousande prysoners and mo.
The chase lasted swythe longe,
Tyll the tyme of evensonge. *the sixth canonical hour (sunset)*
Richard rode after tyll it was nyght,
So many of them to deth he dyght, *he put to death*
That no nombre it may accounte.
How many of them it wolde amounte.
Rycharde lefte without the towne, *remained (stopped) outside*
And pyght there his pavylyowne; *pitched*
And that nyght with mylde herte,
He comforted his barons smarte. *bold*
And ye shall here on the morowe,
How there was a daye of sorowe;
For the gretest batayll, I understonde,
That ever was in ony londe.
And ye that this batayll wyll lere, *learn about*
Herken now, and ye shall here!

As Kynge Rycharde sate at his soupere,
And gladded his barons with mylde chere, *encouraged*
And comforted them with good wyne,
Two messengers came frome Saladyn,
And stode Kynge Rycharde before,
With longe berdes and with hore. *gray hair*
Of two mules they were alyght; *were dismounted*
In golde and sylke they were idyght. *adorned*
Eyther helde other by the honde

And sayd, "Kynge Rycharde, now understonde
Our lorde, Saladyn, the hygh kynge,
Hath thee sente this askynge: *petition*
If that thou were so hardy a knyght,
That thou durste hym abyde in fyght, *dare to face him*
Tyll to morwe that it daye ware,
Of blysse thou sholde ben all bare; *deprived*
For thy life and for thy barons
He wyll not gyve two skalons! *scallions*
He wyll thee take with strength of hondes,
For he hath folke of many londes,
Egyens, and of Turkye,
Of Moryens, and of Arabye, *Moors*
Basyles, and Embosyens, *(see note)*
Well eger knyghtes of defens,
Egypcyens, and of Surrye,
Of Ynde Maior and of Capadocye, *Cappadocia (see note)*
Of Medes, and of Asclamoyne, *(see note)*
Of Samarye, and of Babyloyne, *Samaria; Egypt*
Two hondred knyghtes without fayle,
Fyve hondred of amarayle;
The grounde ne may them unneth bere, *scarcely bear them*
The folke that cometh thee to dere. *injure*
By our rede, do ryght well, *counsel*
And tourne agayne to Jaffe Castell.
In safe warde thou myght there be
Tyll thou have sente after thy meyné,
And yf thou se thou may not stonde, *endure*
Tourne agayne to thyn owne londe." *Go back again (see t-note)*
In anger Rycharde toke up a lofe, *loaf of bread*
And in his hondes it all torofe, *broke it all apart*
And sayd to that Sarasyne:
"God gyve thee well evyll fyne, *wretched end (death)*
And Saladyn, your lorde,
The devyll hym hange with a corde!
For your counseyll and your tydynge,
God gyve you well evyll endynge! *May God give you an entirely wretched end*
Now go and saye to Saladyn,
In despyte of his God, Appolyn, *In contempt*
I wyll abyde hym betyme, *await; in due time*
Though he come to morowe or pryme, *before prime (6:00–9:00a.m.)*
And though I were but my selfe alone,
I would abyde them everychone; *face them in combat*
And yf the dogge wyll come to me,
My pollaxe shall his bane be!
And saye that I hym defye *challenge (declare war on)*
And all his cursed company in fere. *together*

Go now and saye to hym thus:
The curse have he of swete Jhesus!" *(see note)*
The messengers wente to Saladyn,
And told the Sowdane worde and ende. *beginning*
Saladyn mervayled than
And sayde it was none erthly man:
"He is a devyll or a saynt.
His myght founde I never faynt."
Anone he made his ordeynynge, *preparation for battle*
For to take Rycharde the kynge.
Therof Rycharde toke no kepe, *paid no attention*
But all nyght lay and slepe
Tyll ayenst the dawnynge; *about*
Than herde he a shyll cryenge. *melodious (loud)*
Thorugh Goddes grace, an aungell of heven
Tho seyd to hym, with mylde steven: *voice*
"Aryse, and lepe on thy good stede, Favell,
And tourne agayne to Jaffe Castell.
Thou haste slepte longe inough!
Thou shalte it fynde harde and tough
Or thou come to that cyté,
Thou shalte be wrapped and thy meyné. *surrounded (entrapped)*
After the bataile do by myne hees, *command*
With the Sowdan thou make thy peas.
Take trues and let thy baronage *Make truce*
Unto the flome do theyr pilgrimage, *[Go] to the river*
To Nazareth and the Bedlem,
To Calvarye and to Jherusalem,
And let them wende hom after then,
And come thou after with thy shypmen,
For enemyes thou haste, I understonde,
Here and in thyne owne londe.
"Up!" sayd the aungell, "and well thee spede,
Thou ne haddest never more nede!"
Rycharde arose as he wolde wede, *go mad*
And lepte on Favell, his good stede,
And sayd: "Lordynges, Or sus! Or sus! *Arise now*
Thus hath us warned swete Jhesus!
"As armes," he cryed thare, *To arms*
Ayenst the Sarasynes for to fare;
But Saladyn and his tem *troop*
Was bytwene Jaffe and them.
That was to Rycharde moche payne,
That he ne myght his hoost ordayne, *command*
But prekyd forth upon Favel,
And garte hys launse byte fol wel. *prepared his lance to pierce*
Therwith he slowgh withouten doute,

Three kynges of the Sawdones route. *troop*
Hys steed was strong, hymselven good,
Hors no man hym non withstood. *Horse nor man, none withstood him*
He hew upon the hethene cors, *cut into*
That unto grounde fel here hors. *bodies*
Who so hadde seen hys cuntynaunse, *behavior (appearance)*
Wolde evere had hym in remembraunce.
They gunne on hym als thykke to fleen,[1]
As out of the hyve doth the been; *bees*
And with hys ax doun he sweepe *mowes down*
Of the Sarezynys as bere doth scheepe. *bear; sheep*
Ynglyssche and Frenssche gunne aftir ryde,
To fyghte they were ful fressche that tyde;
Upon the Sarasynes faste they donge *beat*
With swerdes and with sperys,
And layden on with al here myght,
And slowen the Sarezynes dounryght;
But therof was but lytyl keepe: *service (protection)*
So many ther were upon an hepe *in great quantity*
That no slaughtyr in that batayle
Myghte be sene, withoute fayle.
  A myr ther was withouten Jaffes, *swamp*
A myle brod withouten les. *lying*
Mawgré the Sarazynes, Richard the syre, *In spite of*
Three thousand Sarezynys drof into the myre.
Thoo myghte men se the hethene men *Then*
Lyggen and bathen hem in the fen! *Lying and wallowing in the marsh*
And thoo that wolden have come uppe,
They drank of Kyng Richardis cuppe.
What there were drowenyd, and what were slawe,
The Sawdon loste of the hethene lawe,
Syxty thousand in lytyl stounde,
As it is in Frensch ifounde.
Kyng Richard wente again
To helpe hys hoost with myght and mayn;
Now was there, now was here,
To governe hys hoost with hys powere. *ability (vigor)*
Seygh nevere man I have herd telle,
One man so many to grounde quelle;
And the moste peryle of the batayle
Kyng Richard seygh, withouten fayle;
Hys eme, Sere Henry of Champayn, *nephew*
Feld off hys horse doun on the playn.
The Sarezynys hadde hym undyr honde, *captive*

[1] *They spread (went) upon him as thick as flies*

To slen hym ful faste they fonde. *endeavored*
It hadde ben hys day laste,
Ne hadde Kyng Richard comen in haste.
Kyng Richard cryede with lowde voys:
"Help, God and the holy croys!
This ylke day myn eme thou schylde *protect*
Fro deth of these doggys wylde!
Lordynges," he sayde, "lays upon! *deliver blows*
Letes of these houndes ascape non!
And I my self schal prove to smyte, *try to strike*
Yif my polax can ought byte." *can at all bite*
Men myghten see hym with myghte and mayne,
Schede the Sarezynys blood and brayn.
Upon the place that grene was,
Many soule wente to Sathanas. *Satan*
Be the dymmyng of the more, *By the darkening of the marshland*
Men myghte see where Richard fore. *attacked*
The Templers comen hym to socour;
There began a strong stour. *combat*
Thay layden on as they were wood,
Tyl valeys runnen al on blood.
The Longespay was a noble knyghte;
As a lyoun he gan to fyghte.
The Eerl of Leycetre, Sere Robard,
The Eerl of Rychemound, and Kyng Richard,
Many Sarezyn they slowgh, saun fayle.
Soo layde they on in that batayle,
There these ylke knyghtes rod, *Where*
There was slayn a way so brod *a path so wide*
That foure waynes myghte on mete — *four carts might pass*
So manye Sarezynes les the swete — *lost the lifeblood*
On bothe half was many body
Slayn, strong, bold, and hardy;
And at the laste, with gret payne,
Kyng Richard wan the Eerl of Champayne, *rescued*
And sette hym upon a stede
That swythe good was at nede,
And bad hym wenden by hys syde, *travel*
And nought a foote fro hym ryde.

With that came a messenger reke *quickly*
With kynge Rycharde for to speke,
And sayde, "Sere, pour charyté,
Turne agayn to Jaffe cytee!
Helyd is bothe mount and playn. *Covered*
Kyng Alisaundyr, ne Charlemayn,
Hadde nevere swylk a route *an army*

As is the cyté now aboute!
The gates ben on fyre set, *set on fire*
Ryght of Jaffe castellet: *On the right side*
Thy men may nether in ne oute.
Lord, of thee I have gret doute, *fear*
For ye may nought to the cyté ryde,
In felde what aventure yow betyde! *danger may befall you*
And I yow warne, withouten fayle,
Mekyl apayryd is youre batayle. *reduced; army*
The patryark itaken is, *patriarch*
And Jhon the Neel is slayn, iwis.
William Arsour, and Sere Gerard,
Bertram Braundys, thy goode Lumbard,
All these ben slayne and many mo!"
Kyng Richard bethoughte hym thoo, *devised a plan*
And gan to crye, "Turne arere, *Turn to the rear*
Every man with his banere!"
And many thousand before hym schete *rushed before him*
With swerdes and with launses grete,
With fauchouns and with maces bothe;
Kyng Richard they made ful wrothe;
They slowen Fauvel undyr hym:
Thenne was Kyng Richard wroth and grym. *angry and fierce*
Hys ax fro hys arsoun he drowgh; *saddlebow*
That ylke Sarezyn sone he slowgh *same*
That stekyd undyr hym his stede; *killed*
Therfore, he loste hys lyf to mede. *as recompense*
On foote he was, and he on leyde: *delivered blows*
Manye undyr hys hand ther deyde.
Alle that hys ax areche myghte,
Hors and man he slowgh dounryghte:
What before and what behynde. *Those; those*
A thousand and moo, as I fynde,
He slowgh whyl he was on foote;
That hem come nevere help ne boote.[1]

Saladynes twoo sones come ryde,
Ten thousand Sarezynes by here syde,
And gan to crye to Kyng Richard:
"Yelde thee, thef, traytour, coward, *thief*
Or I schal sloo thee in this place!"
"Nay!" quod Richard, "be Goddes grace!"
And with hys ax he smot hym soo,
That hys myddyl flowgh in twoo. *waist; flew*
The half the body fel adoun,

[1] *So that to them came neither help nor remedy*

And that othir half lefte in the arsoun.
"Of thee," quod Kyng Richard, "I am sekyr!" *From you; secure*

Hys brothir com to that bekyr
Upon a stede with gret raundoun. *with great speed*
He thoughte to bere Kyng Richard doun, *overthrow*
And gaf hym a wounde thorwgh the arme
That dede oure kyng mekyl harme:
Upon the spere hed was venym. *poison*
And Kyng Rychard stoutly smot hym
That man and hors fyl ded to grounde. *So that*
"Lygge there," he sayde, "thou hethene hounde!
Schalt thou nevere telle Saladyne
That thou madyst me my lyf to tyne!" *to lose*
With that, fyve dukes of hethenys
Come with here hoost, withouten mis, *unquestionably*
Bysette aboute Richard, oure kyng,
And thoughten hym to dethe bryng.
Kyng Richard in a lytyl thrawe, *little time*
The fyve dukes hadde islawe,
And fele hyndryd aftyr then *many*
Of stronge, hethene men.
And at the laste, though it were late,
Rycharde wanne to Jaffe gate. *succeeded in passing to*
Thenne were oure Crystene men ful sekyr *fully assured*
That they scholden overcome the bekyr. *withstand (win); encounter*
  The Eerl of Leycestre, Sere Robard,
Broughte oure kyng hys stede, Lyard.
Kyng Richard into the sadyl leep,
Thenne fledde the Sarezynes as they were scheep.
Oure kyng rode aftyr tyl it was nyghte,
And slowgh of hem that he take myghte.
There were slayn in playn and den, *plain and valley*
Ten hundryd thousand hethene men
That nyght withouten les.
Kynge Richard wan into Jaffes, *attained*
And thankyd Jhesu, kyng of glorye,
And hys modyr of that victorye:
For siththen the world was ferst begunne, *For since*
A fayrere batayle was nevere iwunne. *more fortunate (just)*

  At morwen he sente Robert Sabuyle
And Sere Wyllyam Watevyle,
Huberd and Robert Tourneham,
Gawter, Gyffard, and Jhon Seynt Jhan,
And bad hem seye to the Sawden
That hym self agayn fyve and twenty men

In wylde feeld wolde fyght *uncultivated*
To derayne Goddes ryghte; *To vindicate God's just cause*
Yif he it wynne, to have the land
Evere in Crystene mennys hand;
And yif the Sarezynes myghte hym slee,
The land scholde evere the Sawdonys bee.
And yif he wole nought here hys sawes, *proposals*
"Says three yer, three monethis, and thre dawes, *Designate*
I aske trewes of the Sawdan *demand truce*
To wenden home and come agayn than." *then*
The messangerys gunne to wende,
And tolde the Sawdon wurd and ende, *beginning and end*
He wolde nought consente to that batayle:
Fyve hundryd agayn Richard, saun fayle!
At morwen, yif he wolde come,
The trewes scholde ben inome, *be received (established)*
Thus he tolde the messangers,
And they it tolde Richard, the fers, *noble*
The nexte day he made foreward *The next day he made an agreement*
Of trewes to the Kyng Richard. *Of truce with King Richard*
Thorugh all the londe to the flome *Throughout all the land to the sea*
Fro Acres that wolde come. *Who [Richard] would come away from Acre*
Thoo aftyrward all the thre yere
Crystene men bothe fer and nere,
Yeden the way to Jerusalem,
To the Sepulcre and to Bedlem,
To Olyvete and to Nazarel, *Mount of Olives; Nazareth*
To Jaffe and to Mayden Castell,
And to alle othere pylgrymage,
Withote harme or damage.

Thus Kynge Rycharde, the doughty man, *(see t-note)*
Peas made with the Sowdan,
And syth he came, I unerstonde,
The waye towarde Englonde;
And thorugh treason was shotte, alas,
At Castell Gaylarde there he was.
The Duke of Estryche in the castell *Austria*
With his hoost was dyght full well.
Rycharde thought there to abyde;
The weder was hote in somer tyde.
At Gaylarde under the castell,
He wende he myght have keled hym well.[1]
His helme he abbated thare, *cast (threw) down*

[1] *He thought he might have cooled himself off*

And made his vysage all bare.
A spye there was in the castell
That espyed Rycharde ryght well,
And toke an arblaste swythe stronge,
And a quarell that was well longe,
And smote kynge Rycharde in tene — *wrongfully*
In the heed, without wene. — *without doubt*
Rycharde let his helme downe fall,
And badde his men dyght them all,
And swore by the see and the sonne,
Tyll the castell were iwonne
Ne sholde neyther mete ne drynke
Never into his body synke.
He let up robynet that tyde
Upon the castelles syde;
And on that other halfe the one,
He set up the matgryffone.
To the castell he threwe stones,
And brake the walles, for the nones,
And so within a lytell tyde,
Into the castell they gan ryde,
And slewe before and behynde
All tho that they myght ayenst them fynde;
And ever was the quarell by the lede, — *arrow [from a crossbow]; leaden tip*
Stycked styll in Rychardes hede.
And whan it was drawen out,
He dyed soone, without doute,
And he commaunded in all thynge,
To his fader men sholde hym brynge.
That they ne let, for nesshe ne harde, — *soft*
Tyll he were at the Font Everarde. — *Fontevraud*
At Font Everarde, wytterly,
His bones lye his fader by.
Kynge Harry, forsothe, he hyght:
All Englonde he helde to ryght.
Kynge Rycharde was a conquerour.
God gyve his soule moche honour!
No more of hym in Englysshe is wrought,
But Jhesu that us dere bought,
Graunte his soule rest and ro, — *peace*
And ours whan it cometh therto,
And that it may so be,
Saye all amen for charyté.

EXPLANATORY NOTES

ABBREVIATIONS: **A**: MS London, College of Arms HDN 58 (formerly: Arundel); ***a***: part of the manuscript tradition (see pp. 3–10 of the introduction); **B**: MS London, BL Additional 31042 (formerly: London Thornton); ***b***: part of the manuscript tradition (see pp. 3–10 of the introduction); **C**: MS Cambridge, Gonville and Caius College 175/96 (base text); ***CT***: Chaucer, *Canterbury Tales*; **D**: MS Oxford, Bodleian 21802 (formerly Douce 228); ***DMA***: *Dictionary of the Middle Ages* (ed. Strayer); **E**: MS London, BL Egerton 2862; **H**: MS London, BL Harley 4690; **L**: MS Edinburgh, National Library of Scotland Advocates' 19.2.1 (the Auchinleck manuscript); **ME**: Middle English; ***MED***: *Middle English Dictionary*; **OE**: Old English; **OF**: Old French; ***RCL***: *Richard Coer de Lyon.* **W**: Wynkyn de Worde's 1509 printed edition (*Kynge Rycharde cuer du lyon*, Oxford, Bodleian Crynes 734; and Manchester, John Ryland's Library Deansgate 15843); **W²**: de Worde's 1528 printed edition (*Kynge Rycharde cuer du lyon,* Oxford, Bodleian S. Seld. D. 45 (1); and London, BL C.40.c.51);**Whiting**: Whiting, *Proverbs, Sentences, and Proverbial Phrases*.

Incipit — *Hic incipit vita Ricardi Regis primi.* For a discussion of *RCL*'s application of the terms *vita* (life), "story" (line 4886), and "hystorye" (from the beginning of de Worde's two printings), see Mills, "Generic titles," pp. 126–29; see also his discussion of *Sir Gowther* and *Roberte the Deuyll,* romances whose heroes, like Richard, have demonic pedigrees.

1–35 — *Lord Jhesu . . . . herkenes before*. Patterned after the formal openings in OF texts, prologues to ME romances may include conventional elements: an invocation (lines 1–4); an exhortation to listen (line 35); a statement of the subject (lines 29–32); praise of the hero (lines 31–32); and a blessing or prayer (lines 33–34), (*Havelok*, ed. Smithers, p. 83n). *RCL's* prologue stresses the poem's "historical nature and establishes a tone that is both secular and nationalistic" (Turville-Petre, *England the Nation*, p. 122).

As with other members of the *a* group of manuscripts, the prologue is comprised of four-stress couplets. Loomis argues that this prologue is the addition of a Kentish translator of the original Anglo-Norman text (Review, p. 463). In contrast, L opens with two tail-rhymed stanzas followed by five couplets:

> Lord Ih[es]u, kyng of glorie,
> Swiche auentour & swiche victorie
> Þou sentest king richard,
> Miri it is to heren his stori
> & of him to han in memorie

Þat neuer no was coward.
Bokes men makeþ of latyn,
Clerkes witen what is þ[er] in,
Boþe almaundes & pikard.
Romau[n]ce make folk of frau[n]ce
Of kniȝtes þat wer[e] in destaunce,
Þat dyed þurth dint of sward:

Of Rouland & of Oliuer
& of þe oþer dusse per,
Of alisander & charlimeyn,
& ector þe gret werrer,
& of danys le fiz Oger,
Of Arthour & of Gaweyn.
As þis romau[n]ce of frenys wrouȝt,
Þat mani lewed no knowe nouȝt.
In gest as so we seyn,
Þis lewed no can freyns non:
Among an hundred vnneþe on,
In lede is nouȝt to leyn.

Noþeles wiþ gode chere,
Fele of hem wald yhere
Noble gestes, ich vnderstond
Of douȝti kniȝtes of inglond.
þerfore now ichil ȝou red[e],
Of a king douȝti of dede,
King Richard þe werrour best
þat men fineþ in ani gest.
Nou al þat listen þis ginni[n]g,
Ih[es]u hem grau[n]t god[e] ending.

Compare Brunner, *Löwenherz*, pp. 81n–82n; and see also his discussion of the prosody of L's prologue and related analogues at pp. 25–26. Prologues from the other members of the *b* group — A, D, E, and H — do not survive. As evidence for the intervention of an editor designing the Auchinleck Manuscript, Turville-Petre cites L's unique prologue together with revisions to other texts, (*England the Nation*, p. 114).

5 *jeste*. Compare Latin *res gestae*, exploits. In contrast to narratives of argument, a *jeste* (geste) could refer "to any written account of actions — historical or fictitious, secular or divine" (Strohm, "*Storie, Spelle, Geste*," pp. 348, 354). Accordingly, "jeste" carries a wide range of meanings: "a poem or song about heroic deeds, a chivalric romance . . . a prose chronicle or history, a prose romance or tale . . . a noteworthy deed . . . a military enterprise; entertainment . . . an amusement," (*MED*, s.v. *gest(e*, (n.1)). See also Mills, "Generic titles," p. 130.

7 *romaunces*. Derived from *romanz*, originally a linguistic term that referred to vernacular, romance languages, especially French, *romaunce* was later applied to a range of texts; see Strohm, "*Storie*, *Spelle*, *Geste*," pp. 354–56.

11–19 *Of Rowelond . . . . of Achylles*. Arguing that the *b* version of the romance was "a work of the vigorously heroic type," Finlayson suggests the heroes listed derive from epics and *chansons de geste*, sources that emphasize historical, not romance figures ("'*Richard, Coer de Lyon*,'" p. 161; the Introduction discusses the two versions of *RCL*, *a* and *b*). Jordan Fantosme in his *Chronique* gives similar praise to Henry II, illustrating the conventionality of such descriptions within an historical context (*Chronique*, p. 212, lines 112–17); for translation and discussion, see Fleischman, "On the Representation," p. 286. Compare Trotter's discussion of the Old French Crusade Cycle, whose references to heroes and incidents in *chansons de geste* established an epic frame of reference and suggested a continuity between the crusades and previous exploits (*Medieval French Literature*, pp. 110–15). ME versions of texts associated with these heroes were found, for example, in L, the Auchinleck MS, which contains a fragmentary version of *RCL* and includes *Of Arthour and Merlin*, *Of Roland and Vernagu*, and *Kyng Alisaunder* (Weber, *Metrical Romances*, 3.347–48). For discussions of this list and the list at lines 6713–22, see Liu, "Prototype Genre" (pp. 340–48); Mehl, *Middle English Romances*, pp. 243–44; Mills, "Generic titles," pp. 128 and 136n35; Fewster, *Traditionality and Genre*, p. 4; and Blurton, *Cannibalism*, pp. 122–23. Because the distinction between history and literature was less than clear, a medieval audience likely conceived of this list of heroes as both historical and legendary: for example, a chronicle account of Richard's exploits in defense of Jaffa compares the king to many of these same heroes (Nicholson, *Itinerarium*, 6.23, pp. 366–67).

11 *Of Rowelond and of Olyver*. Preeminent *chanson* heroes. In *La Chanson de Roland*, these two peers of Charlemagne died fighting Muslims at the Battle of Roncevaux. While historical references to Oliver are lacking, Einhard states in his *Vita Karoli Magni* that Roland, lord of the Breton March, died in the Pyrenees in an ambush by the Basques. See Dutton, *Charlemagne's Courtier*, pp. 21–22.

12 *doseper*. OF *douze pairs*. A reference to the twelve peers or principal warriors of Charlemagne who appear in various iterations in *La Chanson de Roland*, Geoffrey of Monmouth's *History*, where they attend Arthur's coronation feast at Caerleon (p. 228), and *The Sultan of Babylon*, among other texts. See Lupack, *Charlemagne Romances*, p. 97n241.

13 *Alisaundre and Charlemayn*. Two of the nine worthies, Alexander the Great, and Charlemagne, King of the Franks and the first Holy Roman Emperor, served as the heroes of such ME texts as *Kyng Alisaunder*, *The Wars of Alexander*, *The Sultan of Babylon*, and *The Siege of Milan*. The nine are often cited for their exemplary exploits, in conjuction with Fortune's Wheel. E.g., *Alliterative Morte Arthure* (lines 3408–37), *The Parlement of the Thre Ages*, Chaucer, and Langland. Three are ancient (Alexander, Hector, Julius Caesar); three are Hebrew (Judas Maccabee, Joshua, David) and three are Christians (Arthur, Charlemagne, Godefrey of Bouillon).

14 *Of Kyng Arthour and of Gawayn.* Among the numerous medieval accounts of this legendary British king and his nephew, none are as influential as Geoffrey of Monmouth's *History of the Kings of Britain.* Scholarship on these figures is vast. Hahn discusses the representation of Gawain in ME romance (*Sir Gawain*, pp. 1–35); for Gawain in Old French romance, see Busby, *Gauvain.*

16 *Turpyn and Oger Daneys.* The son of Geoffrey and king of Denmark, Ogier the Dane first appears in *The Song of Roland* leading part of Charlemagne's army against the Saracens. In this same poem Archbishop Turpin, one of the Twelve Peers, dies at the battle of Ronceveaux fighting infidels and exemplifying "the twin goals of the active chivalric life, fame in this world and salvation in the next," (Keen, *Chivalry*, p. 54). Ogier and Turpin were primarily *chanson* heroes; see also the *Pseudo-Turpin Chronicle*, a popular but forged twelfth century presentation of Charlemagne's legendary conquest of Spain, and *The Siege of Milan.* This last text, a ME romance in which Turpin plays a central role, survives in B (the London Thornton MS) which also contains a text of *RCL.* See Lupack, *Charlemagne Romances.*

19 *Of Ector and of Achylles.* Hector, Trojan prince, elder brother of Paris, and one of the worthies, is a prominent hero in the various versions of the Troy story. Achilles, the greatest warrior in the Trojan war, secures victory for the Greeks in part by killing Hector. Medieval versions, including Benoit's OF *Roman de Troie*, and Guido delle Colonne's Latin translation of that work, *Historia destructionis Troiae*, attest to the period's fascination with the story: to overestimate the importance of the Troy story to medieval culture would be difficult. From the ruins of Troy came the Roman empire, and later, Trojan ancestors for nearly every Western European kingdom. For the story's influence upon Britain, see Ingledew, "Book of Troy."

21 *In Frenssche bookys this rym is wrought.* The first of several references to an original French text of the romance; see also lines 5098 and 7008; and, less clearly, lines 3439 and 5667. For a discussion of this narrative's French origins, see the Introduction (pp. 3–4, p. 10n50).

22 *Lewede men ne knowe it nought.* Expressing populist and nationalistic concerns, the narrator describes an unlettered English audience to justify translating a "Frenssche book" (line 21) about "doughty knyghtes of Yngleonde" (line 28) (see Heng, *Empire*, p. 105 and "Romance of England," p. 155; Turville-Petre, *England the Nation*, p. 122). For references to discussions of ME romances, even those derived from French originals, as comprising a textual community with nationalist impulses, see Heng, "Romance of England," pp. 155 and 169n46.

35–250 *Lordynges, herkenes . . . . and conqueroure.* While members of the *b* group of manuscripts identify Eleanor of Aquitaine as Richard's mother — see the note to line 2040 — she becomes Cassodorien in the *a* group's demon-mother episode, which has a number of legendary and folk-tale analogues. Most notable is the story of Black Fulk of Anjou, Richard's ancestor, who married a lady of unearthly beauty. Like Cassodorien, she could not witness the consecration of the host. Compelled to stay in the church by Fulk's men, she escaped with two children by flying through a window of the church. Chapman classifies Cassiodorien as "a demon or fairy mistress of the widespread 'Swan-Maiden' type" and examines similar legends attached to Eleanor, Richard's mother. See Walter Map's account of Henno-with-the-Teeth, for example, in *De Nugis Curialium*, 4.9, pp. 345–49; Chapman, "Demon Queen," pp. 393, 395; and Broughton, *Legends of Richard I*, pp. 11–12, 78–82.

Recent scholarship gives prominence to this episode and to Richard's demonic origins. McDonald, for example, argues that "*Richard*, like *Sir Gowther*, is . . . a narrative of exorcism: an account of how Richard . . . purges himself of his devilish inheritance. Significantly, Richard's anthropophagy, far from being a sign of that inheritance, not only marks, but produces, his return to the Christian community. Cassodorien's alterity is a function . . . of her inability to sit through the mass" ("Eating People," p. 140). See also Heng, *Empire*, pp. 97, 343n29, 351n58; and Akbari, "Hunger," pp. 200–01.

35 *Lordynges, herkenes before*. The narrator's exhortation to listen, a common feature of ME romance, reflects the genre's association with oral tradition; see, e.g., the openings of *Havelok* and *Athelston*.

37 *Kyng Henry*. Richard's father, Henry II, king of England from 1154 to 1189.

40 *Seynt Thomas*. Thomas Becket (1118–1170) became chancellor to King Henry II in 1155, whom he served with distinction; but when Henry designated Thomas archbishop of Canterbury in 1162, their close relationship ended. An amiable and able chancellor, this noble, genial, and worldly man became stubborn and austere as archbishop. Disputes arose over Henry's ecclesiastical policies. Henry II's annoyance at Thomas's refusal to compromise over the crown's jurisdictional claims was well known. As a result, Henry was believed to be complicit in Thomas's murder before his altar in 1170. Thomas was canonized in 1173. See Alexander, "Becket, Thomas" (*DMA* 2.151–53).

45–52 *He wolde . . . . to wyf.* The motif of a lord who refuses to marry, yields to his subjects' advice to wed, and then searches for a bride frequently recurs in medieval romance; see, e.g., the Tristan story; Chrétien's *Cligés*, p. 128; *Roberte the Deuyll*, pp. 219–20; and Chaucer's *Clerk's Tale*. See Broughton, *Legends of Richard I*, p. 83 and Loomis, Review, p. 465.

60–72 *Another schip . . . . it was*. Texts with parallels to this fabulous ship include Marie de France's *Lay of Guigamar*, and *Partenope of Blois*. See Broughton, *Legends of Richard I*, pp. 83–85.

62 *ruel bon*. This reference to whale bone, a common simile in ME romance, likely referred to walrus or narwhal tusks. See *MED*, s.v. *rouel* (n.1) and Weber, *Metrical Romances*, 3.350; *Sir Degrevant*, line 1445: "All of ruelbon"; Sir Thopas (*CT* VII[B^2]878): "his sadel was of ruel bone." The implication is "white," but also radiant or bright. See *MED*'s quotation 8a from St. Greg (Auch) 169/994: "An Angel can fram heven adown, Briȝter þan þe rowwel bon." See lines 75–76 below.

66 *samyte*. A rich silk cloth, embroidered or interwoven with gold or silver. See *MED*, *samit(e* and medieval Latin *examitum*.

67 *Tuely sylk*. Among its definitions of *tuli*, the *MED* defines *tuli silke* as fabric of a deep red color, but the context will not allow such a reading. Compare *Bevis of Hampton*, line 1158: "The broider is of Tuli selk," where its accompanying gloss reads "silk from Toulouse."

69 *al with oute*. In all aspects of its outward appearance. See *MED*, *withouten* (adv.), sense 3.

71 *loof*. "A spar holding out and down the windward tack of a square sail while going into the wind" (*MED*, s.v. *lof* (n.4)).

89 *charbocle ston*. See *The Peterborough Lapidary*: "Carbuncculus is a precious stone [that] schineþ as feyre whose schynyng is not overcom by nyȝt. It schineþ in derk places, & it semeþ as it were a feyr." It has "a maner myȝt as it wer about sperkynge of fyre þat beclyppeth him [the wearer] withowte [i.e., all about] (p. 82). Compare the ship in *RCL*, line 69. See also Chaucer's translation of *The Romaunt of the Rose*, where Rychesse wears "a fyn charboncle" so bright that it illuminates even at night a mile or two on both sides and illuminates her faces and all about her wonderously (lines 1120–28). It has such power that no venom can effect its possesser and it can cure palsy and tooth ache (lines 1085–1107). See also Chaucer's *House of Fame* (line 1363), where a carbuncle perpetually adds radiance to the "femynyne creature" (line 1365) who is the "noble quene" and "lady schene" of the House of Fame (lines 1535–36).

118 *vysyoun*. In this context, *visioun* likely denotes a supernatural revelation or a prophetic dream. As attested in its literature, the medieval period manifested a profound interest in dreams, visions, and related revelations; see Loftin, "Visions" (*DMA* 12.475–78).

133 *the Tour*. Built by William the Conqueror in the southwest corner of London c. 1080, the Tower of London served as a fortress and stronghold, as well as a palace and a prison for men and women of exalted status.

148 *menstralles*. The minstrels represented here are likely professional musicians of high status. See Olson, "Minstrels."

153 *Westemenstre*. Westminster is the principal residence of English kings even before the conquest and the site of the Abbey Church where English kings were invested with the crown. It became the home of various governmental institutions including Parliament, law courts, and the exchequer. See Lyon, *Legal History*, p. 424. So, the connection between the English monarchy and Westminster is profound.

163 *Corbaryng*. This name may derive from "Corborans," the Saracen leader in the *Chanson d'Antioche*, which is evidently a corruption of the historical "Kerbogha," the atabeg of Mosul who is reported to have converted to Christianity in the thirteenth-century *Chrétienté Corboran*. See Akbari, "Hunger," p. 201, and Heng, *Empire*, p. 343n29.

164 *Antyoche.* Ancient, eastern, and exotic, Antioch is a site rich in associations. Situated on an important trade route in present-day Turkey, especially holy to Christians — St. Peter founded his first bishopric there — Antioch under Byzantine rule became a chief trading center for Greek and Moslem commerce: its fortress was the most formidable on the Syrian frontier. See Runciman, *History of the Crusades*, 1:93, 213. Conquered in 1098 after a long siege whose rigors may have included crusader cannibalism (see Heng, *Empire*, pp. 23–24 for a discussion of sources), it served as the capital of the Latin principality of Antioch. After 1187, all Crusader colonies besides Tyre, Tripoli, and Antioch had fallen to Saladin. Akbari argues that Richard's success in conquering eastern lands derives from his mother through whom he "lays claim to both supernatural powers and legitimate descent from the former Saracen rulers of Antioch and its region" ("Hunger," p. 201).

172 *wyght.* Here, Henry uses *wight* to denote a living creature, but in this context, the word's other meanings bear mentioning: "an unnatural or monstrous being; a supernatural creature, [a] demon" (*MED wight* (n.), sense 1c).

173 *Cassodorien.* The *a* group of manuscripts provides Richard with a "demon mother" instead of Eleanor of Aquitane, his historical mother; hence, the narrative trades a dominant French mother for an exotic Oriental, thus making Richard, an historical figure accused of sodomy, more masculine (Heng, *Empire*, p. 97). Noting John of Salisbury implied that Eleanor had incestuous relations with Raymond of Antioch and that a minstrel accused her of having "an affair with Saladin himself," Akbari argues that the "replacement of Eleanor with Cassodorien, Aquitaine with Antioch, produces a Richard whose alien nature is not French, but Oriental" ("Hunger," pp. 204–05).

189–94 *Beforn the elevacyoun . . . . no sacrement.* For references to medieval discussions of the power of sacred objects like the Eucharist over demons, see note to line 222 below.

199–201 *Twoo knaves and a mayde.* At this point, the poet indicates the demonic mother by not following the birth order and number of children born to Eleanor of Aquitaine. Henry II and Eleanor of Aquitaine actually had eight children in the following order: William, who died in infancy, Henry, Matilda, Richard, Geoffrey, Eleanor, Joan, and John.

202 *romaunce.* See notes at lines 7 and 6711–13.

206 *To the fyftenthe yere.* The age at which childhood ended, fifteen, became in late antique and medieval Europe "the vital age for both combat and majority" (James, "Majority," p. 24). Thus, Richard would be of age when he ascends to the throne at line 243. In fact, Richard was 32 when he ascended to the throne on 8 September, 1189 (Jentsch, "Quellen," p. 232).

222 *The preest scholde make the sakeryng.* The "sakerying" is the point at which the elevated host is transformed into the blood and body of Christ; see McDonald's discussion ("Eating People," pp. 140–41). Hagiographic literature abounds in representations of demoniacs being healed through the

use of such sacred objects as the consecrated host. See, e.g., Arnold of Bonneval, *Vita primi Bernardi*, 2.11–14; *Patrologia Latina* 185: cols. 275–77, which Newman discusses ("Possessed," pp. 738–40).

241 *Crowned after Kynge Harry*. Compare the more detailed account from L:

> In heruest, after þe natiuite,
> King Richard fenge his dignete
> [Boþe] þe kinges ȝerd and the croun,
> At Winchester in þe gode toun.

Paris suggests that "Winchester" is a scribal error ("Le Roman," p. 356). English monarchs, both before and after the Conquest, were crowned at the Abbey Church at Westminster (Lyon, *Legal History*, p. 425).

252–426 *At Salysbury . . . . hym drowe*. The Three Days' Tournament together with the use of disguise is a fixture of medieval romance. (See, e.g., Weston, *Three Days' Tournament;* Loomis, Review, p. 465). But there is an historical component there as well. A celebrated tourneyer, Richard I in his licensing edict of 1194 designated five official tourneying sites, one being between Salisbury and Wilton (Barker, *Tournament*, p. 11). In "Tournament," Nickel provides a good discussion of the medieval tournament, an institution central to chivalry and its arts, which included heraldry, coats of arms, specialized tournament equipment, elaborate armor and gear for knight and horse, and codes of conduct, for example, knightly service to ladies. In setting forth three functions for the tournament, including associating Richard with such romance heroes as Cliges, Ipomedon, and Lancelot, Finlayson argues that the tournament, a redaction from the *b* version, "reflects the intermingling of 'history' and romance motifs which is typical of 'chronicle' and 'ancestral' romances" ("Legendary Ancestors," p. 303; see also Broughton, *Legends of Richard I*, pp. 90–92). In the *a* group, Fouk Doly, and Thomas of Multon acquit themselves so well that Richard chooses them to accompany him on his pilgrimage; but in some witnesses to the *b* group (A, D, and H), Richard defeats all knights equally. Since no link exists between tournament and pilgrimage in manuscripts from the *b* group, Brunner argues that *a* stands closer to the original text than does *b* (*Löwenherz*, p. 21), a conclusion Loomis supports (Review, pp. 461–62). L omits this episode.

273 *All togyder cole blacke*. The king mysteriously appears in three different disguises — first black, then red (line 333), then white (line 387) — the same successive colors of disguise worn by another devil's son, Sir Gowther, as he battles a sultan (*Sir Gowther*, lines 403–633). Discussing the Christian and alchemic symbolism of these colors in general and within the ritual of knighting, Marchalonis argues that the order — first black (humility), then red (passion, blood), and finally white (purity) — reflects the process of Gowther's spiritual development. She observes that in *RCL*'s tournament, as in *Sir Gowther*, these colors are associated with chivalric testing ("*Sir Gowther*: The Process," pp. 20–24). For a general treatment of the use of successive, colored

disguises in medieval romance, see Weston, *The Three Days' Tournament*, especially pp. 9–11 and 23–38.

275 *Upon his creste a raven stode*. A crest was an heraldic device affixed to the helmet; see line 523. Knights came to attach symbols and devices to their helmets for purposes of identification. One of the earliest heraldic birds, the raven had been in use by the Normans from the Conquest onwards, (Fox-Davies, *Heraldry*, p. 186), perhaps as a sign of the feast the knight plans for the scavengers after he kills his opponents. Also noteworthy is the hunter's practice of leaving the corben bone for the raven — "at the death he will be" — as a talisman of self defense. See Peck, "Careful Hunter," pp. 336–37.

280 *In travayll for to be*. For the raven, the travail is obvious. *Travayll* may signify "spiritual or physical labor as a religious obligation" (*MED*, s.v. *travail* (n.), sense 1b). This accords with the crusades references in lines 281–84. Compare Hugh of Fouilloy's account: "On the Sacred Page the raven is perceived in various ways, so that by the raven is understood sometimes a preacher, sometimes a sinner, sometimes the Devil" (Clark, *Aviarium*, p. 175).

297 *gorgere*. Plate armor for the chin and neck.

321 *pusen*. "A piece of metal or mail attached to the helmet and extending over the neck and upper breast" (*MED*, s.v. *pisan(e* (n.), sense a).

323 *gorgere*. Synonymous with *gorgette*; see note at line 297 above.

337–42 *Upon his creste . . . . the grounde*. The note to line 275 above discusses crests as heraldic devices. While the Talbot, an English hunting dog, served as a common heraldic symbol (Fox-Davies, *Heraldry*, p. 154), a number of details in this description emphasize the peculiarity of both knight and crest: the dog's color, the position of its tail, the stated significance of the crest, and Multoun's comment in lines 522–23 that that the red knight seemed to be a devil (*qued*). One of several representations that link Richard to the devil (see note at 500 below), this portrayal entwines a complex set of associations: the king's demonic pedigree; the perception by Saracens and others that he is a devil; and the king's and his people's status as *taylardes*, tailed-ones (see line 1776 and note, and the Introduction, p. 14).

341 *Them to slee for Goddes love*. For a discussion of the relation between chivalry, the church, and the crusades, see Keen, *Chivalry*, pp. 44–63. For an expression of a militant chivalric perspective, see Gautier's sixth commandment of chivalry: "Thou shalt make war against the Infidel without cessation and without mercy" (*Chivalry*, p. 26). For the peculiarities of knightly piety, see Kaeuper, *Holy Warriors*.

375 *acketton*. "A quilted or padded jacket worn under the armor for comfort and protection" (*MED*, s.v. *aketoun* (n.), sense a). The term derives from Moorish-Spanish, *al coton*, cotton (Nickel, "Tournament," p. 218).

387–89 *All his atyre . . . . crosse rede*. A likely allusion to the Templars, a military and religious order founded c. 1119 to guard the site of the Temple of Solomon and to protect pilgrims in the Holy Land. The Templars wore white to symbolize their rejection of women. Later, each Templar added a red cross to his coat of arms (Broughton, *Dictionary*, p. 445).

388 *croper*. "A cover for the hindquarters of a horse, or a crupper" (*MED*, s.v. *crouper* (n.), sense a).

392 *To wynne the Crosse*. One goal of the Third Crusade was to regain the True Cross lost to Saladin at the Battle of Hattin in 1197 (Runciman, *History of the Crusades*, 2:455–60).

393 *Upon his heed a dove whyte*. See note on crests at line 275. Doves with olive branches in their beaks are common heraldic devices. See Fox-Davies, *Heraldry*, p. 183. Among other sources, medieval bestiaries associated the dove with Christ and the Holy Ghost. Compare line 5711.

399 *Fouke Doly*. Of undoubted historicity, Fulk D'Oilly and Thomas Moulton (line 433) were Lincolnshire knights connected by marriage in the thirteenth century. As they do not appear in chronicles of the Third Crusade, Finalyson suggests that the large role these knights play in *RCL*'s *a* version represents an early redactor's efforts "to glorify his or a patron's family," since the names do not occur in L, the fragment that Finlayson believes to contain the story's basic form ("'*Richard, Coer de Lyon*,'" p. 166; and "Legendary Ancestors").

403 *bassenet*. "Bacinet" refers to a variety of head coverings from the "hemispherical helmet, without a visor, worn under the fighting helmet" to "a pointed helmet with a visor" (*MED*, s.v. *bacinet* (n.)).

428 *Herodes*. A herald. "An officer of a tournament who makes announcements, introduces knights, and reports their actions, awards prizes, etc." (*MED*, s.v. *heraud* (n.), sense 1a).

433 *To Syr Thomas of Multon*. See note to line 399 above.

453 *paramours*. The convention of knights gaining their ladies' affections through prowess at tournaments appears as early as c. 1135 in Geoffrey of Monmouth's *History* (pp. 229–30). See Nickel, "Tournament," p. 236. But *RCL*'s virulent crusading propoganda overwhelms this quaint, chivalric convention.

500 *This is a devyl and no man*. Variations of this statement recur throughout the text and thus emphasize Richard's demonic pedigree: *Hym semyd weel to ben a qued* (line 522); *Sayden he was a devyl of helle* (line 2580); and *The Englysshe devyl icome is* (line 6818). See also lines 568, 2679, 3166, 3664, 4354, and 6935; though less direct, see also line 1776. These references likely reflect contemporary accounts linking Richard to the devil: for references, see Prestwich, who notes that Richard himself "was fond of mentioning the legendary descent of the Angevin dynasty from the devil," and who quotes contemporary chronicles, both Muslim and Christian, that link the king to the devil ("*Rex Bellicosus*," pp. 2–3). The recurring association of Richard with demons and devils distinguishes *RCL* from other ME crusading texts that demonize

Saracens: compare, e.g., *The Sultan of Babylon*, lines 356–57. Other ME romances with demonic heroes include *Sir Gowther* and *Roberte the Deuyll.*

521–22 *Hys hors . . . . a qued.* See notes to lines 337–42 and to line 500 above. Compare Borgström, *Proverbs of Alfred*, number 37, p. 25: "The rede mon he is a quet [qued] / for he wole thee thin iwil red."

528 *renge.* "An area designated for a tournament or sport" (*MED*, s.v. *ring* (n.), sense 4a). See also *renge* (n.2), sense b.

568 *pouke.* See the note to line 500.

595 *Al in palmeres gyse.* Identity and disguise are central themes of romance, ancient and medieval. For a discussion of the motif of kings in disguise, see Walsh, "King in Disguise." Hibbard notes chronicle and romance accounts of the use of pilgrim garb as disguise during the Crusade period (*Mediæval Romance*, p. 93 and 93n9); see note at line 613 below. The note to line 273 discusses Richard's three disguises at the Salisbury tournament, the Three Days' Tourney, and romance analogues.

605–08 *On the book . . . . to bee.* Swearing an oath upon the bible, as here, reflects the religious nature of oaths, which are invocations of the divine name in witness to the truth. From the oath of fealty to those that knights took after dubbing, oaths "secured the bonds of medieval society" (Lynch, "Oath," *DMA* 9.207). The person swearing often pledged his or her faith, that is, future salvation, that he or she would perform a certain task. See Pollock and Maitland, *English Law*, 2.189–92.

607 *And kyste hem thenne alle three.* Kissing often formed part of medieval rituals. As part of the ceremony of homage, for example, "the lord then kissed the vassal on the mouth and said that he took him as his man" (Major, "'Bastard Feudalism,'" p. 510). See also the note to line 1588.

613 *With pyke and with sclavyn.* The staff and cloak of a pilgrim is a disguise frequently adopted by the heroes of medieval romance. For example, when Orfeo puts aside his kingship to search for Herodis, he puts on a *sclavyn* as he makes his pilgrimage into the wilderness (*Sir Orfeo*, line 228). Likewise, Horn trades his clothes for a palmer's *sclavyn* (*King Horn*, line 1064). In Richard's historical return to Europe from the Third Crusade, Roger of Howden reports that "Richard and his followers were disguised as pilgrims" (*Chronica* 3:185–86, cited in Gillingham, *Richard I*, p. 232).

615–50 *Now they dyghten . . . . here myght.* Richard's pilgrimage to the Holy Land. This episode appears in *a* and in all texts of *b* save L and E, the latter being defective at its beginning.

619 *Into Flaundrys.* Flanders, loosely the "land of the Flemings," occupied parts of present day Belgium, France, and the Netherlands.

623 *Braundys.* Brindisi, a port in southern Italy on the Adriatic, became part of the Norman kingdom of Naples in 1070.

630 *Famagos*. Famagusta, a seaport on the east coast of Cyprus.

634 *Acres*. Located on a peninsula on the northern part of Haifa bay, first taken by crusaders in 1104 (Boas, *Archaeology*, p. 222), Acre was the main port for the kingdom of Jerusalem and its largest city when it fell to Saladin in 1187 (Gillingham, *Richard I*, p. 155). In part, *RCL* recounts the crusaders' retaking of Acre in 1191 after a lengthy siege. The city served as the administrative capital of the kingdom of Jerusalem and the main headquarters for all of the military orders until its fall in May of 1291 (Boas, *Archaeology*, p. 222) at which time the crusaders, most notably the military orders, lost their last citadel in the Holy Land (Nicholson, *Templars*, pp. 1, 125).

635 *Massedoyne*. Macedonia, ruled by Byzantines from 298 CE.

637 *Cesare*. Caesarea. Situated between Haifa and Arsuf and held by crusaders from 1101–87 and from 1191–1265, this fortified coastal city served as an important port for the kingdom of Jerusalem which relied heavily upon its maritime connections to western Europe. See La Monte, *Latin Kingdom*, pp. 226–27; and Pringle, *Secular Buildings*, p. 43. After its capture by Baldwin I in 1101, the crusaders brutally massacred most of its inhabitants (Runciman, *History of the Crusades*, 2:73–74). See also line 4931.

638 *Nynyve*. See note to line 5189.

641 *Sudan Turry*. A likely reference to Sidon and Tyre. See Brunner, *Löwenherz*, p. 472. These two cities are grouped together, for example, in the note to line 1307 below which describes Conrad of Montferrat's purported offer to Saladin to attack Acre in exchange for Sidon and Tyre.

642 *Ebedy*. A city in the Holy Land, perhaps Ebron. See Brunner, *Löwenherz*, p. 465.

643 *Castel Orglyous*. Perhaps named after the Saracen commander *Orgayl* in line 4151, this castle's name evokes romance castles: e.g., the adventure at "Castell Orgulus" in Malory, *Works*, 2:463; Finlayson notes a parallel to "Castle Orellous" from later prose redactions of *Perceval* ("Legendary Ancestors," p. 300).

644 *Aperyous*. Perhaps Piraeus, a port on the Greek coast. See Brunner, *Löwenherz*, p. 462.

645 *Safrane*. A town in the Holy Land, possibly the "Safoire" mentioned in the *Estoire*, which may correspond to Sephoria in Galilee. See Brunner, *Löwenherz*, p. 472. Loomis suggests this reference is to a hamlet near Acre (Review, p. 456).

646 *To Taboret and Archane*. *Taboret* is likely a reference to Tiberias, a city on the Sea of Galilee. After the fall of Jerusalem during the First Crusade, it became the capitol of Tancred's Principality of Galilee. In 1197 at the Battle of Hattin, Saladin defeated crusaders who were coming to relieve the Muslim siege of Tiberias. See Runciman, *History of the Crusades*, 1:304–07; 2.452–58. Loomis suggests that *Archane* is a corrupt form of Archas, a fortified town near Tripoli (Review, p. 456).

651 *the Grykys se.* Frequently encountered in ME romance, the "greckes see" ("Greeks' sea") denotes the eastern Mediterranean, the boundary between the Christian and the Muslim world. See Hudson, *Four Middle English Romances*, p. 32, and compare *Sir Isumbras* (line 359); *Octavian* (line 407); *Sir Eglamour* (line 894), and The Man of Law's Tale (*CT* II[B[1]]464).

657–1242 *A goos . . . . schal bene.* This episode of Richard's captivity in Germany appears in *a* and in all non-defective texts of *b* save L: e.g., E, missing initial leaves, begins on line 1857.

676 *mynstrale.* While *minstrali* (*MED*) may denote musical entertainment, it may also be an aberrant form of *minstralsi(e*, which may signify "the art of performing music or story-telling" (*MED*, s.v. *minstralsi(e* (n.), sense 1d). This is a concise statement of an important motivation for the patronage of minstrels or *jongleurs*, some of whom are associated with texts, the Oxford *Roland*, for example. See Taylor, "Minstrel Manuscript," p. 44; but also see line 3780.

694 *And chose thy selfe a ryche towne.* This bequest would endow the minstrel with noble status, not an unusual effect of patronage.

722 *treason.* Felony (*felonia*) constituted a breach of fealty to one's lord; it was a crime "involving some breach of the feudal bond between lord and man." See Barron, "Penalties for Treason," p. 188. Treason involved a crime against the crown (Pollack and Maitland, *English Law*, 2.501–08). Before its expansion in late thirteenth-century England, treasonous acts included "compassing or imagining the king's death, sedition . . . by the vassal or by others at his instigation, and affording aid to the king's enemies" (Kaeuper, "Treason," 12.165).

739 *pryme.* The Catholic Church divided the day into seven canonical hours. Prime occurred approximately at daybreak and lasted roughly from 6:00 am to 9:00 am.

740–98 *The kynges . . . . ony stone.* The exchange of blows episode recounted here represents the game of "pluck buffet," a form of dueling by alternate blows. Representations of this game in folktales, romances, and chronicles are numerous and include, most famously, *Sir Gawain and the Green Knight*. Broughton discusses analogues in *Legends of Richard I*, pp. 120–23. In his use of wax, and in the lethality of his rage, Richard's response lies well outside the norms of heroic, not to mention chivalrous, behavior.

763 *And sware his othe by Saynt Martyn.* Like holy books, saints were invoked in the swearing of oaths because they (and their relics) had power. One of the most popular saints, Martin of Tours (c. 316–397) was born in Hungary, enrolled among the catechumens at an early age, and later was imprisoned for refusing to carry out his duties as a Roman soldier. After establishing the first monastery in Gaul, he became bishop of Tours in 372. A "pioneer of Western monasticism," he established monasteries, destroyed heathen temples and sacred trees, and is reported to have healed lepers, among other miracles.

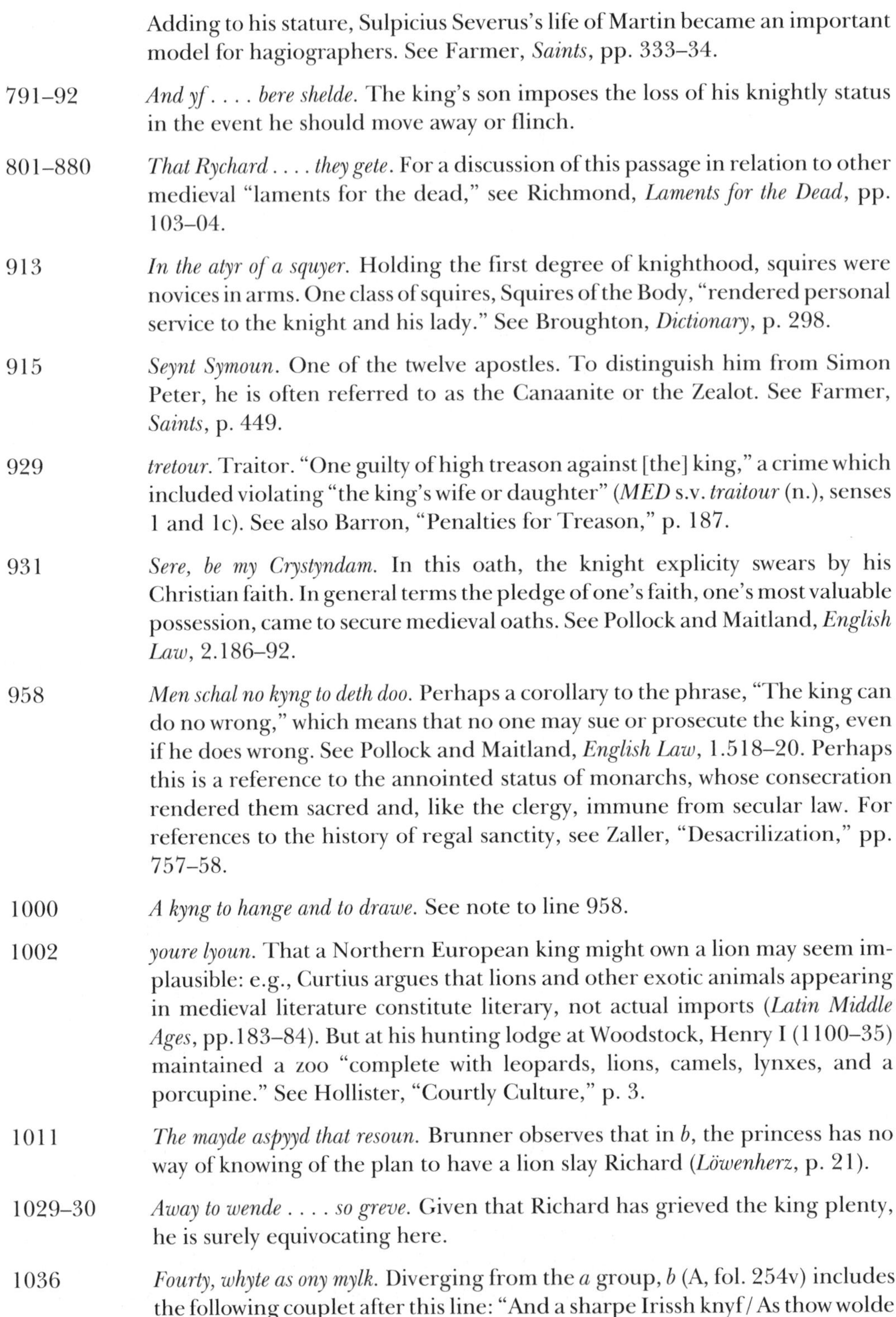

Adding to his stature, Sulpicius Severus's life of Martin became an important model for hagiographers. See Farmer, *Saints*, pp. 333–34.

791–92 *And yf . . . . bere shelde.* The king's son imposes the loss of his knightly status in the event he should move away or flinch.

801–880 *That Rychard . . . . they gete.* For a discussion of this passage in relation to other medieval "laments for the dead," see Richmond, *Laments for the Dead*, pp. 103–04.

913 *In the atyr of a squyer.* Holding the first degree of knighthood, squires were novices in arms. One class of squires, Squires of the Body, "rendered personal service to the knight and his lady." See Broughton, *Dictionary*, p. 298.

915 *Seynt Symoun.* One of the twelve apostles. To distinguish him from Simon Peter, he is often referred to as the Canaanite or the Zealot. See Farmer, *Saints*, p. 449.

929 *tretour.* Traitor. "One guilty of high treason against [the] king," a crime which included violating "the king's wife or daughter" (*MED* s.v. *traitour* (n.), senses 1 and 1c). See also Barron, "Penalties for Treason," p. 187.

931 *Sere, be my Crystyndam.* In this oath, the knight explicity swears by his Christian faith. In general terms the pledge of one's faith, one's most valuable possession, came to secure medieval oaths. See Pollock and Maitland, *English Law*, 2.186–92.

958 *Men schal no kyng to deth doo.* Perhaps a corollary to the phrase, "The king can do no wrong," which means that no one may sue or prosecute the king, even if he does wrong. See Pollock and Maitland, *English Law*, 1.518–20. Perhaps this is a reference to the annointed status of monarchs, whose consecration rendered them sacred and, like the clergy, immune from secular law. For references to the history of regal sanctity, see Zaller, "Desacrilization," pp. 757–58.

1000 *A kyng to hange and to drawe.* See note to line 958.

1002 *youre lyoun.* That a Northern European king might own a lion may seem implausible: e.g., Curtius argues that lions and other exotic animals appearing in medieval literature constitute literary, not actual imports (*Latin Middle Ages*, pp.183–84). But at his hunting lodge at Woodstock, Henry I (1100–35) maintained a zoo "complete with leopards, lions, camels, lynxes, and a porcupine." See Hollister, "Courtly Culture," p. 3.

1011 *The mayde aspyyd that resoun.* Brunner observes that in *b*, the princess has no way of knowing of the plan to have a lion slay Richard (*Löwenherz*, p. 21).

1029–30 *Away to wende . . . . so greve.* Given that Richard has grieved the king plenty, he is surely equivocating here.

1036 *Fourty, whyte as ony mylk.* Diverging from the *a* group, *b* (A, fol. 254v) includes the following couplet after this line: "And a sharpe Irissh knyf / As thow wolde saf my lyf." In addition to other details, Brunner considers the knife a rationalization and therefore a revision of the original text (*Löwenherz*, pp. 20, 22).

1057–1428 *Sertes, henne . . . . hys mede*. For a variant passage in A, see the corresponding Textual Note. In these lines from *b*, the king's daughter reveals her relation with Richard by admitting to her father that Richard promised her the lion's heart. Considering such a revelation unlikely, Brunner regards the daughter's statement as evidence that *b* is more distant from the original text than is *a* (*Löwenherz*, p. 22).

1103 *sat on des*. The *dais* was a raised platform on which was set the table reserved for the king and guests of honor. Compare line 3451 where, during Richard's second act of cannibalism, the Saracen ambassadors are seated at a side table while Richard sits "on des."

1109 *Wythouten bred the herte he eet*. A joke in itself, Richard's eating the heart without bread may imply a lack of courtesy or proper etiquette: bread was often used as a trencher or platter upon which to eat. Compare lines 3447–48 and its corresponding note. Akbari argues that Richard gains the lion's strength by consuming its heart, a result that mirrors the effect of the Eucharist ("Hunger," p. 208). See also McDonald's arguments referenced in the note to line 1118 below.

1112 *This is a devyl, and no man*. See note to line 500.

1118 *Stronge Rychard, Coer de Lyoun*. Romances often provide heroes with nicknames and calling brave men "lions" is a practice of long standing. McDonald lists early instances of Richard's epithet in her argument that *RCL* transforms the metaphoric — a lion's heart that stands for bravery — into a "mimetically coherent" narrative that renders the lion's heart both literal and edible: "That Richard's identity is contingent on an act of ingestion accords with the narrative's alimentary logic" ("Eating People," pp. 138–39).

1132 *traytour*. See note on *tretour* at line 929.

1136 *Raunsum for hys body take*. For a discussion on the historical Richard's capture and ransom, see Gillingham, *Richard I*, pp. 222–53.

1137 *For my doughtyr that he has schent*. In an aristocratic culture based on nobility of blood, a maiden's virginity was prized and heavily controlled; its loss was considered a disaster. For a discussion of the Church's not entirely successful prohibition upon sex outside of marriage, see, e.g., Brundage, *Law, Sex, and Christian Society*, p. 459.

1175 *chaunceler*. The king's chief administrative officer, the chancellor, "served as an itinerant justice, supervised the work of the exchequer, carried on various judicial services, administered all vacant holdings in the king's hand, handled diplomatic contacts and received important visitors, and dispensed royal patronage," (Alexander, "Becket," p. 151). In addition, the chancellor held special assignments like governing England during the king's absence.

1186 *Bothe myn erchebysschopys tway.* The archbishop of Canterbury and the archbishop of York. During Richard's reign (1189–1199), the archbishops of Canterbury were Baldwin (1184–1193) and Hubert Walter (1193–1207), both of whom saw action in the Crusades. Having travelled to the Holy Land with Richard on the Third Crusade, Walter brought the army back to England and also raised Richard's ransom of 100,000 marks. Geoffrey Plantagenet, illegitimate son of Henry II, served as archbishop of York from 1191 to 1212.

1191 *seel.* Attached to documents, the Great Seal of the Realm signaled the king's official approval.

1223 *Of every kyrke, lesse and more.* The lesser and greater churches, cathedrals as opposed to parish churches.

1258–68 *The kyng . . . . to undyrstande.* As with the summons to a parliament at Lincoln in *Havelok*, the king's broad summons here emphasizes a national framework (Turville-Petre, *England the Nation*, p. 147). Ruling through parliament and caring for one's people were ideal traits for an English king: compare Turville-Petre's discussion of the *Short Metrical Chronicle* (*England the Nation*, p. 109). The summons, by including both high and low classes, formulates an assembly of "an especially broad range of constituents," thus expressing both populist and nationalist impulses (Heng, "Romance of England," p. 158).

1267 *Serjauntes and every freholdande. Seriaunt* or *sergeaunt* is a broad term that included a rank of troops in both cavalry and infantry (Broughton, *Dictionary*, p. 415). Here, the term likely signifies a "tenant by military service under the rank of knight" (*MED* s.v. *sergeaunt* (n.), sense 2a). *Freholdande*, a participle used as a noun, denotes a freeholder (*MED* s.v. *fre-holding* (n.)). A freeholder is a tenant whose land is a freehold, that is, land held in fee simple in consideration for explicit services or payments (*MED* s.v. *fre-hold* (n.)).

1270 *Grykkyssche see.* See note to line 651.

1273 *And the croys that Cryst was on ded.* See note to line 1287 below.

1287 *Duke Myloun.* The defeat of the Christians under Duke Myloun motivates the crusade in *RCL*; he corresponds to Guy of Lusignan, who was king of Jerusalem from 1186–1192 through his marriage to King Baldwin's widow, Sibylla, a cousin of Richard's and a member of the house of Anjou (Gillingham, *Richard I*, p. 122). Guy's defeat by Saladin at the Battle of Hattin in 1187 and his loss of the True Cross prompted the Third Crusade, the effort to restore the kingdom of Jerusalem. Though a brave soldier, he was considered "a most incompetent general and an ineffective king" (Painter, "Third Crusade," p. 51). See also note to line 1307; Brunner, *Löwenherz*, pp. 51, 469; and Jentsch, "Quellen," p. 196. "Myloun" or "Milon" is perhaps a copyist's mistake for "Guion" (Paris, "Le Roman," p. 362n6).

1291 *Erl Renaud.* A likely reference to Reynald of Châtillon, Prince of Antioch, whom the chronicles report was beheaded by Saladin himself after the battle of Hattin (Nicholson, *Itinerarium*, 1.5, p. 34; Jentsch, "Quellen," p. 196; and Brunner, *Löwenherz*, p. 471).

1295 *Of Sarezynys that mysbelevyd.* For a discussion of the medieval West's use of the term "Saracen" as a Muslim Oriental, "a racial and religious marker," see Heng, *Empire*, p. 334n2. The growing scholarship on the medieval West's misperceptions of Islam includes Tolan, *Saracens*, and Frasetto and Blanks, *Western Views*.

1296 *Sawdon.* The title "sultan" (as well as "emir") historically referred to Muslim governors who gave allegiance to a caliph; more generally, *sawdon* may denote the ruler of a Muslim state.

1298 *Eerl Roys.* Brunner equates Earl Roys with Reginald of Kerak, one of many crusaders massacred by Saladin at Hattin. As Roys's betrayal of the Christians results in the loss of the True Cross and Acre, Brunner suggests he may also represent Raymond II of Tripoli (Brunner, *Löwenherz*, pp. 52, 471). Many believed Raymond guilty of treachery because he was one of the few to escape massacre at the Battle of Hattin, perhaps an unfair conclusion; see Ambroise, *Estoire*, 2:68n195. Ambroise states that Raymond and Saladin's notorious alliance led to the loss of the Holy Cross and to Christian suffering, in short, Saladin's victory at Hattin (*Estoire*, 1:39, lines 2443–47). He was also accused of betraying the Christians at the Battle of Tiberias (Paris, "Le Roman," p. 363n1).

1307 *Markes Feraunt.* A northern Italian nobleman, Conrad was the marquis of Montferrat from 1191 and, shortly before his death in 1192, the king of Jerusalem by marriage to Isabella of Jerusalem. A controversial figure in the Third Crusade, he arrived in Tyre after its residents agreed to terms with Saladin following the fall of Jerusalem in 1187; but under Conrad's able leadership, the city rallied and withstood a Muslim siege (Runciman, *History of the Crusades*, 2:471–72). After Saladin released Guy of Lusignan, king of Jerusalem, Conrad denied him entry into Tyre, ostensibly over the latter's failures at Hattin. In Guy and Conrad's feud over the kingship of Jerusalem, Richard had originally sided with Guy, which did not help the relationship between Richard and Conrad. Their difficult relationship led many Franks to believe Richard played a role in Conrad's assasination in 1192.

Conrad's dubious diplomatic activities rendered him suspect: among other acts, he had offered to attack Acre if Saladin, in return, ceded Sidon and Tyre. (In 1192, galleys under Conrad's command, in fact, attacked Acre in an attempt to wrest control from Guy.) In like manner, Richard's open dealings with leading Muslims earned the distrust of other crusaders and helped justify his capture and imprisonment by the German emperor, Henry VI (Gillingham, *Richard I*, pp. 23, 147–150, 183, 193, 195).

1310 *Crystyndom he forsook.* Conrad's dealings with Saladin no doubt inform this characterization; see note at line 1307 above. Analogues of Christians betraying their fellow warriors to Muslims — though without forsaking Christianity — are numerous and include Ganelon from the *Song of Roland*.

1311–12 *Thus thorwgh . . . . Holy Croys. RCL* revises history by diminishing Saladin's role and implying Christian control of Syria; but the battle of Hattin in 1187 enabled Saladin to consolidate his already substantial control of the territory. These lines equate Roys with Raymond II of Tripoli; see notes to lines 1298 and 1318.

1318 *Kyng Bawdewynys sone*. Duke Myloun corresponds historically to Guy of Lusignan, who was not King Baldwin IV's son, but the spouse of Baldwin's sister, Sibylla. Through this marriage Guy became king of Jerusalem; in 1187, he lost the kingdom at the Battle of Hattin as well as the True Cross. See Brunner, *Löwenherz*, p. 54, and Runciman's discussion of Guy (*History of the Crusades* 2:424–60).

1323 *Urban*. Pope Gregory VIII, not Urban, led the Third Crusade (Brunner, *Löwenherz*, p. 54). Urban II, though, attained fame in part from his advocating a crusade at the Council of Clermont in 1095; compare Paris, "Le Roman," p. 363n4. For a discussions of Urban's role and sources of his speech, see, e.g., Runciman, *History of the Crusades*, 1:106–118.

1325 *And asoylyd hem of here synne*. Promoting crusade at his famous speech at the Council of Clermont, Urban II is reported by Guibert de Nogent, among others, to have absolved all those who vowed to go on crusade (Peters, *First Crusade*, p. 37; Runciman, *History of the Crusades*, 1:108).

1331 *The duke of Bloys, the duke of Burgoyne*. Theobald V, count of Blois (1130–91) and a crusade participant, died during the siege of Acre (Brunner, *Löwenherz*, p. 463). Hugo III, duke of Burgundy (1143–92), accompanied the king of France on crusade but remained in the Holy Land as leader after Philip Augustus's departure (Brunner, *Löwenherz*, p. 463).

1332 *The duke of Ostrych, and duke of Cessoyne*. Leopold V, duke of Austria (1167–94), participated in the siege of Acre (Brunner, *Löwenherz*, p. 463). He quarrelled with Richard after Richard removed his banners and returned to Austria soon thereafter. See the note to lines 5997–98 below. No count of Soissons is known to have participated in the Third Crusade. Nor did Henry the Lion, Duke of Saxony, participate in this crusade (Brunner, *Löwenherz*, p. 464).

1335 *The eerl of Flaunders, the eerl of Coloyne*. Philip of Alsace died on 1 June, 1191, during the siege of Acre (Brunner, *Löwenherz*, p. 466). The Earl of Colyne is a fictitious person (Brunner, *Löwenherz*, p. 464).

1336 *The eerl of Artays, the eerl of Boloyne*. At the time of the Third Crusade, Louis, the eldest son of Philip II Augustus of France, was the count of Artois. He inherited the county at the age of three when his mother, Isabelle, died in 1190. Renaud de Demmartin (Reginald of Boulogne) was count of Boulogne from 1190 until his death in 1227. He is not known to have participated in the Third Crusade.

1343 *At Westemynstyr heeld a ryal feste*. See the notes to line 153 and line 241 above.

1348–75 *My leve frendes . . . . ye or nay*. Though the passage is simplified and condensed, *RCL* presents typical crusading propaganda. Such propaganda is widely studied, especially with regard to the First Crusade; see, e.g., Cowdrey, "Pope Urban II's Preaching" and its substantial references.

1351 *lewyd and lerde.* Proverbial: compare *The Ormulum*, line 19930; Chaucer's Physician's Tale (*CT* [VI(C)]283); and Whiting L157.

1354 *Hys bulle.* Granting privileges or issuing instructions, papal bulls were a form of charter or diploma whose name reflects the *bulla*, a bubble-like circular plate, source of the pope's authenticating seal: the name of the seal came to stand for the document.

1363 *Crystene men, children, wyf, and grome.* Altering history to demonize Muslims, *RCL* reports the savage slaying of women and children by Muslims; but Saladin was humane in his conquest of Jerusalem in 1187: not a single person was injured nor a building looted (Runciman, *History of the Crusades*, 2:466). In contrast, the crusaders who took Jerusalem in 1099 massacred so many Muslims that they waded in blood: "[M]addened by so great a victory after such suffering, [they] had rushed through the streets and into the houses and mosques [of Jerusalem] killing all that they had met, men, women and children alike" (Runciman, *History of the Crusades*, 1:286).

1387 *Mekyl folk that the croys have nomen.* The defining ritual of crusading, "taking the Cross," was also the earliest ceremony that distinguished holy war as a religious activity: copies of the ceremony were widely dispersed (Tyerman, *God's War*, pp. 480, 892). Urban II's role in founding this ritual is clear in Guibert de Nogent's report of his speech at the Council of Clermont: "He instituted a sign well suited to so honorable a profession by making the figure of the Cross, the stigma of the Lord's Passion, the emblem of the soldiery, or rather, of what was to be the soldiery of God. This, made of a kind of cloth, he ordered to be sewed upon the shirts, cloaks and *byrra* of those who were about to go" (Peters, *First Crusade*, p. 37). See also note to lines 1700–01 and line 2143.

1392–93 *Thrittene schyppys . . . . Of bees.* Heng argues that these bees with their hives and honey express economic and symbolic values that constitute "[i]n a single image, an ideological assertion of the [English] nation's character and unity, and an indelibly memorable romance weapon" (*Empire*, pp. 101–02). See lines 2902 (and its corresponding note) and 2910.

1394 *He leet make a tour ful strong.* An important element in siege warfare, towers protected attackers and their ladders as they stormed a fortress wall.

1398 *With an engine hyghte robynet.* As lines 2921–24 indicate, this engine is likely a trebuchet, a lever and sling designed to hurl large stones hundreds of feet.

1399 *mangenel.* A *mangonel* is a machine used to hurl stones and other heavy objects during sieges and defences of cities and castles. See also line 2904.

1407 *maystyr Aleyn Trenchemere.* Appropriately named, Alan Trenchemer ("Cut the sea") was a celebrated twelfth century mariner who commanded the ship that brought the king from Germany to England after his captivity (Roger of

Howden, *Chronica* 3:206, 3:235; Jentsch, "Quellen," p. 222; and Brunner, *Löwenherz*, p. 58). The historical commanders of the departing fleet were "Gerard, Archbishop of Aix, Bernhard, Bishop of Bayonne, Robert de Sabloil, Richard de Camville, and Willaim de Fortz of Oleron" (Nicholas, *Royal Navy*, p. 87). See also note to line 2479.

1415 *Catayl, dromoun, and galeye*. *Catail* designates the principal ship (*MED*); a *dromoun(d)* was a fast and large seagoing vessel (*MED*); and *galei(e)* referred to a seagoing ship with both sails and oars (*MED*, sense 1a).

1417 *Marchylé*. Marseille. Richard's sending his fleet ahead with orders to wait for him in Marseille is historically accurate (Brunner, *Löwenherz*, p. 52).

1423 *Modard, the kyng*. Heng observes that the name of this king who serves as Richard's chief Christian foe recalls "Mordred," who betrayed Arthur in Geoffrey's *Historia*, and thus serves as one instance of *RCL*'s "repeated invocation of Arthur as Richard's forbear in cultural mythology" (*Empire*, pp. 66, 336n8). See also Jones, "Richard the Lionheart in German Literature," p. 71n3, and Blurton, *Cannibalism*, p. 124.

1430 *Goddys owne palmere*. As the crusades were conceived as both military expedition and pilgrimage, crusaders were both soldiers and pilgrims; see the Introduction (p. 2 and p. 2n7).

1432 *The erchebysschop, Sere Bawdewynys*. While the text indicates that Baldwin, the Archbishop of Canterbury, departed in advance directly from England, Baldwin and others sailed from Marseille to Outremer, arriving in Tyre on 16 September, 1190 (Gillingham, *Richard I*, p. 129; and Brunner, *Löwenherz*, p. 54).

1437–1666 *Three hoostes . . . . Holy Londe*. Richard's journey of revenge to Germany is not included in the *b* version. Brunner does not consider this episode to have been part of the lost Anglo-Norman original, in part due to the present participle in *-and(e)* in lines 1522 and 1525 (*Löwenherz*, p. 19). In contrast, witnesses of *b* take Richard to Marseille (A, fol. 255v).

> To Marcelly he wente ful right
> With Barons and many a knyght,
> W[ith] shipp[es] galies grete and smale,
> Ne couthe no man but god that tale.

See Brunner (*Löwenherz*, p. 157n).

1450 *Traytours lookes ye honge and drawe*. Punishments for treason included hanging, drawing, quartering, emasculation, disemboweling, and beheading. Some traitors were even flayed alive: see Barron's discussion of these severe punishments ("Penalties for Treason," pp. 189–200) and the note to line 722.

1452 *The bysschop of York, my chauncelere*. Richard's chancellor was actually William Longchamp, Bishop of Ely (Gillingham, *Richard I*, pp. 121–22). See the note at line 1175 for a discussion of the chancellor's duties.

1481 *styward*. A steward is the "principal officer in charge of the domestic affairs of a royal or imperial household, a seneschal" (*MED* s.v. *steuard*, (n.), sense 1b).

1512 *servyse*. "Service" here refers to the sequence of dishes.

1549 *Marburette*. Perhaps Marbourg (Paris, "Le Roman," p. 358n1).

1565 *Carpentras*. Located in southeastern France, Carpentras, never part of Germany, was part of the Holy Roman Empire (Paris, "Le Roman," p. 358n3).

1588 *Ye schole be kyssyd*. A common practice, the exchange of kisses between men formed part of such rituals as the ceremony of homage where the lord "kissed his [new] vassal on the mouth" (Major, "'Bastard Feudalism,'" pp. 509–10). Overtly representing reconciliation, kisses between males are frequent in *RCL*; see lines 607, 1613, 1673, 1749, and 2687.

1639 *Twoo ryche rynges of gold*. A folklore motif, rings that bestow invulnerability occur in a number of ME romances; see, e.g., *Sir Eglamour of Artois*, lines 607–12; and *Sir Perceval of Galles*, lines 1839–64.

1649 *Serjauntes of armes*. A sergeant of arms is an officer in the service of the king or other person of rank who is usually armed (*MED* s.v. *sergeaunt* (n.), sense 2b).

1657 *Roberd of Leycester*. The historical Robert de Beaumont, fourth Earl of Leicester, accompanied Richard I on the Third Crusade. As he does with Fulk D'Oilly and Thomas Moulton, Finlayson suggests that Robert's extensive role in Richard's crusading exploits in the *a* version of *RCL* may serve to glorify the redactor's patron or family ("'*Richard, Coer de Lyon*,'" p.166).

1659 *Robert Tourneham*. Mentioned in lines 2102, 2120, 4051, 4900, 6133, and 7151, Robert de Turnham (of Thornham) (d. 1211) was a soldier and administrator closely associated with Richard I during the Third Crusade and afterward. Having commanded half the naval force during the conquest of Cyprus, Turnham and Richard de Camville served as joint administrators of Cyprus after the crusaders departed. As Richard's *familiaris*, he carried the king's equipment from the Holy Land to Europe. He also served Richard as seneschal of Anjou (Gillingham, *Richard I*, pp. 150–52, 329).

1661 *Al redy they founde there here flete*. Historically, Richard did not find his fleet in Marseille but waited there for days before giving up and proceeding to the Holy Land in hired ships (Brunner, *Löwenherz*, p. 55; and Gillingham, *Richard I*, pp. 129–30).

1669–2040 *Before the gates . . . . he wente*. For a discussion of the turbulant relations between Richard, Philip, Tancred, and other historical points of tension that characterized Richard's adventures in Sicily, see Runciman, *History of the Crusades*, 3:38–43; and Gillingham, *Richard I*, pp. 132–39. By reproducing only Philip's aggression, not Tancred's, *RCL* clearly displays its anti-French bias.

1669 *Gryffouns.* Crusaders and others insulted Byzantine Greeks by calling them gryphons, the name of a fabulous animal with the front of an eagle and the rear of a lion. Sicily formed part of the Byzantine empire until the late eleventh century, but the insult applied to Muslims as well. See Nicholson, *Itinerarium,* p. 155n45. As the West believed Greeks to be thieves, the insult may stress the gryphon's rapacious nature (Livingston, "Grifon," p. 48).

1677 *tresoun.* See the note on *treason* at line 722 above.

1679 *a wryt.* Philip sent not a writ — a legal document that compels action — but a letter to Tancred of Lecce, the illegitimate cousin of the late William II of Sicily, maligning Richard as a traitor. Tancred delivered the letter to Richard who declared his innocence immediately. See Roger of Howden, *Chronica,* 3:98 (trans. Archer, *Crusade,* pp. 49–50); cited by Brunner, *Löwenherz,* p. 55. See note to line 1726 below.

1700–1701 *Kyng Richard . . . . Holy Lande.* These lines refer to Richard's protected status as both pilgrim and crusader. Having taken the cross — *croysyd* — he has taken crusade vows that both impose obligations and afford protections; see Brundage, *Medieval Canon Law,* pp. 30–65.

1712 *Rys.* Reggio di Calabria, the capital of Tancred's kingdom of Sicily (Brunner, *Löwenherz,* p. 471).

1726 *mysdede thee.* Historically, Richard held legitimate grievances against Tancred. After William II, king of Sicily, died in 1189, Tancred became king. Not trusting William's widow, Joanna (Richard's sister), he held her in confinement and would not release her dower. Tancred also withheld from Richard a large legacy that William II had left to Richard's father, Henry II (Runciman, *History of the Crusades,* 3:38).

1762 *Quarters.* A quarter is "a unit of dry measure of approximately eight bushels" (*MED, quarter(e* (n.), sense 3e).

1768 *Under the house of the Hospytall.* The Knights Hospitallers of St. John of Jerusalem. Originally a group of men attached to an Amalfi hospital that cared for pilgrims to the Holy Land, the Hospitallers became a military order after the conquest of Jerusalem in 1099. They were the earliest order of crusading knights, a chivalric order that combined Christian asceticism with chivalric ideals. Organized to protect the pilgrims' hospital in Jerusalem, they took vows of poverty, chastity, and obedience. They became powerful through donations and built castles and hospitals in the Holy Land and in Europe. Hospitaller influence in Sicily can be dated to the time of Roger II, king of Sicily (1130–54) but increased during the reign of Frederick II, king of Sicily and Jerusalem. From their headquarters in the Holy Land, the Krak de Chevaliers, "one of the largest castels ever built," the Hospitallers played a vital, well-documented role in the crusades, as did the Templars (Nickel, "Chivalry," 3.303–04). The Knights of St. John exist today as the Knights of Malta. See also line 3152.

1771–72 *The Frensshe . . . . Englyssche knyghtes.* Chronicle accounts report that conflict with the local citizens prompted Richard's conquest of Messina. See, e.g., Nicholson, *Itinerarium*, 2.11–22, pp. 154–70; and Brunner, *Löwenherz*, p. 52.

1776 *Of the Englysshe taylardes.* In *RCL*, the French and Greeks repeatedly abuse the English by calling them "tailed ones;" see lines 1878, 1886, 1960, 2006, 2124–25, and 2158. As beasts and devils have tails, the insult "makes the English over into devilish unbelievers and bestial animals," the very heathen hounds they considered their enemies — Muslims, Jews, heretics — to be while mocking English sexual practices, especially those of Richard I (Heng, *Empire*, pp. 94–95). The only instances of this term of abuse noted by the *MED* occur in *RCL*: s.v. *tailarde* (sense a). The epithet *caudatus Anglicus* or "tailed English" likely derives from a legend that has pagan Englishmen growing tails after the devil urged them to abuse St. Augustine of Canterbury: for a discussion of sources and scholarship, see Broughton (*Legends of Richard I*, pp. 93–97).

1807–09 *The table . . . . in haste.* Compare *The King of Tars*, lines 101–05:

> He shuld venge him wiþ his swerd,
> He swore bi seyn Mahoun.
> Þe table so heteliche he smot
> It fel into þe fire fot-hot,
> & loked as a lyoun.

1810 *He wolde not wende for Crystes faste.* The conflict in Messina actually broke out on 4 October and lasted not days but hours (Nicholson, *Itinerarium*, 2.16, p. 159; for additional sources, see Brunner, *Löwenherz*, p. 55).

1814–16 *The erle . . . . Longe Spaye.* William Longespée, the third Earl of Salisbury, an illegitimate son of Henry II and Countess Ida de Tosny, took no part in the Third Crusade. See Loomis, Review, p. 456; and Brunner, *Löwenherz*, p. 468. He should not be confused with William Longespee II, an English hero of the Battle of Mansura during the Seventh Crusade. (Lloyd, "William Longespee II," p. 41).

1842 *mayster maryners.* Wardens of the ports.

1849–50 *I have . . . . tembre of Englonde.* Present in the earliest manuscript witness, L (the Auchinleck MS), c. 1330, this line, a "charming nationalist fiction," is set within *RCL*'s representation of an historical event — Richard's subjugation of Sicily — and may reflect English nationalist sentiment "on the eve of Edward III's long-lasting war with France" (Finlayson, "'*Richard, Coer de Lyon*,'" p. 171).

1856 *mate-gryffon.* Frequently used — see lines 2898, 2943, 6090, and 6109 — the *mate-gryffon* was a portable siege engine whose name means "harm (evil) of the Greeks." Historically, Richard's mate-gryphon was a wooden castle erected on a hill overlooking Messina. See Nicholson, *Itinerarium*, 2.20, p. 167; Gillingham, *Richard I*, p. 136; and Brunner, *Löwenherz*, pp. 55–56.

1858 *And holde up well your manshippes.* "Do up your manshyppes" may be paraphrased as "maintain or raise your spirits" (*MED* s.v. *manship(e* (n.), sense 1c). Heng includes this phrase in her discussion of *RCL*'s phallic imagery, bestial puns, and sodomy (*Empire*, p. 195).

1878 *The tayled dogges.* See note at line 1776.

1902 *wylde fyre.* Also known as Greek fire, this incendiary, which the Byzantines developed, burned on water and enabled them to break the Arab siege of Constantinople in the late seventh century. Arab use of the weapon during the Crusades produced superstitious awe among the Christians. Frequent mention of Greek fire in chronicles, *chansons de geste*, and recipe books indicates a cultural preoccupation with the weapon that *RCL*, no doubt, reflects; see lines 2477, 2589, 2624, 2644–45, 2650, 2760, 4398, 5269, 5395, 5432, 5439, 6051, 6101, and 6161. Wildfire became an integral part of crusading warfare. Defenders poured or shot the incendiary onto besiegers through a variety of means. See Partington's *Greek Fire* for a sustained treatment of the weapon.

1909 *londe gate.* As its name implies, a fortified entrance on land as opposed to a water gate; compare *Bevis of Hampton*, lines 4491–92: "And afterward, ase ye mai hure, / Londegate thai sette a fure."

1919 *a gate one.* Chronicles describe Richard's forces entering Messina through an unguarded back gate. See Nicholson, *Itinerarium*, 2.16, p. 162; Brunner, *Löwenherz*, p. 59.

1931 *His baner upon the wall he pulte.* Chronicles report King Philip's anger at seeing Richard's banners above Messina. The people of Messina must have deemed Philip's presence a guarantee of their safety, so Richard's victory humiliated him: "He [Philip] demanded that the banners should be taken down and his own hoisted up in their place. To plant a banner in a captured town was to stake a claim to a share in its government and its plunder" (Gillingham, *Richard I*, p. 135).

1939 *Porcules.* A portcullis is a "heavy wooden or metal grating . . . housed in a castle room immediately above the entrance passage and dropped vertically in grooves in the wall to block a passageway" (Broughton, *Dictionary*, p. 376).

1967 *vyage.* OF *voiage* came to convey both "pilgrimage" and "crusade"; see Trotter, *Medieval French Literature*, pp. 38–39.

1975 *so sayth the boke.* A reference to the French source; see note at line 21.

1984–85 *And bad Rycharde . . . . agayne than.* This demonstration of Philip's avaricious hypocrisy is another example of *RCL*'s anti-French bias.

2003 *Margaryte.* This comical French justice's name may derive from Tancred's admiral, Margaritus (Runciman, *History of the Crusades*, 3:39).

2016 *And Rycharde was soone at his tayle.* See Heng's discussion of the varied resonances in *RCL*'s use of "tail" (*Empire*, p. 95). See also the note to line 1776.

2019 *Ternes and quernes.* When used non-figuratively, these terms refer to casts in which both dice yield either three or four respectively. See MED, *terne* (n.2).

2040 *And than on his waye he wente.* After this line, E, D, A, and H — each manuscript of the *b* group (except L) — contains a passage that refers to Richard's historical mother, Eleanor of Aquitane, and his future wife, Berengaria of Navarre:

> His moder sent hym a fair[e] p[re]sent:
> Elianor[e] brought hym Beringer,
> The kynges dought[er] of Nauern[e].
> King Ric[hard], the p[re]cou[n]s,
> Beringer he shulde spouse,
> And he sayde, "Nay, not in þ[at] sesouns."
> He nolde her spouse amonge þ[e] G[ri]ffouns.
> Aft[er] Est[er], yf he hadde lyf,
> He wolde her spouse to his wyf.
> Alianore her leue toke
> And wente home, so seþ þe boke. (A, fol. 258r)

2046 *With moche store of sylver and golde.* Lacking in the *a* group, after this line in *b* appears the following passage that mentions both Berengaria and Joan, Richard's sister:

> Joh[a]n and Beringer, his wyf,
> Dude him byfor[e] to arif.
> K[ing] R[ichard] come after, so seith þe boke,
> All his grete nawes for to loke,
> Ffor the tempeste and for the wawes,
> And eke for the maistres outlawes. (A, fol. 258r)

2049–2457 *Charged with tresour . . . . helde afterwarde.* *RCL*'s account of the storm, the three wrecked ships, their plundering by Cypriots, and Richard's conquest of Cyprus reflect historical events; see, e.g., Gillingham, *Richard I*, pp. 144–53; and Edbury, *Conquest of Jerusalem*, pp. 175–82. Though not religiously significant like Jerusalem, Cyprus was of great strategic value: it offered "a rich and secure supply and naval base close to the coast of Palestine"; and its emperor, in alliance with Saladin, had been denying supplies to the starving crusaders at Acre (Prestwich, "*Rex Bellicosus*," pp. 8–9). While Acre, the last possession of the Kingdom of Jerusalem, fell in 1291, Cyprus did not fall to the Turks until 1571 (Prestwich, "*Rex Bellicosus*," p. 16). For Richard, taking Cyprus was "the most far-sighted and the most enduring of all of his achievements on the Crusade" (Runciman, *History of the Crusades*, 3:46). See the Explanatory Note to line 2040 above, which mentions an additional or fourth ship whose passengers included Richard's historical mother, Eleanor of Aquitaine, his sister, Joan, and his betrothed, Berengaria of Navarre.

2051 *A grete tempest arose sodaynly.* While such tempests are frequent plot devices in the romance genre, a storm in fact made travel difficult for Richard's fleet (Gillingham, *Richard I*, p. 144).

2069 *Grete slaughter of our Englysshe maked.* An exaggeration. The English "who reached dry land were imprisoned and their money taken" (Gillingham, *Richard I*, p. 144).

2102 *Roberte of Turnam.* See note to line 1659.

2107 *Saynt Denys.* St. Denys, bishop of Paris, martyr and patron of France. The abbey built over his and his fellow martyrs' tomb became the burial place for French kings. Richard's swearing by the patron saint of France may reflect the French source that the narrator repeatedly invokes; see lines 21 and 3012 and related notes. Of course, the exigencies of rhyme may have influenced the choice: Ailes and Barber note a similar instance involving a Welshman in Ambroise (*Estoire*, 2:84 and 2:84n265). That a cult of St. Denys existed in England with "no fewer than forty-one ancient churches in his name" lessens the oddity of an English king swearing an oath on the name of France's patron saint (Farmer, *Saints*, p. 135). See also line 3278.

2135 *stewarde.* "Steward" refers to the official in charge of the domestic affairs of a house or estate, a seneschal. The position, "high stewarde," refers to a position in charge of the domestic affairs of a great or royal house, in this case, that of the emperor of Cyprus. See lines 2345 and 2435.

2143 *For he is crossed and pylgrym.* See note to line 1387.

2147–62 *The eyen . . . . tourne agayne!* Paris suggests a story as a source for this event from the songs of the First Crusade, that of *Estatin l'esnasé* (Tatinus the noseless). In Pierre Langtoft's chronicle account of Richard's conquest of Cyprus, the emperor mistreats a seneshal named Statin (Paris, "Le Roman," p. 389). Jentsch notes Roger of Howdon's account of the Emperor of Cyprus removing a baron's nose upon receiving unwelcome advice ("Quellen," p. 223). Ambroise reports that the emperor cut off the hands, feet, and noses of captured crusaders and of Cypriots who had surrendered to Richard (*Estoire*, 1:31–32, lines 1944–55). See also Brunner, *Löwenherz*, pp. 64–65, 64n5.

2185–86 *The erle . . . . he layed.* In the medieval West, chess was viewed more as a noble game than as a frivolous or harmful pastime. Peter Damien's imposing a penance in 1061 to a bishop for playing chess and St. Louis's ban of chess in France in 1254 were isolated events. Even though chess was viewed as "ennobling men's minds instead of corrupting their souls" (Nickel, "Games," p. 351), playing chess for money likely tarnished the nobility of the pursuit: for example, the author of the pseudo-Ovidian *De vetula* praises the game's honorable, noble status but rebukes those who play chess for money (Adams, *Power Play*, pp. 167–68n19). Here, *RCL's* populist tendencies emphasize not nobility and honor but gambling and aggressive, virile competition. Compare, for example, the opening of the Middle Dutch *Roman van Walewein* in which a chess board magically floats through a window and bedazzles

Arthur's court before disappearing. In this courtly romance, Arthur's quest to find the magic chess board expresses a connection between the game and political order, between playing "chess and improving one's ability to govern one's kingdom (and, implicitly . . . one's self)." This connection is made explicit in such thirteenth-century treatises as Jacobus de Cessolis's *De ludo scachorum* (Adams, *Power Play*, p. 4). As a popular romance, *RCL* presents the virile hero's victorious wagering, not the privileged status of chess or its ties to the political order. See Adams, *Power Play*, pp. 3–4.

2194 *In dede lyon, in thought, lybarde*. A formulation that stresses the bravery of the lion and the craftiness or cunning of the leopard.

2202 *the hayle stone*. For a discussion of the collective singular, see Brunner, *Löwenherz*, p. 43.

2209–11 *Kynge Rycharde . . . . the nones*. Intended for Saracens and deployed by the English king, this ax symbolizes the nationalism that characterizes the poem's crusading ideal (Turville-Petre, *England the Nation*, p. 123). Favored by Anglo-Saxon warriors, used by Normans at the battle of Hastings and by Anglo-Normans afterwards, the battle-ax, as used by Richard, "unites two opposing military and political lineages, signaling their combination in the now-English king" (Heng, *Empire*, p. 101; see also Akbari, "Hunger," p. 203). One chronicle reports that Richard, upon arriving to relieve the siege of Jaffa, "armed himself with his hauberk, hung his shield at his neck and took a Danish axe in his hand" and "jumped into the sea followed by his men" (Edbury, *Conquest of Jerusalem*, p. 117). An illustration in L (fol. 326), which depicts in the bow of a galley, "a bearded knight, on whose red surcoat white leopards are distinguishable, grasping a large ax in his hands," likely refers to this chronicle report. See Loomis's description of the illustration ("Pas Saladin," pp. 522–23). See also the note to line 4594.

2251 *The emperours doughter*. The emperor's daughter, a child, was captured after the siege of Kyrenia. Richard entrusted her into the care of his queen (Ambroise, *Estoire*, 1:18, lines 1076–83; Nicholson, *Itinerarium*, 2.41, p. 195).

2334 *That one hyght Favell and that other Lyarde*. According to Ambroise, Richard seized several horses in Cyprus, including the emperor's own "Fauvel," who became his war-horse (*Estoire*, 1:30, lines 1840–42; 1:31, line 1927; 1:107, lines 6597–98; 1:115, line 7104; and 1:125, line 7735). The second name, "Lyarde," need not be historical as both names indicate color: *fauvel* designates a dun, fallow, or fawn-colored horse, and *liard*, the color gray (Brunner, *Löwenherz*, p. 59). Broughton argues that "Favel" means "favor" and cites its occurrence in the *chanson de geste*, *Otinel* (*Legends of Richard I*, p. 100).

2345 *hygh stewarde*. See note to line 2135.

2353–54 *Homage by . . . . hym helde*. Expressing feudal vassalage, the emperor submits to Richard in the ritual of homage that makes Richard his lord. The emperor's submission and other details correspond to historical accounts; see, e.g., Ambroise, *Estoire*, 1:32–33, lines 2006–61 (Brunner, *Löwenherz*, p. 52).

2383–85 *He fell on . . . . good entent.* The emperor fulfills Richard's two demands from lines 2372–73: "And crye me mercy with sorowe, / Homage by yere me to bere." In the traditional ceremony of commendation, "the man doing homage clasped his hands together, placed them between the hands of his superior, and briefly acknowledged himself to be his 'man'" (Reedy, "Commendation," p. 490).

2387 *Fewté he dyde hym, and homage.* A reference to the oath of fealty that normally accompanied the ritual of homage discussed above in the note to lines 2383–85. By this oath, the vassal swore — that is, invoked the divine name in witness to the truth — to be faithful to his master.

2443 *treuth.* See note at line 2387 above.

2455 *He made hym stewarde of that londe.* Richard left the governance of Cyprus, not to Robert of Leicester but to Richard of Camville and Robert of Turnham (Roger of Howdon, *Chronica*, 3:111; Brunner, *Löwenherz*, p. 56).

2472–2606 *They sawgh . . . . Seynt Edmound. RCL*'s depiction of the capture and sinking of the Saracen ship reflects chronicle accounts of a similar incident, for example, the Saracens' claim of being French (line 2489), and the richness of the ship's stores of weapons and food (lines 2588–98). See, e.g., Gillingham, *Richard I*, pp. 157–58. The passage, though, omits one weapon found in the chronicles: 200 deadly snakes (Nicholson, *Itinerarium*, 2.42, pp. 195–99; and Ambroise, *Estoire*, 1:35–36, lines 2141–99). Since this portion follows historical accounts, Brunner argues that it formed part of the original French poem (*Löwenherz*, p. 52).

2477 *wylde fyre.* Wild fire. See note at line 1902.

2479 *Aleyn Trenchemer.* Compare Nicholson, *Itinerarium*, 2.42, p. 196, which names Peter des Barres as the sailor Richard commands to approach the vessel. See also note to line 1407.

2495 *Seynt Thomas of Ynde.* The Saracen swears by St. Thomas, the apostle who doubted Christ's Resurrection. By one tradition, Thomas evangelized the Syrian Christians in Malabar and was killed and buried at Mylapre, near Madras (Farmer, *Saints*, pp. 470–71).

2541 *The galey rente with the bronde.* Compare Nicholson, *Itinerarium*, 2.42, p. 198. The *bronde* was an ornamental timber on the bow.

2580 *Sayden he was a devyl of helle.* See note to line 500 above.

2589 *Many barel ful of fyr Gregeys.* See note at line 1902 above.

2590 *And many a thousand bowe Turkeys.* Though requiring greater strength than other bows, the shorter Turkish or Turco-Mongol form of composite bow was well suited for use on horseback. For a discussion, see Tarassuk and Blair, *Arms and Weapons*, pp. 98–99.

2600–04 *For hadde . . . . ben iwunne!* An accurate assessment: "How great a loss this was to the Muslims is clear from Baha al-Din's claim that Saladin took the news 'with perfect resignation to God's will.' For Imad al-Din, it was a critical turning point" (Gillingham, *Richard I*, p. 158; citations omitted).

2606 *Seynt Edmound.* This reference to Edmund, king of East Anglia (841–69 CE), links Richard's crusading exploits to an early English warrior-saint. After his defeat and capture by the Vikings, Edmund would neither deny his Christian faith nor rule as a Viking vassal; thus, he became a martyr and hero and "fulfilled the ideals of Old English heroism, provincial independence, and Christian sanctity" (Farmer, *Saints*, pp. 151–52).

2635–36 *And whan . . . . it atwayne.* For a chronicle reference to a chain drawn across the entrance to the Acre's harbor, see Ambroise, *Estoire*, 1:63–64, lines 3940–54.

2641 *clarré.* Clary, a wine sweetened with honey and then clarified by straining.

2656 *melle.* Heng argues that the "English king's supernatural windmill," which appears to grind not grain but bones, "is a hyperbolic expression of English, and Western, technological superiority. . ." (*Empire*, p. 102).

2679 *And sayd he was the devyll of hell.* For *RCL*'s frequent association of Richard with the devil, see the note to line 500.

2693–94 *The archebysschop . . . . his servyse.* The historical record indicates that the Pisans swore allegiance to Richard upon his arrival, and that the archbishop of Pisa, Ubaldo Laufranchi, was their leader. For references, see Brunner, *Löwenherz*, p. 52n; and Paris, "Le Roman," p. 378.

2699–2884 *Kynge Richard . . . . to felle.* The archbishop's account of the siege of Acre. One chronicle reports that the siege of Acre began in August of 1189 and lasted four years, not seven (Nicholson, *Itinerarium*, 1.26, p. 70). See also Brunner, *Löwenherz*, pp. 52–53. For an historical discussion of the siege, see Rogers, *Latin Siege Warfare*, pp. 212–36.

2710 *Saladyn the Sawdon.* Saladin (Salah ed-Din Yusuf, 1138–1193), a Kurdish soldier and brilliant military commander who became Sultan of Egypt, Damascus, and Aleppo, and who founded the Ayyubid dynasty. Militarily, he is noted for defeating the crusaders at the Battle of Hattin in 1187 and for re-taking Jerusalem and regaining control of Syria from the crusaders; only Tyre, Tripoli, and Antioch remained under Frankish control. Saladin's reputation for chivalry and for charity is equally impressive. See the Introduction, pp. 15–17.

2713–20 *And with hym . . . . hys name!* Though his behavior was considered treasonous by some, Conrad of Montferrat never converted to Islam. In fact, after the conquest of Acre, his personal standard accompanied those of Richard and Philip as they were borne into Acre (Runciman, *History of the Crusades*, 3:51). Both he and Richard held negotiations with Saladin that damaged their reputations with contemporaries (Ambroise, *Estoire*, 1:41–44, lines 2574–2737; Gillingham, *Richard I*, pp. 157–58, 162, 183–84). See note at line 1307, and Brunner, *Löwenherz*, p. 56.

2714 *Mahoun and Termagaunt*. Typical of the medieval West's inaccurate conception of Islam, *Richard* portrays Muslims as polytheists who worship *Termagaunt*, a fictitious deity, and Muhammad, not the prophet but a god. References to other Muslim gods include Jupiter (*Jubiterre*) at line 4451, Apollo (*Appolyn*) at line 3744, and Pluto (*Plotoun*) at line 6476. For a broad discussion of this misrepresentation of Islam, see Tolan's *Saracens* and his *Sons of Ishmael*.

2732–46 *Befel that .... withouten pyté!* Ambroise recounts a similar story of a German horse that led to many crusader deaths (Ambroise, *Estoire*, 1:47–49, lines 2952–3071). See Brunner, *Löwenherz*, p. 56. For a list of Christian nobles who fell before Richard and Philip's arrival in Acre, including William of Ferrers, Earl of Derby (at line 2741), see Ambroise, *Estoire*, 2:6.

2744 *Janyn, the Eerl of Playn Spayne*. This earl, as yet unidentified, may be fictitious. Compare Brunner, *Löwenherz*, p. 467.

2743 *And the Emperour of Alemayne*. As he and his army approached Antioch from Armenia, the Emperor of Germany, Frederick I, in fact drowned in a river on 10 June, 1190 (Runciman, *History of the Crusades*, 3:15; Brunner, *Löwenherz*, p. 56).

2749–52 *He leet .... to quelle*. Ambroise reports that "Saladin had all the bodies of the dead taken and returned to us by throwing them into the river of Acre" (*Estoire*, 2:76, lines 3072–93). In 1192 at a later point in the crusade, Saladin reacted to Richard's victory against a caravan by destroying cisterns and filling in wells (Gillingham, *Richard I*, p. 208). Heng suggests that Saladin's acts recall the libel of well-poisoning made against medieval Jews and so conflates the two groups (*Empire*, p. 79; "Romance of England," p. 143).

2775 *On Seynt Jamys even*. The eve of St. James, 25 July. See the note on St. James at line 4817.

2822 *Sente us sone socouryng*. Compare Nicholson, *Itinerarium*, 1.41–42, pp. 97–99, noted by Brunner, *Löwenherz*, p. 53.

2823 *The doughty eerl of Champayne*. Actually Henry II, the Count of Champagne (1181–1197), one of the most powerful barons of France. He was the nephew of both Richard I and Philip II; his mother, Mary, was the daughter of Eleanor of Aquitaine and king Louis VII of France, a marriage later annulled. After the death of Conrad of Montferrat, he married Isabel, Conrad's widow, and so became King of Jerusalem. Undeservedly maligned in *RCL*'s biased picture of the French, he played an important role in the Third Crusade and remained loyal to Richard; see, e.g., Runciman, *History of the Crusades*, 3:28–29, 55, 64–67, and 72–73; Gillingham, *Richard I*, pp. 165n49, 192n1, 201–03, and 219–20; and Heng, *Empire*, p. 109.

2825 *Randulf, the Glamvyles*. Ranulf de Glanville, chief justiciar for Henry II, resigned upon Richard's accession in 1189 and then took the Cross: compare Nicholson, *Itinerarium*, 1.42, p. 99 and 99n210; Loomis, Review, p. 456.

2826 *Jhon the Neel.* A reference to Jean de Nesle, a hero of the Fourth Crusade (Loomis, Review, p. 456).

2831 *Huberd Gawter of Yngelande.* Bishop of Salisbury, Hubert Gautier or Hubert Walter became in 1193 the Archbishop of Canterbury. His deeds feature prominently in chronicles of the crusades; see, e.g., Nicholson, *Itinerarium*, 1.78, pp. 135–36, and 6.34, pp. 377–79.

2837–65 *At Myghhylmasse . . . . for woo.* The crusaders' periodic shortages of food — during the winter of 1190, for example — are well attested (Runciman, *History of the Crusades*, 3:27), but the manner in which the shortages are recounted — the listing of prices — follow a typological pattern also found in chronicles of the First Crusade: "The most common strategy of the *Gesta* [*Francorum*] for illustrating the severity of the famine was to list the prices of food; the same strategy is used in 4 Kings 6" (Rubenstein, "Cannibals and Crusaders," p. 549n100). For the significance of typological patterns in *RCL*, especially those related to cannibalism, see the Introduction, pp. 6–9 and 17–20.

2855 *For fourty pound.* A "pound" is "an English monetary unit based on a Tower pound of silver; a pound sterling" (*MED*, s.v. *pound(e* (n.1), sense 2a).

2857 *A swyn for an hundryd floryn.* The "floren" was "an English gold coin worth 6s. 8d [6 shillings, 8 pence]" (*MED*). It may refer to a "gold coin minted at Florence and stamped with the figure of a lily," but the term may refer to any foreign gold. The Muslim and Jewish prohibition on swine would have made their meat rare, and hence expensive, in the Middle East.

2858 *A goos for half mark.* A "mark" is a "monetary unit equal to 160 pennies or 2/3 of a pound sterling" (*MED*, s.v. *mark(e* (n.2), sense 2a).

2860 *of penyes, fyftene schillinges.* A *penye* or penny was an "English silver coin, weighing approximately 22 grains, decreasing in weight and value from about 1300 A.D., equal to 1/12 of a shilling or 1/240 of a pound" (*MED*, s.v. *peni* (n.), sense 1a). After the Norman Conquest, the English monetary unit known as the shilling, was "worth twelve pence or one twentieth of a pound" (*MED*, s.v. *shilling* (n.), sense 1a).

2876 *whyt tourneys.* "A denier of Tours worth four fifths that of Paris; also, a debased coin imitative of the French silver tournois" (*MED* s.v. *tourneis* (n. 2)).

sterlyng. This refers to the English silver penny (*MED* s.v. *sterling*, sense a).

2898 *And arerede hys mate-gryffoun.* See note at line 1856 above.

2902 *shyppes full of been.* Arguably part of a symbolic vocabulary for imagining the English nation, bees and their hive were a "figure for the polity since the time of Bede." And since the West imported sugar from the East but exported honey to the East, *RCL*'s use of bees as weapons may serve as "a defiant statement of economic and ideological superiority" (Heng, *Empire*, pp. 101–02). See also note to lines 1392–93.

2904 *magnel.* See note to line 1399.

2926 *mynour.* One who undermines fortifications.

2983 *With thre gryffouns depayntyd weel.* A fabulous animal often represented in Western heraldry, the gryphon "is formed by the body, hind-legs and tail of a lion conjoined to the head and claws [and wings] of an eagle, the latter acting as its forepaws" (Fox-Davies, Heraldry, pp. 222–24; insertion mine). This representation of the knightly culture of the East using herladic symbols common in the West evinces the transnational nature of chivalry. "Gryphon" was also a term of abuse for Greeks; see note at line 1669.

2989–90 *And on everylkon . . . . a lyoun.* The dragon serves as an appropriate heraldic symbol for Saracens: likening the animal to the devil, bestiaries described the dragon as the worst serpent. As no other figure "plays such an important or such an extensive part in armory as the lion" (Fox-Davies, *Heraldry*, p. 133), this lion opposing a dragon conjures not only Richard but stands as a chivalric symbol of the West.

2998 *Myrayn-Momelyn.* The name given to the nephew of Saladin is likely a corruption of *Amīr al-Mu'minīn*, which means "Leader of the Faithful," another title of the Caliph. For this reference, the editor thanks Ishan Cakrabarti, a graduate student at the University of Texas. In a related mistake, the *Itinerarium* states that Saladin "was from the nation of Mirmuraenus" (Nicholson, 1.3, p. 26).

3000 *With thre Sarezynes hedes of sable.* The depiction of Saladin's banner — three heads of sable [black] upon a white background — provides an heraldic prelude to the racial use of color that occurs later in the poem. For a variant herladic device, see the Textual Note for line 2994.

3005–08 *The footmen . . . . in myghte.* A conventional stratagem in crusading romances: compare, e.g., *The Sultan of Babylon*, lines 282–93.

3012 *Susé seynours, has armes tost!* One of several passages entirely in French, the angel's exhortation to arms partly supports the text's citing of a French source (Hibbard, *Mediæval Romance*, p. 147). W and B include English; see related Textual Note.

3027–3124 *Kyng Richard . . . . his maladye.* This passage marks the first of a series of scenes that increasingly emphasize, even celebrate, the king's cannibalism: Richard later asks for the head of the swine that he had eaten and is presented with that of the Saracen (lines 3194–3226); his performance of cannibalism before the Saracen messengers (lines 3409–3562); and the messengers' report of Richard's cannibalism to Saladin (lines 3563–3655). This notorious episode from *a* is absent from the *b* group of manuscripts. Though E depicts Richard's second act of cannibalism at lines 3409–3562, the defective state of this manuscript obscures whether E does, in fact, present the first incidence of cannibalism. B is partially defective, missing lines at this interval. For a table listing these and other lacunae, see Brunner, *Löwenherz*, pp. 15–17. See the

Introduction (pp. 3–4, 6–8, 13, and 17–20) for a discussion of the complex manuscript situation and the varied interpretations of Richard's cannibalism.

3027 *Kyng Richard was syke thoo.* Accounts of the siege report that both Richard and Philip fell ill with "*Arnaldia* or *Léonardia*, a fever [likely scurvy or trench mouth] which caused their hair and nails to fall out" (Gillingham, *Richard I*, p. 160 and 160n25. Compare Brunner, *Löwenherz*, p. 53).

3052 *to loken hys uryn.* A first diagnostic step in matters of internal medicine, picked up frequently in literature to indicate a doctor's wise involvement, it is usually the only detail in a diagnosis. Compare the Ellesmere drawing of Chaucer's Physician holding a urine flask on high even as he rides his horse while the Host (in the Introduction to the Pardoner's Tale) mocks his gestures, saying, "God so save thy gentil course, / And eek thyne urynals and thy jurdones" (*CT* VI(C304–05). Or note the *Gesta Romanorum*'s "Tale of the Ring, the Brooch, and the Cloth," where Jonathas poses as a physician and "whenne he hadde i-seyne hir vryne," diagnoses Falicite's moral illness (p. 191). See also *The Croxton Play of the Sacrament*, where another Jonathas is called "the most famous phesysyan / That ever sawe uryne" (lines 535–36); and Machaut's *Le Jugement dou Roy de Navarre* (in *The Debate Series*), where it is said, "Premiers, s'orine resgarderent" (line 1903) ["First they examined her urine."]

3071 *But aftyr pork he was alongyd.* Later in his campaign, chronicles report that Richard had longed for pears and peaches while ill (Gillingham, *Richard I*, p. 217). Cited by Loomis (Review, p. 466) and others as a source for Richard's feats of anthopophagy is the Tarfurs' cannibalism in *La Chanson d'Antioche*, 2:219, lines 4073–75: "The pilgrims ate with pleasure, without bread and without salt, saying as they did, 'This is most tasty, better than any pork or even cured ham. Cursed be anyone who would die now where is such abundance!'" (trans. Rubenstein, "Cannibals and Crusaders," p. 549 and 549n113). The ban against pork, considered an unclean and forbidden food, distinguishes Muslims and Jews from Christians in medieval culture. The substitution of Muslim for pork thus makes the enemy bestial, subhuman (Heng, *Empire*, pp. 37, 63–64). In another analogue, Bevis's mother lures her aged husband into a trap by feigning a fever that she reports can be cured by eating boar: "Ye," she seide, "of a wilde bor / I wene, me mineth, boute for / Al of the fevre!" (*Bevis of Hampton*, lines 184–86, cited by Jentsch, "Quellen," p. 238).

3077 *An old knyght.* Heng reads this old knight as "a residual figure from the First Crusade" (*Empire*, p. 334n2).

3088–93 *Takes a Sarezyn . . . . good colour.* McDonald argues that this passage largely mimics the language and grammar of conventional medieval recipes: *Sarazyn* was a "term current in medieval cookery books to denote exotic foods of Eastern origin" ("Eating People," pp. 134–35). Thus, the recipe in *RCL* transforms "a young Muslim into a plate of pork (the meat that is the ubiquitous mark of a Christian diet) . . . by subjecting the unfamiliar flesh to the normal rules of English cooking" ("Eating People," p. 147n28).

3092–93 *With powdyr . . . . good colour.* The spices would mask the taste, and the "good colour" of the saffron would alter the 'bad' color of the Saracen's head. Due to a variety of influences including the Arab civilization in Spain and crusader experiences in Antioch, Arabic culinary emphasis upon color, notably a range of saffron-induced colors, penetrated the West, and "saffron became one of the most popular ingredients in England" (Adamson, *Food*, p. 100). "Saffron" was not only used as a spice in medieval recipes but also as a dyestuff (*MED* s.v. *saf(f)roun* (n.), sense 1c).

3113–14 *And whenne . . . . and lowgh.* See note to lines 3210–15 for a reference to Heng's analysis of Richard's two acts of cannibalism as a joke that conjures a collective identity — the English — by means of dietary habits as well as through a racializing discourse that relies upon biological and religious difference.

3123–24 *And thankyd . . . . his maladye.* Together with lines 3061–64 — the English folk's prayers for his cure — these lines present Richard's recovery through the cannibalism of Saracen flesh as being divinely sanctioned (Heng, *Empire*, p. 64). Noting Richard's eastern origins, Akbari argues that the king's consumption of Saracen flesh heals him because the roast Saracen is "food from home" ("Hunger," p. 209–10).

3125–50 *The Sarezynes . . . . so fele.* With the exception of E, which is defective, the *b* group of manuscripts depicts Richard's healing, not by means of Saracen flesh, but as found in the passage from A (fol. 264r) below:

The Saracennis p[ro]ued nyght & day
To wynne the diche, if they may.
The barbycan they broken a doune,
And hadden almost jn jcome
And al most jnne jcome.
But god that made mone and sonne
Heled kyng Ric[hard] of his sekenesse
In that nede and that destresse,
And whenne Ric[hard] that bataylle und[er]stod,
Ffor wrath hit brent negh his blode,
And dude him arme wel tho
As a knyght myght do.
His arblasters byfore him cast
That many a Sarasyne deyde in hast.

Compare *Löwenherz*, p. 252n. Brunner argues that Richard's healing from Saracen flesh formed part of the original text and that the passage above represents a revision (*Löwenherz*, p. 22).

3134 *houndes.* In ME romances, Christians frequently abuse Saracens by referring to them as *hounds* (see lines 4054, 5113, 5231, 6136, 6786, 7120) or as *heathen hounds* (line 6480; see, e.g., *The King of Tars*, lines 93 and 1097). Shores observes that the epithet *hethen hounde* is a "popular romance insult for the pagans" (*King of Tars*, p. 202n93). While the Saracens describe the Christians with the same slur in line 6070 — *Crystene houndes* — the portrayal of the enemy as a hound, and, in particular, a tailed hound, achieves particular resonance in *Richard*. This begins with a description of the English as *taylardes* (tailed ones) at line 337, and continues emphatically with the description of the English as taylardes (tailed ones) at line 1776, and as dogs with tails at line 1830: "Go home, dogges, with your tayle." As noted in the Introduction p. 14 the romance celebrates these insults — and Richard's demonic pedigree — as markers of English identity.

3140 *ax*. See note to lines 2209–11 for a discussion of the historic and symbolic uses of Richard's ax.

3151–52 *Before wente . . . . his Ospytalers*. The origins of the Templars — the Knights Templar, the Order of the Temple — can be traced to 1118 when two knights, Hugh of Payns and Godfrey of Saint-Omer, gave their vows of poverty, chastity, and obedience to the Patriarch of Jerusalem. King Baldwin II gave them as their base the south side of his palace, the Temple of the Lord, the name the Franks gave the Dome of the Rock. The main role and distinctive duty of this fraternity — later, a military order — was to ensure the safety of the roads travelled by pilgrims (Barber, *New Knighthood*, pp. 6–7); even after the victories of the First Crusade, pilgrims and other travellers faced great peril even in regions under Frankish control (p. 3). Through recruitment, donations, and well-placed friends, he Templars became a powerful, wealthy order. Though suppressed in 1312, the Templars in the preceding century may have had as many as 7000 knights and 870 castles, preceptories, and subsidiary houses throughout Western Europe and the Holy Land (p. 1). See note at line 1768 for a discussion of Hospitallers.

3165–66 *Whenne the Sawdon . . . . hem among*. See the note to line 500.

3170 *Gage*. Perhaps Gaza (Brunner, *Löwenherz*, p. 466).

3177–93 *Thus al . . . . ten myle*. In this interval, A (fol. 264v) includes the following passage:

They hem assailled with arblast & bowe
And many a Saraseyne they slewe.
So last the strong fyght,
Twey dayes & twoo nyght;
And ev[er]e in eyther half, saunz faille,
Was jlliche strong bataylle.

In contrast to C and W, A lengthens the fighting: "Twey dayes and twoo nyght." Brunner argues that *b*'s lengthening of the fighting, an absurd exaggeration, indicates that *a*'s account of the battle for Acre stands closer to the original (*Löwenherz*, p. 22).

3210–15 *"Loo, here . . . . were wood*. Arguing that *RCL* presents Richard's cannibalism as an aggressive, communal joke that unites nationalist and colonialist ambitions, Heng points to these lines that instantly define Muslim identity through biological, ethnic, and religious markers ("Romance of England," pp. 140–42). These lines stage "the horror of the head, its color difference, and its inhuman devilish nature" as a joke in a popular romance about an historical king that, amazing to say, embellishes rather than condemns his legend (*Empire*, pp. 64–65, 76).

3231 *And cryeden trewes and parlement. Trewes* here refers to pledges for a temporary cessation of hostilities to allow the Saracens to decide whether their position is viable; see *MED*, s.v. *treu(e*, (n.1), sense 1a. *Parlement* signifies parley or discussion.

3244 *besauntes*. A reference to gold coins of Byzantium or to "any of several similar coins minted in Western Europe" (*MED*, s.v. *besaunt* (n.), sense 1a).

3254–55 *Markes is . . . . Saladynys hand.* In a text that consistently represents Conrad of Montferrat as base — see the notes to lines 1307 and 1310 — Richard accuses Conrad of treason, of betraying his realm to the enemy, and of bribing Saladin: his "whitening" with silver of Saladin's presumably black hand forms part of the poem's pervasive black/white color imagery. Compare a similar use of this racial imagery in *The King of Tars*.

3264–68 *He robbyd . . . . to governy.* Richard's accusations conflate Conrad with the historical misdeeds of Tancred of Lecce ("Tanker" in *RCL*). The previous ruler of Sicily, William II, was married to Richard's sister, Joan. When William died, Tancred confined Joan and withheld her dower. William had also bequeathed to Richard's father, Henry II, a large legacy intended to finance Henry's crusade. Tancred also withheld this legacy from Richard despite his status as Henry's crusading heir (Gillingham, *Richard I*, pp. 132–33).

3274 *With wylde hors he schal be drawe.* Being drawn by horses is a punishment historically associated with treason in medieval England. Reflecting the horror aroused by a crime of betrayal, punishments for treason included a series of lethal acts: hanging, disemboweling, beheading, and quartering (Barron, "Penalties for Treason," p. 189).

3278 *Seynt Denys*. See note to line 2107.

3283 *I am hys borwgh: Loo, here the glove*. In becoming surety for the behavior of the Marquis of Montferaunt, Philip invokes not the French term, *plege*, but its OE and ME equivalent, *borh* or *borwgh*. The king's glove serves as evidence of his obligation, a pledge. See Pollock and Maitland, *English Law*, 2.85, 185. Compare, *Havelok*, lines 1666–67: "Bi the fey that I owe to thee, / Ther of shal I me self borw be."

3287–88 *Ne hadde . . . . hys tresoun.* Part of *RCL*'s inaccurate, anti-French revision of history. For discussions of Conrad, see notes to line 1307, to lines 2713–20, and to lines 3254–55; for a brief discussion of treason, see the notes to lines 722 and 3274.

3289–90 *Yif he . . . . gret honour.* This reference to Henry's treasure is to the large legacy that William II of Sicily bequeathed to Richard's father, Henry II, to finance Henry's crusade; see note to lines 3264–68 above. For the dispute over Jerusalem, see the note to line 1307 and Gillingham, *Richard I*, pp. 148–49.

3306 *croys*. See note to line 392 and to lines 3330–3755.

3326 *In myn half, I graunte thee forward*. Not found in the *a* group, here begins a passage in the *b* group in which Richard demands guarantors at the conclusion of the treaty of Acre (A, fol. 265r):

> "Sey thugh me, myscreaunt,
> Who shal be borgh oth[er] waraunt
> Of the tres[ou]r th[o]gh byhotest vs
> Yf we leteth yogh passe thus?"
> "Sire." He seyde, "we haveth herjnne
> Sarasyne of ryche kunne
> That ye mogh take to ostage,
> Fort ye have yo[ur] payage.
> Hit shal be payed att Halwe-Masse,
> Ev[er]y ferthyng more & lasse."

Compare Brunner, *Löwenherz*, pp. 260n–64n. For arguments that place this passage in the original, though lost, Anglo-Norman text, see Brunner, *Löwenherz*, p. 20.

3330–3755 *They token . . . . wan Acrys*. This episode pairs two brutal acts, one historical (Richard's slaying of the prisoners at Acre) and one fabulous (the second act of cannibalism). At the fall of Acre, the Muslim defenders agreed to peace terms in exchange for their lives. They were to make money payments, liberate 1500 Christian prisoners, and return the True Cross (Nicholson, *Itinerarium*, 3.17, p. 219; and Runciman, *History of the Crusades*, 3:50). Difficulties ensued which gave Richard an excuse for not honoring the agreement. On his orders, 2700 Muslim prisoners and their wives and children were brutally slaughtered. For contemporary and modern reactions to this event, see Gillingham, *Richard I*, pp. 167–71. The Introduction (pp. 17–20) discusses the potential sources, critical reception, and interpretations of Richard's repeated cannibalism. Unique among witnesses of the *b* group, E depicts portions of this second cannibalism. See the notes to lines 3027–3124 and to lines 3409–3655.

3346 *And took hem into hys partyes*. Diverging from the *a* group at this point, manuscripts from *b* depict Philip returning to France after the surrender of Acre, an historically accurate sequence that Brunner deems likely to have been represented in the original, lost Anglo-Norman text (*Löwenherz*, p. 20). For the variant reading from A, a *b* group witness, see the corresponding Textual Note.

3391 *doande*. Brunner argues the presence of a participle with the ending *—ande* indicates that this section of the romance —the serving of the heads of the Saracen envoys — could not have been part of the lost, Anglo-Norman original (*Löwenherz*, p. 19).

3409–3655 *They grauntyd . . . . playn werk!* Richard's second act of cannibalism, his serving the heads of Saracen princes to Saladin's emissaries, and the emissaries' report to Saladin. Unique among witnesses of *b*, E depicts this second act of cannibalism.

3410 *marchal.* A marshal was a court official who maintained discipline at court and who, in times of war, performed a variety of functions (Broughton, *Dictionary*, p. 326). *Fifteenth-Century Courtesy Book*, eds. Chambers and Seton, makes clear that a marshal's duties included maintaining the meal hall (p. 11).

3420 *And bere the hedes to the kechyn.* The presentation of enemy heads as trophies is an historical practice attributed to both Christians and Muslims alike. During the siege of Antioch during the First Crusade, the *Gesta Francorum* (p. 42) reports that crusaders outside the city walls exhumed bodies from graves to accurately count the dead, after which they sent "severed heads as gifts to legates of the emir of Egypt" (Rubenstein, "Cannibals and Crusaders," p. 542n85). At the final siege of Acre in 1291, "the Prince of Hamah, after defeating a body of Franks, cut off the heads of the dead, slung them round their horses' necks, and sent horses and heads as a present to the Sultan of Egypt" (Archer, *Crusade*, pp. 382–83).

3423–24 *And loke . . . . of lyppe.* Heng reads the removal of the beards from the corpses of these Saracen princes as a process of emasculation (*Empire*, pp. 38, 74). See McDonald's discussion of Richard's preparation of the Saracens' heads as "a conventional *[entremet]*," an argument that likens Richard's efforts to other successful *entremets* that articulate "with inescapable clarity, the nature and extent of the host's authority" ("Eating People," p. 137).

3428 *Lay every hed on a platere.* As Heng observes, "If Richard's demand for a head on a platter seems uncannily to resemble typological revenge for the biblical decapitation of the forerunner and cousin of Christ, we recall that the killing of Jews was an integral part of crusade history, as well as the history of Richard's ascension to the throne of England" (*Empire*, p. 78).

3446 *They were set a syde-table.* By placing himself on a raised platform and the Saracen ambassadors on a lower "syde-table," Richard begins the embassy with an insult (Heng, *Empire*, p. 73).

3447–48 *Salt was set . . . . whyt ne red.* By not offering his guests wine, Richard may distance his cannibalistic feast from the Eucharist. Compare *La Chanson d'Antioche*, 2:220, lines 4102–06, when Duke Godfrey learns of the Tarfurs' cannibalism; he "responds not with anger or shame, but with a [Eucharistic] joke, offering the King of the Tafurs wine with which to wash down his Saracen meat" (Rubenstein, "Cannibals and Crusaders," p. 549). Not offering bread and drink may constitute an insult as well. *Fifteenth-Century Courtesy Book*, eds. Chambers and Seton, details the proper presentation of food in part as follows: "And anone forthewyth þe amener shall bryng in þe almesse dyshe with a loofe [of bread] þer Inne and set it bynethe þe lordes salt or elles vppon þe copborde yf no Rome by yppon þe borde" (p. 12). Bread was often used as a trencher or platter upon which to eat. Compare Richard's consumption of the lion's heart with salt but no bread at lines 1105–09; see also the note to line 1109.

3458–60 *A Sarezynys hed. . . . hys forheved.* While both W and E read *cleved*, C's reading, *leued* — see Textual Notes to line 3459 — is contextually compelling and grimly humorous. The labels attached to the princes' heads, Heng suggests, mirror the identity badges that the Statute of Jewry of 1275 required the Jews in England to wear ("Romance of England," p. 148).

3484 *develys brothir*. See the note to line 500.

3547–52 *Kyng Richard . . . . a Saryzyne!* Richard's declaration not only defines an Englishman's identity through his delight in eating his non-Christian enemies (Heng, *Empire*, p. 74.), but, as McDonald argues, it presents edible Saracen flesh as conforming to "established linguistic and culinary codes of English cuisine" ("Eating People," p. 136). This "theatrical" cannibalism, no doubt, constitutes a form of psychological warfare (Ambrisco, "Cannibalism," pp. 503–05). In an historical parallel from the First Crusade, Bohemond, according to William of Tyre, staged crusader cannibalism (*Chronicon*, 4.23.267, cited by Rubenstein, "Cannibals and Crusaders," p. 541n82). See lines 3088–93 and the related note.

3581–82 *No bred . . . . othir lycour.* The reiteration of this detail — salt but no bread — emphasizes Richard's lack of proper courtesy. See note to lines 1109 and to lines 3447–48.

3610 *As a wood lyoun he farde.* Proverbial. See Whiting L327, who cites thirteen passages, though not *RCL*. Compare Malory, *Works*, (1:30): "he fared woode as a lyon."

3641 *saf coundyte.* Safe conduct is "the officially granted privilege of passing through an overlord's domain undisturbed or under escort" (*MED* s.v. *sauf* (adj.), sense 6a).

3656–57 *His clothis . . . . for yre.* Saladin rends his garments in a traditional Jewish gesture of mourning. This representation of the Muslim leader as a Jew accords with Heng's arguments that *RCL* conflates Muslims and Jews (*Empire*, pp. 78–91). For the historiographical significance of this representation and for references to the rending of garments in the Old Testament, see the Introduction (pp. 16–17 and 17n86). Compare the Soudan's angry response to the King of Tars's refusal of his marriage proposal: "His robe he rent adoun" (*The King of Tars*, line 99).

3664 *It is a devyl, withouten fayle.* See the note to line 500.

3668–69 *To wynne . . . . and us!* In this expression of Richard's plan, "English Christians will swallow up lineages and sweep away succession, consuming the future itself, in world domination" (Heng, *Empire*, p. 75).

3670–98 *Lord Saladyn . . . . lyves endes.* In similar fashion, the emir suggests to Charlemange that he become the emir's vassal. Compare *The Song of Roland*, lines 3593–94.

3688 *Conferme it hym and hys ospryng.* Legal language granting an hereditary fief. Among other meanings for *confermen*, the *MED* includes: "to ratify or confirm a grant of (property, privilege, or office); bestow (to sb.) by charter or by virtue of authority" ((v.), sense 2).

3703–14 *And yif. . . . Preter Jhon.* Compare Baligant's offer that Charlemagne become his vassal, and Charlemagne's response that Baligant accept Christianity (*The Song of Roland*, lines 3589–99); Blancandrin's advice that King Marsile make large gifts to Charlemagne and pretend to convert to Christianity in order to retain Saragossa (*The Song of Roland*, lines 24–46); and Genyonn's (Ganelon) advice to Charlemagne that he become the vassal of a Saracen (*The Siege of Milan*, lines 589–600).

3707 *Darras.* This reference may refer to Dara, a fortress on the Persian front that Runciman mentions as one of the few areas in which the Christians provided organized opposition to the Arabs during their conquest of Syria in the seventh century (*History of the Crusades*, 1:17). Perhaps the reference is to Damascus and resulted from a scribal misreading of *Damas*, an early name for this Syrian city.

Babyloyne. A geographic reference to Cairo and a place-name from the Bible that chroniclers associated with the birth and rearing of the Antichrist (Tolan, *Saracens*, p. 112 and 112n35).

3708 *Cessoyne.* A possible reference to Cesson or Kesoun, a bishropic east of Edessa located in present-day eastern Turkey. The previous reference to *Cessoyne* (Soissons) at line 1330 is unrelated.

3709 *Bogye.* As yet unidentified, perhaps a reference to the Buqaia, or to the Beqaa Valley. Buqaia, a district in central Lebanon, was the site of the Battle of al-Buqaia in 1163, one of the rare crusader victories over Nur ad-Din Zangi. The Buqaia is near the Beqaa Valley in Lebanon as indicated by Runciman's statement: when "Saladin was besieging Aleppo, Raymond of Tripoli invaded Beqa'a from the Buqaia" (*History of the Crusades*, 2:410).

3714 *Preter Jhon.* Prester John. In perhaps the first reference, Otto of Freising describes Prester John — *Presbyter Johannes* — as a Christian monarch and priest who ruled a Far Eastern empire, a Nestorian descended from the magi, who campaigned against Persians and Medes and who attempted to help the Christians of Jerusalem. Not being able to cross the Tigris, he and his army returned East (Beckingham and Hamilton, *Prester John*, p. 2). Because this mysterious Christian ruler was viewed as a potential ally against the Muslims, legends about him flourished during the crusades.

3732 *They nyste where the croys was become.* Though chronicle accounts report that both sides had difficulties in fulfilling the agreement, English envoys were actually shown the Cross (Gillingham, *Richard I*, p. 166–67).

3739 *And taken Sarezynes syxty thousandes.* A typical romance or *chanson* exaggeration: Richard slaughtered 2600–3000 Muslim prisoners and their wives and children (Runciman, *History of the Crusades*, 3:53).

3744 *Appolyn*. Apollo. The misrepresentation of Muslims worshipping such pagan gods as Apollo typified the medieval West's misconception of Islam.

3748–54 *There they . . . . foul dyke*. Except for the exaggerated number and the angelic intervention, *RCL*'s presentation of the slaughter of the hostages reflects the historical record. Runciman indicates that Richard, in breaking the agreement, used Saladin's refusal to free specifically named Christian prisoners of rank as a pretext to slaughter the Saracen prisoners at Acre (*History of the Crusades*, 3:53). In a letter to the abbot of Clairvaux, Richard himself states that the time limit in which to complete the agreement had expired and was therefore void (Gillingham, *Richard I*, pp. 168–69, citing Howden's *Chronica*, 3:131). For contemporary responses to the slaughter, including Saladin's as well as modern assessments, see Gillingham, *Richard I*, pp. 170–71.

Divine aid against God's enemies is a convention of *chansons de geste* — compare, *Song of Roland*, lines 3609–13. Certainly, divine interventions recur throughout *RCL*: for example, the appearance of St. George at line 4887, and the angelic warning of the enchanted horse at lines 5548–75. But this passage's use of the Christian supernatural to sanction an historical atrocity may distinguish *RCL* from other ME crusade romances (Hamel, "*Siege of Jerusalem*," pp. 184–85; Finlayson, "Marvellous," p. 376). Common to heroic and religious literature, instances of angelic intervention may exemplify *RCL*'s generic affiliation by enhancing "Richard's status as a divinely guided Christian warrior" (Finlayson, "'*Richard, Coer de Lyon*,'" pp. 166–67). The massacre may follow a typological pattern: Rubenstein cites Bartolph of Nangis (*Gesta Francorum Iherusalem expugnantium*, 35.515) who "appeals to Old Testament precedent (3 Kings 15) to explain the [First Crusade's] massacre in Jerusalem. The Franks, he says, did not wish to be like Saul, who had spared Agag against God's orders to destroy all of the Amalekites" ("Cannibals and Crusaders," p. 546 and 546n100). See the Introduction's discussion (pp. 17 and 19–20) of *RCL*'s representation of the English as God's chosen people, as well as that of Cordery ("Cannibal Diplomacy," pp. 154, 166).

3759–71 *Merye is . . . . strokes hard!* The placement of this lyrical passage or "seasonal headpiece" immediately following the beheading of 60,000 Saracen prisoners is jarring. See White, "Saracens and Crusaders," p. 190 and 190n1. Citing Statius, Smithers suggests the form reflects an epic tradition that rarely occurs in ME texts outside the *Kyng Alisaunder* tradition (*Kyng Alisaunder*, 2.35–39); but see *The Sultan of Babylon*, lines 41–48. Kölbing cites this passage as evidence that *RCL*, *Arthour and Merlin*, and *Kyng Alisaunder* were written by the same hand (*Arthour and Merlin*, pp. lxii–lxiii); instead of evidence of authorship, the uniqueness of the passage within an often brutal narrative leads Hibbard to argue that the passage was produced by a redactor familiar with the Kentish romances, not the original translator (*Mediæval Romance*, p. 147). See also Pearsall, "Development," p. 101. In McDonald's interpretation of *RCL*'s alimentary logic, this abrupt and contextually inappropriate passage "confirms the formal rupture that the anthropophagy effects"; in short,

Richard exorcizes his demonic origins through the consumption of Saracen flesh, thus gaining an assured Christian identity ("Eating People," p. 141).

3780–81 *Thorwgh here . . . . and free.* Compare line 676 and note.

3788 *serjaunt of mace.* An officer who bears the mace as a symbol of authority.

3823–28 *In Goddes name . . . . take Crystyndome!* Muslim conversion to Christianity was a rare occurrence. Having few historical analogues, the forced, mass conversions in *RCL* represent a cultural fantasy (Heng, *Empire*, pp. 81–84). Not only was Muslim conversion rare; but the historical record includes measures taken by the Templars and by Richard to prevent Muslim conversion (Heng, "Romance of England," pp. 146, 165n18). See also Kedar, *Crusade and Mission*, p. 82.

3834–4780 *He gan . . . . ayther cyté.* These lines, which depict a series of conquests by Philip, Richard, Fouk Doyly and Thomas of Moulton, are not related in *b*; nor do they occur in W. Brunner suggests these passages, as well as the conquest of Babylon (lines 5381–5890), did not form part of the lost, Anglo-Norman original (*Löwenherz*, p. 21).

3860 *mystere*. The likely gloss is "a time of peril or distress." See *MED* s.v. *mister* (n.) sense 6. The word may also denote "an occupation" (sense 2a), or "a guild of craftsmen" (sense 2b). Heng argues that the application of a term that denotes a craft or trade practiced by merchants, to warfare — an aristocratic occupation — demonstrates *RCL*'s appeal to a broad audience (*Empire*, pp. 110–11; "Romance of England," p. 158). Another potential gloss is "display or outward show." See *MED* s.v. *moustre* (n.), sense a. Brunner offers "necessity" (from OF *mestier*) (*Löwenherz*, p. 461).

3865 *Slake a bore of here boost.* "?May a boar retreat (in the face of their boasting)" (*MED* s.v. *slaken* (v.1), sense 5). The ferocity of boars may render the comment ironic. Though the editor disagrees with Brunner's observation that C reads *bere* (bear) rather than "boar," given a bear's reluctance to face loud noises, a reading of "bear" may increase the irony (*Löwenherz*, p. 287n2865).

3868 *Taburette*. Brunner suggests that this city may refer to Mount Tabor *(Löwenherz*, p. 472).

3910 *With flour delys of gold and asour.* Adopted by King Louis VII in the twelfth century, the *fleur-de-lis* ("flower of lily"), a stylized iris flower, became the royal badge of France, the armorial emblem of French kings (Gough and Parker, *Glossary*, p. 266).

3938 *And hys eme, Henry of Chaumpayn.* See the note to line 2823.

3939 *And hys maystyr, Robert of Leycetere.* Robert de Beaumont, fourth Earl of Leicester (d. 1204), accompanied Richard I on crusade.

3946 *Bertram*. A likely reference to Bretram III de Verdun, a nobleman influential in the courts of Henry II and Richard I. The historical Bertram III went on the Third Crusade with Richard, was put in charge of Acre, and died at the

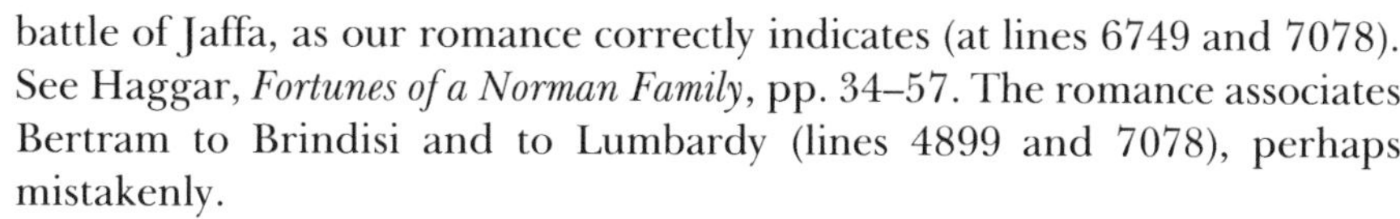

battle of Jaffa, as our romance correctly indicates (at lines 6749 and 7078). See Haggar, *Fortunes of a Norman Family*, pp. 34–57. The romance associates Bertram to Brindisi and to Lumbardy (lines 4899 and 7078), perhaps mistakenly.

3948 *And Templeres, and hys Hospytaleres*. See the notes to lines 1768 and 3151–52.

3972 *Sudan Turry*. Perhaps a reference to Sidon and/or Tyre, both coastal cities (Brunner, *Löwenherz*, p. 472). See note to line 641.

3974 *Orgylous*. The name of this unidentified and likely fictitious location recalls the names of castles in various romances. See the note to line 643.

3991 *Grandary*. Perhaps a combination of *grand* and ME *are*, which denotes honor, grace, mercy: see *MED*, *ore* (n.2) , senses 1a and 4a.

3998 *arweblast of vys*. An arbalest is a medieval device that operated like a crossbow but hurled large objects such as stones and quarrels or bolts: "a crossbow drawn by a screw mechanism" (*MED* s.v. *arblast* (n.), sense 2c).

4077 *That hadde ben Crystene in hys youthe*. See Heng's discussion of this renegade's reconversion (*Empire*, pp. 86–87).

4221 *For wollewarde on my bare feet*. The apostate describes two penitential acts: walking barefoot and doing so *wolleward*, while wearing of woolen clothing next to the skin (*MED* s.v. *wol-ward* (adj.)).

4354 *He is no man: he is a pouke*. Like Richard, Fouke is now described as a devil or demon; see the note to line 500. The recurring association of English leaders with demons and devils distinguishes *RCL* from other ME crusading texts which portray Saracen leaders as devils: compare *The Sultan of Babylon*, lines 356–57.

4368 *brymme*. Brunner argues for a reading of *brymm* (OE *bank*) instead of *brymm* (OE *surf, sea*) (*Löwenherz*, "nachtrag" or addendum).

4393 *A sory beverage there was browen*. Proverbial: *breuen a bitter (sory) beverage*, denotes "inflict great harm" (*MED* s.v. *breuen* (v.), sense 3a). Compare Whiting B529.

4450–52 *And made . . . . here werre*. These lines typify *RCL*'s and the West's inaccurate portrayal of Muslims as polytheistic pagan idolaters.

4461–67 *The fyrste . . . . the ferthe*. Likely fictitious, the names of these five Saracen knights — Sir Arcade, Sir Cudary, Sir Orphias, Sir Materbe, and Sir Gargoyle — reflect the West's conflation of Greek culture and mythology with Islam as well as the geographic sweep of Islam and the Crusades. "Arcade" closely resembles the Greek Arcadia, a central region of the Pelopennese as well as the Greek town, Arcadia, which became part of the Frankish states in Greece after falling in 1204 to Geoffrey of Villehardouin and William of Champlitte (Longon, "Frankish States," p. 237). "Cordary" may be a name of Indian origin and thus reflects *Richard*'s repeated references to "Ynde" as part of Saladin's empire and the origin of part of his army. "Orphias" is the name of the mythical singer who was the son of Apollo and a Muse; see also *Sir Orfeo*, a ME romance that blends Greek and Celtic mythology. As gargoyles were most often in the shape of grotesque figures and animals, the name "Sir Gargoyle" is an obvious slur. Associations from the name "Sir Materbe" remain unclear.

4531 *fawchoun*. The weapon conventionally wielded by Saracens, a falchion is "a large, broad sword with a curved blade" (*MED* s.v. *fauchoun* (n.)).

4539 *Sir John Doyly, Sir Foukes nevew*. Though the historicity of John Doyly's uncle — Fulk D'Oilly, a Lincolnshire knight — has been confirmed, he does not appear in chronicles of the Third Crusade. Finlayson argues that an early redactor of *Richard* may have placed Fulk in the romance in order to glorify a patron ("'*Richard, Coer de Lyon*,'" p. 166; see also Loomis, Review, p. 460). The same rationale may apply to the nephew whose historicity and crusade participation remains unconfirmed.

4594 *wessayl*. Heng argues that the Anglo-Saxon toast, *wessayl*, and Richard's ax — see, e.g., lines 2211, 4848, 4865 — form "nostalgic echoes" that aid *RCL*'s populist representations (*Empire*, p. 104).

4603–20 *Of sylvyr . . . . here ovyrlord*. This sharing of Muslim wealth and lands depicts two strands in *RCL*'s discourse of nation: a leveling discourse that represents the fantasy of Anglo-Norman leaders directly accountable to their people; and the militant, colonialist discourse that "anticipates . . . Victorian and modern imperial England" (Heng, *Empire*, pp. 104–05).

4812–13 *Cogges, drowmoundes . . . . crayeres fele*. A cog was a medium sized ship used for military expeditions (*MED*, s.v. *cogge* (n.1), sense 1a); a dromond was "a large, fast, sea going vessel" (*MED*, s.v. *dromoun(d* (n.)); a galley was a "sea going vessel having both sail and oars or a large row boat" (*MED*, s.v. *galei(e* (n.), sense 1a); a shout was a "flat-bottomed boat, barge" (*MED*, s.v. *shout(e* (n.2), sense a); a crair was a type of small ship (*MED*, s.v. *craier* (n.)).

4817 *Seynt James tyde*. The anniversary or feast day of Saint James is 25 July. St. James, the patron saint of Spain, was an apostle and martyr whose relics were translated to Compostela, Spain, the third most-revered pilgrimage site after Jerusalem and Rome. Through numerous miracles, James came to be viewed as a powerful defender of Christians against the Moors, a military aspect that flourished during the crusading movement. Artistic images of James often depict him on horseback, trampling a Moor (Farmer, *Saints*, p. 256).

4855 *Thorwgh a carte that was Hubertes Gawtyr*. For an historical analogue to this incident, complete with the loss of one crusader's arm, who nevertheless continues to fight, see Nicholson, *Itinerarium*, 4.10, p. 238. See also Jentsch, "Quellen," pp. 208–9; and Brunner, *Löwenherz*, p. 57.

4886 *story*. For references to the term *story*, see the note on *incipit* at the beginning of these notes.

4887 *He seygh come Seynt George, the knyght.* Martyr, warrior saint, and patron of England, George was a Roman soldier in Palestine whom Diocletian executed in 303 for refusing to renounce Christianity. His body was returned to Lydda where he was revered as a martyr. George's cult became widespread even before the *Golden Legend* circulated the story of his slaying of a dragon. In the First Crusade, a vision of St. George, St. Mercurius, and St. Demetrius aided the Christians during the siege of Antioch, hence his association to the crusades (Farmer *Saints*, pp. 202–03). Representations of such combatant saints on the battle field, a conventional type of divine intervention, helped to create an "atmosphere of pious violence" that supported the crusading propaganda of chronicles and crusading poems (Cook, "Crusade Propaganda," pp. 161–62). For a discussion of historical cults of St. George, his roles in *chansons de geste*, in romance, and in *RCL*, see Broughton, *Legends of Richard I*, pp. 104–07. Finlayson suggests the appearance of this warrior-saint and other instances of divine intervention reflect *RCL*'s affiliation, not to romance, but to heroic and religious literature ("'*Richard, Coer de Lyon*,'" p. 166).

4916 *To the cyté of Palestyn.* Perhaps a reference to *Caesarea Palaestinae*, which lay between Acre and Jaffa (Jentsch, "Quellen," p. 186).

4925–46 *To bete . . . . no recette.* In *RCL*, Saladin destroys a group of castles and cities in Palestine before the battle at Arsur. Historically, Saladin ordered fortifications and cities near Gaza and Jerusalem destroyed after the battle; see, e.g., Ambroise, *Estoire*, 1:110–111, lines 6826–6860; Nicholson, *Itinerarium*, 4.23, pp. 261–62. For a brief discussion of these fortifications, see Ambroise, *Estoire*, 2:124n442 and the notes below. Strategically, the crusaders needed these strongholds to protect the inland supply lines needed to take and to defend Jerusalem; so Richard had to rebuild them (Gillingham, *Richard I*, p. 181).

4928 *Myrabele.* Located inland, east of Arsur, Mirabel (Arabic *Majdal Yaba*) formed part of the lordship of Ibelin (Kennedy, *Crusader Castles*, p. 38). It was one of the few castles destroyed by Saladin that did not belong to the military orders (Ambroise, *Estoire*, 2:124n442; Nicholson, *Itinerarium*, 4.23, p. 261).

4929 *castel Calaphyne.* Unidentified.

4931 *Sessarye.* Perhaps a reference to Caesarea; see the note to line 637 and Brunner (*Löwenherz*, p. 472).

4932 *And the tour of Arsour al.* Arsur (Arabic *Arsuf*), a coastal city between Jaffa and Caesarea, was taken by Baldwin I in 1101 but fell to Saladin in 1187. Recaptured by the Franks following the Battle of Arsuf in 1191, it was taken by Babyars in 1265 (Boas, *Archaeology*, p. 225; Pringle, *Secular Buildings*, p. 20). It was not listed by Ambroise among castles and cities Saladin ordered destroyed (*Estoire*, 1:110–111, lines 6826–56).

4934 *castel Touroun. Toron des Chevaliers* (Castle of the Knights) (Arabic *al-Atrun*, corrupted French *Latrun*), an extensive Templar castle located on a hill above the road from Jerusalem to Jaffa (Ambroise, *Estoire*, 2:124n442; Pringle, *Secular Buildings*, pp. 64–65). Though Saladin had destroyed Toron, Richard I and the crusading army camped at its ruins in December of 1191 during their first attempt to reach Jerusalem (Boas, *Archaeology*, p. 255).

4935 *Castel Pylgrym.* Pilgrims' Castle (Arabic *'Atlit*, French *Chastel Pelerin*), a Templar castle built on the coast between Caesarea and Acre (Kennedy, *Crusader Castles*, p. 124). As its construction began in 1218 to replace the inadequate *Le Destroit*, Pilgrims' Castle is not found among chronicle lists of castles that Saladin destroyed.

4936 *castel La Fere.* Chronicles report that as Richard travelled from Darum to Ascalon, he raided the Castle of Figs (French *Le Fier*, Latin *Castrum Ficuum*, Arabic *Qal'at al-Burj*) located 28 miles southwest of Hebron, but he found it abandoned (Nicholson, *Itinerarium* 5.41, pp. 320, 320n89; Pringle, *Secular Buildings*, p. 37). *RCL* associates similar events with *Lefruyde* at line 6298.

4937 *The castel of Seynt George Dereyn.* A reference to *Saint Jorge Labane* (*de la Baene*) (Arabic *al-Ba 'ina*), an independent lordship located inland east of Acre (Pringle, *Secular Buildings*, pp. 24–25). Paris suggests this line results from a mistake, either from a name of the castle — Saint George of Rames — or from a line from Ambroise in which Saladin directs the destruction of the castle Saint George and the fortified inland city Ramla: "Abatez moi Seint Jorge, Rames" (*Estoire*, 1:111, line 6846; "Le Roman," p. 382 and 382n4). See also Nicholson, *Itinerarium*, 4.23, p. 261, which reads as follows: "St. George [Lydda] and Ramula [Ramla]."

4939 *The walles they felde of Jerusalem.* Paris ("Le Roman," p. 382) suggests this historically inaccurate detail resulted from a mistranslation of Ambroise's *Estoire*, 1:111, lines 6855–56: "Que tut ne seit agraventé, / Fors le Crac e Jerusalem" ("[T]hat nothing will be left standing except for Kerak and Jerusalem"; trans. Ailes and Barber). Compare Nicholson, *Itinerarium*, 4.23, p. 261: "Destroy everything, throw everything down, except for Crac and Jerusalem."

4940 *Bedlem.* Historically inaccurate, the destruction of the walls of Bethlehem in *RCL* may be motivated by rhyme (Paris, "Le Roman," p. 382n4).

4941 *Maydenes castel.* Loomis suggests this reference is to *Castrum Puellarum* near Dana in the Principality of Antioch (Review, p. 456).

4942 *Aukes land.* This unidentified place name may signify "Perverse Land": *auk(e* is an adjective that can denote "perverse" (*MED*, (adj.) sense b).

4963 *On Seynt Marye even, the natyvyté.* 8 September is the feast of the Nativity of the Blessed Virgin Mary.

4965–72 *Many was . . . . another empire.* Saladin's army is composed of men from a list of lands that closely resembles the lands listed in lines 3703–14, lands that Saladin was prepared to hand over to Richard should he convert to Islam.

This parallel suggests a feudal relation between the lands Saldin holds and his army, a likely misconception.

4969 *Of Aufryk and of Bogye*. "Aufryk" is likely a reference to some region of North Africa. For "Bogye," see the note to line 3709.

4999 *pensel of sykelatoun*. A *pencel* in this context is "a small pennon, usually attached to a lance, often used to identify a lord and his men-at-arms; a small company standard" (*MED* s.v. *pencel* (n.1), sense a); *sykelatoun* is a fabric of silk woven with gold (*MED* s.v. *siclatoun* (n.), sense a).

5006 *With bowe Turkeys and arweblaste*. For the Turkish bow, see the note to line 2590. For *areweblast*, see note to line 3998.

5021 *Jakes Deneys and Jhon de Neles*. Chronicle accounts of the conduct and death of Jacobus [James] of Avesnes at the Battle of Arsuf correspond to *RCL*'s account (Jentsch, "Quellen," p. 211). Compare, e.g., Nicholson, *Itinerarium*, 4.17–20, pp. 246–59. During the early part of the siege of Acre, James served as one of the leaders of the crusading army (Nicholson, *Itinerarium*, p. 258n56). Loomis suggests that "Jhon de Neles" is Jean de Nesle, a hero of the Fourth Crusade (Review, p. 456).

5098 *The Frenssche says he slowgh an hundrid*. One of several references to an original French text of the romance. See note at line 21.

5159–62 *Manye were . . . . kyng Richard*. While descriptions of a visual work of art, the shield of Achilles, for example, can become thematically significant digressions, in *RCL*, the description portrays the art as a commodity, as exotic plunder.

5173 *Sere Gawter*. A likely reference to Garnier de Nablus, master of the Hospitallers and an Englishman (Paris, "Le Roman," p. 380). See the note on the Hospitallers at line 1768.

5187–5380 *At morwen . . . . hym noughte*. This passage recounts the conquest of Nineveh, an unhistorical episode that does not appear in *b* or in W.

5189 *Nynyvé*. Nineveh was located on the banks of the Tigris River on an important trade route between the Mediterranean and the Indian Ocean opposite present day Mosul, Iraq. Though unhistorical, Richard's assault upon this city may allude to the emperor Heraclias's campaign against the Persians. During the Persian War against the empire, Jerusalem fell to King Chosroes II in 614. His queen, a Nestorian, later received the Holy Cross and other sacred relics. In a campaign memorialized by William of Tyre and translated into French in the *Livre d'Eracles*, Heraclias defeated the Persians at Nineveh in 627. In 629, he received back the Holy Cross, which he returned to Jerusalem in 629. To later generations, Heraclias thus "figured as the first of the Crusaders" (Runciman, *History of the Crusades*, 1:10–11).

5194 *Babyloyne*. For a discussion of the military significance of Babylon (Egypt) in its relation to Jerusalem, and for Richard's intended Egyptian campaign, which he announced by letter dated 11 October, 1191, see Gillingham, *Richard I*, pp. 182–83.

5267 *With trepeiettes.* The *trepeget* or *trebuchet* was a siege weapon that used a counterweighted arm to swing or hurl heavy objects against ramparts and other defenses (Broughton, *Dictionary*, p. 458).

5314 *For Kyng Richard was his preeste.* Presided at his death. A parodic reference to the administration of last rites.

5325 *spawdeler.* "A piece of armor protecting the shoulder" (*MED* s.v. *spaudeler*).

5359–62 *On knees . . . . body froo.* The beheading of a prisoner who pleads for mercy may appear unchivalric, but see Gautier's sixth commandment of chivalry: "Thou shalt make war against the Infidel without cessation and without mercy" (*Chivalry*, p. 26).

5367–76 *Yif he . . . . crystynyd wore.* Compare lines 3823–28 and see Heng's discussion of *RCL*'s fantasy of the forced conversion of entire Saracen populations (*Empire*, pp. 81–84).

5381–5891 *The chef . . . . fourtene nyght.* The conquest of Babylon appears in all witnesses of the *a* version: C, B, and W; in the *b* version, this episode appears only in E. Brunner argues that this episode did not form part of the original, Anglo-Norman version (*Löwenherz*, p. 20).

5381 *The chef Sawdon of Hethenysse.* I.e., Saladin. See Loomis, Review, pp. 456–57.

5399 *Was, as we in booke fynde.* A reference to the original, French version; see the Introduction (pp. 3–4, p. 10n50) and the note to line 21.

5444 *trewes.* See *MED treu(e)* (n.1), sense 1a, indicating a pledge for a temporary cessation of hostilities.

5479–5794 *The nexte . . . . the rygges.* Richard's duel with Saladin. Often perceived as an historical event, the unhorsing of the sultan is one of the king's most famous exploits. Recounted in the chronicles of Pierre Langtoft and Walter de Hemingburgh and represented in numerous medieval images, this victory held particular significance for medieval audiences; see Loomis, "Pas Saladin," especially pp. 512–19. Noted for his generosity, humanity, tolerance, and prodigious military skill, Saladin was more often praised than demonized by the West; texts from the thirteenth to fifteenth centuries often depict him as the pinnacle of chivalry (Tolan, *Sons of Ishmael*, pp. 79–100). In contrast, the details surrounding this duel, in particular, Saladin's unchivalric use of enchanted horses to gain an advantage, depict the sultan as a "*chanson* villain who little recalls the noble emir of history" (Heng, *Empire*, p. 80). See the Introduction (pp. 15–17) for a fuller discussion.

5489 *Slees hys men and eetes among.* Among the meanings of the adverb, *among*, the *MED* (s.v. *among(es)*) lists "besides, in addition, also" (sense 6).

5499–5500 *Whether is . . . . or Jubyter?* A conventional and propagandistic formulation in crusading poems; see, e.g., *The Sultan of Babylon*, lines 196–99.

5502 *Yif thou wylt have an hors of his?* The narrative of the enchanted horse which follows may reflect several influences. Three derive from chronicles. Ambroise reports that after Richard's heroic defense of Jaffa (5 August, 1192), Saladin's brother, Safadin, was so impressed that he sent the king two steeds (*Estoire*, 1:186–87, lines 11,544–64), cited by Gillingham (*Richard I*, p. 216; Nicholson, *Itinerarium*, 6.22, p. 364). Other chronicles report that Saladin generously sent Richard a magnificent mount after learning that Richard's had been killed from under him (Broughton, *Legends of Richard I*, pp. 100–02). According to another chronicle, after Richard's magnificent defense of Jaffa, Saif al-Din maliciously sent a dangerously restive horse to Richard in an effort to capture him (Edbury, *Conquest of Jerusalem*, pp. 117–18). Yet another version derives from the devilish steeds frequently encountered in *chansons de geste*; Finlayson argues that the incident serves as evidence that *RCL* stands generically closer to *chansons de geste* than to romance ("'*Richard, Coer de Lyon,*'" p. 166).

5510 *Seynt Mychel.* The archangel, one of the chief princes of heaven (Daniel 10:13). He and his angels prevail in their battle against the dragon and his angels in Apocalypse 12:2–9.

5530–33 *A maystyr . . . . the eyr.* A reference to the medieval belief that demons made bodies of animals out of the air and then assumed their form (MacCulloch, *Medieval Faith*, pp. 75–88). For a discussion of a medieval necromantic handbook's directions on how to conjure demonic, illusory horses — a popular spell, apparently — see Kieckhefer, *Forbidden Rites*, pp. 42–47. Ambrisco argues that Richard's use of a demon horse "associates him with hell's minions, and in doing so, caps off a long series of references that identify Richard as subhuman and demonic" ("Cannibalism," p. 501).

5545 *And knele adoun and souke hys dame.* The basis of the ruse, the dependence of a militant male upon his mother, articulates in romance fashion Richard's relation to Eleanor of Aquitaine (Heng, *Empire* pp. 97–98).

5548–75 *Al thus . . . . is wente.* One of several instances of divine intervention; see lines 3010–11, 3748–54, 4887 and 6943–62. For discussions, see the Introduction (pp. 1, 16, 19) and the notes to lines 3748–54, 4887, and 6943–62.

5557 *Purveye a tree.* Heng argues that this tree's use as a weapon against Saracens vengefully recalls the True Cross won by Saladin at Hattin (*Empire*, p. 350n54).

5587–99 *And sayde . . . . me at wylle.* An expression of a commonplace of demon lore: "[A]nd if a fiend commissioned for an evil purpose was commanded in the name of the Trinity by the person whom he was sent to afflict, to become his servant, and turn his powers against his sender, he was compelled to obey" ("On Good and Bad Fairies," p. 17). Necromantic manuals advise magicians against making the sign of the cross when flying upon an illusory horse, because doing so could cause the horse to flee from the magician (Kieckhefer, *Forbidden Rites*, p. 47).

5591 *And sufryd grymly woundes fyve.* Christ suffered five wounds: one on each hand and foot, and one in his side. These wounds appear frequently in medieval devotional writing. A notable reference in ME romance occurs in *Sir Gawain and the Green Knight*, lines 642–43.

5595–96 *And aftyr . . . . names sevene.* God in His redemptive relation to man bears seven names in ancient Hebrew tradition: El, Elohim, Elyon, Shadday, Olam, Adonay, Seba'ot (Jeffrey, *Dictionary of Biblical Tradition*, p. 535). In all likelihood, rhyme controls the number of God's names in the couplet. For a similar couplet, see *Lay le Freine*, lines 79–80 and its corresponding Explanatory Note, which lists these seven names from the Hebrew tradition. For a brief discussion, see Marshall, "'Sacral Parody,'" pp. 728–29 and 728n44.

5667 *jeste.* See the note to line 5.

5696 *Bothe in gerthes and in peytrel.* A *gerth* denotes "a belt or strap passing under a horse's belly to secure a saddle, harness, load, etc.," (*MED*, sense a). A *peytrel* is "a protective breastplate or pectoral armor for a horse" (*MED* s.v. *peitrel* (n.1), sense a).

5697 *queyntyse. Queyntyse* may refer to ornamental battle trappings for horse or man, or, in this context, it may denote "a surcoat or mantle worn over armor and bearing a heraldic device" (*MED* s.v. *queintise* (n.), sense 3d).

5710 *ventayle.* A *ventaile* is a "piece of chain mail protecting the lower face, neck, and part of the upper chest, later extending around the upper back" (*MED*, sense a).

5711–12 *On his . . . . Holy Speryte.* See the note to line 393.

5719–20 *Upon his . . . . was grave.* Demon lore has it that "[n]o evil sprite could endure to be touched with any thing on which the holy name of God was written" ("On Good and Bad Fairies," p. 17).

5737 *Thertoo, my glove, as I am knyght.* See the note to line 3283.

5744 *Aftyr here feet sprong the fure.* Sparks shooting from the hooves of a horse often appear in scenes involving the supernatural. Compare *Sir Gawain and the Green Knight* as the Green Knight leaves Arthur's court: "þe fyr of þe flynt flaȝe fro fole houes" (line 459).

5750 *mere.* Muslims perferred to ride mares into battle (Gillmor, "Horses," 1:274). The heavily armored crusaders rode stallions, who could handle the weight, but this weight was often a disadvantage given the heat of the Holy Land.

5768 *Was ipayntyd a serpent.* In the crusading context of *RCL*, Saladin's heraldic emblem is — appropriately enough — the instrument of man's Fall, the serpent; but serpents were not uncommon symbols in heraldry; see Gough and Parker, *Glossary*, pp. 529–31.

5769–79 *With the . . . . the grene.* See the note to lines 5479–5794.

5864 *Wurschepyd hym and hys names sevene.* See the note to lines 5595–96.

5879–82 *Sarezynes before . . . . fourty thousynde*. One of several depictions of mass conversions of Saracens; see also lines 5367–76 and the note.

5884 *And here Mawmettes leet doun drawe*. An instance of the medieval West's confused notion that Muslims worshipped idols.

5889–90 *Erl, baroun . . . . wolde have*. Among foreign themes in *RCL* that may reflect domestic issues in England, the romance, Heng argues, conflates Saracens and Jews. The profit in these lines may recall how violence against Jews in England during Richard's ascension benefited Christians, some of them crusaders ("Romance of England," p. 147–48).

5895–5928 *Kyng Richard . . . . were wrothe*. Unlike the *b* version, *a*'s representation of Philip and Richard's conflict and Philip's departure is chronologically inaccurate (Brunner, *Löwenherz*, p. 22–23). See note to line 3346. Chroniclers blamed strife among the Third Crusade's leaders for the venture's failure to realize its main goal: retaking Jerusalem. See Tolan, *Sons of Ishmael*, pp. 85–91; and Heng, *Empire*, p. 351n57.

5906 *I wyl come the cyté no nere!* A justification for Richard's not taking Jerusalem, a primary goal of the Third Crusade; see the Introduction's brief discussion (p. 13 and 13n64).

5907 *arweblast of vys*. See note at line 3998.

5918 *Alhalewe-messe*. The festival of All Saints, or All Saints' Day is 1 November in the Western Church.

5930 *To Jaffe*. Jaffa served as the main port for Jerusalem (Ambroise, *Estoire*, 2: 124n442).

5937 *Sarezyneys*. See *MED* s.v. *Sarasinesse* ((n.), sense a), that is, Saracen territory, or lands under Saracen control.

5949–50 *Fro thennes . . . . al torente*. *Chaloyn* or Ascalon, from OF, *Eschaloine* (Paris, "Le Roman," p. 366n6). Located on the southern coast of Palestine and replenished by sea from Egypt, Ascalon remained in Muslim hands until 1153. From Ascalon, Muslims raided the southern parts of the Kingdom of Jerusalem. After falling to Baldwin III of Jerusalem in 1153, the fortified city was organized as a fief and became the double county of Jaffa and Ascalon, thus securing the southern borders of the kingdom (La Monte, *Latin Kingdom*, p. 19). Richard I is associated with construction at Ascalon in 1192 (Pringle, *Secular Buildings*, p. 21). See also Jentsch, "Quellen," p. 211. In negotiating a truce — see note to lines 7177–84 — one term that Saladin demanded and obtained was the destruction of this strategic castle: for a chronicle account of this treaty, see Nicholson, *Itinerarium* 6.27, p. 371.

5959–64 *Kyng Richard . . . . myght, everylkon*. While these lines may exaggerate cooperation between classes, chronicles do report that Richard personally labored in the rebuilding of Ascalon; they also describe how Richard and his nobles themselves carried stonethrowers from the shore in preparation for the siege of Darum (Nicholson, *Itinerarium*, 5.39, p. 316; Ambroise, *Estoire*,

1:148–49, lines 9170–237, and Prestwich, "*Rex Bellicosus*," p. 14). After four months of construction, Richard's forces made Ascalon the strongest fortress on Palestine's coast, thus threatening the road between Syria and Egypt (Gillingham, *Richard I*, p. 192). Despite these historical parallels, these lines may well exemplify a utopian fantasy; as Heng argues, "a nascent impetus toward horizontal leveling under conditions of cooperative labor in the service of a religious war" articulates an emerging nationalism (*Empire*, p. 103; "Romance of England," pp. 159–60).

5974–76 *My fadyr . . . . to make!* This statement angers Richard to such an extent that he flings the Duke's banner into the river (lines 5977–97); this exchange thus presents "the fiction of class solidarity through combined physical labor," a bold formulation indeed for a feudal culture, and one that demonstrates *RCL*'s popular appeal (Heng, "Romance of England," pp. 159–60).

5982 *It was evyl don, be Seynt Mathewe.* A likely reference to Richard's imprisonment and ransom by Leopold or Henry VI, even though the romance inaccurately depicts the imprisonment and ransom as occurring before rather than after the crusade. See the note to line 6007 below.

5993 *glotoun*. Compare *MED glotoun* (n.), sense b for the unusual definition of this term: "villain, wretch; worthless fellow, parasite."

5997–98 *I schal . . . . the revere.* These events correspond to the Duke of Austria's humiliation at Acre. Wishing to take part in the plunder of this city, Duke Leopold entered Acre with his banner carried before him to signify his claim, "but it was thrown down and insulted — if not on Richard's direct orders, at least with his consent" (Gillingham, *Richard I*, p. 224). This humiliation motivated in part Leopold's later capture of Richard.

6007 *He heeld hym al to weel foreward.* A likely reference to the historical capture of Richard by Duke Leopold and his imprisonment by the German emperor, Henry VI, which occurred as Richard was returning from the Holy Land. Among numerous discussions, see Gillingham, *Richard I*, pp. 222–53. Considering the abrupt close of C, this reference to the Duke of Austria's revenge leads Paris to argue that the English translation of *RCL* derived from an incomplete manuscript of an Anglo-Norman original to which the English reviser inserted the narrative of Richard's captivity and ransom in an historically inaccurate position: before, rather than after the crusade ("Le Roman," pp. 357–58); but Brunner argues that both W and A provide a justification for this reference to revenge — the Duke of Austria's presence at *castelle Gaylarde* where King Richard is mortally wounded — that does not depend upon Richard's captivity (*Löwenherz*, pp. 18–19). For the variant endings from C, A, and B, see the Textual Note to lines 7185–7240.

6042 *Famelye*. Perhaps a reference to *Famiya* (Arabic *Qalaat al-Madiq*), also known as *Famiyyah* and *Afamiyya*, a town and medieval fortress in northwestern Syria situated on the eastern bank of the Orontes River.

6055–6212 *Of castel . . . . hys benysoun!* For chronicle accounts of the siege of Darum Castle, see Ambroise, *Estoire*, 1:148–51, lines 9127–9369; and Nicholson, *Itinerarium*, 5.39, pp. 316–19.

6055 *castel Daroun.* In 1150, King Baldwin III fortified Gaza on the Egyptian side of Ascalon with this four-tower castle (Kennedy, *Crusader Castles*, p. 31). A stronghold for the military orders located in Gaza, Deir al-Balah (Darum) became a staging area for attacks against Ascalon. Saladin captured Darum Castle in 1187, Richard I retook it in 1191, and it was razed in 1192 (Pringle, *Secular Buildings*, p. 47).

6062 *Seynt James day.* 25 July. See note on St. James at line 4817.

6089 *By water they were ibrought anon.* Chronicles report that Richard transported his catapults by ships from Ascalon to Darum (Nicholson, *Itinerarium*, 5.39, p. 316; Jentsch, "Quellen," p. 189).

6118 *myddylerd.* The terrestrial earth that exists between the underworld and heaven.

6205 *And he that payde a thousand pound.* Chronicles report that Richard would not negotiate with the defenders of Darum Castle but made slaves of the survivors (Ambroise, *Estoire*, 1:149–50, lines 9238–9309; Nicholson, *Itinerarium*, 5.39, p. 317–18). Nicholson argues that Richard, "according to the custom of war," would have let the defenders depart in peace had they surrendered upon his arrival (*Itinerarium*, p. 317n79).

6215 *To Gatrys.* This city in the Holy Land has been variously identified as Gasdres or Guadres of the *Estoire*, as Gaza, and Gazara of Celesyria, which crusaders called Montgizard (Brunner, *Löwenherz*, p. 466).

6280 *He was an aungyl and no man. Aungyl* can mean both celestial being and devil (*MED* s.v. *aungel*, (n.), senses 1a and 4). See note to line 500.

6296 *Castel Pylgrym.* The Castle Pylgrym previously was taken by Saladin; see line 4935 and note.

6298 *Lefruyde.* Unidentified. In an analogous historical event, Richard, who was preparing to besiege the Castle of Figs, instead found it deserted (Nicholson, *Itinerarium*, 5.41, p. 320).

6309 *Gybelyn.* Arabic *Bait Jibrin* (French *Bethgibelin*, Latin *Ybelin Hospitalariorum*, Greek *Eleutheropolis*). Built in 1136 by King Fulk and located to the north of Hebron and east of Ascalon. Initiating the military orders' holding of castles, the Knights Hospitallers were given the castle (Kennedy, *Crusader Castles*, p. 31). For parallels, see Nicholson, *Itinerarium*, 5.44, p. 322; Jentsch, "Quellen," p. 190; and Brunner, *Löwenherz*, p. 466.

6313 *Whenne Bawdewyn was slayn with bronde.* Though Brunner notes that Baldwin IV died from leprosy, he suggests the reference is nonetheless to Baldwin IV of Jerusalem (*Löwenherz*, p. 463).

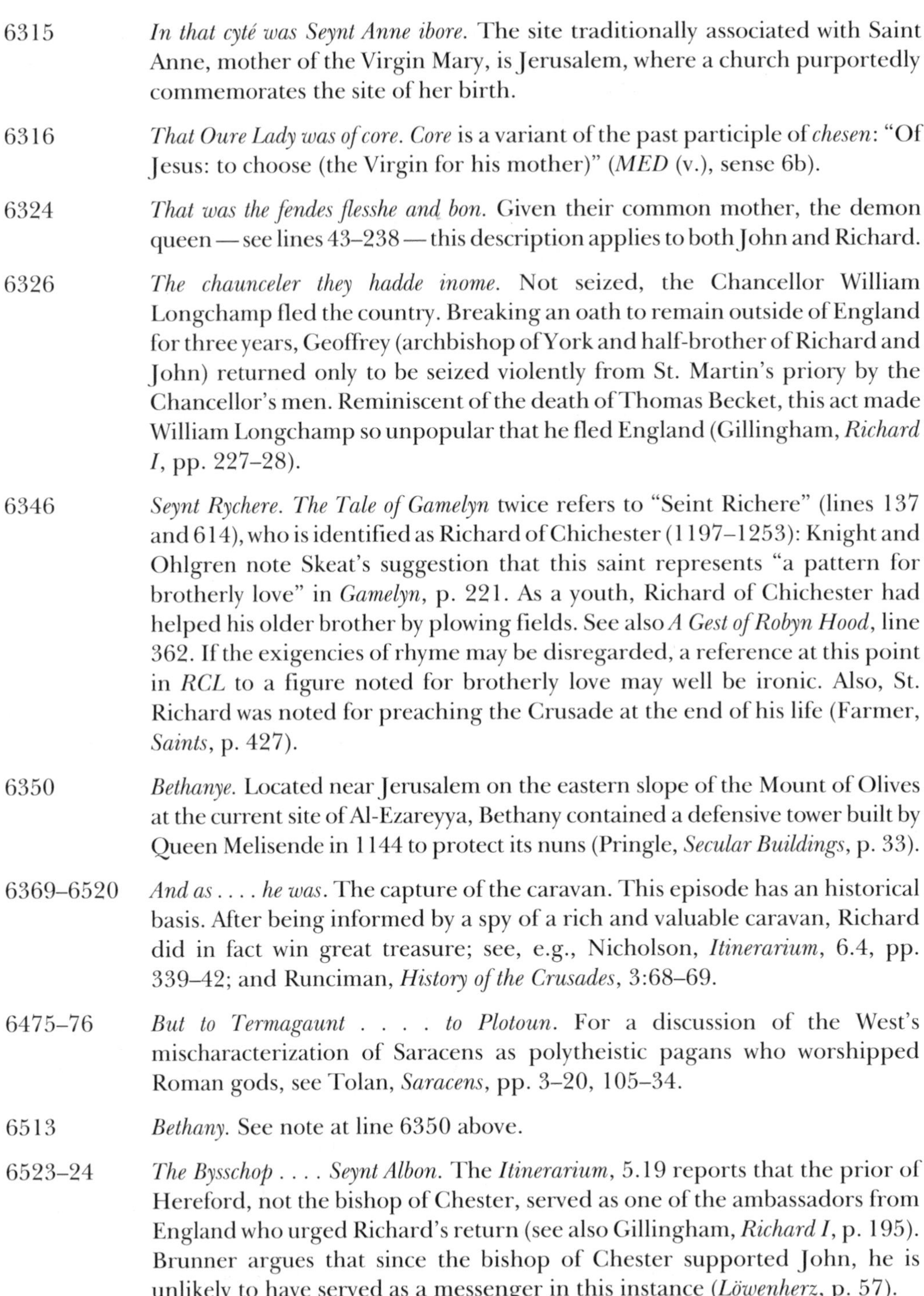

6315 *In that cyté was Seynt Anne ibore.* The site traditionally associated with Saint Anne, mother of the Virgin Mary, is Jerusalem, where a church purportedly commemorates the site of her birth.

6316 *That Oure Lady was of core. Core* is a variant of the past participle of *chesen*: "Of Jesus: to choose (the Virgin for his mother)" (*MED* (v.), sense 6b).

6324 *That was the fendes flesshe and bon.* Given their common mother, the demon queen — see lines 43–238 — this description applies to both John and Richard.

6326 *The chaunceler they hadde inome.* Not seized, the Chancellor William Longchamp fled the country. Breaking an oath to remain outside of England for three years, Geoffrey (archbishop of York and half-brother of Richard and John) returned only to be seized violently from St. Martin's priory by the Chancellor's men. Reminiscent of the death of Thomas Becket, this act made William Longchamp so unpopular that he fled England (Gillingham, *Richard I*, pp. 227–28).

6346 *Seynt Rychere. The Tale of Gamelyn* twice refers to "Seint Richere" (lines 137 and 614), who is identified as Richard of Chichester (1197–1253): Knight and Ohlgren note Skeat's suggestion that this saint represents "a pattern for brotherly love" in *Gamelyn*, p. 221. As a youth, Richard of Chichester had helped his older brother by plowing fields. See also *A Gest of Robyn Hood*, line 362. If the exigencies of rhyme may be disregarded, a reference at this point in *RCL* to a figure noted for brotherly love may well be ironic. Also, St. Richard was noted for preaching the Crusade at the end of his life (Farmer, *Saints*, p. 427).

6350 *Bethanye.* Located near Jerusalem on the eastern slope of the Mount of Olives at the current site of Al-Ezareyya, Bethany contained a defensive tower built by Queen Melisende in 1144 to protect its nuns (Pringle, *Secular Buildings*, p. 33).

6369–6520 *And as . . . . he was.* The capture of the caravan. This episode has an historical basis. After being informed by a spy of a rich and valuable caravan, Richard did in fact win great treasure; see, e.g., Nicholson, *Itinerarium*, 6.4, pp. 339–42; and Runciman, *History of the Crusades*, 3:68–69.

6475–76 *But to Termagaunt . . . . to Plotoun.* For a discussion of the West's mischaracterization of Saracens as polytheistic pagans who worshipped Roman gods, see Tolan, *Saracens*, pp. 3–20, 105–34.

6513 *Bethany.* See note at line 6350 above.

6523–24 *The Bysschop . . . . Seynt Albon.* The *Itinerarium*, 5.19 reports that the prior of Hereford, not the bishop of Chester, served as one of the ambassadors from England who urged Richard's return (see also Gillingham, *Richard I*, p. 195). Brunner argues that since the bishop of Chester supported John, he is unlikely to have served as a messenger in this instance (*Löwenherz*, p. 57).

6525 *lettres speciele.* Letters issued under extraordinary circumstances.

6531–32 *For the kyng . . . . in Normandye.* The Introduction (p. 14–15) discusses the poem's portrayal of King Philip II Augustus. The historical record documents well Richard and Philip's turbulent relations, one point of contention being Philip's numerous invasions of Normandy; see, e.g., Gillingham (*Richard I*, pp. 81, 229, 235n51, 240–42, and 249–50).

6552 *That hys tresore robbyd was.* See note to lines 6369–6520 above.

6574 *Fro his body kyttes the tayle.* Compare lines 1776 and the related note.

6587 *Kyng Richard with hys grete tayle.* See note to line 1776 above.

6592 *Capados and of Barbarye.* "Capados" is likely a reference to Cappadocia, a region in central Anatolia (Asia Minor) now located in Turkey. See the reference to "Capadocye" at line 6898. "Barbarye" of Barbary, the land of the Berbers, refers to "the Saracen north coast of Africa" (*MED*, s.v. *barbarie* (n.), sense 3).

6598 *the Grekyssche see.* See note at line 651 above.

6663 *Henry of Champayn.* See note at line 2823 above.

6684 *He fledde ayen, be Jhesu Cryste.* Not an accurate portrayal of Henry of Champagne. See note at line 2823.

6711–13 *Now herkenes . . . . romaunce non.* For a similar rejection of romance in favor of history, see *Kyng Alysaunder*, lines 668–70; and Mills, "Generic Titles," p. 128 and 128n14. *RCL*'s use of generic labels, though, can be inconsistent: "Rychard hyghte the fyrste, iwis, / Of whom this romaunce imakyd is" (lines 201–02).

6714–22 *Of Partinope . . . . ne of Achylles.* Despite overlap between this list and that found in lines 11–19, differences bear mentioning: the initial list includes heroes from the Charlemagne romances; this tendentious list "draws most heavily upon the romances of Troy, of Arthur, and of native English heroes" (Mills, "Generic Titles," pp. 128n13 and 136n35). See also the note to lines 11–19.

6718 *Sere Vrrake.* Loomis suggests that this name appoximates that of "Urake," the name of a lady in *Partonope of Blois*, and, as such, does not belong in a list of romance heroes but was inserted for the sake of rhyme by a writer without adequate knowledge (Review, p. 457).

6761 *wayte.* "A military or civic functionary responsible for signaling the hour, sounding an alarm, etc. by blowing a trumpet, ringing a bell, or the like; also, a palace retainer assigned to blow a trumpet at designated times, a herald" (*MED* s.v. *wait(e* (n.), sense 1d).

6800 *With my pollaxe I am come.* A poleaxe was "a staff weapon whose head had a Danish-type ax offset by either a thick fluke, straight or curved, or a flat ridged hammer; at the top of the haft was a sturdy spike. The term, 'poleax,' . . . came into use in the early 15th century" (Tarassuk and Blair, *Arms and Weapons*, p. 382).

6802 *Wesseyl I schal drynke yow too.* Like Richard's ax, this toast in a popular romance may nostalgically recall an Anglo-Saxon past; see Heng, *Empire*, pp. 104, 106–07.

6815–16 *Malcan staran . . . . me moru.* These lines appear to be gibberish — a mock Arabic flourish.

6818 *The Englyssche devyl icome is.* See note to line 500.

6893 *Egyens.* An unidentified people.

6894 *Moryens.* Possibly a reference to the Moorish people from Mauretania, a part of North Africa in what is now Morocco.

6895 *Basyles, and Embosyens.* Unidentified peoples in Saladin's army (Brunner, *Löwenherz*, pp. 463, 365).

6898 *Capadocye.* Cappadocia, a region in central Turkey.

6899 *Of Medes, and of Asclamoyne.* The Medes, an ancient Iranian people who lived in Media. Brunner suggests that "Asclamoyne" refers to Slavic lands (*Löwenherz*, p. 462).

6930 *The curse have he of swete Jhesus.* See Matthew 21:18–19: "And in the morning, returning into the city, he [Jesus] was hungry. And seeing a certain fig tree by the way side, he came to it and found nothing on it. And he saith to it: May no fruit grow on thee henceforward for ever. And immediately the fig tree withered away." See also Mark 11:13-14. Richard's curse of Saladin invokes the parable of the barren fig tree, used by medieval theologians who repeatedly compared the Jews to this barren tree (Whitman, "The Body and The Struggle," p. 53). As Richard replaces the Jews with Saladin, his curse serves as further evidence of Heng's assertion that *Richard* depicts Muslims as virtual Jews (*Empire*, p. 79).

6932 *And told the Sowdane worde and ende.* For a discussion of the phrase, "worde and ende," see Onions, "Middle English 'Ord and Ende.'" See also *MED*, *ende* (n.1), senses 24(2–3).

6934–35 *And sayde . . . . a saynt.* See note to line 500.

6943–62 *Thorugh Goddes grace . . . . more nede!* One of several angelic interventions, a convention of *chansons de geste* and crusading poems; see the Introduction, pp. 1, 16, 19. See also lines 3011, 3748–54 and related note, 5548–75 and, though less clearly, lines 3123–24.

6953–57 *Take trues . . . . after then.* These lines express the notion that crusade combined holy war with the concept of pilgrimage, and, in particular, the lines refer to that part of the crusading vow that imposed on crusaders the obligation to worship at the Holy Sepulchre: see Merrilees; "Crusade," p. 16.

7003–04 *And thoo . . . . Richardis cuppe.* Akbari argues that these lines parody the poem's repeated presentation of ritual feasting to demonstrate the reconciliation of former enemies ("Hunger," pp. 205–06).

7008 *As it is in Frensch ifounde.* One of several references to an original French text; see the Introduction (pp. 3–4, p. 10n50) and the note at line 21.

7017 *Hys eme, Sere Henry of Champayn.* In the *Itinerarium*'s description of the battle of Joppa, Richard saves not Henry of Champagne but the earl of Leicester, "who had been thrown from his horse" (Nicholson, *Itinerarium*, 6.22, p. 363). Thus, this substitution serves as another example of *RCL*'s revision of history to humilate the French (Jentsch, "Quellen," p. 194).

7075 *patryark.* The patriarch, a bishop of one of the "chief sees of Antioch, Alexandria, Constantinople, Rome, or Jerusalem" (*MED* s.v. *patriark(e* (n.), sense c). The reference is likely to the Bishop of Jerusalem.

7076 *Jhon the Neel.* A reference to Jean de Nesle, a hero of the Fourth Crusade. See also line 2826 and Loomis, Review, p. 456.

7077 *William Arsour, and Sere Gerard.* Both of these knights remain unidentified. Though the name "Arsour" may refer to Arsur — also known as Arsuf (a coastal city between Jaffa and Caesarea) — William was not one of the lords of Arsuf.

7078 *Bertram Braundys, thy goode Lumbard.* For information on Bertram III de Verdun, see the note to line 3946.

7087 *They slowen Fauvel undyr hym.* Ambroise reports that after Richard's heroic defense of Jaffa (5 August, 1192), Saladin's brother, Safadin, was so impressed that he sent the king two steeds (*Estoire*, 1:186–87, lines 11,544–64; cited by Gillingham, *Richard I*, p. 216; Nicholson, *Itinerarium*, 6.22, p. 364). Other chronicles report that Saladin generously sent Richard a magnificent mount after learning that Richard's had been killed from under him (Broughton, *Legends of Richard I*, pp. 100–02). See the discussion of Saladin in the Introduction (pp. 15–17) and the note to line 5502.

7149–52 *At morwen . . . . Jhon Seynt Jhan.* Of this list of emissaries that Richard sends to Saladin, only "Gawter" (Hubert Walter), can be confirmed as an actual participant (Gillingham, *Richard I*, p. 217): Walter, who figures prominently in chronicles of the Third Crusade, is described more fully by the note at line 2831. "Robert Sabuyle" likely refers to Robert de Sabloel. A commander of Richard's fleet and a treasurer of the crusade, Robert served as one of the messengers to Tancred and later became master of the Temple from 1191 to 1193 (Nicholson, *Itinerarium*, p. 165 and n72). Though "Huberd Tourneham" remains unidentified, Robert Tourneham was a soldier and administrator closely associated with Richard I. His career is described at the note to line 1659. "Wyllyam Watevyle" and "Gyffard" have not been unidentified, nor has "Jhon Seynt Jhan," though the latter's name may intimate some relation to the Knights Hospitaller of St. John.

7162 *Says three yer, three monethis, and thre dawes.* Similar durations are reported in the chronicles of William of Newburgh and Walter of Heminburgh (Jentsch, "Quellen," p. 226; and Brunner, *Löwenherz*, p. 54).

7166 *And tolde the Sawdon wurd and ende.* See note at line 6932 above.

7177–84 *Thoo aftyrward . . . . or damage.* For a chonicle's record of the terms of the three-year truce, which include the destruction of Ascalon, see Nicholson, *Itinerarium*, 6.27, p. 371.

7181 *Olyvete.* Mount Olivet of the Mount of Olives is a mountain ridge east of Jerusalem. Among other associations, it is the site of Jesus's prophecy of the Last Judgment (Matthew 24:2–3) and of his ascension into heaven (Acts 1:1–12). As a result, the Mount of Olives became an important pilgrimage destination.

7182 *Mayden Castell.* See the note to line 4941.

7190 *At Castell Gaylarde there he was.* Richard did not fall outside Castle Gaillard (Chateau-Gâillard), an impressive fortification and palace on an isle in the Seine that was the favorite residence of Richard during his last two years (Gillingham, *Richard I*, p. 302). Rather, he fell outside the less impressive Chaluz; see Brunner's discussion of Walter of Hemmingburgh's similar mistake (*Löwenherz*, p. 58n), and Jentsch, "Quellen," p. 227.

7228 *at the Font Everarde.* A likely corruption of the place of Richard's burial, at Fontevraud, an abbey near Chinon in Anjou. As described by Gillingham: "His brain and entrails were buried on the Poitou-Limousin border at Charroux — an abbey which claimed none other than Charlemagne as its founder. His heart went to Rouen, where it was buried next to his elder brother. . . . The rest of him, together with the crown and regalia he had worn at Winchester, reported the Winchester annalist, was buried at Fontevraud, at his father's feet on Palm Sunday, 11 April (*Richard I*, pp. 324–50. See also Brunner, *Löwenherz,* p. 465). For an ambitious study of such aristocratic burial practices, see Westerhof's *Death and the Noble Body*.

Textual Notes

Abbreviations: A: MS London, College of Arms HDN 58 (formerly: Arundel); ***a***: part of the manuscript tradition (see pp. 3–10 of the introduction); **B**: MS London, BL Additional 31042 (formerly: London Thornton); ***b***: part of the manuscript tradition (see pp. 3–10 of the introduction); **D**: MS Oxford, Bodleian 21802 (formerly: Douce 228); **Br**: *Der Mittelenglische Versroman über Richard Löwenherz*, ed. Brunner. **E**: MS London, BL Egerton 2862; **H**: MS London, BL Harley 4690; **L**: MS Edinburgh, National Library of Scotland Advocates' 19.2.1; **MS**: MS Cambridge, Gonville and Caius College 175/96 (C; base text); ***RCL***: *Richard Coer de Lyon*; **W**: Wynkyn de Worde's 1509 printed edition; **W**^{2}: de Worde's 1528 printed edition.

1–35	For L's unusual prologue, the only prologue from the *b* group to survive, see the corresponding Explanatory Note.
24	MS: Below this line appears a crossed-out couplet corresponding to lines 25–26.
27	*jestes*. So W. MS: *ʒyiftys*. B: *geste*. L: *gestes*.
49	*sondes*. So Br. MS is illegible. W: *sonde*. B: *sandys*.
50	*londes*. So Br. MS is illegible. W: *londe*. B: *landis*.
52	*hym to wyf*. Illegible in MS. W: *hym to wyve*. B: *hyme to weyffe*.
181	*she*. So W. MS: *they*. B: *they*. Brunner argues that MS and B form a group within the *a* version of manuscripts because their joint mistake — *they* for *sche* — is not encountered in W (*Löwenherz*, p. 13). See note to line 522.
183	*hym*. So W, B. MS: *here*.
228–448	*And Johan . . . . to me*. Due to missing leaves, these lines are lacking in MS and are supplied by W.
237	*he*. So B. W: *she*.
241	*Crowned after Kynge Harry*. See the corresponding Explanatory Note for an additional passage from L.
269	*He came out of a valaye*. Defective at its beginning, D begins here.
279	*kynde*. So B, D. W: *oynge*.
290–318	*Full egerly . . . . he bare*. For the passage from D corresponding to these lines, see *Löwenherz*, p. 93n.
297	*gorgere*. So B. W: *forgette*.
324	*he came*. So B. W: *be came*.
343	*thore*. Br: *þore*. W: *yore*. B: *thare*.
357	*peres*. So B. W: *speres*.
397–426	*To the . . . . hym drowe*. For D's version of these lines, see *Löwenherz*, pp. 98–101n.
405	*foundred*. So B. W: *swouned*. W^{2}: *sounded*.

435 *Doly*. So B. W: *Dely*.

439 *messengere*. B: *messangere*. W: *messengers*.

455–58 *And whiche . . . . the loos*. Absent in MS, these lines derive from W. A variation of these lines is found in B.

495–96 *The aventurous . . . . knyght betydde*. Absent in MS, these lines derive from W.

498 *off his stede*. So Br. MS: *off stede*. W, B: *of his stede*.

506 *shelde*. So W. MS: *schuldre*. B: *schelde*.

522 *Hym semyd*. So MS, B. W: *He semed*. Though less convincingly than in line 181, Brunner argues that a joint error in MS and B — *Hym semyd* — indicates that MS and B form a subset within the *a* group distinct from W (*Löwenherz*, p.13). The form, *him semed*, though, is not rare; see, e.g., *MED* s.v. *semen* (v.2). sense 1f: "him semeth (them semed), etc., he seems (they seemed, etc.) to be."

558 *culvere*. So MS. W: *dove*. B: *dofe*.

568 *pouke*. So MS. B: *puk*. W: *symple man*.

582 *stonyd*. So Br. MS: *stornyd*. B: *stonayde*. Omitted in W.

608 The *b* version includes at this point an 18-line passage that offers a concise reiteration of the knights' summary of the tournament at Salisbury:

Whan her couen[a]nt was jmade
The kyng spake w[ith] hert glade
"My leue ffrendes, w[ith] gode entent
How ferde ye atte t[or]nament?
Cam any strong knyght to yo[ur] play?"
"Ye," they seiden, "p[ar]mafay,
Auentures knight ther cam ryde
In dyu[er]s atyre, w[ith] muche p[ri]de
He felde both hors and man
Hym ne myght non w[ith]stond þan."
"Ye," q[uo]the þe kyng, "my frend[es] be ye
Of that knyght j shall yow say
Jch was thuder jgon for certe."
Tho wer[e] they glad and blithe in herte
That he loued her felawred.
Ffor he wax dowty man of dede,
And also queynte in many case;
Therfor they maden gret solas.

The text of this passage is taken from A (fol. 252r).

667 *bad that he scholde goo*. So Br. MS: *bad that sche scholde goo*. W: *bad hym thens go*. B: *we will ryse & goo*. A, D: *and seyde nay*. H: *& seid nay*. Omitted in L.

674 *mynstrall*. So MS. W: *glee men*. B: *glewe men*. Omitted in *b*.

677 *He*. So B, Br. MS: *Sche*. W: *They*. Omitted in *b*.

679–796 *Forthe he wente . . . . a swoughe*. These lines are absent in MS and are supplied by W.

679 *Forthe*. So Br. B: *And forthe*. W: *For*.

721 *put*. So B. W: *uot*.

741 *Wardrewe*. So Br. W: *Mardrewe*. B: *Sir Andryne*. H: *Ardoure*. See note to line 851.

763 *Saynt Martyn*. B: *Saynt Martyne*. D: *Seynt Elyne*. A: *Gemelyne*.

790 *As thow art a stalworth knyght*. So A. W: *Thou hast Jfared well this nyght*. B: *Euene als þou arte a stalworth knyght*. H: *As þu arte a stalleworth knyghte*. D: *As þou art a trowe knyth*.

795 *droughe*. So B. W: *tare*. A: *drowe*. D: *drew*. H: *drowghe*.

796 *swoughe*. So B. W: *care*. A: *swowe*. D: *swone*. H: *sowghe*.

803 *worde*. So W, B, A, D. MS: *noyse*.

805 *He*. So B, W. Omitted in MS. Absent in *b*.

827 *Her kerchers she drewe and heer also*. So W. Omitted in MS. B: *Hir kerchefes sche drewe hir hare also*. A: *Her kerchefs she to drowe*. D: *Here kerchys sche drow here here also*. H: *Here kerchews sche alle to drowghe*.

828 *Alas, she sayd, what shall I do?* So W. Omitted in MS. B: *Allas sche seide what schall I doo*. A: *Alas she seide me is woo*. D: *Alas, sche seyde, me ys woo*. H: *Alas sche seide me is woo ynoughe*.

829 *qahchyd*. So MS. W: *cratched*. B: *skrattede*.

830 *was in a rage*. So W. MS: *wolde be rage*. B: *was alle in a rage*. Omitted in A, H, D.

841 *The knyght*. So MS. W: *The knyghtes*. B: *the knyghte*. A: *The kyng*. D: *The knyth*. H: *The kyng*. From common errors found in this line — *king* for *knyght* — Brunner argues that in the *b* version, A and H form a group distinct from L, E, and D, (*Löwenherz*, p. 13). E, being defective, begins with line 1857, and L does not include the exchange of blows episode.

842 *he scholde*. So B. MS: *the he scholde*. W: *he sholde*.

849 *I fette*. So W. MS: *fette*. B: *j fetchede*. A: *ich hem fette*. D: *j hem fettys* (*hem* inserted above *fettys*). H: *y ham fette*.

851 *Wardrewe*. So W. MS: *Ardru*. B: *Ardrene*. See note to line 741.

857 *Wardrewe*. So W. MS: *Ardu*.

871 *wylle*. So MS. A, H: *mode*. This "error" that destroys the rhyme in A and H forms part of a cluster of shared features within the *b* group that distinguish A and H from L, E, and D: see note at line 841 above and *Löwenherz*, pp. 13–14.

873 *And fetters upon theyr fete feste*. So W. MS: *And feteres hem for þe best*. B: *And grete ffettirs one hym loke þou do feste*.

875 *he*. MS: This word is inserted above the line.

886 *soone*. MS: *sone* with *o* inserted above the line.

927–1018 *The kyng . . . . to ded*. Instead of these lines, *b* (A, fols. 254r–v) reads as follows:

Thanne was the kyng sor[e] amayde,
"Alas," he seide, "ich am betrayed!
That traito[ur] hath my sone aslayne,
And my fayr[e] dought[er] forlayne."
Smertly the kyng, w[ith]oute faille,
Let ofsende all his counseill,
And of hem he axed rede
How he myght do Ric[hard] to dede.
He tolde hem all hough he he had done,
The barons radde him also sone.
He hadde a lyon in a cage,

A wilde best and a sauage.
Men seide if they wer[e] togeder steke,
On him wolde þis best awreke.
All they seiden hit shulde be so,
Thanne was the kyng[e] dought[er] wo.
Whenne eu[er]ych man slepte in the castell,
The mayde wente to the gayler[e].
Her bedde she hadde therin jdight[e]
Bi Ric[hard] she lay all the nyghte.
And alltogedres she tolde hy[m] tho,
How they hadde dampned hy[m] to slo

Compare Brunner, *Löwenherz*, pp. 128n–130n.

933 *The kyng in herte sykyd sore*. So MS. Brunner argues that *b*'s account of the decision to battle the lion, which begins here, abbreviates the original version (*Löwenherz*, p. 21).

939 *messangers*. So B. MS: *messangrys*. W: *messengers*.

945 *welcome*. So W, B. MS: *welcomes*.

975–76 *And stryvenn . . . . egere mode*. Absent in MS, these lines derive from W. B: *And stryvenn faste als þay were wode / With grete erroure and egere mode*.

1017 *ordeynyd thee*. In MS, *þe* is inserted above the line. W: *ordeyned*. B: *ordaynede*.

1057–1428 *Sertes, henne . . . . hys mede*. Instead of these lines *b* (A, fols. 254v–55v) reads as follows:

Ric[hard] seide, "lady free,
Ich the p[ra]y wynde hennes fro me,
Or els þ[ou] wilte g[re]ve me sor[e]
Go hennes lemman, for goddes or[e]!"
The mayde aros and wente her way;
Ric[hard] slepte fort hit was day.
Ric[hard] the kerchyues toke on honde,
And aboute his arme wonde,
Vnder his slyve harde icaste.
In hert was he noughte agaste.
Ric[hard] thought in that wyle
To sle the lyon w[ith] his gyle.
The sharpe knyf foryate he noght,
Of grounde style hit was iwrought.
And semeliche in his kertyll stod,
Abode the lyon fers and wode.
With that come the Gayler,
And the knyghtes all ifeer,
And lad the lyon hem amonge
W[ith] pawys bothe sharpe & strong.
The chambr[e] dore they hadde vndo,
And the lyon they ladde him too.
Whan the lyon sey him skete,
He ramped on with his fete.
He yoned wyde and ganne to Rage,
As wilde best that was sauage;

And kyng Ric[hard] also sket[e],
Jn the lyones throte his arme he shete.
All in kerchefs his arme was wonde:
The lyon he strangeled in that sto[n]de.
With his pawys his kyrtell he roff;
W[ith] þat þ[e] lyon to the erthe he droff.
Ric[hard] w[ith] that knyf so smert,
He smote the lyon to þe hert.
Oute of his kerchefs his honde he drogh,
And at that game Ric[hard] lough,
And the kercheffes stille he lette;
Thus the lyon his make mette.
He opened him atte brest bone,
And toke his hert oute anone,
And thonked God om[n]ipotent
Of the grace he hadde hem sent,
And of his dede of grete renoune
Cleped he was quer[e] lyon.
Now wente thes knyghtes all fyve,
And tolde kyng alle blyve
That Ric[hard] and the lyon
Togeders wer[e] in prisone.
Than seide he, "By heuen kyng,
Jch am glad of that tything.
By this tyme, Ich wote full well,
The lyon hath of him his dell!"
Vp aros the dought[er] yong,
And seide thus to her fader the ky[n]g:
"Nay," she saide, "So god me rede,
J ne leve that he be dede.
He by hete atte sop[er] tyme
The lyons hert today by p[ri]me!"
The kyng comaunded his knyght[es] anon
To the p[ri]son for to gone;
And loke hasteliche and blythe,
If that the devyll wer[e] alyue,
And the knyghtes al sone
The prison dor[e] have vndone,
And in they yede all sone.
Ric[hard] seide, "Ye beth wellcome!"
They sey the lyon lye dede thar[e].
They orne and tolde the kyng for[e]
That Ric[hard] was all hole and sounde,
And the lyon ded vpon the grounde.
The kyng seyde to the q[ue]ne so,
"Yf he dwelle her, he wole vs sloo.
Do we him raunson tho[ur]gh our[e] honde,
And swythe flen oute of þis londe,
And also his felawes twey
His wikked hefd hit shall away."
Of lyme and stone he had an house;
The kyng than swor[e] by Jh[esu]s,

The house kyng Ric[hard] fullyng shuld,
Fful of seluer and of golde,
And ell in prisou[n] ligge ev[er]mor[e].
Th[us] haþ the kyng his oth iswor[e].
Anon kyng Ric[hard] v[er]ement
L[ett]res into Engelonde he sente
To the kynges chaunceller.
The l[ettr]e speke as ye mowe her[e]:
"Kyng Ric[hard] lithe in p[ri]sou[n],
And most haue grete raunsou[n]:
Treso[ur] with an house to fille,
Other elles in p[ris]on he shall spille."
That was ther maked, J understonde,
A taxion in Engelonde;
In abbeys and in cherches bo,
Ther ner chalis but to,
That on they toke w[ith]oute lesyng;
Thus raunsomed Engelond for our[e] ky[n]g.
Whenne the t[re]sour[e] com ther hit shold be,
They hadde brouten swiche three
Also they had nede for[e],
But all togeder hit leued ther.
Kyng Ric[hard] swor by Seynt John,
He wolde haue to for[e] on.
Thane the kyng, Jch vnderstond,
Toke his dought[er] by the honde,
And bade hur w[ith] Ric[hard] goo
Oute of his londe for ev[er] mo.
He swor as he was kyng or page,
Thare she sholde haue none heritage.
Thus come Ric[hard] oute of p[ri]son,
God yeve vs all his benesou[n].
Jnto Engelond wente they thoo,
And alle bothe ffrendes com to.
With ham they mande muche glady[n]g,
And many a feyr[e] justyng,
Ffor joy that her lorde was com to lond[e];
Þ[er]of þey thonket Goddes sonde.
Hom þey wente to her contres all,
And lefte the kyng w[ith] his mayne all.

1058 *I shall take the grace that god wyll sende*. So W. MS: *Here J wole take myn ende*. B: *I will take here þe grace þat god will sende*.

1077 *thay hafe undo*. So B. Absent in MS. W: *they undone*. A: *hadde undo*. D: *dede undo*.

1078 *lyoun lete hym to*. So B. Absent in MS. W: *lyon to hym is gone*. A: *lyon they ladde him too*. D: *lyoun gon hym to*.

1125 *hys*. In MS, *hys* appears as a correction above the line.

1140 *Messe is sayd*. MS: *Messe in sayd*. Br: *Messe in saye*. W: *And matyns synge*. B: *Matyns sayes*. Omitted in *b*.

1147 *And my doughter for her outrage*. So W. Omitted in MS. B: *And my doghetir for hir owtrage*.

1148 *Shall forgoo her herytage*. So W. Omitted in MS. B: *Shall forgo hir herytage*.

1164 *me too*. So W. MS: *me* is inserted as a correction.

1178 *travayle*. MS: *turvayle*.

1205 *rede*. So W. MS: *redy*. B: *red*.

1254 *travayle*. MS: *turvayle*.

1287–1312 *Of Surry . . . . Holy Croys*. See Paris's discussion of this passage in relation to the much shorter account — four lines — in L; ("Le Roman," pp. 354–56).

1290 *it*. In MS, *it* appears as a correction above the line.

1317 *Surry lande*. So B. MS: *þat lande*. W: *Surrey londe*.

1343 *Westemynstyr*. So MS. L: *Winchester*. See the Explanatory Note at line 241 above.

1387 *have nomen*. So W. MS: *wolde have nomen* (*wolde* appears as a correction above the line). B: *has nome*.

1410 *other londe*. So W. MS: *Crystene londe*. B: *other landes*.

1437–1666 *Three hoostes . . . . Holy Londe*. For a variant passage in A, see the corresponding Explanatory Note.

1477 *mayre*. So W. MS: *men*. B: *mayere*.

1487 *he*. So W, B. MS: *ye*.

1507 *for to wende*. So W, B. MS: *swythe sende*.

1521 *They waschede as it was lawe of land*. Omitted in MS. B: *Þey waschede þane als was lawe of lande*. W: *They wysshe as it is lawe in lande*.

1522 *rydand*. Brunner argues that the use of the present participle in *-ande* here and in line 1525 (*ryngangde*) and in 3430 (*grennand*) serves as evidence that the episode — either the journey of revenge through Germany or the second act of cannibalism — did not form part of the original, Anglo-Norman text (*Löwenherz*, p. 19).

1535 *made at ease*. So MS, W. In MS, *at ease* appears as a correction above *ryght merye*. B: *welcomed full fayre*.

1536 *semblaunt*. So W. MS: *herte*. B: *semblande*.

1566 *in*. In MS, *in* appears as a correction above the line.

1602 *skylle*. So Br. MS is defective here. B: *skille*. W: *skyll*.

1629 *to beker in fyght*. So W. MS: *and bykyr and ffyght*. B: *to bekir in fighte*.

1645 *it*. In MS, *it* appears as a correction above the line.

1660 *Gret Ynglys peple*. So B. MS: *Gret peple*. W: *Moche englysshe people*.

1712 *Rys*. So A. MS: *rys*. B: *pys*. W: *thys*. L: *Riis*. D: *Pys*. H: *Ryse*.

1737–2468 *And I . . . . and styll*. Due to missing leaves in MS, these lines derive from W.

1739 *men*. So W, B, D, Br. Omitted in L, H, A.

1744 *Lo, here the letter forsothe, iwys*. So D, Br. W: *Lo here are the letter forsothe Jwys*. B: *Loo here þe lettre there of Jwysse*. A: *Lo here the lettre Jwys*. H: *Lo here the letter wreten ys*.

1761 *Whete and benys twenty thowsande*. So B. Omitted in W. A: *And of whete & benen quarters xx* m^{t}. L: *Wiþ . . . seuen to þousinde*. D: *Of wete & benys tuenty þousand*. H: *Of wete quarters twenty þowsende*.

1762 *Quarters he boughte als that I fynde*. So B. Omitted in W. A: *he bought as we fynde*. D: *Qwarters he bowte also J fond*. H: *he bowghte as iche ffynde*. L: *He bouȝt also y finde*.

1764 *account*. W: *acccount*.

1769 *into the chepynge*. So B. W: *to shyppynge*. A: *into þe chepyng*. L: *into the chepeinge*. H: *to chepyng*.

1773 *Kynge*. So Br. W: *Kynke*.

1775 *helde*. So B, A, H, Br. W: *had*. D, L: *held*.

1784 *feste*. So B, A, D, H, Br. W: *faste*. L: *fest*.

1785 *erles*. So B, Br. W: *clerkes*. D: *erl*. L: *erle & clerke*. Omitted in A, H.

1818 *Full*. So Br. W: *fulll*. B: *ffull*.

1830 *Go home, dogges, with your tayle*. W: *Awaye dogges with your tayle*. B: *And seid gose home dogges with ȝour taylles*. A: *Go hom dogges with your taill*. D: *Go home doggys with ȝoure vitayle*. H: *Go home dogges wyth youre tayle*. L: *Goþ home dogges wiþ ȝour tayl*. Br: *"Go hom, dogges, with your tayle!"*

1832 *Men shall threste in your cuyle*. So W. B: *Righte sall mene garre ȝow habide*. A: *Me shall thrust in youre cull*. D: *Men schal þrestyn in ȝoure koyl*. L: *Man schal þrest in ȝour coyl*. H: *menne schall threste yn yowre cule*.

1838 *pavylyouns*. B: *pauylyons*. Br: *pauylyouns*. W: *pavylyous*.

1851 *With syxe stages full of tourelles*. So W. B: *With sere stages full of torells*. D: *With sex stages & tureles*. L: *Wiþ sex stages ful of turels*. A: *With vi. stages jmade of stirells*. H: *wyth sexe stages ymade of styrelles*. On the basis of *stirelles* and other "errors" shared by A and H, Brunner argues these manuscripts form a group within *b* that is distinct from L, E, and D (*Löwenherz*, pp. 13–14).

1855 *surnownne*. So B. W: *sory nom*. L: *sornoun*. A: *surnum*. D: *sirename*. H: *surname*.

1857 *Maryners, arme your shyppes*. E, missing a few initial leaves, begins here, but only the last two words are legible: *shippes blyve*.

1858 *And holde up well your manshippes*. So A. Br: *And holde up your manshyppes*. W: *And do up your manshyppes*. B: *And haldis up wele oure manchippys*. L: *& holdeþ vp our manschippes*. H: *And holde uppe ȝour manneschippes*. Omitted in D and in E.

1861 *For joye come never to me*. So Br. A: *ffor Joy come neuer to me*. W: *For come ye neuer to me*. B: *ffor certis joye commys never vnto me*. D: *Joye comyth never non to me*. H: *ffor y ioy cometh never unto me*. L: *Joie ne comeþ þer neuer to me*.

1867 *With ore, sprete, and sayle*. B: *With are and sprete and saile*. W: *Syth ore spredde and sayle*. A: *With bowsprete and saille blyve*. L: *Wiþ ore & seyl & spere*. D: *With ore and sayle spret*. H: *With bowsprete and sayle blyve*.

1871 *kynge of Fraunce*. So B. W: *kynge fraunce*.

1873 *Englysshe cowardes*. So W. B: *Inglys cowardes*. A: *Englissh taylardes*. D: *englische taylardes*. L: *Inglische cowardes*. H: *englysche taylardes*.

1874 *mosardes*. So A. Br, L: *mossardes*. W: *losardes*. B: *moserde*. D, H: *cowardes*.

1875 *But reyse up*. So W. B: *Do drisses now*. A: *Dighteth he seide*. D: *Ordeyne now*. L: *Drisses now*. H: *dyghte he seyde*.

1881 *Targes and hurdis*. So L, Br. W: *Terges and hardes*. B: *Targis and hurdas*. D: *Torches bordes*. A, H: *Targes and dores*.

1885 *mosardes*. So A, D, H, W: *losardes*. B: *moserde*. L: *musardes*.

1888 *in hast*. So B. W: *on fast*. A: *unto*. D: *on hast*. L: *anon*. H: *uppe*.

1895 *hade so*. So B. W: *harde*. A: *So harde*. D: *hadde ny*. L: *hadde so*. H: *So Harde*.

1898 *Felde*. W: *Helde*. B: *felle*. A: *ful*. D: *feldyn*. L: *fel*. H: *fylle*.

1905 *wele*. So B, Br. W: *welee*. A: *well*. D: *wel*. Omitted in H.

1915 *Kynge Rycharde come*. So B. W: *Kynge Rychard and*. A: *When he come to him*. L: *King Richard com*. D: *Kyng Richard came*.

1928 *After hym prycked upon*. W: *After prycked upon*. B: *Aftire hym prekede appone*. L: *After him priked on*.

1930 *felawrede*. So B, A. W: *ferhede*. D: *felarede*. H: *felawrade*.

1942 *tholed schame*. So B. W: *gave bane*. D: *casche here bane*. A: *her schame*. H: *to take schame*.

1943 *hous*. So A, D. B: *howsses*. H: *howse*. W: *horse*. Using W's *horse* seems out of context given that line 1944 describes the barring of windows and doors; B provides an exemplar from *a* to corroborate the emendation.

1945 *Oure Englissh with grete levours*. So A. W: *And ever men bare them up with levours*. B: *Bot the Ynglismen rane to with levours*. H: *Englysche menne with lewwres*. D: *The Englische have brostyn with levauns*.

1946 *Breke hem up with grete vigours*. So A. W: *And slew them with grete vygours*. B: *And brake thame up with grete vigours*. D: *And slowin hem with gret vemauns*.

1949 *tresoure*. So B, A, D. W: *tresours*.

1950 *covertoure*. So B, D. W: *countours*. A: *couerters*. H: *couerture*.

1969 *one hande*. So B. W: *have honde*. A: *an hande*. D: *one honde*.

1974 *knee*. So B, H. W: *kene*.

1978 *towne*. So A, Br. W: *twone*. B: *townne*. D: *town*.

1982 *itelde*. So D, Br. W: *itelbe*. B: *telled*. A: *itolde*.

1989 *thy*. So A, H. W: *theyr*. B: *thi*. D: *þat*.

2004 *Syr Hewe Impetyte*. So W. B: *Hewe of Pympotit*. A: *Sir Penpetite*. D: *Hewe Pimperise*.

2006 *Cleped hym taylarde and hym myssayde*. W: *Cleped taylarde and myssayde*. B: *And called hym vile foule tayliarde*. A: *They cleped him tailarde & hym mysade*. D: *Clepid hym taylarde & hym myssayde*. H: *And fulle foule hym myssayde*. E is illegible.

2025 *Of Kynge Richarde he asked mercy*. So Br. B: *Of Kyng Richerd he asked mercy*. W: *Of kynge Rycharde he had his grace*. A: *And for goddess loue he cried mercy*. H: *And for goddes loue he cryed mercy*. D: *Tto kyng Richard he seyde mercy*.

2026 *That he wolde ther sesy*. So D, Br. W: *That he would leue his stryfe in that place*. B: *Ffor Jhesu lufe & for þe lufe of myld Mary*. A: *That he shulde secy*. H: *that he schulde sessey*.

2029 *graunted hym*. So H. B: *granted hym*. W: *graunted*. D: *hym graunted*. A: *graunted hem*.

2040 *And than on his waye he wente*. See the corresponding Explanatory Note for an additional passage from the *b* group of manuscripts.

2046 *With moche store of sylver and golde*. See the corresponding Explanatory Note for an additional passage from the *b* group of manuscripts.

2051 *sodaynly*. So Br. B: *sodeynly*. W: *sondaynly*.

2055 *bowe spret*. So B. W: *bothe sprett*.

2063 *The ferde schippe behynde duellede*. So B. W: *That shyppe lefte in the shelde*. A: *The ferthe ship byhynde dwellyd*. D: *The fferd chipe behynd dwellyd*.

2064 *Unnethes the maryners it helde*. So B, Br. W: *The maryners vnneth it with helde*. A: *Vnneþ the mareners hit ahelde*. D: *Vnethe þe mariners had yt welmyd*.

2065 *And that schippe lefte righte in the depe*. So B. Omitted in W. A: *The ship lasted in the depe*. D: *þus yt befel jn depe*. H: *The schype lanched in the depe*.

2066 *That the folkes one the lande myghte wepe*. So B. Omitted in W. A: *ffolke on þe londe myght wel wepe*. H: *ffolke of the londe myght wel wepe*. D: *The folke on londe myth wepe*.

2067 *Gryffons*. So Br. W: *Pryffons*.

2071 *of lyve*. So B, D, H. W: *on lyve*. A: *of lyf*.

2083 *borne*. So B, D, A, H. W: *lorne*.

2096 *dyshonoure*. So B. W: *byshonoure*.

2108 *double*. So B. W: *bouble*.

2111 *hastely*. So B, W^2. W: *hasteyl*.

2141 *Thou hast thy selfe tresoure enoghe*. So Br. W: *Thou hast the selfe tresour grete plente*. B: *Thou hase thi selfe tresoure enoghe*. A: *Thow hauest thi self tresor jnoghe*. H: *For þou haste tresoure ynowghe*. D: *Þou hast þiselfe tresoure jnow*.

2142 *Yelde hym his tresour or thou getis grete woghe*. So B. A: *yelde him his tresour thow hauest þe wogh*. W: *Yf thou it withhelde it were grete pyte*. H: *yelde hym his tresour þou hast þe wowghe*. Note that the order of lines 2141–42 is reversed in A and H. D: *Ȝelde hym his þou hast done wow*.

2152 *And seid he wolde tellene hym a consaile*. So B. W: *And sayd he wolde hym accounsayle*. A: *And seide he wolde telle him a consaill*. D: *And seyde he wolde spekyn Jn counsaill*. H: *For to herkenne a cownceylle*.

2176 *bryght*. So H. W: *bryghe*. B: *brighte*. A: *bright*. D: *bryth*.

2180 *done us*. So B. W: *done vo*.

2204 *flenne*. W: *fleune*. B: *to fly*. A: *to flen*. D: *to fle thenne*. Omitted in H.

2216 *he toke*. So B, D, L. W: *toke*.

2219 *cleved*. So Br. B: *clevede*. W: *claved*. A: *sleed*.

2220 *therby leved*. So W, A. B: *þer he relevede*. D: *ther he levyd*.

2231 *jewells*. So B. W: *meles*. A: *jewels*. D: *juelys*. L: *iuwels*.

2232 *He sesyde als his owne catells*. B: *He sesyde als his awenne catells*. W: *He toke to his owne deles*. D: *He nam & all here chateles*. A: *Right for his owne cattels*. H: *Right for ys owne catelles*. Br: *He toke to his owne cateles*.

2247 *He*. So B, D. W: *She*. Omitted in A, H.

2253 *The keyes also I betake thee here*. W: *The keyes also in batayll here*. B: *And alswa alle þe keyes J betake þe here*. D: *The keyis also J take þe here*.

2276 *Stowte in armes and stronge in fighte*. So Br. B: *Stowte in armours & stronge in fighte*. W: *Well armed in armure bryght*. A: *Stout in Armes & strong in fighte*. L: *Stout in armes & strong in fiȝtes*. D: *Steffe jn Armys & bold jn fyth*.

2279 *pavylyoune*. So B. W: *pauylywne*. L: *pauilons*. A: *pauilion*. D: *pauylouns*. H: *paueloune*. Br: *pauylyowne*.

2280 *trompis*. So B, D. W: *turmppettes*. A: *trompes*. L: *trumppes*.

sowne. So B. W: *swone*. D: *souns*. L: *sounes*.

2295 *As armes lordynges, all and some*. So B, A, L. W: *Horse and harneys lordes all and some*. H: *To armes lordes alle and somme*. D: *Lordis as armys all & some*.

2296 *We bene betrayed and inome*. B: *We bene bytrapped and bynommene*. W: *We betrayed and Jnome*. A: *We buth bytrayed and jnome*. D: *We bene jtrayde & jnome*. L: *We beþ bitreyd & ynome*. H: *For whe ben trayed and ynome*.

2303 *felled downe*. So B. W: *fell downe*.

2317 *He fande his clothis and his tresoure*. So B. Omitted in W. D: *He ffond his clodes & his tresoure*. L: *he fond his cloþes & his tresour*.

2318 *Bot he was fled, that vile traytoure*. So B. Omitted in W. D: *And flowin was þat fowle tratour*. L: *Ac he was flowen þat vile traytour*.

2334 *hyght*. E: *hyȝt*. W: *hygh*. B: *highte*. D: *heyte*. L: *hete*. Omitted in A, H.

2356 *let me be*. So E. W: *leve me*. B: *late me bee*. A: *to bee*. H: *in pees be*. L: *lete me*.

2361 *Goth and seithe*. So H. W: *Go and sayd*. B: *Gase and says*. A: *Goth and siggeth*. E: *To sauȝtle*. L: *Goþ and siggeþ*.

2367 *And also saye*. W: *And all that*. B: *and alswa saye*. A: *And also sey*. D: *& seye þus*. L: *& siggeþ also*.

2376 *out of*. So E, L. B, A: *oute of*. D: *owte of*. W: *but of*. Omitted in H.

2391 *In grete solace*. So B. W: *Grete solace*. D: *In solas*. E: *In solace*. A: *In grete delyte*. H: *With grete delyte*.

2401 *Bonevent*. So B. W: *Boffenent*. H: *Bonnevente*. A: *Bonnent*. E: *Bowent*.

2430 *dy*. So B. A: *die*. D: *dye*. H: *dyghe*. W: *abye*.

2440 *Pyse*. So B, A, D, H. W: *pryse*.

2442 *not loke*. So D. W: *no love*. B: *noghte loke*. A: *Wolde loke*. H: *Wolde lowke*.

2449 *by Hym*. So B, D, A, H. W: *by Jhesu*.

2453 *Erle*. W: *elre*.

2456 *To kepe his realme to his honde*. After this line, *b* (A, fol. 260v) includes the following verses:

Ther[e] Kyng Ric[hard] spoused berenger,
The kyng[es] doughter of Nau[er],
And made ther Richest spousyng
That ev[er] maked any kyng,
And corouned himself Emp[er]o[ur]
And her Emp[er]ice w[ith] honour[e];
And thus Kyng R[ichard] wonne Cipres.
God g[ra]unte his soule heuene blys!

2545 *on borde*. So A, D, H. MS: *to borde*. W: *aborde*. B: *one borde*.

2580 *a devyl*. So MS, D. W, B: *the devyll*. A: *a fende*. H: *a ffende*. E: . . . *com fro helle* (line partially illegible).

2631 *The galey yede as swyfte*. So W. Omitted in MS. B: *Þat the galy went alswa swyfte*. D: *The galey ȝede also wyth*.

2632 *As ony foule by the lyfte*. So W. Omitted in MS. B: *Als any foule by the lifte*. D: *so any ffowle þat flyith in fflyth*.

2635 *to the chayne*. So W. MS: *the cheyne too*. B: *unto the cheyne*. A: *þe cheyne*. D: *þe chayne*.

2636 *atwayne*. So W. MS: *on twoo*. B: *in twayne*. A: *atweyne*. D: *mayne*.

2651 *Gunnes he hadde on wondyr wise*. A (fols. 261v–62r) provides the *b* group's shorter account of Richard's arrival in Acre:

The saracen[es] that wer[e] in acres toune
To þe walles ronne abondoune.
Of þe far[e] þey hadde wonder:
The see brent aboue & vnder;
And alle c[ri]sten kyng[es] & pages
Erles barons and bondages
To þe see wente afterward

To see the comyng of Kyng Ric[hard],
ffor to see the galies saile,
His mynstrallsye & his app[ar]aille.
ffor they ne sey neu[er] suche a comyng
Jnto Acres of no C[ri]sten kyng,
And whenne jdo was þis m[er]vaill[e],
Kyng Ric[hard] wente to londe saunz faill[e].

2675 *For it was within the nyght*. So W. Omitted in MS. B: *Ffor þat it was appone þe myrke nyghte*.

2676 *They were agrysed of that syght*. So W. Omitted in MS. B: *Þerfore þay were all awondrede of þat sighte*.

2679 *And sayd he was the devyll of hell*. So W. Omitted in MS. B: *And saide þan it was þe fende of helle*.

2680 *That was come them to quell*. So W. Omitted in MS. B: *Þat was comen þam alle to quelle*.

2695 *ledden hym*. So B. MS: *ledde*. W: *syth ledde hym*.

2722 *deedly*. So W. MS: *manly*. B: *dedy*. A: *dethliche*. D: *dedlyche*. H: *dethelyche*.

2755 *and that brethe*. So W. MS: *wiþouten drede*. B: *& þat stynke*. A: *of þat brethe*. E: *of þe breeth*. D: *& þat breth*.

2756 *toke theyr dethe*. So W. MS: *þeroff were dede*. B: *als I thynke*. A: *toke her deth*. D: *tok here deth*. E: *token her deeth*.

2765 *And so they*. MS: *So þey*. W: *And so we*. B: *And soo þay*. D: *& so þay*.

2770 *bore*. So B, A, D. MS: *ibere*. Omitted in W. L: *ybore*.

2775 *On Seynt Jamys even, verrayment*. H ends here.

2780 *And alle it*. So B. MS: *And it*. Omitted in W. A: *And all hit*. L: *& alle it*. D: *And al yt*.

2804 *With there swerdes doun thay hewe*. Omitted in MS. B: *With there suerdys doun þay hewe*. W: *Were with swerdes all to hewe*. L: *Wiþ her swerdes adoun þai hewe*. D: *& here swerdis al to hewe*. E: *With her swerdes al to hew*.

2827 *Bawdewyne*. So W, B. MS: *Bawdekyn*. A: *baudewyne*. L: *Baudewines*. D: *blandewyne*.

2880 *But blessyd be the Holy Goost*. So W. MS: *ffadyr & sone be þankyd & holy gost*. B: *There louyde now be the holy goste*. D: *blyssyd be þe holy gost*. A: *But jhered be that holi gost*. L: *& herd be þat holy gost*.

2892 *And pryckyd out of that felawred*. W: *And prycked out that felowrede*. MS: *And preykyd forþ wiþ his felawred*. B: *And prikked owte of that forehede*. D: *Richard tok leue of þat ffered*. Note that the order of lines 2891–92 is reversed in D. L: *& rode him out of þat ferred*. A: *And priked oute of that felawerede*.

2896 *Seynt John*. So A, D. MS: *Seynt Thomas*. W: *saynt Johan*. B: *seyne John*. L: *seyn Jon*.

2899 *That was a tree castell ful fyne*. W: *That was a tree castelle full fyne*. MS: *It was off tree castel fful ffyn*. B: *Þat was a tre castelle full fyne*. L: *Þat was a tre castel ful fine*. D: *That was a tre castel ful ffyne*. A: *That was a castell gode and fyne*.

2902 *shyppes full of been*. MS: *schyp fful been*. W: *shyppes full of bene*. B: *schyppes ful of bees*. A: *shippes full of been*. D: *schippis of ben*. L: *schippes of hiuen of ben*.

2934 *ben and stones*. L: *ben & stones*. MS: *bond and stones*. W: *bente and stones*. B: *grete stanys and bees*. A: *stones*. D: *stonys*.

2945 *Sarazenes*. So B. MS: *archers*. W: *the Sarazynes*. D: *Sarazynys*. L: *þai*. Omitted in A. *flowen*. So MS. B: *fflowe*. W: *drewe*. D: *flew*. L: *flowe*. Omitted in A.

2954 *In ynde armyd to all ryghtes*. At this point, the fragmentary L breaks off.

2994 *In ynde armyd to all ryghtes*. Absent in MS, A includes the following couplet after this line: *Her baner was peynted, so seith þe Latyn, / Wiþ iij bores hefdes of golde fyne*. See *Löwenherz*, p. 245n.

3010 *But*. So W, A, D, E. MS: *And*. B: *Warne*.

3012 *Susé seynours, has armes tost*. So MS. W: *Soyes seygnyours for the holy goost*. B: *And knyghttis hase þaire armours takyne*. A: *Sus seignours as Armes tost*. D: *Sus seygnunzs As Armes tost*. E: *Suse seignours as armes toste*.

3023 *And many a knyghte loste his armys*. W: *Many a knyght lost his harnes*. MS: *Manye knygtes þere loste here armes*. B: *And many a knyghte lese his armys*. A: *And many a knyght þere los his armes*. D: *And many A man þere les his armys*.

3024 *And many a stede drewe theyr tharmes*. W: *And many a stede drewe theyr tharnes*. A: *And many a stede drough his tharmes*. D: *& many a stede þere drow his tharmys*. MS: *And manye stedes drowȝ to harmes*. B: *And many a stede drewe after þam þaire tharmes*. E: *And mony a stede þere drewe his* . . . (line partially illegible).

3025 *manye a*. W, B, D: *many a*. MS: *manye*. E: *mony*.

3035 *But holde them all within*. So W. Omitted in MS. B: *Bot halde þame alle it with inne*. A: *But holde hem all stille þerinne*. D: *Therfor þer holdyn hem withinne*.

3036 *That the Sarasynes sholde them not wyn*. So W. Omitted in MS. B: *That the Sarazenes ne scholde thame wynne*. A: *That no Saracens sholde in wynne*. D: *That þe sarazynys schulde hem not wynne*.

3040 *For them yede no raunsoun*. So W. MS: *Ther yede no*. B: *Ffor þame that noþer go rawnsone*.
to mede. So MS, W. B: *no mede*.

3058 *laye in grete*. So W. B: *laye in so grete*. MS: *was in swylk*.

3062 *To the Fadyr*. So W. MS: *Ffadyr*. B: *To god þe ffadir*.

3066 *her*. So W. MS: *hys*. B: *for hir*.

3083 *And ye*. So W, B. MS: *Ye may*.

3099 *broweys*. So MS. W, B: *brothe*.

3108–3613 *Thorwgh grace . . . . to sterve*. Missing leaves, B is defective for this interval.

3114 *Hys folk hem turnyd away and lowgh*. So MS. Omitted in W. B is defective.

3119 *Kyng*. MS: *Kyn*.

3125–50 *The Sarezynes . . . . so fele*. See the corresponding Explanatory Note for a variant passage from the *b* group of manuscripts.

3128 *entred an in icome*. So W. MS: *entryd in þe comoun*. A: *almost in icome*. D: *made entre comoun*.

3151 *Before wente his Templers*. So W. Omitted in MS. A: *Byfor him wente his templers*. D: *Beforn went his templers*.

3152 *His Gascoynes and his Ospytalers*. So W. Omitted in MS. A: *His gascons & his hospitalers*. D: *his gascons & his ospitalers*.

3177–93 *Thus al . . . . ten myle*. See the corresponding Explanatory Note for a variant passage from A.

3212 *hys whyte teeth*. So MS. W: *tethe whyte as snawe*.

3234 *without dystaunse*. MS: *with off here dystaunse*. W: *without dystaunce*. A: *withoute distaunce*. D: *for here dystance*.

3237 *Heris*. MS: *Here is*. W: *here*. D: *Herkenyth*. A: *lusteth*.

3296 *To underfonge of*. So W, A. MS: *To styrte undyr off*.

3298 *That kynge myght not be Syr Markys*. So W. MS: *Þat þe kyng louyd nouȝt þe markys*. A: *That kynge ne moste noght be marcus*. D: *That malkows schulde not be marchis*.

3304 *Without dente and without harme*. So W. MS: *Þat non off hem have ony harme*. A: *Withoute dunt, withoute harme*. D: *Withowtyn dynt withowtyn harm*.

3312 *ye may fynde*. MS: *I may ȝow ffynde*. W: *ye may fynde also*. A: *ye may fynd*. D: *Ȝe schul ffynde*.

3320 *defensable*. So W, A. MS, D: *fensable*.

3326 *In myn half, I graunte thee forward*. See the corresponding Explanatory Note for an additional passage from A.

3331 *put them thore*. So W. MS: *token hem ȝare*. Omitted in A. D, E: *put hem þore*.

3346 *To venge God of hys enemyes*. See below for the reading from A, fols. 265r–v:

Sone theraft[er] bitidde a chaunce
Bytwene Richard & the kyng of ffraunce
Als they pleiden atte ches.
Thanne seyde kyng phelip in a res:
"Kyng Richard, they thugh wynne
Al this lond thurgh thy gynne
J am lord, siker thugh be,
And j wille have the dignyte."
"The dignite?" quath kyng Richard.
"Thugh lixt, by seynt Leonard!
I the swere, by seynt marie,
Of my p[ur]chas ne getest thugh w[u]rth a flye!
Yf thugh w[u]lt haue dignite,
Go wyn hyt with thy meyne!
& fonde if thugh hauest g[ra]ce
Of the Soudan to gete p[ur]chace.
I swere by Seynt Thomas of Inde,
Of my p[ur]chas thugh art byhynde."
Ffor wratth worth sike the kyng of ff[ra]unce,
His lechis seyde without distaunce
That he ne sholde neu[er] hol be
Bute he to ffraunce to[ur]ne aye.
The kyng of ffraunce tho vnd[er]stode
That hur[e] consail was trywe & goode.
His shypes he dighte, more & lasse.
& wente hom atte halwe masse.
Kyng Richard on hym gan to crie,
And seyde he dude vileynye;
That he wolde for any maladie
Wende of the lond of Surrye
Er he hadde do godes s[er]uyse
For lif or deth in any wise.
The kyng of ffraunce wolde hy[m] nogh here,
But wente forth on this manere.
For they departede thus, forsoth,
Ev[er]e aft[er] were they wroth.

On the morwe Kyng Richarde
Dyghte hym to Jafes ward
& ladde with hym a gret oste
In the name of the holy goste.
Saladyn that heigh Soudan,
Lay logged with many a man,
With many a tente & pauyloun
To kepe Nazares toun.
The wey was narwe saunz doute,
Ther fore kyng Richard rod aboute.
Byside fflum Jordan he gan hym reste,
To sle the Sarasyne he was preste
For to fighte vppon the pleyn
That nolde the Soudan Saladyn,
For he hadde in memorye,
That he ne sholde wynne the vittorye.

For variations among the *b* group, see *Löwenherz*, pp. 262n–64n.

3383 *Our Sawdon*. So W, E. MS: *Þe sawdon*.
3384 *ever more*. So W, E. MS: *ffor evere more*.
3408 *bode*. So MS. W: *worde*. E: *word*.
3411 *alone*. So W. MS: *anon*. E: *alloone*.
3413 *Pryvely*. So W, E. MS: *Stylly*.
3431 *that they be nought rowe*. So MS. W: *they be no thynge rawe*. E: *they be nothing rowe*.
3436 *Faste therof ete I shall*. So W. MS: *Ete þeroff ryȝt faste I schal*. E: *Faste þerof ete y shalle*.
3459 *He broughte oure kyng — was it nought leued*. So MS. W: *He brought to kynge Rycharde not cleuede*. E: *He bare to Richard it was not cleued*.
3464 *Therof they had all grame*. So W. MS: *Theroff thoughte hem but lytyl game*. E: *Þereof þey hadden al grame*.
3512 *a Sarezynys hede al hoot*. MS: *sarezynys hedes abouten al hoot*. W: *a Sarasynes heed all hote*. E: *a Saryzyns hed al whoot*.
3516 *In saf condyt*. MS: *In saff cundyt*. W: *safe to wende*. E: *In saf condit*.
3519 *so vylayne*. So W. MS: *so euyl*. E: *velayn*.
3520 *For to*. So W, E. MS: *Þat I wolde*.
3530 *and tell thy Sowdan*. So W. MS: *to ȝoure sawdan*. E: *and biddeth ȝoure Soudan*.
3531 *he*. So W, E. MS: *ȝe*.
3539 *Brede, wyne, flesshe, fysshe and kunger*. So W. MS: *Bred & wyn ffysch fflesch samoun & cungir*. E: *fflessh and fyssh samon and kungour*.
3541 *Whyle that*. So W. MS: *Whyle we*. E: *While þat*.
3547 *Kyng Richard sayd: "I you waraunt."* W: *Kyng Rychard sayd J you wraunt*. MS: . . . *ng Richard j schal waraunt* (line partially illegible). E: *King Richard seide y ȝow waraunt*.
3548 *Ther is no flesch so norysshaunt*. W: *There is no flesshe so nouryssaunt*. MS: . . . *no fflesch so norysschaunt* (line partially illegible). E: *Þer is no flesshe so noresshaunt*.
3549 *Unto an Ynglyssche Crysten man*. Br: *Vnto an Ynglyssche Cristen-man*. MS: . . . *an ynglyssche man* (line partially illegible). W: *To none englylshe crysten man*. E: *To myn Jnglyssh cristen men*.

3552 *As is the flessh of a Saryzyne*. So E. MS: *As þe hed off a sarezyn*. W: *Than is the flesshe of a sarasyne*.

3556 *Lyvande*. So MS. W: *Alyue*. E: *Lyuyng*.

3563 *tournyd*. MS: *tourn*. . . (line partially illegible). E: *tornyd*. W: *dyde tourne*.

3564 *mournyd*. MS: *mour*. . . (line partially illegible). E: *mornyd*. W: *dyde mourne*.

3566 *Kyng*. MS: *Kyn*. W: *That kynge*. E: *King*.

3571 *Of thy gold wolde he non*. MS: *Off þy gold wolde he take non*. W: *Of our golde wolde he none*. E: *Of þy golde wolle he noon*.

3579 *Rychardes table*. MS: *þe k*. . . . (line partially illegible). W: *stode Rychardes table*. E: *stood Richard is table*.

3580 *But non of us before hym segh*. W: *But none of vs before hym sygh*. MS: *But non off v . . . re hym segh* (line partially illegible). E: *What þeron com wel we syȝe*.

3591 *feres*. So Br. MS: *seres*. W: *felawe*. E: *men*.

3596 *For sorwe we wende for to deye*. Below are two couplets that follow this line in E (fol. 15v), but not in MS or in W:

> When we dede rede þe letter ryȝt,
> Whos sone he was and what he hight,
> The teers ron doun[e] by oure berde
> To be þere slayn[e] we were aferde.

3598 *Nynyve*. MS: *nynyue*. W: *rube*. E: *Nauerne*.

3609 *With teeth he gnew the flesch ful harde*. MS: *Wiþ teeþ . . . fflesch ful harde* (line partially illegible). W: *With his tethe he grynded flesshe harde*. E: *With teeth he gnew þe flessh herde*.

3612 *He*. So W, E. MS: *And*.

3613 *For drede we wende for to sterve*. W omits lines 3613–40.

3617 *that he be*. So B, E. MS: *to ben*.

3618 *soure*. So Br. MS: *oure*. B: *so soure*. E: *sory*.

3631 *Be servyd ferst, I and myn hynys*. E omits lines 3631–38.

3636 *Ne drank of wyn*. MS: *drank off whyt*. B: *Ne drynke no wyne*.

3656 *His clothis of gold unto his scherk*. MS: *Off þy cloþis off gold vnto þy scherk*. W: *His clothes of golde and his sarke*. B: *His clothes of golde vnto his serke*.

3660 *here bodies*. MS: *here blood*. B: *their bodies*. E: *oure boody*. Omitted in W.

3664 *It is a devyl, withouten fayle*. After this line in B (fol. 144r), the following passage occurs, which is not found in other manuscripts:

> And for serwe þay fallen[e] doun[e] in swoune,
> Dukes & Erles & Barouns bathe vp & doun.
> Many a lady and many a quene
> Ffor þare childre þ[at] slayne thus bene,
> Ffelle full flatte doun[e] appon[e] þe flynte,
> And for þ[e] sorowe fulle nere þaire lyfes tynte.
> Owte of þaire swounyng when þay myghte ryse,
> þane þayre god Mawhoun[e] þay disspyse,
> þay spittede one hym and seyden[e] "Fy!"
> And one all þaire oþ[ere] goddes bothe by & by.
> "Allas, Mawhoun[e] þat þ[ou] suffre wilte
> Oure childre thus for thi laye to be spilte!

Of thi myghte whatte es worthe to ȝelpe
Whene þ[ou] ne will thy s[er]vandes nothynge helpe.
We prey to the bothe lowde and softe,
And dose to the full grete wirchipes & ofte,
And hono[ur]es full heghely thyn[e] holy name,
Why soffre þ[ou] þam[e] thus to done vs this schame?
We prey the with full mylde bysekynge,
Of ȝone kynge Richerd to take wrekynge!
Confou[n]de hy[m], Lerde, throrow thyn[e] holy vertue,
And also alle those þ[at] leves appon[e] þat Jh[es]u.

3667 *he may go forth*. So Br. MS: *he may forth*. W: *he go forth*. B: *may he goo forthe*. E: *he may for sooth*.

3669 *oure chyldren and us*. So W. MS: *boþe oure chldren & us*. B: *oure childre & us*. E: *oure children and us*.

3673 *yif*. C: *ȝyff*. This word appears either as *yyff* or *ȝyff* throughout the text, and has been emended to *yif* at lines 3703, 3723, 3791, 3805, 3806, 3807, 3821, 3965, 3968, 4101, 4192, 4358, and 5523.

3683 *that he his travayle lese*. MS: *hys trauayle þat he lese*. W: *that he his trauayll lese*. B: *þat he his travelle lesse*. E: *þat he his trauaile lese*.

3690 *thee to*. MS: *& go*. W, B: *the to*. E: *þe to*.

3691 *folk*. So E, Br. MS: *land*. W: *folke*. B: *folkes*.

3692 *thy maltalent*. So Br. MS: *al maltalent*. W: *thy malatent*. B: *þat gilte*. E: *þy male talent*.

3696 *wynne*. So W, E. MS: *bere*. B: *wyne*.

3697 *And so shall ye leve and be frendes*. So W. Omitted in MS. B: *Lyffe togedire & be gud ffrendys*. E: *Loueþ togeder and beth frendes*.

3698 *With joye to your lyves endes*. So W. Omitted in MS. B: *With vnto ȝour lyffes endes*. E: *Euer to ȝoure lyues endes*.

3701 *besoughte*. So Br. MS: *beþouȝte*. W: *besought*. B: *bysoughte*. E: *bysouȝt*.

3704 *Mahowne*. So W. MS: *appolyn*. B: *Sir mahownne*. E: *mahon*. A: *mahunde*. D: *mahond*.

3726 *So God do my soule boote*. After this line, the following 10-line passage appears in *b* (A, fols. 265v–66r):

The messagere gonne forth wende
& tolde the Soudan word & ende;
Than was he in gret dolo[ur],
A morwe he sende hym more t[re]so[ur],
An hundred thousende pounde of gold,
So much for Acres pay he wold.
The messager that t[re]so[ur] broughte
And for the ostage hym bysoughte.
Than askede Kyng R[ichard] the roude anone,
That god was on to dethe don[e].

Compare D, fols. 28r–v and Brunner, *Löwenherz*, p. 281n.

3727 *I wolde nought lese my lordes love*. So A. Omitted in MS. W: *J wyll not leue my lordes lawe*. B: *J ne wolde noghte lese my lordes lufe*. D: *Ffor lesyn J nold myn lordes loue*. E: *Ffor lese y ne wold my lordes loue*.

3728 *For al the londes under heven above*. Omitted in MS. W: *Of all the londes vnder heuen ahawe*. B: *Ffor alle þe londis vndir heuen abofe*. A: *For all the gold vnder heuene aboue*. D: *Ffor al þe landis vnder heuene above*. E: *Ffor al þe londe vnder heuyn aboue*.

3731 *They answered at the frome*. W: *They answered at the forme*. MS: *Þenne answeryd off hem some*. B: *Bot þay ansuerde alle þerto full sone on none*. E: *. . . y him . . . wered at þe froome* (line partially illegible). A: *And they answerden atte frome*. D: *They hym answerd at frome*.

3735 *nought so slye*. So W, D. MS: *nought slye*. B: *slee*. E: *so slyȝe*. A: *so sley*.

3737 *sone anon*. So A. MS: *euerlkon*. W, D: *anone*. B: *sone on nane*. E: *anoon*.

3748 *an aungell*. So E, A. MS: *aungeles*. W: *aungell*. B: *ane angelle*. D: *an angel*.

3749 *That seyde, "Seygnyours, tues, tues."* So W. MS: *Þey seyde seynyours tuez tuese*. B: *Þat cried sayntours tues tues*. E: *Þat cryed seignours touz touz*. D: *Þat cryid sargnures tues tues*. A: *& seyde seynours twyes twyes*.

3759–71 *Merye is . . . . strokes hard!* The descriptive passage or seasonal headpiece does not appear in W, which omits lines 3759–4816. Compare *Löwenherz*, p. 16. See the related discussion in the Explanatory Notes.

3779 *his los*. MS: *here los*. B: *his lose*.

3780 *his renoun*. MS: *here renoun*. B: *his renownne*.

3942 *was here wone*. MS: *was his wone*. B: *werene acostome & wonne*.

3944 *here*. MS: *his*.

4110 *Coverde*. So B. MS: *Corue*.

4124 *Where it is no man may seen*. For an 8-line passage that occurs after this line in B (fol. 147r), see below:

Thom[a]s askede the Sarazene thare,
"Es slikke trappes any ma there?
Vs to bytraye or to grefe?"
"Nay, S[ir], for sothe, þ[ou] may me lefe!
With any lyes gif þ[ou] me fynde,
Bynd myn[e] handes me byhynde
And gare me be hangede & alswa drawenn[e]
And of thies tydandes Thom[a]s was fayne.

4127 *has horsmen*. MS: *horsemen*. B: *hase horsemen*.

4221 *For wollewarde*. So B. MS: *Barefoot*.

4285 *ying*. MS: *ȝyng*.

4408 *weel hem*. So Br. MS: *hem weel hem*. B: *þame ful harde*.

4435 *we*. So B, Br. MS: *he*.

4507 *Sarazynes comen with gret wylle*. So Br. MS: *Sarazynes comen wiþ gret wy . . .* (line partially illegible). B: *Þe Sarazenes come þane with full grete will*.

4508 *When the Crystene myghte drawe hem tylle*. MS: *When þe crytene myȝte draw . . .* (line partially illegible). B: *Bot whene þat þe Cristyne myghte come þame till*. Br: *When þe Crystene myȝt drawe hem tylle*.

4509 *To schete the arweblasteres hem dresse*. MS: *To schete þe aweblasteres he . . .* (line partially illegible). B: *To schotte faste þe alblasteres þame drisses*.

4510 *And the archeres to hem gesse*. After this line, B (fol. 149v) includes three couplets not found in MS (see Brunner, *Löwenherz*, p. 312n):

> þay smate þan[e] at ev[er]ilke schote,
> Thurghe sydis and thurgh throte,
> And staffe slyngers w[ith] grete stanes,
> Slewe many of þam[e] for þ[e] nanes.
> Off the vawarde a thowsande score
> þ[e] Crystyn[e] men wexe þ[e] baldere þ[er]fore.

4536 *For bost he prekyd a gret pas*. So Br. MS: . . . *bost he prekyd a gret pas* (line partially illegible). B: *Ffor boste prikkande a full grete pase*.

4537 *A gret fawchoun in hand he bar*. MS: . . . *houn in hand he bar* (line partially illegible). B: *A grete schafte in his hande he bare*. Br: *A gret ffawchoun in hand he bar*.

4538 *"Come fyght with me now hoo that dar!"* MS: . . . *with me now hoo þat dar* (line partially illegible). B: *Come feghte with me he bade what sa dare*. Br: *"Come ffyȝ wiþ me now hoo þat dar!"*

4539 *Sir John Doyly, Sir Foukes nevew*. MS: . . . *ffoukes nevew* (line partially illegible). B: *Sir Johne Doly Sir ffukes kyne*. Br: *Jhon Doyly, Sere Ffoukes nevewe*.

4540 *A yonge knyghte of gret vertew*. MS: . . . *off gret vertew* (line partially illegible). B: *A ȝonge knyghte full of joye within*. Br: *A ȝong knyȝt off gret vertew*.

4541 *In hande he took*. MS: . . . *took* (line partially illegible). B: *Jn hande he toke*.

4546 *And sayde, "Dogge, there thou ly."* So Br. MS: . . . *dogge þere þou ly* (line partially illegible). B: *And sayd heythyne doge ly þere þou ly*.

4549 *mete*. MS: *meten*. B: *mett*.

4579 *sene*. So B, Br. MS is illegible.

4582 *werk*. So Br. MS is illegible. B: *werke*.

4750 *syne*. So B, Br. MS: *ffyn*.

4817 *Seynt James*. MS: *Seynt Jamys*. W: *Saynt James*. B: *Sayne James*. A: *Saynt Johnes*. D: *Seynts Johnnys*. E: *Seynt Joones*. W, A, D, and E resume here.

4819 *Kynge Richard turnde his ost to pas*. So A. Omitted in MS. D: *The kynge dede his men turne here pas*. E: *The kinge dede turne his pas*. W: *Kynge Rychard wente forthe a pace*. B: *Þe oste remowed to Cayphas*.

4837 *In this world at grete nede*. So E. Omitted in MS, W, A. B: *Ffor in alle þe worlde at nanekyns nede*. D: *In þis werde at gret nede*.

4838 *Was nevere founde a better stede*. So E. Omitted in MS, W, A. B: *Was þer nane þat hade a bettir stede*. D: *Was never ifoundyd a betire stede*.

4846 *fall doun*. MS: *doun*. W: *fall downe*. B: *falle downne*. A: *adoun*. D: *ago doun*. E: *go doun*.

4849 *He them tohewed and tocarfe*. So W. MS: *He gan to hewe ffaste and to kerue*. B: *He theym hewed and in sondre schare*. A: *he to heogh & to carf*. E: *He hem to hew and to kerue*. D: *he hem hew and al to carfe*.

4851 *Never was man in erthe ryght*. So E. Omitted in MS, W, A. B: *Never was mane in erthe righte*. D: *Never was man on erthe ryth*.

4852 *That better with hem gon fyght*. So E. Omitted in MS, W, A. B: *Þat better agaynes the Sarazenes gane fighte*. D: *That better cowthe with hem ffyth*.

4857 *For Saladynes sones theder came*. W: *For Salandynes sones theder came*. Omitted in MS. B: *Sir Saladynes sones ther come jwys*. A: *Saladines two sones come*. E: *Saladyne sone þere com*. D: *Saladynys sone þer came*.

4858 *And the harneys them bename*. So W. Omitted in MS. B: *And toke þe carte with alle þe harnasse*. A: *And the armes hem bynome*. E: *And her harneyse hem bynome*. D: *& here hernyse he bename*.

4864 *Yet almoost he came*. So W. MS: *Almost hadde he come*. B: *And ȝitt almoste he come*. A: *But almost he come*. D: *& almost he came*.

4865 *In honde he helde his axe good*. So W. MS: *He layde on wiþ hys ax good*. B: *And in his hande he helde his axe gud*. A: *Jn his hand he huld a trenchon good*. E: *Jn his honde an axe ful good*. D: *Jn his hond his ax ful good*.

4875 *hete*. So W, B, A, D. MS: *wynd*.

4882 *pouder*. So W, E. MS: *smoke*. B: *powdir*. D: *pouodur*.

4892 *he felde*. So W. MS: *wenten*. B: *alle wente*. A: *he drof*. *D*: *fell*. E: *he fel*.

4931 *Sessarye*. So B. MS: *serarye*. W: *sezary*. A: *Cesarie*. D: *Sesarye*. E: *Sesary*.

4936 *La Fere*. So MS. W: *laffere*. B: *Jasare*. A: *Offere*. D, E: *lazare*.

4971 *grete Grece*. So W, A, E. MS: *grece*. Omitted in B. D: *gret Grece*.

4972 *another empire*. MS: *empyre & kyndom moo*. Omitted in B. W: *an other ryche empyre*. A: *another heigh empire*. D: *anodir empire*. E: *anothe empire*.

4984 *There was many a doughty man*. So W, D, E. MS: *Þere were douȝty men off mayn*. B is defective. A: *He hadde with hym many a doghty man*.

4987 *that*. So W. MS: *there*. B is defective. Omitted in A. D, E: *þat*.

5035 *his*. So W, E, D, A. MS: *þe*.

5040 *no thynge*. So W. MS: *non helpe*. B is defective. A: *nought that*. D, E: *no thyng*.

5043 *by Jhesu Cryste*. So W. MS: *theroff, be Cryste*. D: *be Jhesu Crist*. E: *by Jhesu Crist*. Absent in A.

5059 *had non*. So D. MS: *non*. W, E: *had no*. B is defective. A: *hadde non*.

5061 *Nevertheles doughtely he faught*. So W. Omitted in MS. B is defective. A: *But natheles wel he faught*. E: *Neuerþeles douȝly he fauȝt*. D: *But netheles doutylyc he fawt*.

5062 *The Sarazynes yet felde hym naught*. So W. Omitted in MS. B is defective. A: *That the Sarasyns slogh hym naught*. E: *And slowe al þat he ouercauȝt*. D: *Ȝet þe Saraxynys slowin him nowt*.

5081 *honde*. So W, E. MS: *arme*. B: . . . *ande*. A, D: *hond*.

5093 *And of som he pared so the croune*. So Br. Omitted in MS, A. W: *And some he pared the crowne*. B: . . . *e parede so the crownne* (line partially illegible). D: *& summe he paryd of þe croune*. E: *And of four he pared so þe croune*.

5094 *That helme and hed fel adoun*. So E, Br. W: *That they ne helped mahowne*. Omitted in MS, A. B: . . . *and ~~hede~~ helme felde þer ryght doune* (line partially illegible). D: *That helm & heuyd fel adoun*.

5107 *And that Rycharde with theyr folke fares*. So W. Omitted in MS. B: *And also kyng Richerd with þere mene faris*. A: *& that with hure folk fare*. D: *And þat þer wiþ sarazynnys faryne*. E: *And þat Richard dide with hem fare*.

5108 *As hende grehoundes do with hares*. So W. Omitted in MS. Br: *As grehoundes do with hares*. B: *Als grewhoundes dose with hares*. A: *As gryhund doth with the hare*. D: *Os grehondis done with þe haryne*. E: *As þe Grehound doth with þe hare*.

5119 *empty*. So A, D, E, Br. MS: *voyde*. W: *emty*. B: *tome*.

5120 *in the cradyl*. So W, B, A. MS: *in cradyl*. Omitted in D, E.

5126 *of here god Mahoun*. So D. MS: *here mahoun*. W: *of theyr god mahowne*. Omitted in B. A: *of mahun*. E: *of her god mahoun*.

5133 *for the drede*. So W, B, A, MS: *ffor drede*. D: *& for þe dynt*. E: *for dout of*.

5134 *fell*. So W. MS: *fflowen*. A: *fulle*. E: *felle*. D: *fellyn*.

5136 *to lyve than*. So Br. MS: *to lyue off hem*. W: *to lyue ayan*. B: *lufed aftir þane*. A: *to gode of ham*. D: *lyue þan*. E: *to lyf þan*.

5139 *lefte*. So W, A, E. MS, B: *lofte*. D: *les*.

5141 *fleande*. So W, D. MS: *prykande*. B: *flyande*. A: *flyngynge*. E: *flyngande*.

5158 *sylvyr were the*. So B. MS: *and syluyr þe*. W: *syluer were theyr*. A: *& seluer &*. D, E: *gold were þe*.

5159 *noble geste*. So B, A. MS: *ffayre geste*. W: *noble Jeste*. E: *noble gest*.

5160 *of wylde beste*. So W. MS: *& wylde beste*. A, B: *wilde beste*. D: *& wyld beste*. E: *wylde best*.

5169 *rested hym there*. So W. MS: *restyd þere*. B: *ristede hym there*. A: *restid him there*. D: *festyd hym þer*. E: *rested him þere*.

5170 *And thanked Jhesu ful of myght*. So E, Br. MS: *On morwe whene it was day lyȝt*. W: *And thanke Jhesu cystes myght*. B: *And gaffe louynge to god full of myghte*. A: *& thankede god full of myght*. D: *& þankyd Jhesu ful of myth*.

5171 *On the morowe Kynge Rycharde arose*. So W. MS: *Kyng richard fful erely ros*. B: *And at þe morne þe kyng of his bedde rasse*. A: *Erly a morwe kynge Richard aros*. D: *On morwe qwane þe kyng ros*. E: *A morwe when þe kyng aroos*.

5337 *Galabre*. So Br. MS: *Salabre*. B: *Galabere*.

5408 *On batayll*. So W. MS: *And batayllyd*. B: *And bekeride*. E: *And to bataile*.

5428 *wolde be*. So B, E. MS: *was al*. W: *was full*.

5448 *latemere*. So W. MS: *Sarezynes*. B: *latymere*. E: *messengers*.

5456 *Sowdan*. So W. MS: *þenne were þey*. B: *Sawdane*. E: *þan had Richard*.

5496 *To deraye*. MS: *Deraye*. W: *To detreyue*. B: *To dresse*. E: *Þy selue*.

5552 *That thee*. MS: *Þe*. W: *That the*. B, E: *Þat þe*.

5554 *To betraye*. So W, E. MS, B: *Betraye*.

5573 *perce be thou*. So Br. MS: *perce it*. W: *percysshed be thou*. B: *perche be þou*. E: *persh be þow*.

5616 *a coost*. So W, Br. MS: *acoost*. B: *of that coste*. E: *of the cost*.

5619 *To Kynge Phelyp*. So W. MS: *To Phelyp*. B: *To the noble kyng Richerde*. E: *To King Philip*.

5634 *gradde*. So W, Br. MS: *badde*. B: *sayde*. E: *gred*.

5637 *we*. So W, B, E. MS: *ȝe*.

5692 *And good rynges that wolde duren*. So W. MS: *þat wondyr weel wolde laste & duren*. B: *And with gud rynges and with fyne*. Omitted in E.

5695 *they*. So W. MS: *þoo*. B: *þay*. Omitted in E.

5742 *stedes*. So W, E. MS: *stede*. B: *stedis*.

5777 *His*. So W, B, E. MS: *Þe*.

5780 *smote*. So W. MS: *prekyd*. B: *strykes*. E: *smot*.

5795 *wysten*. MS: *wyste*. W: *wyst & his men*. B: *wystyne*. E: *wisten*.

5796 *Crysten*. So W. MS: *cryste*. B: *cristyn*. E: *cristen*.

5857 *Astray they yeden with grete pride*. MS: *Astray þay ȝeden wiþ þe brydyl*. E: *Aboute þey ȝede with grete pride*. W: *All astraye aboute they yede*. B: *Gud stedis rane with grete pryde*.

5858 *The man that wolde myght ryde*. So E. MS: *To ryden on hem men were nouȝt ydyl*. W: *What man wolde myght ryde*. B: *Ilke mane þat walde myghte þane ryde*.

5861 *that they myghte*. So W. MS: *þey myȝt*. B: *þat þay myghte*. E: *þat þey myȝt*.

5900 *noghte half*. MS: *halff*. W: *not halfe*. B: *noghte halfe*. E: *nouȝt oo*.

5916 *And sayd it was trewe and good*. So W. MS: *And þouȝte it was boþe trewe & good*. B: *þat his conselle was ryghte gude*. E: *And seide it was trew and good*.

5931 *fair and fyne*. So B. MS: *affyn*. W: *good and fyne*. D: *fayr & fyne*. E: *feire and fyne*. A: *afyn*.

5932 *He leete tylde*. So Br. MS: *Þe leete tylde*. W: *They gan dyght*. B: *Was pighte*. A: *Was teld*. D: *He dede yt teldyn*. E: *There he tilde*.

5938 *So strong wrought and of gret ryhcheys*. After this line in *b* (D, fol. 33v) is found the following passage:

> þ[er]ynne he dede ber[e]nger
> His quen[e] þ[at] was his lef & der[e]
> And Jhone his sust[er] þ[at] was a quene
> Ffor þ[ey] schulde at ese bene.

Compare A, (fol. 268v), and Brunner, *Löwenherz* (p. 380n).

5941 *Theder myght come by the see*. So W. MS: *Þedyr myȝte men come be þe see*. A: *Ther myghte come by the sea*. E: *Þeder myȝt men come by the see*. D: *To hem came goods from þe se*. Omitted in B.

5946 *withouten*. MS: *wiþouten wiþouten*.

5948 *Tyl that Jaffe was maad al sure*. After this line, the following passage occurs in A (fol. 268v):

> To turrien they dude hem by drem
> Ffour myle fro Jerusalem.
> Tho made oure c[ri]sten ost gret blisse,
> For they wente wel to wisse
> Haue wonne Jer[usa]lem cite all,
> So they hadde do withoute faill.
> Sire Gauter of Naples hospitiler,
> Ther was he no good consailer.
> "Kyng Richard," he seide, "& thugh winne
> Jerusalem with thy gynne,
> Alle the folk shal seche the stede anon
> That was god was on to dethe don
> High and lowe sweyn & grom,
> Smartly than wille wende hom;
> Ac t[ur]ne ayen to Chaloyne,
> The wey lith toward Babiloyne,
> & drawe the vp to the paynym,

And thugh shalt wel bisette thy tym.
Saladyn, the heygh Soudan,
Thugh shalt hym sle or al quyke tan."
Kyng Ric[hard] to his consail luste,
They hit nere with the beste.
Many Eorles & barons bothe,
For that consail were wrothe,
& wente hom to hure contre,
And left Kyng Richard stille be.

Compare D (fol. 34r), E (fols. 28v–29r), and Brunner, *Löwenherz* (pp. 381n–382n). Needler provides this passage as found in D (*Richard*, pp. 41–42).

5977 *Kyng Richard pykkyd gret errour*. MS: *Kyng Richard pokyd gret errour*. W: *Kynge Rycharde was in grete erroure*. B: *Kyng Richerd thoghte he spake grete erroure*. E: *Tho king Richard pykked errour*. A: *Kynge Richard thanne peckyd errour*. D: *Kyng Richard pickyd gret errour*.

5987 *By the sydes of swete Jhesus*. MS: *Ffor be mary þat bar ihesus*. W: *By the sydes of cryste Jhesus*. B: *Be the sydes of swete Jhesu*. E: *By the sydes of Jesus*. A: *for by marie that bar Jhesus*. D: *Be þe sydys of swete Jhesus*.

6018 *Scholde have holden undyr hym*. MS: *Scholde holden vndyr hym*. W: *Solde all holde of hym*. B: *Solde hafe bene holden hally of hym*. E: *Shulde haue be hoolden of hym*. D: *They haddyn holdyn all of hym*. A: *Shold haue holde vndyr hym*.

6037–43 *Than Kynge . . . . arme wele*. So W. Absent in MS, this 7-line passage appears in both the *a* version (W and B) and in *b* (E and A). D omits lines 6037–6218. Found in four of six manuscripts, this passage forms part of a lengthy section that Brunner considers part of the original text of *RCL* (*Löwenherz*, p. 19).

6045 *he*. So W, A, E. MS: *þey*. B: *þay*.

6089 *By*. So W, B, A, E. MS: *To*.

6099 *playne*. So W, B. MS: *plener*. A, E: *playn*.

6128 *gave*. So W. MS: *goue*. B: *gaffe*. A: *smete*. E: *ȝeue*.

6130 *was clevede*. So B. MS: *wiþ þe heuyd*. W: *all to cleved*. E: *was cleuyd*. Omitted in A.

6141 *he*. So W, B, E. MS, A: *þey*.

6143 *plenteuous*. So W, B. MS: *plenté*. A: *large*.

6153 *brethe*. So W, E, A. MS: *brekyng*. B: *Sauoire*.

6155 *Alle that*. So A. MS: *Off þoo*. B: *Alle thase that*. W: *All that*. E: *Al þat*.

6156 *None amendes must they make*. So W. MS: *Myȝte he non amendes make*. B: *Ffor none amendis ne myghte þay make*. A: *non other amendis he wolde make*. E: *Noon amendes most þey make*.

6157 *He*. So W, E. MS: *þey*. B: *The kyng*. Omitted in A.

6180 *leve*. So A. MS: *wurþy*. W: *good*. B: *lefe*. E: *lyue*.

6195 *To honge or drawe, brenne or sle*. So W. Omitted in MS. B: *To hange or bryne or ells to slee*. A: *brenne vs lord hange other sle*. E: *To honge vs to burne to drawe or to sle*.

6196 *Our fredome, lorde, is in thee*. So W. Omitted in MS. B: *Oure lyfe and dede nowe alle ligges in the*. A: *al oure fredom is in the*. E: *At þy wille lord al it be*.

6202 *Kynge Rycharde let them faste bynde*. So W. MS: *þe kynge hem comaundyd faste to bynde*. B: *Kyng Richerde garte þame faste bynde*. A: *Kyng Richard hem leit faste bynde*. E: *King Richarde let hem fast bynde*.

6218 *And ye shall here*. So W. MS: *And may here*. B: *And heris now*. A: *Ye mogh hure*. D: *ȝe schul heryn*. E: *Ye shul here*.

6238 *There assaute he began bydene*. So W. MS: *At þat cyte he þouȝte be sene*. B: *Swythe layde assawte vnto þe toune*. A: *his saut he gan all bydene*. E: *Bygan þe assaut al bydene*. D: *Began asawt al bedene*.

6253 *Kynge Rycharde stode, so sayth the boke*. So W, B, E. Omitted in MS. A: *Kynge Richard as we fyndeth in boke*. D: *Richard stood so seyth þe bok*.

6254 *And on the ymage he gan for to loke*. So W. Omitted in MS. B: *And one the ymage gane he loke*. E: *And on þe ymage fast gan looke*. A: *on that ymage gan to loke*. D: *And on þat ymage faste he lok*.

6255 *How hewge he was wrought and sterne*. So W. Omitted in MS. B: *How hogge he was wroghte thowe steryne*. A: *hogh huge he was wroght & seurne*. E: *How houge he is and how sterne*. D: *Wou houge he es as wiþout & how stern*.

6256 *And sayd to them all yerne*. So W. Omitted in MS. B: *And seyd to them thane alle ȝerne*. E: *And to þe men he seide ȝerne*. A: *to hem he saide also yerne*. D: *& to þe men he seyde ȝerne*.

6277 *That the hede flowe fro the body insundyr*. B: *That the hede flowe fra the Body in sondire*. MS: *Þe hed & þe body ffel in sundyr*. W: *The heed tho flowe the body asonder*. A: *The hed fleigh fro the body onsoynder*. D: *That þe hed fley from þe body onsonder*. E: *That þe hed fley fro þe body asounder*. Br: *Þe hed flowe from þe body insundyr*.

6293 *They pyght pavylyons fayre and well*. So W. MS: *On morwen he leet arme alle wel*. B: *Þay pighte thare pavelyounis faire & welle*. E: *And pyȝt his pauyloun faire and welle*. A: *There Kyng Richard armed hym well*. D: *He put his pauylounes ffayr & wel*.

6301 *Theyr hertes were full of wo*. So W. Omitted in MS, A. B: *Þaire herttis weren all ille bystedde*. E: *In hert þey were ful sore adredde*. D: *Here hertes were ful of care & wo*.

6302 *All by nyght awaye they flo*. So W. Omitted in MS, A. B: *And alle by nyghte awaye they fledde*. E: *And al nyȝt awey þey fledde*. D: *And all be nyth þei gonne to go*.

6324 *the fendes*. So W, D, E. MS: *a cursyd off*. B: *alle þe fendys prey*. A: *the deuelus*.

6369–6658 *To fulfylle . . . . hys way*. B omits these lines.

6388 *So as thou bylevest on Termagaunt*. So W. Omitted in MS. A: *As thugh leuest on Termagaunt*. D: *I wot þu leuyth on termegant*. E: *As þou leuyst in Termegane*.

6456 *nyne or ten*. So W, E. MS: *ffyue & ten*. Omitted in B. A: *nyne & ten*. D: *sexti & ten*.

6513 *Into the cyté off Bethany the noble*. So MS. W: *Jnto betanye that cyte noble*. Omitted in B. A: *into Constantyn the noble*. E: *And to Bytany þe nobel Citee*.

6525 *brought*. So W, E. MS: *bouȝte*. A: *broghte*. Omitted in B.

6546 *Frome Yngelond, as he had tyghte*. MS: *Ffor to yngelond he has tyȝte*. W: *Frome englonde god it dyght*. Omitted in B. A: *Fro Engelond as he hadde tighte*. E: *Ffrom Jnglonde as he had tyȝt*.

6567 *he hath stored*. So W, E. MS: *was astoryd*. A, D: *he hath storid*. Omitted in B.

6595 *grete Grece*. So W, E, A. MS, D: *grece*.

6613 *hadde ben fro*. MS, A: *hadde ffro*. W: *had ben from*. D: *hade ben from*. E: *hadde be*. Omitted in B.

6623 *the cyté nome*. So W, A. MS: *haue þe cyte take*. D: *þe cete nome*. E: *þe citee noome*.

6624 *To theyr will and to theyr dome*. So W. MS: *Þe crystene men þey þouȝte to awake*. A: *to hure wille and hure dome*. D: *To her will & to her dome*. E: *To her wille and her doome*.

6643 *The Sarezynes, for no nede*. Here ends D.

6649 *That he scholde to hem come*. MS: *Þat he scholde come to hem þan*. W: *That he sholde to helpe come*. Omitted in B. A: *That he sholde to hem come*. E: *That he shulde to hem come*.

6650 *were al inome*. So W, A, E. MS: *scholde ben alle itan*.

6659 *I nele for hym to hem wende*. Gap in B resumes here.

6660 *But soone I wyll hem socour sende*. W: *But soone J wyll them socour sende*. MS: *But sum socour J schal hem sende*. B: *Bot sone J sall theym socoure sende*. A: *but good socour J wol hem sende*. E: *But sone y wyl hem socoure sende*.

6675 *Gascoynes, Spaynardes and Lumbarde*. So W. MS: *Spaynulff gavscoyn & lumbard*. B: *Gascoyns Spayneelfes ffrance men & lumbardes*. A: *Both ffrenssh & lumbarde*. E: *Gascoynes spaynardes and lumbardes*.

6682 *Swythe towarde them*. So W. MS: *Agayn hem also soone*. A: *Smartly ayenst hem*. E: *Swith to hem ward*. Omitted in B.

6697 *beth*. So W, A, E. MS: *bee*. B: *ware*.

6698 *They may wyte thee of theyr deth*. So W. MS: *Ȝiff þe be slayn I wyte it þee*. B: *May wele whitte þe alle þayr care*. A: *Mowe wite the hure deth*. E: *Mow wite þe her deethe*.

6712 *none oth*. MS: *an oþ*. W: *none othe*. B: *nane othe*. E: *noon othe*. A: *non oth*.

6717 *de Lake*. So W, B. MS: *þe lake*. A: *du lake*.

6719 *Ne of Ury, ne of Octavyan*. So W. MS is illegible. B: *Nor of Uly nor ȝitt of Sir Octouyane*. A: *of Oliuer ne of Otuan*. E: *Ne of Ely ne of Octauyan*.

6720 *Ne of Hector, the stronge man*. So W. MS is illegible. B: *Nor ȝitt of Sir Ecter the strange mane*. A: *Ne of Ector the strongeman*. E: *Ne of Ettor þe stronge man*.

6721 *Ne of Jason, ne of Hercules*. W: *Ne of Jason neyther of Hercules*. MS: *Off Jason* . . . (line partially illegible). B: *Of Jasone ne ȝitt of Ercules*. A: *Of Jason ne of Ercules*. E: *Ne of Jasyne ne of Ercules*.

6728 *At Jaffe*. So W. MS: *At þe cyte off Jaffe*. B: *Att Jaffe*. A: *At Jafes*. E: *At Jaffes*.

6731 *heyghe myd night*. MS: As a correction, *heyȝe* is inserted above *myd*.

6753 *They ben slayne and all totore*. So W. MS: *Þey ben sla*. . . . (line partially defective). B: *Was slayne ȝisterdaye at morwe*. A: *beth nogh slawe & al to tore*. E: *They be slawe and toterye*.

6771 *herde*. So W. MS: *wyste*. B: *herden*. Omitted in A. E: *herd*.

6783 *ne have lyfe*. So W. MS: *have he seyde lyff*. B: *ne hafe lyfe*. E: *ne haue lyȝf*. Omitted in A.

6784 *we it dere*. So W, B, E. MS: *we it*. Omitted in A.

6789 *Take me myn axe in myn honde*. So W, E. Omitted in MS. B: *Take me myn axe in myn hande*. A: *Taketh me myn axe an honde*.

6790 *That was made in Ingelonde*. So E. Omitted in MS. W: *Jt was made in englonde*. B: *Þat was wroghte in mery ynglande*. A: *that was mad in Engelonde*.

6791 *Here armure no more I ne doute*. So MS. B: *Ffor þair harnys no mare j no dowte*. A: *no more hure armure J doute*. E: *No more her armes y ne dout*.

6799 *inome*. So W. MS: *itake*. B: *strete*. A, E: *nome*.

6800 *With my pollaxe I am come*. So W, E. MS: *Vnwynnely j schal ȝow wake*. B: *With myne axe j schall þame mete*. A: *With myn axe J am come*.

6834 *mette*. So W, B, A. E: *met*. MS: *fond*.

6842 *Fared ryght lyke wood lyouns*. So W. MS: *And hospytalers egre as lyouns*. B: *Ffaughte als þay hade bene wode lyouns*. A: *Gunne to fighte as wode lyons*. E: *Ffauȝt as egre lyouns*.

6846 *awaye*. So W, B. MS: *agayn*. A: *Ayen*. E: *awey*.

6850–6972 *The Sowdan . . . . hoost ordayne*. Due to missing leaves, MS omits these lines.

6850 *The Sowdan loste that same daye*. So W. B: *Of Sarazenes kene was slayne þat daye*. E: *Þe Sawdan lost þat ylke day*. Omitted in A.

6870 *ever*. So A, E. W: *never*. B: *ever ȝitt*.

6875 *with good wyne*. So A, E. W: *ale and wyne*. B: *with gud wine*.

6876 *Saladyn*. So B, E. W: *Salandyn*. A: *Saladin*.

6883 *Saladyn*. So E. W: *Salandyn*. B: *Saladyne*. A: *Soudan*.

6910 *Tourne agayne to thyn owne londe*. After this line, the following couplet appears in B: *And thus thou may fra the dede flee / Hame to thi contree by the see*. A: *So thugh myght thi deth fle / Hom to Engelond by the see*. This couplet is absent in W and in E.

6914 *fyne*. So A. W: *pyne*. B: *to tyme*. E: *fynes*.

6915 *Saladyn*. So E. W: *Salandyn*. B: *Sarazyne*. A: *Sarasyn*.

6926 *pollaxe*. So Br. B: *polaxe*. W: *bollaxe*. A: *Axe*. E: *pollax*.

6927 *defye*. So E. W: *desyre*. B: *this*. A: *abie*.

6932 *And told the Sowdane worde and ende*. So B. W: *And all the begynnynge tolde hym*. E: *And tolde þe begynnynge and þe fyn*. A: *to do hure lordes comaundement*.

6933 *Saladyn*. So B, E. W: *Salandyn*. A: *Saladin*.

6948 *shalte it fynde*. So Br. W: *shalte fynde*. B: *þou salle fynd þe passage*. A: *shalt hit fynde*. E: *shalt it fynde*.

6951 *bataile do by myne hees*. So E. W: *batayll without leas*. B: *Batelle þou do thyne ese*. A: *bataille do by my hes*.

6954 *pilgrimage*. So A, E. W: *vyage*. B: *pilgremage*.

6967 *"As armes," he cryed thare*. So E. W: *On armes he let crye thare*. B: *he blewe he cryede as armres whatt*. A: *he blew and cried as armes wate*.

6969 *Saladyn*. So E. W: *Salandyn*. B: *Sir Saladyne*. A: *Soudan*.

6973 *But prekyd forth upon Favel*. MS resumes here.

6979 *cors*. So W, A, E. MS: *vpon here hors*. MS appears to modify the initial letter of *cors* to produce *hors*; and *hors* is written above line. B: *corses*.

6980 *hors*. So W, A. MS: *cors*. B: *horses*. E: *fors*.

6989 *Upon the Sarasynes faste they donge*. So W. Omitted in MS. A: *Upon the Sarasynes they flonge*. B: *And appon þe Sarazenes full faste dange þay*. E: *Uppon þe Saryzyns faste they donge*.

6990 *swerdes and with sperys*. W: *swerdes and with launces*. Omitted in MS. B: *swerdis lange & sperys*. A: *swerdes & with sper*. E: *axes and with swerdes*.

7014 *One man so many to grounde quelle*. W: *One man so many to grounde fell*. MS: *Halff so manye Sarezynys ffelle* (*quelle* appears in the margin). B: *Þat with his awnne handis so many heythyn gunne quelle*. A: *on man so many men to quelle*. E: *That oo man so mony gan quelle*.

7031 *hym with myghte and mayne*. So B. MS: *crystene with al here mayn*. W: *with mayne*. A: *with myghte & mayn*. E: *him with mayn*.

7059 *With that came a messenger reke*. So W. MS: *A messanger come swyþe rydyng*. B: *Bot a messangere came there swythe one a reke*. A: *Than a messager ther reke*. E: *With þat come a messenger reke*.

7060 *With kynge Rycharde for to speke*. So W, A, E. MS: *To speke wiþ Richard oure kyng*. B: *And sayde þat with Kynge Richerd wolde he speke*.

7079 *All these ben slayne and many mo*. So W. MS: *Þey are slayn & ȝit moo*. B: *Alle thes are slayne and many mare*. A: *Thes beth slaw and wel mo*. E: *Þese ben slaw and wel moo*.

7100 *That hem come*. MS: *Þat hym come*. W: *That came there*. B: *Þat to þam ne come*. E: *Come þer neuer*. A: *That hem ne come*.

7132 *Rycharde wanne to Jaffe gate*. So W. MS: *Þey wunne unto jaffes ȝate*. B: *Kyng Richerde wanne to Jaffe ȝate*. A: *Kynge Ricard wan Jafes gate*. E: *Richard wanne to Jaffys gate*.

7141 *in playn and den*. So E, Br. MS, A: *in playn den*. W: *in playne and den*. B: *in playne & den*.

7142 *Ten*. So W, B, A, E. MS: *Two*.

7175 *Thorugh all the londe*. So W. MS: *Þree ȝer & more*. B: *Ffor thre ȝere thane went þay*. A: *Thurgh all the lond*. E: *Þat þrouȝ þe lond*.

7182 *To Jaffe and to Mayden Castell*. So W. MS: *And to Emaus castel*. A: *To Jafes & to Maide Castell*. E: *To Jaffys and to Maiden Castel*. E ends here. Omitted in B.

7185–7240 *Thus Kynge . . . . for charyté*. Taken from W, this conclusion, similar to that from A, provides a more satisfactory ending to *RCL* than does the brief, even abrupt, 10-line conclusion of C (fol. 97v) that appears below:

Kyng R[ichard], douȝty off hand,
Turnyd homward to yngeland.
Kyng R[ichard] reynyd here
No more but ten ȝere.
Siþþen he was schot, allas, *After that*
In castel gaylard, þ[er] he was.
Þus endyd Rychard oure kyng,
God geve vs alle good endyng,
And hys soule rest & roo, *repose (peace)*
And oure soules when[n]e we come þerto.

Amen. Explicit. (Glosses mine)

Even more concise, B (fol. 163v) follows C but omits the penultimate couplet to end as follows: *And god grante vs alle gude Endynge. Amen.*

It is to be noted that A's text is inserted into *The Chronicle of Robert of Gloucester*. At times, A shifts between verse and prose, as happens in its conclusion (fols. 275v–76r), which appears below:

Thus kyng[e] Rich[ard] the doghty man,
Made pes betwyne hym & the Soudon,
And sithe he cam, I understonde,

The wey towarde Engalonde;
And hamward was shoten, allas,
At Castel Gailard ther he was.
The Duk[e] of Ostrich in the castel
With his ost was dight ful wel.
The wedur was hot in som[mer]es tide.
Kyng Richard thoghte ther to abide
At Gailard vnd[er] the castel.
He wende he myghte haue kelid hy[m] wel;

And bysegid the Castel Gailard byside Lemones, and strongly assailed hit, So that the vij k[a]l[e]n[des] of Aprill, as the kyng went aboute the castell to avise hit, vnarmed, a knyght cleped Peris Besile sodenly bende his arblast vppon the walles & haply with a gayn smot the kynge in the lifte shuldr[e] and made dedely wounde.

Kyng Richard tho let his men calle,
And bad hem dighten alle;
& swor by see and su[n]ne,
Tyl that castel weren wonne,
Sholde mete ne drinke
Never in his body sinke.
He sett up Robynet in that tide,
On that on castel side,
& on that oth[er] half of the toun[e],
He let arere the Maudegriffoun[e];
And to the castel hij threw stones,
& broke the walles, for the nones,
And withinne a litel tide,
Into the castel he gan ryde.
& slogh bifore & byhinde
That he myghte tofore hym fynde;
And ev[er]e by leved the quarell, *ever present remained*
Stikyng faste in his sheldere.

And when the kyng sey that he was in peril of deth he let ofsende iij abbotes of Cristeaux ordr[e], that is of grey londes of the kyng of Engelonde. . . .

BIBLIOGRAPHY

MANUSCRIPTS AND PRINTINGS

MS Edinburgh, National Library of Scotland Advocates'19.2.1 [formerly the Auchinleck MS] fols. 326r–27v [1330–40; the oldest manuscript extant, though fragmentary, and a good portion of its text survives in separated leaves: the Laing leaves, MS Edinburgh, Edinburgh University Library — 218, fols. 2 and 7, and MS St. Andrews, St. Andrews University Library — PR 2065 R.4, 2 fols.]

MS London, BL Egerton 2862, fols. 1r–44v [formerly: Sutherland or Trentham MS] [late fourteenth c.]

MS Badminton House 704.1.16, single folio [1400–1425]

MS Cambridge, Gonville and Caius College 175/96 (pp. 1–98) [1400–1450; used by Brunner and by Weber as their base manuscript]

MS London, BL Additional 31042 [formerly: London Thornton], fols. 125r–163v [1425–1450]

MS London, College of Arms HDN 58 [formerly: Arundel], fols. 250–275 [c. 1448]

MS London, BL Harley 4690, fols. 106–115 [1450–1500]

MS Oxford, Bodleian 21802 [formerly: Douce 228], fols. 1–40v [late fifteenth century]

Kynge Rycharde cuer du lyon, Oxford, Bodleian Crynes 734, and Manchester, John Ryland's Library – Deansgate 15843 [1509; a London printing by Wynkyn de Worde that Brunner used to complete gaps in his base MS, Gonville and Caius College 175/96; *STC* 21007; *ESTC* S120269]

Kynge Rycharde cuer du lyon, Oxford, Bodleian S. Seld. D. 45 (1), and London, BL – C.40.c.51 [formerly Harleian] [1528; a second London printing by de Worde nearly identical to his 1509 printing; *STC* 21008; *ESTC* S101588]

BIBLIOGRAPHY

Adams, Jenny. *Power Play: The Literature and Politics of Chess in the Late Middle Ages*. Philadelphia: University of Pennsylvania Press, 2006.

Adamson, Melitta Weiss. *Food in Medieval Times*. Westport, CT: Greenwood Press, 2004.

Adémar de Chabannes. *Ademari Cabannensis Chronicon*. Ed. P. Bourgain, Richard Allen Landes, and Georges Pon. Turnhout: Brepols, 1999.

Ailes and Barber. See Ambroise.

Akbari, Suzanne Conklin. "The Hunger for National Identity in *Richard Coer de Lyon*." In *Reading Medieval Culture: Essays in Honor of Robert W. Hanning*. Ed. Robert M. Stein and Sandra Pierson Prior. Notre Dame, IN: University of Notre Dame Press, 2005. Pp. 198–227.

Alexander, James. "Becket, Thomas, Saint." In Strayer. 2:151–53.

Alighieri, Dante. *Dante Alighieri's Divine Comedy*. Ed. Mark Musa. Bloomington, IN: Indiana University Press, 1996.

Ambrisco, Alan. "Cannibalism and Cultural Encounters in *Richard Coeur de Lion*." *Journal of Medieval and Early Modern Studies* 29 (1999), 499–528.

Ambroise. *The History of the Holy War: Ambroise's Estoire de la Guerre Sainte*. Ed. and trans. Marianne Ailes and Malcolm Barber. 2 vols. Woodbridge: Boydell Press, 2003.

Anderson, Benedict. *Imagined Communities: Reflections on the Origin and Spread of Nationalism*. London: Verso, 1983.

Anderson, Carolyn B. "Constructing Royal Character: King Richard in *Richard Coer de Lyon*." *Proceedings of the Medieval Association of the Midwest* 6 (1999), 85–108.

Archer, Thomas A., ed. and trans. *The Crusade of Richard I, 1189–92: Extracts from the Itinerarium Ricardi, Bohâdin, Ernoul, Roger of Howden, Richard of Devizes, Rigord, Ibn Alathîr, Li Livres de Eracles, &c.* London: David Nutt, 1888.

Arnold of Bonneval. *Vita primi Bernardi.* 2:2.11–14. *Patrologia Latina* vol. 185: col. 275–77.

Arthour and Merlin. Ed. Eugen Kölbing. Leipzig: O. R. Reisland, 1890.

Athelston. In Herzman, Drake, and Salisbury. Pp. 341–84.

Baker, Craig. "Editing Medieval Texts." In *Handbook of Medieval Studies: Terms – Methods – Trends*. Ed. Albrecht Classen. Vol. 1. Berlin: De Gruyter, 2010. Pp. 427–50.

Barber, Malcolm. *The New Knighthood: A History of the Order of the Temple*. Cambridge, UK: Cambridge University Press, 1994.

Barker, Juliet R. V. *The Tournament in England, 1100–1400*. Woodbridge: Boydell Press, 1986.

Barron, W. R. J. "The Penalties for Treason in Medieval Life and Literature." *Journal of Medieval History* 7 (1981), 187–202.

———. *English Medieval Romance.* London: Longman, 1987.

Bartolph de Nangis. *Gesta Francorum Iherusalem expugnantium.* In *Recueil des historiens des Croisades*, Historiens occidentaux. Vol. 3, part 3. Paris: Imprimerie Impériale, 1844–95; Reprint. Farnborough: Gregg Press Limited, 1967.

Beckingham, Charles F. and Bernard Hamilton, eds. *Prester John: The Mongols and the Ten Lost Tribes.* Aldershot: Variorum, 1996.

Benoît, de Sainte-Maure. *Le Roman de Troie*. Ed. Léopold Constans. 6 vols. Paris: Firmin Didot, 1904-12.

Benson, Larry D., ed. *King Arthur's Death: The Middle English Stanziac Morte Arthur and Alliterative Morte Arthure*. Rev. ed. Edward E. Foster. Kalmazoo, MI: Medieval Institute Publications, 1994.

Bevis of Hampton. In Herzman, Drake, and Salisbury. Pp. 187–340.

Blurton, Heather. *Cannibalism in High Medieval English Literature.* New York: Palgrave Macmillan, 2007.

Boas, Adrian. *Archaeology of the Military Orders: A Survey of the Urban Centres, Rural Settlement and Castles of the Military Orders in the Latin East (c. 1120–1291).* London: Routledge, 2006.

Borgström, Edvard. *The Proverbs of Alfred.* Lund: Ohlsson, 1908.

Boyle, David. *The Troubadour's Song: The Capture and Ransom of Richard the Lionheart.* New York: Walker and Co., 2005.

Braswell, Mary Flowers, ed. *Sir Perceval of Galles and Ywain and Gawain.* Kalamazoo, MI: Medieval Institute Publications, 1995.

Broughton, Bradford B. *The Legends of King Richard I, Coeur de Lion: A Study of Sources and Variations to the Year 1600.* The Hague: Mouton and Company, 1966.

———. *Dictionary of Medieval Knighthood and Chivalry: Concepts and Terms.* Westport, CT: Greenwood Press, 1986.

Brundage, James A. "'Cruce Signari': The Rite for Taking the Cross in England." *Traditio* 22 (1966), 289–310.

———. *Medieval Canon Law and the Crusader.* Madison, WI: University of Wisconsin Press, 1969.

———. *Law, Sex, and Christian Society in Medieval Europe.* Chicago: University of Chicago Press, 1987.

Brunner, Karl, ed. *Der Mittelenglische Versroman über Richard Löwenherz.* Vienna: Wilhelm Braumüller, 1913.

Busby, Keith. *Gauvain in Old French Literature.* Amsterdam: Rodopi, 1980.

La Chanson d'Antioche. Ed. Jan A. Nelson. Tuscaloosa, AL: University of Alabama Press, 2003.

La Chanson d'Antioche. Ed. Suzanne Duparc-Quioc. 2 vols. Paris: P. Geuthner, 1976–78.

La Chanson de Roland. See *The Song of Roland.*

Chapman, Robert L. "A Note on the Demon Queen Eleanor." *Modern Language Notes* 70 (1955), 393–96.

Chaucer, Geoffrey. *The Riverside Chaucer*. Ed. Larry D. Benson et al. Third edition. Boston: Houghton Mifflin, 1987.

Le Chevalier au Cygne. Ed. Jan A. Nelson. In *The Old French Crusade Cycle: Le Chavalier au Cygne and La Fin d'Elias*. Vol. 2. Tuscaloosa, AL: University of Alabama Press, 1985. Pp. 2–357.

Chrétien de Troyes. *Cligés*. In *Arthurian Romances*. Ed. and trans. D. D. R. Owen. London: J. M. Dent and Sons, 1987. Pp. 93–184.

La Chrétienté Corbaran. Ed. Peter R. Grillo. In *The Old French Crusade Cycle: The Jérusalem Continuations, part 1*. Vol. 7. Tuscaloosa, AL: University of Alabama Press, 1984.

Clanchy, M. T. *England and Its Rulers, 1066–1307*. Second edition. Malden, MA: Blackwell, 1998.

Clark, Willene B., ed. and trans. *The Medieval Book of Birds: Hugh of Fouilloy's Aviarium*. Binghamton, NY: Center for Medieval and Early Renaissance Studies, 1992.

Cook, Robert Francis. "Crusade Propaganda in the Epic Cycles of the Crusades." In Sargent-Baur. Pp. 157–75.

Cordery, Leona F. "Cannibal Diplomacy: Otherness in the Middle English Text *Richard Coer de Lion*." In *Meeting the Foreign in the Middle Ages*. Ed. Albrecht Classen. New York: Routledge, 2002. Pp. 153–71.

Cowdrey, H. E. J. "Pope Urban II's Preaching of the First Crusade." In *The Crusades: The Essential Readings*. Ed. Thomas F. Madden. Maldwin, MA and Oxford: Blackwell, 2002. Pp. 15–29.

Croxton Play of the Sacrament. Ed. John T. Sebastian. Kalamazoo, MI: Medieval Institute Publications, 2012.

Curtius, Ernst Robert. *European Literature and the Latin Middle Ages*. Trans. Willard R. Trask. Princeton, NJ: Princeton University Press, 1973.

Davis, Norman. "Another Fragment of 'Richard coer de lyon.'" *Notes and Queries* 214 (1969), 447–52 [selections from the single folio that survives from MS Badminton House — 704.1.16].

Dutton, Paul Edwin. *Charlemagne's Courtier: The Complete Einhard*. Peterborough, Ontario: Broadview Press, 1998.

Edbury, Peter. *The Conquest of Jerusalem and the Third Crusade: Sources in Translation*. Aldershot: Ashgate, 1996.

Ellis, George and J. C. Halliwell. *Specimens of Early English Metrical Romances*. London: Henry G. Bohn, 1848.

———. *Richard Coeur de Lion*. In *Specimens of Early English Metrical Romances*. Pp. 282–341 [extracts with linking prose summaries].

Fantosme, Jordan. *Chronique de la guerre entre les Anglois et les Ecossois en 1173 et 1174, par Jordan Fantosme*. In *Chronicles of the Reigns of Stephen, Henry II, and Richard I*. Ed. Richard Howlett. London: Longman, 1886. Pp. 202–377.

Farmer, David Hugh. *The Oxford Dictionary of Saints*. Fourth edition. Oxford: Oxford Universty Press, 1997.

Fewster, Carol. *Traditionality and Genre in Middle English Romance*. Woodbridge: D. S. Brewer, 1987.

Field, Rosalind. "Romance as History, History as Romance." In *Romance in Medieval England*. Eds. Maldwyn Mills, Jennifer Fellows and Carol M. Meale. Woodbridge: D. S. Brewer, 1991. Pp. 163–73.

A Fifteenth-Century Courtesy Book. In *A Fifteenth-Century Courtesy Book and Two Fifteenth-Century Franciscan Rules*. Ed. R. W. Chambers and Walter W. Seton. EETS, o.s. 148. London: Oxford University Press, 1914. Pp. 3–22.

Finlayson, John. "'*Richard, Coer de Lyon*': Romance, History or Something in Between?" *Studies in Philology* 87 (1990), 156–180.

———. "Legendary Ancestors and the Expansion of Romance in *Richard, Coer de Lyon*." *English Studies* 79 (1998), 299–308.

———. "The Marvellous in Middle English Romance." *The Chaucer Review* 33 (1999), 363–408.

Fisher, John H. "A Language Policy for Lancastrian England." *PMLA* 107 (1992), 1168–80.

Fleischman, Suzanne. "On the Representation of History and Fiction in the Middle Ages." *History and Theory* 22 (1983), 278–310.

Fox-Davies, Arthur C. *A Complete Guide to Heraldry.* Rev. ed. J. P. Brooke-Little. London: Thomas Nelson and Sons, 1969.

Frasetto, Michael and David R. Blanks. *Western Views of Islam in Medieval and Early Modern Europe: Perception of Other.* New York: St. Martin's Press, 1999.

Fulcher of Chartres. *A History of the Expedition to Jerusalem: 1095–1127.* Ed. Harold S. Fink. Trans. Frances Rita Ryan. Knoxville, TN: University of Tennessee Press, 1969.

Gautier, Léon. *Chivalry.* Trans. Henry Frith. London: George Routledge and Sons, 1891.

Geoffrey of Monmouth. *History of the Kings of Britain.* Trans. Lewis Thorpe. London: Penguin, 1966.

Gerald de Barri. *Liber de principis instructione*. vol. 8. Ed. George F. Warner. See *Giraldus Cambrensis Opera*.

———. *Giraldi Cambrensis Opera*. 8 vols. Eds. James F. Dimock, J.S. Brewer and George F. Warner. London: Longman & co, 1891. Reprint. Boston, MA: Elibron Classics, 2007.

A Gest of Robyn Hood. In *Robin Hood and Other Outlaw Tales*. Ed. Stephen Knight and Thomas Ohlgren. Kalamazoo, MI: Medieval Institute Publications, 2000. Pp. 90–148.

Gesta Francorum et aliorum Hierosolimitanorum: The Deeds of the Franks and the other Pilgrims to Jerusalem. Ed. and trans. Rosalind Hill. Edinburgh: Thomas Nelson and Sons, 1962.

Gesta Romanorum. Ed. Sidney J. H. Herrtage. EETS e.s. 33. London: Oxford University Press, 1879.

Gillingham, John. "Foundations of a Disunited Kingdom." In *Uniting the Kingdom? The Making of British History*. Ed. Alexander Grant and Keith J. Stringer. New York: Routledge, 1995. Pp. 48-64.

———. *Richard I.* New Haven, CT: Yale University Press, 1999.

Gillmor, C. M. "Horses." *The Oxford Encyclopedia of Medieval Warfare and Military Technology*. Ed. Clifford J. Rogers. 3 vols. Oxford: Oxford University Press, 2010. 1:271–75.

Gough, Henry, and James Parker. *A Glossary of Terms Used in Heraldry.* London: James Parker & Company, 1894.

Guddat-Figge, Gisela. *Catalogue of Manuscripts Containing Middle English Romances.* Munich: Wilhelm Fink, 1976.

Guido delle Colonne. *Historia Destructionis Troiae*. Ed. and trans. Mary Elizabeth Meek. Bloomington, IN: Indiana University Press, 1974.

Haggar, Mark S. *The Fortunes of a Norman Family: the de Verduns in England, Ireland, and Wales, 1066–1316*. Dublin: Four Courts Press, 2001.

Hahn, Thomas, ed. *Sir Gawain: Eleven Romances and Tales.* Kalamazoo, MI: Medieval Institute Publications, 1995.

Hamel, Mary. "*The Siege of Jerusalem* as a Crusading Poem." In Sargent-Baur. Pp. 177–94.

Havelok. Ed. G. V. Smithers. Oxford: Clarendon Press, 1987.

Havelok the Dane. In Herzman, Drake, and Salisbury. Pp. 85–159.

Heng, Geraldine. "The Romance of England: *Richard Coer de Lyon,* Saracens, Jews, and the Politics of Race and Nation." In *The Postcolonial Middle Ages*. Ed. Jeffrey Jerome Cohen. New York: St. Martin's Press, 2000. Pp. 135–171.

———. *Empire of Magic: Medieval Romance and the Politics of Cultural Fantasy.* New York: Columbia University Press, 2003.

Herzman, Ronald B., Graham Drake, and Eve Salisbury, eds. *Four Romances of England: King Horn, Havelok the Dane, Bevis of Hampton, Athelston*. Kalamazoo, MI: Medieval Institute Publications, 1999.

Hibbard, Laura. *Mediæval Romance in England: A Study of the Sources and Analogues of the Non-Cyclic Metrical Romances.* New York: Oxford University Press, 1924.

Higden, Ranulph. *Polychronicon Ranulphi Higden Monachi Cestrensis*. Ed. Churchill Babington and J.R. Lumby. 9 vols. 1865–86. Reprint. Nendeln, Liechtenstein: Kraus Reprint Co., 1964.

Higham, N. J. *King Arthur: Myth Making and History*. London: Routledge, 2002.

Hollister, Warren C. "Courtly Culture and Courtly Style in the Anglo-Norman World." *Albion* 20 (1988), 1–17.

Hudson, Harriet, ed. *Four Middle English Romances: Sir Isumbras, Octavian, Sir Eglamour of Artois, Sir Tryamour*. Second edition. Kalamazoo, MI: Medieval Institute Publications, 1996.

Ingledew, Francis. "The Book of Troy and the Genealogical Construction of History: The Case of Geoffrey of Monmouth's *Historia Regum Britanniae*." *Speculum* 69 (1994), 665–704.

James, T. E. "The Age of Majority." *The American Journal of Legal History* 4 (1960), 22–33.

Jeffrey, David Lyle, ed. *A Dictionary of Biblical Tradition in English Literature*. Grand Rapids, MI: William B. Eerdmans Publishing Company, 1992.

Jentsch, F. "Die mittelenglische Romanze Richard Coeur de Lion und ihre Quellen."*Englische Studien* 15 (1891), 161–247.

Joinville, Jean de. *Joinville's Chronicle of the Crusade of St. Lewis*. In *Chronicles of the Crusades by Jean de Joinville and Geffroy de Villehardouin*. Trans. Frank Marzials. Mineola, NY: Dover Publications, 2007. Reprint. *Memoirs of the Crusades*. London: J. M. Dent, 1908.

Jones, Martin H. "Richard the Lionheart in German Literature." In Nelson. Pp. 70–116.

Kaeuper, Richard W. "Treason." In Strayer. 12:165–68.

———. *Holy Warriors: The Religious Ideology of Chivalry*. Philadelphia: University of Pennsylvania Press, 2009.

Kedar, Benjamin Z. *Crusade and Mission: European Approaches toward the Muslims*. Princeton, NJ: Princeton University Press, 1984.

Keen, Maurice. *Chivalry*. New Haven, CT: Yale University Press, 1984.

Kennedy, Hugh. *Crusader Castles*. Cambridge, UK: Cambridge University Press, 1994.

Kieckhefer, Richard. *Forbidden Rites: A Necromancer's Manual of the Fifteenth Century*. University Park, PA: Pennsylvania State University Press, 1997.

King Horn. In Herzman, Drake and Salisbury. Pp. 11–73.

The King of Tars: Ed. from the Auchinleck MS, Advocates 19.2.1. Ed. Judith Perryman. Heidelberg: Carl Winter, 1980.

Knight, Stephen and Thomas Ohlgren, eds. *Robin Hood and Other Outlaw Tales*. Kalamazoo: Medieval Institute Publications, 2000. Pp. 194–219.

Kyng Alisaunder. Ed. G. V. Smithers. 2 vols. EETS o.s. 227. London: Oxford University Press, 1952; Reprint.1961.

La Monte, John. *Feudal Monarchy in the Latin Kingdom of Jerusalem, 1100 to 1291*. Cambridge, MA: Medieval Academy of America, 1932.

Laborderie, Olivier de. "Richard the Lionheart and the Birth of a National Cult of St George in England: Origins and Development of a Legend." *Nottingham Medieval Studies* 39 (1995), 37–53.

Laskaya, Anne and Eve Salisbury, eds. *The Middle English Breton Lays*. Kalamazoo, MI: Medieval Institute Publications, 2001.

Lay le Freine. In Laskaya and Salsibury. Pp. 61–87.

Liu, Yin. "Middle English Romance as Prototype Genre." *Chaucer Review* 40 (2006), 335–353.

Livingston, A. A. "Grifon. 'Greek.'" *Modern Language Notes* 22 (1907), 47–49.

Lloyd, Simon. "William Longespee II: The Making of an English Crusading Hero." *Nottingham Medieval Studies* 35 (1991), 41–69.

Loftin, Alice. "Visions." In Strayer. 12.475–78.

Longnon, Jean. "The Frankish States in Greece, 1204–1311." In Setton. 2:235–74.

Loomis, Laura Hibbard. See Hibbard, Laura.

Loomis, Roger Sherman. "Richard Cœur de Lion and the Pas Saladin in Medieval Art." *PMLA* 30 (1915), 509–28.

———. Review of *Der Mittelenglische Versroman über Richard Löwenherz*. Ed. Karl Brunner. *Journal of English and Germanic Philology* 15 (1916), 455–66.

Lupack, Alan, ed. *Three Middle English Charlemagne Romances: The Sultan of Babylon, The Siege of Milan, and The Tale of Ralph the Collier*. Kalamazoo, MI: Medieval Institute Publications, 1990.

Lynch, John E. "Oath." In Strayer. 9:207.

Lyon, Bruce. *A Constitutional and Legal History of Medieval England*. Second edition. New York: W. W. Norton, 1980.

MacCulloch, J. A. 1932. *Medieval Faith and Fable*. London: George G. Harrap, 1932.

Machaut, Guillaume de. *Guillaume de Machaut: The Debate Series*. Vol. 1. In *The Complete Works*. 8 vols. Gen. ed. R. Barton Palmer. Kalamazoo, MI: Medieval Institute Publications, Forthcoming.

———. *Guillaume de Machaut: The Boethian Poems*. Vol. 2. *The Complete Works*. 8 vols. Gen. ed. R. Barton Palmer. Kalamazoo, MI: Medieval Institute Publications, Forthcoming.

Major, J. Russell. "'Bastard Feudalism' and the Kiss: Changing Social Mores in Late Medieval and Early Modern France." *Journal of Interdisciplinary History* 17 (1987), 509–35.

Malory, Sir Thomas. *Works*. Ed. Eugene Vinaver. Second edition. Oxford: Oxford University Press, 1973.

Map, Walter. *De nugis curialium: Courtiers' trifles*. Ed. and trans. M. R. James et al. Oxford: Clarendon Press, 1983.

Marchalonis, Shirley. "*Sir Gowther*: The Process of a Romance." *Chaucer Review* 6 (1971/72), 14–29.

Marie de France. "Guigamar." In *The Lais of Maríe de France*. Trans. Robert Hanning and Joan Ferrante. Grand Rapids, MI: Baker Academic, 2009. Pp. 30–55.

Marshall, Linda E. "'Sacral Parody' in the *Secunda Pastorum*." *Speculum* 47 (1972), 720–36.

McDonald, Nicola. "Eating People and the Alimentary Logic of *Richard Cœur de Lion*." In *Pulp Fictions of Medieval England*. Ed. Nicola McDonald. Manchester, UK: Manchester University Press, 2004. Pp. 124–50.

Mehl, Dieter. *The Middle English Romances of the Thirteenth and Fourteenth Centuries*. London: Routledge, 1968.

Merrilees, Brian. "Crusade, Concept of." In Strayer. 4:15–22.

Middle English Dictionary (*MED*). University of Michigan, 2001. Online at http://quod.lib.umich.edu/m/med.

The Middle English Versions of Partenope of Blois. Ed. A. Trampe Bödtker. EETS, e. s., 109. London: Kegan, Paul, Trench, Trübner, 1912. Reprint. Woodbridge: Boydell and Brewer, 2002.

Mills, Maldwyn. "Generic titles in Bodleian Library MS Douce 261 and British Library MS Egerton 3132A." In *The Matter of Identity in Medieval Romance*. Ed. Phillipa Hardman. Woodbridge: D. S. Brewer, 2002. Pp. 125–38.

Mooers, Stephanie L. "Patronage in the Pipe Roll of 1130." *Speculum* 59 (1984), 282–307.

Needler, George Henry. "Richard Coeur de Lion in Literature." Ph.D. Dissertation, Universität Leipzig, 1890.

Nelson, Jan A., et al, eds. *The Old French Crusade Cycle*. 10 vols. Tuscaloosa, AL: University of Alabama Press, 1977-99.

Nelson, Janet L. *Richard Coeur de Lion in History and Myth*. London: Centre for Late Antique and Medieval Studies, King's College, 1992.

Nelson, Paul B. "Swan Knight." In *Medieval Folklore: A Guide to Myths, Legends, Tales, Beliefs, and Customs*. Ed. Carl Lindahl, John McNamara, and John Lindow. Oxford: Oxford University Press, 2002. Pp. 398–99.

Newman, Barbara. "Possessed by the Spirit: Devout Women, Demoniacs, and the Apostolic life in the Thirteenth Century." *Speculum* 73 (1998), 733–70.

Nicholas, David. *The Growth of the Medieval City from Late Antiquity to the Early Fourteenth Century*. London: Longman, 1997.

Nicholas, Nicolas H. *A History of the Royal Navy from the Earliest Times to the Wars of the French Revolution*. 3 vols. London: Richard Bentley, 1847.

Nicholson, Helen. *Templars, Hospitallers, and Teutonic Knights: Images of the Military Orders, 1128–1291*. Leicester: Leicester University Press, 1993.

———. trans. *Chronicle of the Third Crusade: A Translation of the Itinerarium Peregrinorum et Gesta Regis Ricardi*. Aldershot: Ashgate, 1997.

Nickel, Helmet. "Chivalry, Orders of." In Strayer. 3:303–07.

———. "Games and Pastimes." In Strayer. 5: 347–53.

———. "The Tournament: An Historical Sketch." In *The Study of Chivalry: Resources and Approaches*. Ed. Howell Chickering and Thomas H. Seiler. Kalamazoo, MI: Medieval Institute Publications, 1988. Pp. 213–262.

Octavian. In Hudson. Pp. 45–88.

Of Roland and Vernagu. In *The English Charlemagne Romances VI: The Taill of Rauf Coilyear, with the Fragments of Roland and Vernagu and Otuel*. Ed. S. J. Herrtage. EETS e. s., 39. 1869. Reprint. Suffolk: Boydell and Brewer, 2012. Pp. 37–61.

Olson, Claire C. "The Minstrels at the Court of Edward III." *PMLA* 56 (1941), 601–12.

"On Good and Bad Fairies." *The Edinburgh Magazine and Literary Miscellany* 5 (1819), 16–19.

Onions, C. T. "The Middle English 'Ord and Ende.'" *MLR* 24 (1929), 389–93.

Ordene de Chevalerie. In *Ramon Lull's Book of Knighthood and the Anonymous Ordene de Chevalerie*. Trans. William Caxton and Brian R. Price. Union City, CA: Chivalry Bookshelf, 2001. Pp. 107–22.

The Ormulum. Vol. 2. Ed. Robert Holt. Oxford: Clarendon Press, 1878.

Painter, Sidney. "Western Europe on the Eve of the Crusades." In Setton. 1:3–29.

———. "The Third Crusade: Richard the Lionhearted and Philip Augustus." In Setton. 2:45–85.

Paris, Gaston. "Le Roman de Richard Cœur de Lion." *Romania* 26 (1897), 353–93.

The Parlement of the Thre Ages. In *Wynnere and Wastoure and The Parlement of the Thre Ages*. Ed. Warren Ginsberg. Kalamazoo, MI: Medieval Institute Publications, 1992. Pp. 43–79.

Partington, J. R. *A History of Greek Fire and Gunpowder*. Cambridge: W. Heffer and Sons, 1960. Reprint, Baltimore: Johns Hopkins University Press, 1999.

Pearsall, Derek. "The Development of Middle English Romance." *Mediaeval Studies* 27 (1965), 91–116.

———. "The English Romance in the Fifteenth Century." *Essays and Studies* 29 (1976), 56–83.

———. "Middle English Romance and Its Audiences." In *Historical and Editorial Studies in Medieval and Early Modern English for Johan Gerritsen*. Ed. Mary-Jo Arn, Hanneke Wirtjes, and Hans Jansen. Groningen: Wolters-Noordhoff, 1985. Pp. 37–47.

Peck, Russell A. "The Careful Hunter in The Parlement of the Thre Ages." *Journal of English Literary History* 39 (1972), 333–341.

The Peterborough Lapidary. In *English Mediaeval Lapidaries*. Ed. Joan Evans and Mary S. Serjeantson. EETS o.s. 190. London: Oxford University Press, 1933; Reprint. 1960. Pp. 63–118.

Peters, Edward. *The First Crusade: The Chronicle of Fulcher of Chartres and Other Source Materials*. Second edition. Philadelphia: University of Pennsylvania Press, 1998.

Pollock, Frederick and Frederick William Maitland. *The History of English Law before the Time of Edward I*. Second edition. 2 vols. Cambridge, UK: Cambridge University Press, 1898.

Prestwich, J. O. "Richard Coeur de Lion: *Rex Bellicosus*." In Nelson. Pp. 1–16.

Pringle, Denys. *The Churches of the Crusader Kingdom of Jerusalem: A Corpus*. Vol. 1, A–K. Cambridge, UK: Cambridge University Press, 1993.

———. *Secular Buildings in the Crusader Kingdom of Jerusalem: An Archaeological Gazetteer*. Cambridge, UK: Cambridge University Press, 1997.

Pseudo-Turpin Chronicle. See *Turpine's Story*.

Reedy, William T. "Commendation." In Strayer. 3:490–91.

Richard of Devizes. *Chronicon Richardi Divisensis de Tempore Regis Richardi Primi: The Chronicle of Richard of Devizes of the Time of Richard the First*. Ed. and trans. John T. Appleby. London: Thomas Nelson, 1963.

Richmond, Velma Bourgeois. *Laments for the Dead in Medieval Narrative*. Pittsburgh, PA: Duquesne University Press, 1966.

Riley-Smith, Jonathan. *The Crusades: A Short History*. Second edition. New Haven, CT: Yale University Press, 2005.

Roberte the Deuyll. In *Remains of Early Popular Poetry of England*. Vol. 1. Ed. William Carew Hazlitt. London: John Russell Smith, 1864. Pp. 217–263.

Roger of Howden. *Chronica magistri Rogeri de Houedene*. Ed. William Stubbs. 4 vols. London: Longman and Co., and Trübner, 1868-71.

Rogers, R. *Latin Siege Warfare in the Twelfth Century*. Oxford: Oxford University Press, 1997.

Roman van Walewein. Ed. and trans. David F. Johnson. New York: Garland, 1992.

Rubenstein, Jay. "Cannibals and Crusaders." *French Historical Studies* 31 (2008), 525–52.

Runciman, Steven. *A History of the Crusades*. 3 vols. Cambridge, UK: Cambridge University Press, 1951.

Sargent-Baur, Barbara, ed. *Journeys toward God: Pilgrimage and Crusade*. Kalamazoo, MI: Medieval Institute Publications, 1992.

Scofield, C. I., ed. *The New Scofield Reference Bible*. Oxford: Oxford University Press, 1967.

Setton, Kenneth M., et al., eds. *A History of the Crusades*. 6 vols. Philadelphia: University of Pennsylvania Press, 1955; Reprint, 1969.

The Siege of Milan. In Lupack. Pp. 109–56.

Shores, Doris, ed. *The King of Tars*: A New Edition. Ph.D. Diss., New York University, 1969.

Sir Degrevant. In *Sentimental and Humorous Romances: Floris and Blancheflour, Sir Degrevant, The Squire of Low Degree, The Tournament of Tottenham, and The Feast of Tottenham*. Ed. Erik Kooper. Kalamazoo, MI: Medieval Institute Publications, 2006. Pp. 61–105.

Sir Eglamour of Artois. In Hudson. Pp. 97–132.

Sir Gawain and the Green Knight. Ed. J. R. R. Tolkien and E. V. Gordon and revised by Norman Davis. Second edition. Oxford: Clarendon Press, 1967.

Sir Gowther. In Laskaya and Salisbury. Pp. 274–96.

Sir Isumbras. In Hudson. Pp. 5–29.

Sir Orfeo. In Laskaya and Salisbury. Pp. 15–59.

Sir Perceval of Galles. In Braswell. Pp. 1–77.

Skeat, W. W., ed. *The Tale of Gamelyn*. Oxford: Clarendon Press, 1884.

The Song of Roland: An Analytical Edition. Ed. and trans. Gerard J. Brault. 2 vols. University Park, PA: Pennsylvania State University Press, 1978.

Strayer, Joseph, et al., eds. *Dictionary of the Middle Ages*. 13 vols. New York: Scribner, 1982–89.

Strohm, Paul. "*Storie, Spelle, Geste, Romaunce, Tragedie*: Generic Distinctions in the Middle English Troy Narratives." *Speculum* 46 (1971), 348–59.

The Sultan of Babylon. In Lupack. Pp. 7–95.

The Tale of Gamelyn. In *Robin Hood and Other Outlaw Tales*. Ed. Stephen Knight and Thomas Ohlgren. Kalamazoo, MI: Medieval Institute Publications, 2000. Pp. 194–219.

Tarassuk, Leonid and Claude Blair, eds. *The Complete Encyclopedia of Arms and Weapons*. New York: Simon and Shuster, 1982.

Tattersall, Jill. "Anthropophagi and Eaters of Raw Flesh in French Literature of the Crusade Period: Myth, Tradition and Reality." *Medium Ævum* 57 (1988), 240–53.

Taylor, Andrew. "The Myth of the Minstrel Manuscript." *Speculum* 66 (1991), 43–73.

Thompson, John J. *Robert Thornton and the London Thornton Manuscript: British Library MS Additional 31042*. Woodbridge: D. S. Brewer, 1987.

Tolan, John V. *Saracens: Islam in the Medieval European Imagination*. New York: Columbia University Press, 2002.

———. *Sons of Ishmael: Muslims through European Eyes in the Middle Ages*. Gainesville: University Press of Florida, 2008.

Trotter, D. A. *Medieval French Literature and the Crusades (1100–1300)*. Geneva: Librairie Droz, 1988.

Turpine's Story: a Middle English Translation of the Pseudo-Turpin Chronicle. Ed. Stephen H. A. Shepherd. EETS no. 322. Oxford and New York: Oxford University Press, 2004.

Turville-Petre, Thorlac. *England the Nation: Language, Literature, and National Identity, 1290–1340*. Oxford: Clarendon Press, 1996.

Tyerman, *God's War: A New History of the Crusades*. Cambridge, MA: Belknap Press, 2006.

Walsh, Elizabeth. "The King in Disguise." *Folklore* 86 (1975), 3–24.

The Wars of Alexander: An Alliterative Romance Translated Chiefly from the Historia Alexandri Magni de Preliis. Ed. Walter W. Skeat. EETS e.s. 47. London: N. Trübner & Co., 1886.

Weber, Henry. *Richard Coer de Lion.* In *Metrical Romances of the Thirteenth, Fourteenth, and Fifteenth Centuries: Published from Ancient Manuscripts.* Vols. 2 and 3. Edinburgh: Archibald Constable and Company, 1810.

Westerhof, Danielle. *Death and the Noble Body in Medieval England.* Woodbridge: Boydell Press, 2008.

Weston, Jessie L. *The Three Days' Tournament: A Study in Romance and Folk-Lore.* London: David Nutt, 1902.

Whiting, Bartlett Jere, and Helen Wescott Whiting. *Proverbs, Sentences, and Proverbial Phrases.* Cambridge, MA: Belknap Press of Harvard University Press, 1968.

Whitman, Jon. "The Body and the Struggle for the Soul of Romance: *La Queste del Saint Graal.*" In *The Body and Soul in Medieval Literature.* Ed. Piero Boitani and Anna Torti. Camdridge: D.S. Brewer, 1999. Pp. 31–61.

William of Malmesbury. *Gesta Regum Anglorum: The History of the British Kings.* Ed. and trans. R. A. B. Mynors, R. M. Thompson, and M. Winterbottom. 2 vols. Oxford: Clarendon Press, 1998.

William of Tyre. *Chronicon.* Ed. R. B. C. Huygens. *Corpus Christianorum.* Vols. 63–63A. Turnhout: Brepols, 1986.

White, Beatrice. "Saracens and Crusaders: From Fact to Allegory." In *Medieval Literature and Civilization: Studies in Memory of G. N. Garmonsway.* Ed. D. A. Pearsall and R. A. Waldron. London: Athlone Press, 1969. Pp. 170–91.

Wülker, Richard Paul. "*Richard Löwenherz.*" In *Altenglisches Lesebuch.* Vol. 1. Halle: Max Niemeyer, 1874, pp. 95–104 [text of last 479 lines from MS Cambridge, Gonville and Caius College – 175/96].

Zaller, Robert. "Breaking the Vessels: The Desacralization of Monarchy in Early Modern England." *Sixteenth Century Journal* 29 (1998), 757–78.

GLOSSARY

ABBREVIATIONS:

adj.: adjective
adv.: adverb
conj.: conjunction
ger.: gerund
MED: *Middle English Dictionary*
n.: noun
OF: Old French
p.: past
pers.: person
phr.: phrase
pl.: plural
ppl.: participle
prep.: preposition
pr.: present
pron.: pronoun
refl.: reflexive
sg.: singular
v.: verb

abiden (v.) *to wait; to suffer, endure; to stop moving, stop; to stand one's ground (for combat); to face in combat;* **~ to**, *to be in possession of*

abyde (v.) *stay, stayed; stop, stopped; wait, waited; expect, expected*

abye (v.) *buy at a high price; obtain through labor and suffering; to pay the penalty for a crime; to do penance*

aco(o)st (adv.) *nearby; along the side*

affyn (adv.) *completely, fully, thoroughly*

affyr (adv.) *on fire, in flames*

agaste (p. ppl.) *fearful, terrified*

agasten (v.) *to frighten, terrify*

agu(e) (n.) *an acute fever*

amyral(l) (n.) *An emir or prince owing fealty to a sultan; a heathan chieftan or commander*

anon (adv.) *at once, immediately; soon; all the way*

appayre (v.) *to spoil, ruin, impair; to decline; to slander*

arsoun (n.) *A saddle's uptilted front or back; saddlebow*

arwe (adj.) *timid*

arweblast (arblast) (n.) *a crossbow or similar weapon that launches stones instead of quarrels*

aspyde (v.) p. 3rd pers. of **aspye**

aspye (v.) *to observe secretly; wait in ambush; to investigate*

ateynte (p. ppl.) *overcome; achieved; condemned, convicted*

atyr(e) (n.) *the armor, weapons and mount of a knight, his whole equipment*

aught (ought) (adv.) *to any extent, at all*

aunterous (aventurous) (adj., n.) *adventurous, bold, in search of exploits; knight, knight errant*

aventure (n.) *chance, fortune, fate; an event; risk;* **in ~ that** *for fear that*

ay (ei) (n.) *egg*

ay (ayen) (adv.) *in return, in exchange; again*

bacheler(e) (n.) *a young, unmarried man; knight bachelor, a knightly ranking below a knight banneret*

bacynet (n.) *a diminutive of "bacin," a "little helmet" whose early forms were attached to the helmet and protected only the skull.*

badde (v.) p. of **bidden**

bake(n) (ppl. as n.) *pastry; pie*

bar (ber) (v.) *pushed, hurled; wore; carried*

batayllyd (v.) *arrayed for combat*

bed(e) (v.) p. sing. and p. ppl. of **bidden**

beden(e) (adv.) *as a group, all together; completely*

begon (v.) *to cover; covered*

bekyr (n.) *battle, martial encounter, skirmish;* **given ~**, *to attack*

bekyr (v.) *to attack; to make war*

belayd(e) (v.) *see* **bileggen**

bene (bees) (n.) *bees*

beref(f)t (v.) *robbed, deprived; taken away*

beten (v.) *to strike;* **~ doun**, *to level, raze, destroy (a city, castle, wall)*

beut(e) (v.) *beat, whipped, struck*

bidden (v.) *to request, beg, beseech, plea; to command or order; to offer*

bileggen (v.) *to besiege;* **~ aboute** *to encircle, surround*

blasoun (n.) *a shield, one usually bearing a coat of arms*

blyssyd (v.) *struck, knockd.* Compare OF *bleser*

blyve (blive, belyve) (adj.) *rapid, quick;* (adv.) *actively, vigorously; without delay*

bolde (adv.) *boldly; vigorously; quickly*

bon (boun) (adj.) *ready; prepared; at hand*

boote (n.) *remedy; advantage; salvation*

bord (n.) *dining table; plank*

borwgh (borgh, borwe, borh) (n.) *A guarantor of the behavior of another; a thing (gage) deposited as security, a pledge.* **leten to ~** *to allow [a captive] freedom after receiving surety*

brond(e) (n.) *an upright and often carved timber at a ship's bow*

brayd (n.) *sudden movement; hasty act; peculiar event; assault, attack*

brayde (breid) (v.) *dealt (a blow), struck; hurled*

burgeyses (n.) *a citizen or freemen of a town; an inhabitant of a town*

bydde (v.) *see bidden*

byte (v.) *to pierce, penetrate (of a weapon); to sting or bite*

ca(a)s (n.) *event; predicament, circumstances; action; fate*

campeson (n.) *a doublet or padded shirt worn underneath mail*

canst (v.) *see* **connen**

carollyd (v.) *danced or sang*

chaumbyrlayn (n.) *a person who waits upon the king in his private rooms; valet*

chevalry (n.) *the nobility; a troop of mounted and armored knights; the rank of knighthood; warfare; a host of defenders of Christianity*

chepynge (ger.) *trade in goods; a market*

chesen (v.) *to select or choose, to decide, resolve; to elect; to prefer; "Of God or Christ, to choose the virtuous life or the bliss of heaven" (MED)*

clappen (v.) *to strike, strike down;* **~ of**, *to strike off (a head)*

connen (v.) *to be able, have the ability; to possess mastery of a skill; to know*

co(o)st (n.) *coast; region, boundary, limit; side, direction,* **by a ~**, *in a certain direction*

core (v.) p. ppl. of **chesen**: *"Of persons, choice, elegant, distinguished . . ." (MED,* s.v. chesen, sense 5a); *"chosen to heavenly bliss" (MED,* s.v. chesen, sense 6a); *"Of Jesus, to choose (the Virgin for his mother); choose (the Christian community as his bride, the weak to confound the mighty) (MED,* s.v. chesen, sense 6b)

cors (n.) *the human body, living or dead*
countours (n.) *money, coins; that which is used to keep an account, e.g, calculators*
cours (n.) *A charge by knights in a tournament or a battle; route*
covey (n.) *guide or escort, convoy; see MED conveie*
crest(e) (n.) *top of a helmet; heraldic device afixed to a helmet's top; a tuft projecting from the top of a bird or dragon's head*
crouper (n.) *crupper, "a cover for the hindquarters of a horse" (MED)*
croyserye (n.) *crusade*
culvere (n.) *dove*
cuntray (contre(e)) (n.) *a geographic area, territory; a political jurisdiction, country or realm; the land surrounding a walled city; the countryside*
cuyle (n.) *rear, rump.* **thristin in ~** *to shove (something) up (one's) anus (MED)*

debles (n.) *the Devil*
delen (v.) *to divide, split up among persons, chop up (food); to deliver (a blow)*
delyd (deled) (p. ppl.) *see* **delen**
den(e) (n.) *valley*
deray (n.) *ferocity; confusion, disturbance, noise; attack*
derayne (v.) *to vindicate (truth, etc.) by fighting*
dere (n.) *injury, harm*; (v.) *injure, harm*
despyt(e) (n.) *contempt, disdain; disobedience; insult, humiliation;* **itelde ~ on** *disparaged*
destaunce (n.) *strife, discord; interval of space between objects*; **withouten ~** *without delay*
dighten (v.) *to prepare, to arrange, to go, to deliver (a blow)*
dom(e) (n.) *judgment, decision; judicial decision, sentence; act of justice*
doseper (dousse-per) (n.) *One of Charlemagne's twelve peers*
doughty (adj.) *valiant, noble, splendid*
down-ryghtes (adv.) *outright; straight down.*
draven (v.) *to pull, draw; to draw a weapon (sword or arrow); to shoot (an arrow)*
drawe(n) (drauen) (v.) *to breathe; to lead, to bring; to obtain;* **~ doun**, *to tear down (a tree), smash (an idol)*
dred(e) (n.) *fear; anxiety; awe;* **without ~** *without doubt*
duren (v.) *to last; to remain undamaged; to endure, withstand*
durren (v.) *to have the courage; to be able*
durst(e) p. of **durren**
dwelle (v.) *linger, tarry; remain; reside*
dyght (p. ppl.) *prepared, made ready, arranged*

em(e) (n.) *uncle; nephew*
encheso(u)n (n.) *a cause; grounds for conviction*
every dell (n., adj.) *all; completely, wholly*
everylkon (everilkan, everichon) (pron.) *every one, every single one*
eylid (v.) *afflicted, troubled; annoyed*

fallen (v.) *to fall, descend*
fande (fo(u)nd) (v.) *encountered, came upon; discovered in written records*
fawchoun (n.) *a falchion, a short single-edged sword with a sharp, broad point and convex blade*
fawte (faute) (n.) *lack, scarcity; flaw; failure, default; culpability*
fayn (fain) (adj.) *happy; desirous of*
fel (adj.) *treacherous, false, deceitful; fierce*
fel (v.) *fell, dropped; happened; befell*
felawrede (n.) *companions; fellowship*
fel(d)e (v.) *struck down (an enemy)*
fele (n.) *many*
felen (v.) *to perceive with the senses; to taste; to smell*

fere (n.) *a company, group of companions.* **in ~** *together*
ferrede(n) (ferhede(n)) (n.) *a company, band; band of armed men, army, troop*
fers (fers) (adj.) *great, strong, fortified, noble.* Compare OF *ferm*
fet(te) (v.), ppl., imperative sg. *brought, brought into someone's presence, sought; found; received; go and get*
fewte (n.) *feudal relation of vassal to lord;* ***don ~*** *act of acknowledging feudal obligation*
fleand (pr. ppl.) see **flen(ne)**
flen(ne) (v.) *to retreat, flee; to depart from a place*
flien (v.) *to fly; to move quickly*
flingen (v.) *to run, dash;* **comen ~**, *to come running*
flok (n.) *a troop of warriors; a group of people; a group of beasts*
flyngande (fleand) (pr. ppl.) *see* **flingen**
folk (n.) *people;* ***land ~*** *people of a race or nation*
fonde (v.) *endeavored, strove; tested*
forcarf(e) (v.) *to cut or split in two*
fore (for) (v.) *proceeded, travelled; attacked*
forhongred (ppl.) *starving, ravenous*
forlayn (ppl.) *seduced; raped*
forlesen (v.) *to lose (something), to lose or forfeit something completely*
forlorn (ppl. of **forelesen**) *forfeit; lost, completely lost*
forlore(n) (v., p. ppl.) *lost; disgraced, dishonored; wasted; forfeited [forlesen]*
forthought (v.) *regretted;* refl. *to repent of*
forwarde (n., adj.) *agreement; vanguard of an army; afterward, hereafter*
fote hote (fot-hot) (adv.) *immediately*
foysoun (n.) *abundance*
free (fre) (adj.) *noble, gracious, privileged*
ful (adv.) *completely, entirely; very*
fyl (fel, fil) (v., p.) *see* **fallen**
fynde (v.) *to discover, encounter; to learn; to read*

gart(e) (v.) *prepared, equipped; made; see* **geren**
gaynyd (v.) p. of **geinen**
geinen (v.) *to be useful;* refl. *to benefit oneself*
gentyll (adj.) *of noble rank, noble; courteous, refined*
geren (v.) (as an auxiliary verb) *to make, or cause something to be done*
gerte (v.) *struck; beaten down*
geven (v.) *to give gifts, alms, etc.*
gonfanoun (n.) *pennon or banner borne upon a lance; battle standard of an army*
graunted (v.) *granted (boon, request), permitted, allowed; consented, assented; confessed; agreed*
gryth (grith) (n.) *peace; protection; sanctuary;* **pes and ~** *amity and accord*
gunne(n) (v.) *began, started, founded*
gynne (n.) *talent; skill; ingenuity*

hal(f) (n.) *half; side;* **on that ~,** *on that other side*
heden (v.) *to behead*
he(e)ld (v.) p. of **held(e(n))**
held(e(n)) (holden) (v.) *to take hold; to keep, obey, observe; to detain; to hold (land, etc.) from a feudal lord;* **~ holden heygh (heigh) wei**, *follow the main road;* **~ fight (fyght)**, *to do battle*
helme (n.) *a heavy, often cylindrical helmet that enclosed the head and face and nearly reached the shoulders*
hend(e) (adj.) *noble, courtly*
hente (v.) *seized; capture; received blows*
hep(e) (n.) *a company of people; a troop of warriors*
heven (v.) *to raise, lift up, hoist; to raise onself*

hevyd (hed, heved) (n.) *head*
hew(e) (v.) *cut, struck, chopped*
hold(e) (adj.) *loyal, faithful*
ho(o)st(e) (n.) *army, division or company of armed men; retinue*
hoten (v.) *to be named*
hove (v., p.) *raised, hoisted; raised oneself; see* **heven**
hovyd (v.) *lurked, tarried;* ~ **stille** *remained still*
hyghe (v.) *hurry*
hyght (v.) *was named*
hyghtest (v.) *are named*
hynys (n. pl.) *household*
hyyd (v.) *hurried*

icrystenyd (v., p. ppl.) *baptized; Christian*
ilke, eche (pron.) *each; every; each and every;* ~ **a** *each, every, any*
insundyr (adv.) *to pieces, into two parts*
ishent (p. ppl.) *disgraced, shamed; injured; soiled*
iteld(e) (p. ppl.) *judged, considered,* ~ **despite on** *disparaged; narrated; commanded; enumerated*
iwis (adv.) *surely, certainly; indeed, in fact*

jugement (n.) *a trial; court-imposed penalty; verdict*

ken (v.) *make known; instruct; try, test*
kep (n.) *attention, heed; care*
kepe, kepen (v.) *guard, protect, defend;* ~ **batayle**, *engage in combat*
kepte (v.) *guarded, protected, defended*
kernel (n.) *an opening (embrasure) in a protective wall (battlement)*
kynde (n.) *disposition; kindred*

last(e) (v.) *remain useful; continue unchanged*
lat see (v.) *let us see*
latymere (n.) *translator; interpreter*
lay (n.) *religion, faith; law; a set of laws*
le(e)f (lief) (adj.) *dear, beloved*
le(f)ft(e) (p. ppl.) *ceased, discontinued; abandoned; spared;* **ben** ~ *remain, survive*
lem(m)an(n) (n.) *lover, paramour.*
lere (v.) *to find out, learn; to instruct*
lerd (ppl.) *learned, educated*
lesen (v.) *to loosen; set free*
les(se) (n.) *leash for a dog*; **out of** ~ *out of control*
lete (v.) *caused, permitted, see* **leten**
leten (v.) *to allow, permit; to surrender, relinquish (property); to forsake; to depart, leave;* ~ **make** *to make or cause something to be done (often with an infinitive phrase)*
lette (n.) *obstruction, hindrance*; **withouten** ~ *without delay*
leve (v.) *believe, have faith in; stop, leave off*
levere (adj.) comparative of **leef (lief)** *dear, beloved;* **hadde levere** *would prefer*
leyde (layde) (v.) *placed; destroyed;* ~ **on**, *delivered blows*
liken (v.) *to please;* ~ **evil (ille)**, to cause displeasure, be sorry
liven (v.) *to live, to survive; to endure*
loke (v.) *see* **loken**
loken (v.) *to take care, to see to it that. . .; to look*
loof (loft) (n.) *the top-castle of a ship*
lore(n) (v.) *lost*
los(e) (n.) *reputation; honor*. Compare Latin *laus*
lyggen (v.) *to lie down; to be situated or placed; to wallow*

mangenel (mangonel) (n.) *a machine for hurling stones and other objects during sieges*
mansell (masuel) (n.) *mace, club*
manshyppes (manship[e]s) (n.) *dignity; honor;* **do up (hold up) your** ~ *maintain your spirits*
markis (n.) *in English nobility, the rank between duke and earl; in France and Italy, a nobleman*

maryn (adj.) *from the sea;* (n.) *seacoast*
mawgre (prep.) *in spite of; against; despite all that (somebody) could do*
mayn(e) (n.) *vigor, physical strength, power*
mede (n.) *gift, reward, compensation;* **for ~** *for compensation; for a fee or price*
melle (n.) *mill; a military engine*
mes(e) (n.) *food; a course of a meal served at table*
mete (n.) *food; a meal*
meyne (n.) *retinue, body of retainers; a household or its servants; an army; ship's crew*
misprowde (adj.) *arrogant, haughty, vain*
mosard(e) (n.) *wretch, dolt, fool; see MED musard*
most(e) (v.) *to be allowed; to be compelled*; with **liven**, *to be permitted to live*
Myghhylmasse (n.) *the feast of the Dedication of St. Michael the Archangel on September 29*
mysthought (ppl.) **ben ~** *think wrongly*

nimen (v.) *take; seize; take out*
noblay (nobelay) (n.) *graciousness; nobleness; nobility; courage; splendor; wealth; reputation; honor; magnificence*
nome (v.) *took; seized*
nomen (i-nomen) (ppl.) *see* **nimen**
nones (n.) **for the ~** *for the particular occasion*
note (v.) *make use of; use; put to use; to eat or drink; partake of the Eucharist*

ofsent(e) (v.) *sent for*
on *on = won*, preterite of *winnan, to take possession or gain control of*
orguyle (n.) *pride, conceit*
ought (aught) (adv.) *to any extent, at all*
ovyrraughte (v.) *reached*
ovyrsaylyd (v.) *vanquished, overwhelmed*
ovyrspradde *"to become spread out"; "to deploy a military force throughout an area" (MED)*

parayle (n.) *equipment for war, armor, weapons*
paviloun (n.) *"A tent, especially a large or elaborate one used for military encampments, tournaments, hunting parties, etc." (MED)*
pawtener (n.) *scoundrel*
paye (n.) *satisfaction, pleasure;* **in goddes ~** *with God's good will; payment, reward; reprisal, punishment delivered in battle*
payne (n.) *punishment; torture; imprisonment; pain; suffering*
paynym (n.) *heathen lands; heathendom; a heathen*
pekken (v.) *to peck (of a bird), to strike or pluck;* **~ errour**, *to become angry, enraged*
pensel (n.) *standards; pennons*
pes (n.) *peace*; **maken ~** *effect a reconciliation*
picchen (v.) *to set up, erect or build,* **~ paviloun**, *pitch a pavilion, tent, etc.; to array or adorn,* **bodi pight**, *well-built*
playn (adj.) *level; flat; unadorned;* **maken ~** *raze (a structure, city, etc.)*
plyght (ppl.) *sworn, pledged*
pokyd (v.) p. of **pekken**
pouk(e) (n.) *devil, evil spirit, goblin*
pray (n.) *booty, plunder; hostage, captive*
pres(se) (n.) *throng; expedition; war, battle*
prest (adj.) *ready, prepared*
preven (v.) *to test; to prove; to discover; to venture (by combat)*
prove (v.) *see* **preven**
prys (n., adj.) *price, value; fame, renown; prize, booty;* (as adj.) *worthy, of high esteem*

pulte (v.) *to place, put; strike, thrust*
purchas (n.) *plunder, booty; gain, wealth, property*
pusen (n.) *gorget, throat-armor* (OF *pisain*)
putayle (n.) *foot soldiers*
pyght (pight), pyghten (ppl.) *see* **picchen** (v.)

qahchyd (v.) *scratched, lacerated*
quar(r)el (n.) *a bolt for a crossbow or similar weapon*
qued(e) (n.) *a devil; villain; evil*
queyntyse (n.) *strategy, ingenuity; elegance; a marvel*
quyten (v.) *pay; repay; reward; take revenge on*

rabyte (n.) *an Arabian horse*
raunso(u)n (n.) *payment made to secure the release of a prisoner; payment made for a crime or an offense; compensation*
red (n.) *advice, counsel;* **taken to ~** *to agree*
renay (n.) *apostate, one who has abandoned his/her religion*
renayyd (ppl.) *abandoned one's religion*
renge (n.) *a rank, a line or warriors arrayed for battle or a joust*
resoun(e) (n.) *reason, intellectual capacity; proceeding, action*
rout(e) (n.) *company, troop, retinue, army; crowd, gang*
rowe (reue) (n.) *row or line; a group, an army; order*
ryally (adv.) *regally, in a royal manner; splendidly*

sable (n.) *in heraldry, the color black*
sakeryng (ger.) *the consecration of wine and bread at mass*
Sarezynesse (n.) *the lands of the Saracens; heathendom*
Sarezyneys (adj.) *of Saracen style, make, or birth;* (n.) *the territory of the Saracens*
sa(ug)ht (n., ppl.) *peace; reconciliation; at peace; reconciled*
saw(e) (n.) *talk, speech; declaration, claim*
sawt(e) (n.) *assault, attack*
scathe (n.) *injury, harm; misfortune;* **that was ~** *that was a pity*
s(c)heltroun (n.) *an army or soldiers in battle formation*
schentschepe (v.) *to confound, ruin (the devil); to disgrace*
schrewe (n.) *evildoer, rogue; devil*
sclaundre (n.) *renown, fame, repute, information; misrepresentation; calumny*
scounfyte (v.) *to defeat; conquer*
seg(g)e (n.) *the act of besieging a castle or city;* **holden (kepen) ~** *to carry on a siege*
sendell (n.) *an expensive fabric, possibly of linen or cotton*
sene (ppl.) *able to be seen, visible*
sergeaunt (n.) *servant; attendant of a lord or knight*
sethen (v.) *to boil*
seur (adv.) (OF) *fully*
seven (v.) *to follow; to accompany; to obey; to afflict; to go, move forward*
sewyd (v.) p. of **seven**
seyn (seygh) (v.) *saw*
shent(e) (p. ppl.) *harmed; shamed; ruined; mutilated, disfigured; corrupted*
siththen (sitthen) (conj.) *at any time since; after that, subsequent to that time; when; because*
slen (v.) *to strike; to slay, murder*
slowe (sloghe, slowgh) (v.) *slayed, killed*
smot (v., p.) *see* **smyten**
smyten (v.) *to strike; to pierce (with an arrow)*
soden(n)e (p. ppl.) *boiled*
sond(e) (n.) *a sending out, embassy, mission; message, communication, invitation*
sore (adv.) *very; strongly; severely; dearly; forcefully*

soure (adv.) *fully, completely; securely*
span (n.) *a measurement equal to the distance from the end of the thumb to the end of the little finger of a spread hand*
spede (n.) *good fortune; abundance*
speden (v.) *to prosper; to travel swiftly, hasten*
spryngall (n.) *a siege weapon for hurling projectiles, a catapult*
stablen (v.) *to establish, found; to pacify, bring order, secure; to settle*
stand (stond) (v.) *stand, assume upright position;* **~ to**, *to abide (by an agreement)*
stede (n.) *charger, war horse*
sterff (v.) *perished, died*
sterte(n) (v.) *jumped; hastened, rushed, dashed*
sterven (v.) *to die, perish; to kill*
stoor (n.) *provisions, supplies; livestock*
stound(e) (n.) *event, occasion; a short space of time*
stoupe(n) (v.) *to stoop, bend forward; to slump backward from a blow; to make fall*
stout(e) (adj.) *brave; fierce; noble; sturdy*
stykyd (v., p. ppl) *stabbed*
swylke (adj.) *such; so great; certain, particular*
swyre (n.) *neck*
swyth(e) (adv.) *very; eagerly; promptly; with great force; swiftly*
syclato(u)n (n.) *a rich fabric of silk woven with gold*
sykerly (adv.) *indeed, truly; without mistake; well; safely, securely, secretly*

takyl (takel) (n.) *equipment for operating a mangonel.*
taylardes (tailarde) (n.) *people with tails*
telde (v.) *said, recounted; counted; judged, reckoned*
tellen (v.) *to tell, say; to recount, mention; to inform, describe; to count*
than(e) (demonstrative or anaphoric pron.) *that one, it, him* **~ that** *the one which, the one whom*
thar (v.) 3rd pers. sg. impersonal (with infinitive) *it is required, necessary*
thing (n). *attribute of a person or animal*
tho(o) (adv.) *then, at that time;* **~ that,** *at the time that, when*
throwe (throu) (n.) **in a a short time ~** *quickly*
tobrak(e) (v.) *shattered, broken into pieces; (of a ship) suffered shipwreck*
torof(e) (v.) *broke apart; shattered; destroyed*
totar(e) (v.) *destroyed; (of a ship) shattered, broke apart*
tree-castel (n.) *siege tower*
trepeiettes (trepeget) (OF *trebuchet*) (n.) *a siege weapon that hurled stones and other objects by means of a throwing arm*
tresoun (n.) *disloyalty, falseness, treachery; a specific [treasonous] offense*
tuely (tul, tueli) (adj.) *deep red color, crimson*
turnyd (v.) *turned; spun, rotate*
tydde (v.) *happened, befell*
tyt(e) (adv.) *quickly, soon;* **als ~** *immediately*

unnethe (adv.) *with difficulty*
unryght (n.) *wrongdoing, sinful practice*; **haven** ~ *to be wrong*

ven(e)u (n.) *an attack*
venge(n) (v.) *to take vengeance*; refl. *to avenge oneself*
vytayle (n.) *food; provisions*

wan(ne) (v.) *see* **winnen**
wed(de) (n.) *a pledge, security; something risked or forfeited;* **leven in (to) ~**, *leave (something) dead*
we(e)l (adv.) *genuinely; in the customary manner, fittingly; kindly*

wend(e) (v.) *to travel; walk; depart, leave; sail; set out (to accomplish a task)*

wenen (v.) *to suppose, believed, expect; to hope*

weren (v.) *to protect, preserve; to provide defense*

werk (n.) *activity; deed; a structure, fortification*

werken (v.) *to work, act, proceed; to engage in an activity, perform; to make*

wer(re) (n.) *war, battle*

wery and forgone (adj. phr.) *all exhausted*

weved (v., ppl.) *severed; cut deeply; wandered*

winnen (v.) *to exert effort; to take; to proceed*

wol (wel) (adv.) *well, very*

worshyppe (worship[e]) (n.) *esteem, honor, respect; social standing, status;* **with ~** *a ceremony or actions that honor an individual*

wot (v.) *know; find out*

wroken (v., p. ppl.) *avenged, taken vengeance upon*

wrought(e) (p. ppl.) *see* **werken***; made; fashioned; painted; performed*

wurth(e)(i) (adj.) *valiant; deserving; important; of high rank*

wyghte (wight) (n.) *a living being; a man; a creature;* (adj.) *valiant, courageous; swift*

wykke (adj.) *evil, iniquitous; unfavorable; unfortunate, distressing*

wylle (wil(le)) (n.) *the faculty of volition, intention; disposition; a desire,* **at ~**, *according to (one's) desires*

wyndas (n.) *An apparatus for hoisting or hauling, a windlass, winch*

wynne (win(ne)) (n.) (1) *wealth, booty, possessions; benefit, profit;* (2) *happiness, joy*

wyst(e) (wiste) (v.) *knew, discovered, learned*

wytherywynnes (n.) *enemies, foes*

wyttyrly (adv.) *cleverly, skillfully; plainly, clearly*

yar(e) (adj., adv.) *prepared, ready; eager; thoroughly; quickly; eagerly*

yed(e) (v.) *to travel, go, proceed; to walk; to fall*

yelden (v.) *to relinquish (something) voluntarily; to give something up; to surrender to a foe;* **ben yolden**, *to have surrendered; to yield, produce*

yeme(n) (n.) *attention, heed;* **taken ~** *to pay attention, take heed*

yemen (v.) *to protest; to take heed of*

yern(e) (adv.) *keenly;* (adj.) *keen, swift;* (n.) *eagerness*

yet(te) (adv.) *anyway; also; even*

ylk(e) (ech) (pron.) *each; any;* **~ a side***; on every side*

ylke (adv.) *also; similarly; equally*

ylke (ilke) (pron.) *the previously mentioned, the same, the very*

ylkon (ech on) (pron. phr.) *each one; every single one*

Middle English Texts Series

The Floure and the Leafe, The Assembly of Ladies, The Isle of Ladies, edited by Derek Pearsall (1990)
Three Middle English Charlemagne Romances, edited by Alan Lupack (1990)
Six Ecclesiastical Satires, edited by James M. Dean (1991)
Heroic Women from the Old Testament in Middle English Verse, edited by Russell A. Peck (1991)
The Canterbury Tales: Fifteenth-Century Continuations and Additions, edited by John M. Bowers (1992)
Gavin Douglas, *The Palis of Honoure*, edited by David Parkinson (1992)
Wynnere and Wastoure and The Parlement of the Thre Ages, edited by Warren Ginsberg (1992)
The Shewings of Julian of Norwich, edited by Georgia Ronan Crampton (1994)
King Arthur's Death: The Middle English Stanzaic Morte Arthur and Alliterative Morte Arthure, edited by Larry D. Benson, revised by Edward E. Foster (1994)
Lancelot of the Laik and Sir Tristrem, edited by Alan Lupack (1994)
Sir Gawain: Eleven Romances and Tales, edited by Thomas Hahn (1995)
The Middle English Breton Lays, edited by Anne Laskaya and Eve Salisbury (1995)
Sir Perceval of Galles and Ywain and Gawain, edited by Mary Flowers Braswell (1995)
Four Middle English Romances: Sir Isumbras, Octavian, Sir Eglamour of Artois, Sir Tryamour, edited by Harriet Hudson (1996; second edition 2006)
The Poems of Laurence Minot, 1333–1352, edited by Richard H. Osberg (1996)
Medieval English Political Writings, edited by James M. Dean (1996)
The Book of Margery Kempe, edited by Lynn Staley (1996)
Amis and Amiloun, Robert of Cisyle, and Sir Amadace, edited by Edward E. Foster (1997; second edition 2007)
The Cloud of Unknowing, edited by Patrick J. Gallacher (1997)
Robin Hood and Other Outlaw Tales, edited by Stephen Knight and Thomas Ohlgren (1997; second edition 2000)
The Poems of Robert Henryson, edited by Robert L. Kindrick with the assistance of Kristie A. Bixby (1997)
Moral Love Songs and Laments, edited by Susanna Greer Fein (1998)
John Lydgate, *Troy Book Selections*, edited by Robert R. Edwards (1998)
Thomas Usk, *The Testament of Love*, edited by R. Allen Shoaf (1998)
Prose Merlin, edited by John Conlee (1998)
Middle English Marian Lyrics, edited by Karen Saupe (1998)
John Metham, *Amoryus and Cleopes*, edited by Stephen F. Page (1999)
Four Romances of England: King Horn, Havelok the Dane, Bevis of Hampton, Athelston, edited by Ronald B. Herzman, Graham Drake, and Eve Salisbury (1999)
The Assembly of Gods: Le Assemble de Dyeus, or Banquet of Gods and Goddesses, with the Discourse of Reason and Sensuality, edited by Jane Chance (1999)
Thomas Hoccleve, *The Regiment of Princes*, edited by Charles R. Blyth (1999)
John Capgrave, *The Life of Saint Katherine*, edited by Karen A. Winstead (1999)
John Gower, *Confessio Amantis*, Vol. 1, edited by Russell A. Peck; with Latin translations by Andrew Galloway (2000; second edition 2006); Vol. 2 (2003; second edition 2013); Vol. 3 (2004)
Richard the Redeless and Mum and the Sothsegger, edited by James M. Dean (2000)
Ancrene Wisse, edited by Robert Hasenfratz (2000)
Walter Hilton, *The Scale of Perfection*, edited by Thomas H. Bestul (2000)
John Lydgate, *The Siege of Thebes*, edited by Robert R. Edwards (2001)
Pearl, edited by Sarah Stanbury (2001)
The Trials and Joys of Marriage, edited by Eve Salisbury (2002)
Middle English Legends of Women Saints, edited by Sherry L. Reames, with the assistance of Martha G. Blalock and Wendy R. Larson (2003)
The Wallace: Selections, edited by Anne McKim (2003)
Richard Maidstone, *Concordia (The Reconciliation of Richard II with London)*, edited by David R. Carlson, with a verse translation by A. G. Rigg (2003)
Three Purgatory Poems: The Gast of Gy, Sir Owain, The Vision of Tundale, edited by Edward E. Foster (2004)
William Dunbar, *The Complete Works*, edited by John Conlee (2004)
Chaucerian Dream Visions and Complaints, edited by Dana M. Symons (2004)
Stanzaic Guy of Warwick, edited by Alison Wiggins (2004)
Saints' Lives in Middle English Collections, edited by E. Gordon Whatley, with Anne B. Thompson and Robert K. Upchurch (2004)

Siege of Jerusalem, edited by Michael Livingston (2004)
The Kingis Quair and Other Prison Poems, edited by Linne R. Mooney and Mary-Jo Arn (2005)
The Chaucerian Apocrypha: A Selection, edited by Kathleen Forni (2005)
John Gower, *The Minor Latin Works*, edited and translated by R. F. Yeager, with *In Praise of Peace*, edited by Michael Livingston (2005)
Sentimental and Humorous Romances: Floris and Blancheflour, Sir Degrevant, The Squire of Low Degree, The Tournament of Tottenham, and The Feast of Tottenham, edited by Erik Kooper (2006)
The Dicts and Sayings of the Philosophers, edited by John William Sutton (2006)
Everyman and Its Dutch Original, Elckerlijc, edited by Clifford Davidson, Martin W. Walsh, and Ton J. Broos (2007)
The N-Town Plays, edited by Douglas Sugano, with assistance by Victor I. Scherb (2007)
The Book of John Mandeville, edited by Tamarah Kohanski and C. David Benson (2007)
John Lydgate, *The Temple of Glas*, edited by J. Allan Mitchell (2007)
The Northern Homily Cycle, edited by Anne B. Thompson (2008)
Codex Ashmole 61: A Compilation of Popular Middle English Verse, edited by George Shuffelton (2008)
Chaucer and the Poems of "Ch," edited by James I. Wimsatt (revised edition 2009)
William Caxton, *The Game and Playe of the Chesse*, edited by Jenny Adams (2009)
John the Blind Audelay, *Poems and Carols*, edited by Susanna Fein (2009)
Two Moral Interludes: The Pride of Life and Wisdom, edited by David Klausner (2009)
John Lydgate, *Mummings and Entertainments*, edited by Claire Sponsler (2010)
Mankind, edited by Kathleen M. Ashley and Gerard NeCastro (2010)
The Castle of Perseverance, edited by David N. Klausner (2010)
Robert Henryson, *The Complete Works*, edited by David J. Parkinson (2010)
John Gower, *The French Balades*, edited and translated by R. F. Yeager (2011)
The Middle English Metrical Paraphrase of the Old Testament, edited by Michael Livingston (2011)
The York Corpus Christi Plays, edited by Clifford Davidson (2011)
Prik of Conscience, edited by James H. Morey (2012)
The Dialogue of Solomon and Marcolf: A Dual-Language Edition from Latin and Middle English Printed Editions, edited by Nancy Mason Bradbury and Scott Bradbury (2012)
Croxton Play of the Sacrament, edited by John T. Sebastian (2012)
Ten Bourdes, edited by Melissa M. Furrow (2013)
Lybeaus Desconus, edited by Eve Salisbury and James Weldon (2013)
The Complete Harley 2253 Manuscript, Vol. 2, edited and translated by Susanna Fein with David Raybin and Jan Ziolkowski (2014); Vol. 3 (2015); Vol. 1 (2015)
Oton de Granson Poems, edited and translated by Peter Nicholson and Joan Grenier-Winther (2015)
The King of Tars, edited by John H. Chandler (2015)
John Hardyng Chronicle, edited by James Simpson and Sarah Peverley (2015)

Commentary Series

Haimo of Auxerre, *Commentary on the Book of Jonah*, translated with an introduction and notes by Deborah Everhart (1993)
Medieval Exegesis in Translation: Commentaries on the Book of Ruth, translated with an introduction and notes by Lesley Smith (1996)
Nicholas of Lyra's Apocalypse Commentary, translated with an introduction and notes by Philip D. W. Krey (1997)
Rabbi Ezra Ben Solomon of Gerona, *Commentary on the Song of Songs and Other Kabbalistic Commentaries*, selected, translated, and annotated by Seth Brody (1999)
John Wyclif, *On the Truth of Holy Scripture*, translated with an introduction and notes by Ian Christopher Levy (2001)
Second Thessalonians: Two Early Medieval Apocalyptic Commentaries, introduced and translated by Steven R. Cartwright and Kevin L. Hughes (2001)
The "Glossa Ordinaria" on the Song of Songs, translated with an introduction and notes by Mary Dove (2004)
The Seven Seals of the Apocalypse: Medieval Texts in Translation, translated with an introduction and notes by Francis X. Gumerlock (2009)
The "Glossa Ordinaria" on Romans, translated with an introduction and notes by Michael Scott Woodward (2011)

Documents of Practice Series

Love and Marriage in Late Medieval London, selected, translated, and introduced by Shannon McSheffrey (1995)

Sources for the History of Medicine in Late Medieval England, selected, introduced, and translated by Carole Rawcliffe (1995)

A Slice of Life: Selected Documents of Medieval English Peasant Experience, edited, translated, and with an introduction by Edwin Brezette DeWindt (1996)

Regular Life: Monastic, Canonical, and Mendicant "Rules," selected and introduced by Douglas J. McMillan and Kathryn Smith Fladenmuller (1997); second edition, selected and introduced by Daniel Marcel La Corte and Douglas J. McMillan (2004)

Women and Monasticism in Medieval Europe: Sisters and Patrons of the Cistercian Reform, selected, translated, and with an introduction by Constance H. Berman (2002)

Medieval Notaries and Their Acts: The 1327–1328 Register of Jean Holanie, introduced, edited, and translated by Kathryn L. Reyerson and Debra A. Salata (2004)

John Stone's Chronicle: Christ Church Priory, Canterbury, 1417–1472, selected, translated, and introduced by Meriel Connor (2010)

Medieval German Texts in Bilingual Editions Series

Sovereignty and Salvation in the Vernacular, 1050–1150, introduction, translations, and notes by James A. Schultz (2000)

Ava's New Testament Narratives: "When the Old Law Passed Away," introduction, translation, and notes by James A. Rushing, Jr. (2003)

History as Literature: German World Chronicles of the Thirteenth Century in Verse, introduction, translation, and notes by R. Graeme Dunphy (2003)

Thomasin von Zirclaria, *Der Welsche Gast (The Italian Guest)*, translated by Marion Gibbs and Winder McConnell (2009)

Ladies, Whores, and Holy Women: A Sourcebook in Courtly, Religious, and Urban Cultures of Late Medieval Germany, introductions, translations, and notes by Ann Marie Rasmussen and Sarah Westphal-Wihl (2010)

Varia

The Study of Chivalry: Resources and Approaches, edited by Howell Chickering and Thomas H. Seiler (1988)

Studies in the Harley Manuscript: The Scribes, Contents, and Social Contexts of British Library MS Harley 2253, edited by Susanna Fein (2000)

The Liturgy of the Medieval Church, edited by Thomas J. Heffernan and E. Ann Matter (2001; second edition 2005)

Johannes de Grocheio, *Ars musice*, edited and translated by Constant J. Mews, John N. Crossley, Catherine Jeffreys, Leigh McKinnon, and Carol J. Williams (2011)

To Order Please Contact:

Medieval Institute Publications
Western Michigan University
Kalamazoo, MI 49008-5432
Phone (269) 387-8755
FAX (269) 387-8750
http://www.wmich.edu/medieval/mip/index.html

Typeset in 10/13 New Baskerville
and Golden Cockerel Ornaments display

Medieval Institute Publications
College of Arts and Sciences
Western Michigan University
1903 W. Michigan Avenue
Kalamazoo, MI 49008-5432
http:/ /www.wmich.edu/medieval/mip

Printed and bound in the United States of America